# AN AGRARIAN REPUBLIC

# AN AGRARIAN REPUBLIC

Commercial Agriculture
and the Politics of
Peasant Communities
in El Salvador, 1823–1914

*Aldo A. Lauria-Santiago*

UNIVERSITY OF PITTSBURGH PRESS

Published by the University of Pittsburgh Press, Pittsburgh, Pa. 15261
Copyright © 1999, University of Pittsburgh Press
All rights reserved
Manufactured in the United States of America
Printed on acid-free paper
10 9 8 7 6 5 4 3 2 1

Library of Congress Cataloging-in-Publication Data
Lauria-Santiago, Aldo.
    An agrarian republic : commercial agriculture and the politics
of peasant communities in El Salvador, 1823–1914 / Aldo Antonio
Lauria-Santiago.
       p. cm. — (Pitt Latin American series)
    Includes bibliographical references (p.  ) and index.
    ISBN 0-8229-4099-X (alk. paper)
    ISBN 0-8229-5700-0 (pbk. : alk. paper)
    1. Peasantry—El Salvador—History. 2. Land tenure—El
Salvador—History. 3. Peasantry—El Salvador—Political
activity–History. 4. Agriculture—Economic aspects—El
Salvador—History. 5. Coffee industry—El Salvador—History.
I. Title. II. Series.
    HD 1531.S2 L38 1999
    338.1'097284—dc21                                                99-6343
                                                                         CIP

A CIP catalog record for this book is available from the British Library.

# CONTENTS

# ACKNOWLEDGMENTS

This book has been too long in the making. It started in 1992 as a six-hundred-page dissertation at the University of Chicago that read more like a research report. The process of condensing and contextualizing the very extensive case studies and empirical materials I gathered in El Salvador has been a challenging task. I am grateful to the people of El Salvador for their generosity and for the many historical lessons that their recent and old experiences—and sufferings—have given us.

Along the way, many people have contributed to the completion of this book. In El Salvador I received overwhelming support from Joaquin Salaver-ría, director, and Clara Angulo, acting director, of the Archivo General de la Nación of El Salvador. The staff of the Archivo General de la Nación offered me support beyond what I could have ever expected and gave me a free hand at searching and reorganizing the archive's substantial (but chaotic) materials. The vastly underpaid staff offered me assistance, labor, and intellectual vitality. I wish to thank especially Mauricio Costte, Miguel Angel García, Don Luis and Mauricio, with whom I spent many days in the humid heat of Sonsonate cleaning, organizing, and boxing the local archives. Mauricio Costte contributed well beyond the call of duty by traveling with me throughout the western municipalities in search of documents. Staff at the National University Library, the Biblioteca Gallardo, the UCA Library, the Library of the Banco Hipotecario, Patrimonio Cultural, and the National Library also assisted my research, often allowing me to look at those "special" items that only local librarians knew of. And in all real-life, human, and practical matters, Mario, Ana, and Sandra made my stays in El Salvador as normal as they could have ever been, showing me the strength and goodness of a people who deserve so much more than they have received so far.

Since my years as a graduate student at the University of Chicago, the useful and clear advice of John Coatsworth has consistently given me a vision of my project's worthiness. Friedrich Katz contributed to the clarity of discussions over various quarters of course work and discussions of the many parallels between Salvadoran and Mexican agrarian history. Many colleagues have provided encouraging discussions and criticisms of parts of this book—among them John French, Knut Walter, Jeff Gould, Lowell Gudmundson, William Roseberry, Todd Little, Arturo Taracena, Victor Hugo Acuaña, Erik Ching, Patricia Alvarenga, Virginia Tilley, and a handful of intense graduate students at the New School's graduate program in historical studies. Peter Guardino, Avi Chomsky, Charles Walker, and Jordana Dym helped me with their useful comments on the final drafts of this book. I am especially indebted to Hector Lindo Fuentes, whose consistent and supportive attention made this book a much improved product.

I also thank the anonymous readers who read the manuscript in its various incarnations, providing useful suggestions and Eileen Kiley at Pittsburgh University Press, who managed a review process that was only one step ahead of my tenure clock. I'm also very grateful to Jane Flanders, senior editor at the University of Pittsburgh Press, who dramatically improved my often obtuse writing style. Ingrid Vargas, my wife and *compañera,* provided a balanced blend of support and criticism so necessary for completing this kind of project. I thank her for her consistent love and encouragement. I also thank my son Ian for understanding from an early age what it meant to "make" a book and get tenure. Finally, I thank my extended families in Puerto Rico and New York for understanding and never questioning the long-term investment it takes to complete a Ph.D. and (re)write a book.

Fellowships from the Consortium for Institutional Cooperation of the Big Ten Universities, The University of Chicago's Dorothy Danforth Compton program, the Department of Education Fulbright program, the Social Science Research Council, and the Ford Foundation funded the research and writing of the dissertation upon which this book is based. At the New School for Social Research, various faculty research fellowships supported the help of student assistants (Fred Murphy and Noah Yaskin) and research and conference trips related to this book. At the College of the Holy Cross, a junior faculty leave provided most of the time I needed to finish writing and editing the text. Various faculty grants at Holy Cross also facilitated the research process. I thank all of these institutions and programs for their support.

# AN AGRARIAN REPUBLIC

# 1 Introduction

## PEASANTS IN THE AGRARIAN HISTORY OF EL SALVADOR

Over the last two decades, El Salvador's political changes, which include a revolutionary civil war and a transition to civilian rule, have drawn attention to the country's earlier history. Important aspects of recent history have been linked to the changes of the nineteenth and early twentieth centuries. By focusing on land use, export production, and rural class and ethnic relations, this study traces the history of what are considered causal factors in the development of El Salvador's highly stratified and politically conflicted society. Its conclusions may add to our understanding of land use, peasant communities, and politics in other regions of Latin America as well. My research brings together three important literatures in the study of Latin American history. First, it draws on the study of postcolonial agrarian society, including questions of land tenure, labor, and agriculture. Second, it addresses peasant politics and state formation during the nineteenth century. Finally, it contributes to debates on the impact of coffee production on class structure and state power in Latin America. I hope that this book will help insert Salvadoran historiography in a wider Latin American context and end its relative isolation.

## Latin America's Nineteenth-Century Agrarian History

Between the 1950s and early 1980s, the study of Latin American history was framed by theories that emphasized macroeconomic issues, such as developmentalist, dependency, Marxian, and world-system models. These theories stressed Latin America's connections with northern or global economic forces as the key to the region's internal development. Prompted in part by the excesses of these often schematic, rigid, and bipolar models, more recent scholars have incorporated a greater mass of empirical research on local and regional history into their studies.[1] Since the mid-1980s historians have begun to test the ideas proposed by these theories and connect them to the lives and stories of identifiable people.[2] In the process, many have discovered that rural Latin America—especially regions affected by the expansion of export agriculture—was more complex and diverse than originally thought.[3] Recent studies have focused on peasant forms of resistance and adaptation to the impositions and exactions of states and elite groups, emphasizing the experiences and autonomy of subaltern social sectors. This new literature reformulates and reinterprets the effects of long-term, large-scale structural forces in a way more consistent with the heterogeneity of local and regional social history.

This study examines the history of the Salvadoran peasantry, but within the context of processes traditionally perceived as external to the peasantry (agro-exports, state formation, elite political culture). The arguments presented here attempt to compensate for biases in Central American historiography that emphasize elites and global linkages but discount the popular sectors. While acknowledging the diverse responses of peasants to markets, state impositions, and social and political conflict, most historical studies of Central America reflect an emphasis on the dominance of export agriculture and state-based transitions. This literature sees export agriculture as the engine driving the formation of agrarian social relations and political regimes. The export economies that emerged between 1860 and 1929 are usually seen as a negative force, destroying more egalitarian, precapitalist social relations. As a result, discussions of El Salvador's agrarian history have remained top-down, reductionist, and functionalist—and often not backed up by careful study of peasant communities and social structures—emphasizing instead a "development of [export] capitalism" model.[4] Many continue to associate peasants' participation in markets and commercial economies—especially for export—with the dispossession of their lands. "Liberal" privatization—especially in Central America—also continues to be understood mostly as an expression of oligarchic power in which a hovering state, controlled or manipulated by the agro-export elite, tears away the subsistence rights of peasants. My research suggests that the results of peasant commercial participation are more complex and open-ended than these assumptions would have us believe.

This study also seeks to integrate the study of Salvadoran history with recent approaches to politics and the state that focus on peasants' political activities and their involvement in forming the nation-state.[5] In this literature, peasants are posited as integral to the polity, involved in their own struggles over the definition and practice of politics, even creating their own forms of nationalism and national identity, especially between 1820 and 1870. But many historians have turned to popular and peasant culture, nationalism, and politics without fully understanding the underlying structures of the peasant political economy that provided the foundations for collective political mobilization. Many have ignored the political and social impact of changes in peasants' social structure and landowning patterns. While most current studies of peasant politics in nineteenth-century Latin America are framed by the dilemmas of weak, emerging, and conflicted states—problems often exacerbated by foreign invasion, regional conflict, or civil war—important issues such as land tenure, land legislation, how peasant communities actually functioned, and the effects of regional and export markets on these processes are often not integrated into discussions of peasant political mobilization. This inquiry aims to place Salvadoran history within these debates and to advance some questions that might help link these theories to future discussions of nineteenth-century peasants and politics in Latin America.

## Reconceptualizing El Salvador's Agrarian Historiography

The revolutionary movements and wars of the late 1970s and 1980s generated a growing interest in Central American history and a demand for new research into the region's past. The successes of revolutionary movements in Nicaragua, El Salvador, and Guatemala drew particular attention to the region's agrarian history and to the social and historical roots of authoritarian politics; however, little empirical research was done, in part precisely because of the difficulties of carrying out research in war-torn societies.[6] Partially influenced by the ideological polarization of the crises of the late 1970s, scholars emphasized the all-encompassing power of elites over Central American societies. With the emergence of El Salvador's political crisis and revolutionary war after 1980, observers sought the historical sources of the country's social structure and political system, often tracing the origins of mid-twentieth-century elite dominance and authoritarian politics to the nineteenth century. Unfortunately, this meant projecting post-1950 agrarian patterns onto earlier periods. Scholars assumed that the more recent social structure—the dominant landholding oligarchy and landless workers of the 1970s— also existed in the past. This fallacy led to often mythical or romanticized visions of the country's history. El Salvador has remained, both in academic and popular conceptions, a country persistently torn by extremes in the distribution of wealth and power, suffering from large, elite-owned plantations that expropriated and concentrated land and coerced labor, and dominated by authoritarian regimes typically unresponsive to popular pressures or needs that existing only within an "empty shell" of constitutional liberalism.

When dependency theories were at the height of their popularity, much of the blame was placed on the country's linkage to world markets and its reliance on coffee production. Coffee cultivation was usually presented as a homogenizing force controlled by a small oligarchic elite with nearly absolute social power as well as direct control of the state. This has contributed to a highly teleological understanding of the country's history. All that came before was nothing but a prelude to what came after— what followed was nothing but the logical conclusion of a series of originating structures and patterns. Coffee in particular is often presented as the great dividing line—a force that entirely revolutionized or dissolved every agrarian pattern that preceded it.

All this rests on a very narrow empirical base. David Browning's book on Salvadoran land use is cited more often than any other to support this perspective, even though it also suggests that El Salvador did not make the transition to an economy centered on coffee and dominated by an oligarchy until the 1920s. Browning cites evidence from the pre-1900 period that indicates a great diversity in land use patterns. He acknowledges—without specifying a precise time frame—that most coffee cultivation was done by small growers, and that coffee production did not displace other economic activities. But Browning, who relies almost completely on the government's *Diario Oficial* rather than local archival sources, never reconciles his discussion of these trends with more prominent (and often quoted) passages in which he presents coffee and the development of a landholding elite as the key to the period's history. By the late 1870s, Browning suggests, the state was involved in promoting export agriculture, and state leaders realized that the communities and villages could not respond quickly to the opportunities offered by coffee production, a process from which "the majority of the population were excluded."[7]

Browning and others have also assumed that the special requirements of coffee production could be met quickly only on larger plantations with permanent plantings, ready capital, and a massive labor force during the picking season. Furthermore, the elite, assumed to be in firm control of the state, decreed the destruction and appropriation of peasant landholdings:

> An ill-defined and chaotic colonial pattern of land use and tenure . . . persuaded the coffee planters that major reforms were necessary. That these reforms led to a rapid and dramatic transformation of the entire agrarian structure may be attributed to the complete authority of a small oligarchy in whose interests the changes were made, which, freed from colonial restraints, viewed the nation's land and people as resources to be used for its own benefit.[8]

For Browning, as well as other scholars, the transformation of community and municipal landholding patterns was carried out by a small oligarchic elite who controlled state policy.[9]

As a result, discussions of Salvadoran history consistently emphasize how authoritarian politics have determined the fate of the peasantry and land tenure, and how coffee exports served as the elite's battering ram against the peasantry. The arguments presented here question these assumptions[10] and attempt to move Salvadoran historiography away from a rigid economic determinism. The impact on peasants of increasing agro-export production, the emergence of powerful landholding elites, and the rise of increasingly centralized liberal states was not determined simply by economic relations or land tenure patterns. The political position of the peasantry, filtered through myriad local, regional, and national structures, also helped to determine peasant initiatives and responses to the various transformations of the 1820–1930 period. Local power relations—to which peasants were inextricably connected—influenced the structure of land tenure, class formation, and the national state.

This book argues that in the nineteenth century Salvadoran peasants had secure access to land and commercial networks. A weak state, dependent on local power bases and always vulnerable to invasion from other Central American states, and the autonomous role of peasants and their communities gave the peasant economy a certain strength and enabled peasants to participate in commercial and export markets.[11] While they never "seized" the central state, peasants established significant limits and conditions on the actions of other social sectors and the state over questions of power and production. These legacies, fought over for much of the nineteenth century, gave peasants great autonomy—a fact that historians of Latin America are only beginning to research. The result of this legacy is that the transformation of landownership encouraged by liberals and the state took place in a context that provided significant opportunities for peasant landownership and commercial production.

This book reconstructs the agrarian social history of El Salvador in the nineteenth century, especially the western and central regions. Using local archival materials, it traces the formation of a heterogeneous peasantry out of the complex interaction of colonial legacies, peasant practices, and state policies. It focuses on the development of peasant and communal organizations, agriculture, and land use patterns. Contrary to conventional wisdom, the growth of export agriculture and the privatization of land in the nineteenth and early twentieth centuries did not inevitably lead to the immediate expropriation and proletarianization of peasant producers. Instead, these changes created a differentiated class of peasants and small-scale farmers. While the expansion of exports like indigo and coffee revolutionized important aspects of local society, they did not destroy the nation's peasantry. In fact, the clearest result of so-called liberal reforms was the institutionalization of a differentiated, ethnically polarized, freeholding peasantry rather than a transition to a "proletarian" agrarian capitalism.

Despite the importance of new social processes linked to coffee, local agrarian society in most regions retained a degree of continuity with previous patterns. Peasants retained considerable autonomy in relation to other social sectors, as they struggled with, resisted, adapted to, and participated in changing conditions, including the expansion of coffee production. Established social structures provided a framework for coping with the new social relations that began to emerge after the 1870s when coffee became a significant export product. Furthermore, Salvadoran peasants participated in the formation of the nation-state. Peasant communities and peasant-based factions played an important role in local and "national" political struggles—as citizens, insurgents, and soldiers. But this participation developed strong limitations as the century advanced and the administrative and military capacities of the national state expanded, although not in a linear fashion.

## El Salvador's Agrarian Society, ca. 1920

Salvadoran history has often been contrasted with that of Costa Rica. For modern-day observers, the divergence could not be more clear: while Costa Rica has experienced stable, electoral rule and the abolition of its military since 1948, El Salvador remained under military influence for decades, and only after the negotiated settlement of a protracted revolutionary war involving extensive U.S. intervention did it make a transition to civilian rule and stable electoral politics.[12] Similarly, contemporary El Salvador's striking class differences stand in contrast to Costa Rica's less polarized social structure and its social welfare policies.[13] Despite recent reconsiderations and refinements, the predominant view sees the character of Costa Rica's expansion of coffee production, and the associated structures and struggles, as one basis for the development of a more egalitarian and democratic society within a modern welfare state.[14] On the other hand, most observers of El Salvador, with its ethnic divisions, scarce land, and successful elite, focus on the concentration of land in few hands and the violent domination of authoritarian regimes over Salvadoran workers and peasants. Bradford Burns, for example, posits a dramatic contrast between the egalitarian ("leisurely") society of midcentury that produced for the world markets and the plantation-based, oligarchic, export-oriented, coffee-based, authoritarian Salvador of the 1890s—thus pushing back the changes of the 1920s and 1930s by four decades.[15]

This book argues against such simplistic contrasts. In fact, in some important respects El Salvador's history before the 1920s resembles aspects of the Costa Rican experience.[16] We must reexamine the assumptions built into prevailing interpretations of Salvadoran history. This study is motivated by various important questions connected to El Salvador's twentieth-century history. First, how can one explain the successes of the revolutionary movement of the 1980s? By 1983 the Farabundo Martí National Liberation Front (FMLN) controlled vast extensions of El Salvador's national territory.[17] The FMLN's success in holding onto much of the northern and eastern parts of the country cannot be attributed only to the tactical failures of Salvadoran armed forces in dislodging guerrillas from mountainous terrain. Instead, the FMLN clearly developed strong and enduring bases of peasant support in these regions of isolated, neglected, and impoverished peasant agriculture.[18] Decades of poverty and neglect by the central state since the 1950s contributed to the peasants' support, especially in regions with a long tradition of peasant access to land that had survived (if marginally) the dramatic agrarian changes of 1950–1979. The FMLN's success in recruiting peasants went far beyond the foundations laid by pre-1980 popular organizations.[19] In all regions, the effects of post–World War II economic growth on peasants and rural laborers have been crucial to political and social mobilization. Regional differences in the ability of the FMLN to mobilize support raise questions about the local history of class and ethnic relations in El Salvador that this book hopes to begin to answer.

Other questions also emerge from an examination of export production and land use patterns in the first decades of the twentieth century. Historians have assigned a disproportionate role to coffee production, given the actual use of land and labor. The role of coffee has been exaggerated in a teleology shared by perspectives of both left and right: all that was good—or bad—came from the crop, and there was no national history or nation without it. This emphasis obscures the social history of El Salvador's peasants, buried beneath the timeless power of elites and the exploitation of landless wage workers. Yet even a cursory examination of the 1950 agricultural census reveals important pockets of peasant and small-scale agriculture throughout the country, as well as a significant rural middle sector.[20] This raises further questions about the origins of the coffee economy and its impact on the larger society. Could a crop that occupied no more than 40,000 hectares at the turn of the century so clearly have dictated the history of the country's peasantry?

These questions are further fueled by a reading of travel narratives and other descriptions of early twentieth-century El Salvador. Despite their often sweeping generalizations, these accounts present an image of El Salvador very different from the stark polarized scenario reproduced in most depictions of the country. They reflect a surprising consensus that the peasantry and other small-scale producers were an important component of the country's social structure well into the 1920s.[21] One source observed that in El Salvador "the standard of living among the laboring classes is considerably higher than in Guatemala and Nicaragua."[22] In 1910 Dana Munro noticed "plot after plot of coffee grounds as large as village squares, each owned and worked by some peasant proprietor" and argued that the Salvadoran peasants and workers "had never suffered from the rapacity of large landholders."[23] Munro correctly concluded that most of the country's rural residents "earned their livelihood from the cultivation of export crops and from wages, rather than from subsistence agriculture alone."[24] Wallace Thompson wrote in 1924, "Most of the work of El Salvador is done by its independent farmers in their time off."[25] Similarly, Karl Sapper found that "in El Salvador, generally, the small rural property [owner] no longer is always able to produce enough to feed his family. Nevertheless and in spite of differences in detail, the much more equitable division of property results in there being few people without their own land."[26] In 1897 Alexandre Lambert de Sainte-Croix, who observed the peasantry after the privatization of common lands, found an extensive division of property within the coffee economy and even among the Salvadoran elite when compared to Mexico and Guatemala.[27] In 1916, Gulian Lansing Morrill, while contemptuous of Salvadoran poverty, noted that "the peonage or slave system as one finds in Guatemala or Mexico is un-known. The feudal land system isn't fashionable and the people are larger real estate owners than in other Central American countries."[28] Similarly, in 1924 Thompson found that together with clear class distinctions,

> these are the farms, large and small (the numbers of tiny patches prove how many are the individual farms) where food are grown to supply the coffee plantations and for export. . . . The coffee country . . . there, too, there will be many individual properties, for the Salvadoreans are happy in the bits of land that they come to own. . . . The lower classes are apparently well able, also, to take care of themselves in small business, and the percentage of small holdings and tiny coffee "estates" is as high, almost, as in Costa Rica. It is estimated that 75 percent of the coffee of Salvador is raised on properties held by small landowners of the low and lower middle classes. . . . The bulk of the labor of the picking season, however, comes from the small landowners and their families. These independent Salvadoreans, if they are coffee raisers, finish their own picking first, and then go, with their wives and children, to work on one of the big fincas near at hand. . . . There they join the volunteers who have come out from the town, and also, another class like themselves, small farmers who raise other crops than coffee, but who come in to work on the fincas through the picking season. . . . Land is the most approved investment of the upper classes, and in every rank of the lower classes the same instinct appears.[29]

These passages reveal the importance of the Salvadoran peasantry and small producers even within conceptions that emphasize the export economy.

Harry Latourette Foster provides further confirmation. In 1925 he wrote, "Salvador . . . is mainly a coffee country. It is not, however, a country of large estates but of small holdings."[30] In 1917 William Henry Koebel commented, "On the whole . . . the holdings are small, being devoted to such products as coffee, sugar, and tobacco. The country, in fact, is largely one of peasant proprietors."[31] Even an official 1924 government report, probably compiled by Pedro Fonseca, head of the National Statistics Office, reads: "As in our country wealth is very fractioned, production generally satisfies demand, and the average economic standard is higher than in many countries in America." Other observers noted that despite the presence of a few very large coffee producers "the number of small producers is large."[32] For Frank G. Carpenter, El Salvador was "one big farm, with all its people at work, and no land wasted. Practically every man owns a little piece of property, or else has a good home upon one of the many large plantations. Even the poorest have something to lose in case of a revolution, and hence all are peaceful[ly] inclined."[33] Manfredo Vanni, a more sophisticated observer, provides a more detailed assessment of the land tenure situation in the mid-1920s by estimating that around half of all Salvadoran households owned land.[34] While these assertions need not convince us entirely, they do suggest the significance and extent of peasant landownership in El Salvador and provide a set of guiding questions for this study.[35]

## *Region and Geography in El Salvador*

El Salvador is a land of physical and ecological contrasts. (See map 1.) Its relatively small land area includes a multitude of volcanoes, interior elevated plains, coastal lowlands, and coastal and interior mountain ranges and hills of volcanic origin. Volcanic activity provided El Salvador with highly fertile soil. The country contains only one large river, the Lempa, which winds through a dry interior basin before emptying into the Pacific. The alluvial coastal plains are also fertile. While there are many peaks of a few thousand feet, elevation of most of the terrain is below 3,000 feet.

There are two common ways of dividing El Salvador into regions. Dividing it into three north-to-south strips is to stress historical over geographical factors. A second mode, which emphasizes natural features of the landscape, is to divide it into three east-to-west strips separated by mountain ranges.[36] The northern strip, mountainous, arid, and rugged, runs along most of the border with Honduras; the center strip contains mountains and settled valleys, including most urban centers and a large share of the population; the southern coastal plains, valleys, and mountain ranges have until recently been less populated. This study uses both

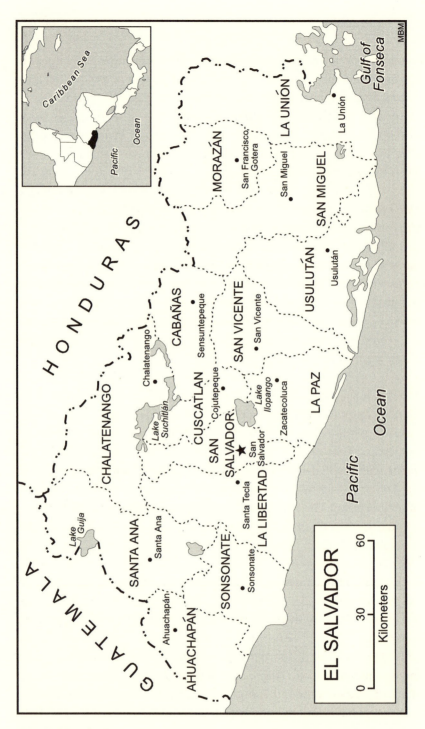

Map 1. El Salvador

perspectives; integrating the ecological variations of the horizontal perspective with the politico-historical variations implied in the vertical is a more useful approach to the diverse landscapes and local histories of El Salvador.

## Organization of the Book

The following chapters focus on the position of the peasantry and small-scale producers in relation to the formation of elite sectors, the state, and the local and national commercial economies. They also provide a framework for future study of El Salvador's regional history that incorporates both the peasantry and the complex story of peasant-elite relations. Chapter 2 examines late colonial landholding patterns, the social structures associated with the production of indigo in this period, and the impositions of the colonial state.[37] It emphasizes the role of small producers and demographic, ethnic, and economic trends. The colonial period left El Salvador three great legacies. It saw the founding of the haciendas, the establishment and expansion of collectively owned lands for both Indian and Ladino communities, and the beginnings of commercial production of sugar, cacao, indigo, cattle, and other products by both peasants and haciendas.

El Salvador's most important characteristics began to emerge in the eighteenth century: the urban centers of Sonsonate and San Salvador were extensively commercialized; community ownership became an important feature of land tenure; the population was ethnically heterogeneous;[38] and large areas of land were privately owned. By the end of the colonial era, El Salvador was Central America's most thoroughly commercialized region, although its commerce was firmly based in peasant forms of production and landholding.[39]

Chapter 3 examines community and hacienda landholding after independence. It reviews national and local land legislation and the effects of politics on land-related issues. It reviews the history of El Salvador's Indian and Ladino communities, municipal landholdings, and internal frontier settlement (which often extended colonial-era forms of common land use). Salvadoran peasants with land could both raise their own crops and produce for the market. In the nineteenth century, community-controlled and municipal land use became more complex. This legacy of strong municipal and community land use, given a relatively weak hacienda sector and expanding commercial agriculture, facilitated the production and export of grains, sugar, indigo, coffee, and other products, especially after the 1850s.

Chapter 4 discusses local economy and society between the 1830s and the 1880s. El Salvador was unusual among the republics that emerged from the Captain Generalcy of Guatemala in combining an extensively commercialized economy with widely distributed trade networks. In addition to producing indigo and raising animals for export, El Salvador added other products in the nineteenth century—silver, coffee, rice, sugar, liquor, tobacco, cigars, and crafts. Internally, El Salvador developed complex and extensive trade networks that became visible in the many commercial fairs and peasant markets. In the fifty years after independence, hacienda-based agriculture and landowning declined in significance, while peasant landholding, production, and commercial involvement increased. Community and village structures sustained the relative prosperity of the peasantry even as social and economic differentiation emerged. In the west, both Ladinos and Indians participated in the commercial economy, but Indians were more likely to become Ladinos if they left home to seek work and opportunity elsewhere. The expansion of regional and export commercial activities in the late 1850s spurred the creation of new sectors of successful farmer-entrepreneurs based on municipal and community lands.

Chapter 5 considers the peasants' role in the political struggles between the 1820s and the 1890s. After independence from Spain and a brief period in which Mexico attempted to annex the region, El Salvador embarked on a long and conflict-ridden process of state formation. Before the emergence of an effective central state with power to implement and enforce laws, a decentralized polity prevailed in which peasant communities, autonomous municipal governments, military strongmen, neighboring states, and weak state institutions were locked in protracted conflicts and unstable alliances. During these tumultuous decades, peasants, artisans, and communities mobilized in various ways, while local and national politics became connected as military caudillos sought alliances with local social forces. Even attempts to defend lands by Indian communities, for example, were related to larger regional, national, and even isthmian political factionalism. An effective national state did not begin to emerge until the 1880s, when export revenues, telegraph service, railroads, a professional military, and foreign pressures slowly brought a measure of stability.

Coffee production is the subject of chapter 6. After the 1850s, coffee was a viable product because it complemented existing commercial activities. Its labor demands were compatible with raising sugar, indigo, and subsistence products, and because it could be grown on previously unused high-elevation forested areas, it did not displace other crops or change landholding patterns. Raising coffee for export supplemented other sources of income for peasants and for larger entrepreneurs, who ultimately benefited most. While coffee was important in the formation of a national elite and as part of the nation's economic development, it did not displace peasant agriculture nor suddenly revolutionize land tenure.

Chapter 7 looks at how communities and municipalities began the partitioning and titling of both possessed and unpossessed lands. After the 1870s, because of population growth and increased commercial farming, tenants wished to own the land they tilled. Legislators from the western coffee region backed laws to privatize community and municipal-owned farms. Thousands of peasants, farmers, and urban investors were able to own their farms, and even to claim unused lands. The privatization of common lands also encouraged the privatization of state-owned *baldíos* (unclaimed lands).

Chapter 8 examines how the protracted partition of community lands weakened ethnic communities and caused the dispersal (even loss) of once-collective resources. This process could take many years and caused many conflicts. Ethnic tensions were heightened as Indian communities clashed with local Ladinos over partitioning. However, conflicts did not necessarily follow ethnic lines, even in localities with significant Ladino and Indian populations, but reflected divisions based on emerging class differences or political alliances within the communities.

Chapter 9 concludes with a survey of the changes in landownership, labor, and how the formation of a peasantry with limited access to land set the stage for the dramatic events of the 1920s and early 1930s. In this period the consolidation of political and economic elites and rural middle sectors established limits to the peasantry's ability to reproduce itself, and a landless rural sector began to emerge. These conditions created the foundations for new politics that relied on clientelistic cross-class alliances mediated by a paternalistic state. This political system that combined liberal and authoritarian elements collapsed with the crisis of the agro-export economy in 1929, contributing to the revolt of 1932 and the reemergence and complete institutionalization of military control over the state.

## 2　Peasants, Indigo, and Land in the Late Colonial Period

During the late colonial period, both subsistence and commercial agriculture expanded in the two provinces that later united to form the State of El Salvador. The second half of the eighteenth century witnessed the steady rise of indigo production and export, as well as related economic activities. Indigo, a blue dye used in textile manufacturing in Europe and the Andes, could be produced and processed by both small and large growers. The colonial-era provinces of San Salvador and Sonsonate became production centers, while the merchants of Guatemala City, and to a lesser extent San Vicente, San Miguel, and San Salvador, controlled most of the financing and marketing of the crop. An important part of the Salvadoran colonial legacy was a strong and heterogeneous peasantry of both Ladinos and Indians deeply connected to these commercial activities but at the same time protective of local political autonomy and resources.

### Indigo, Peasants, and Estates in the Eighteenth Century

Indigo, cattle raising, and other commercial activities encouraged a limited economic expansion in the region, with peasants and communal producers becoming important participants. The term *peasant* refers to small-scale, mostly agricultural producers who grow their own crops but do not necessarily produce for the market. Peasants do not hire others, but instead depend on their own family or community members to work with them. They can be tenants, sharecroppers, owners of land, squatters, or claimants to untitled land. As used here, the term rarely implies a directly subordinate position in relation to a landholding elite or the state.[1]

Indigo production left El Salvador two important legacies. First, it stimulated the formation of haciendas. These estates, most of them undercapitalized and not fully cultivated, created an enduring social structure whose impact would be felt into the twentieth century. Second, a market economy based on indigo, cattle, grain, and other products initiated a pattern of peasant access and titling of lands and the mobilization of community and family resources for commercial production.[2]

Indigo and other commercial products gave peasants important opportunities, especially the expanding group of Ladinos. Whereas Indians were usually identified by their membership in pueblos or communities that dated back to the early colonial era, Ladinos were Indians who had left their native communities and had taken on the dress or language of Spaniards, or simply abandoned their ethnic identity. The term can also mean *mestizo* or mulatto, as many Ladinos were products of unions between Indians and whites or Africans. By the nineteenth century, *Ladino* was more of an oppositional category—anyone not identified as white or Indian—although Ladinos could develop as formal an ethnic consciousness as Indians, especially as members of a landholding community. Ladinos made up about half of the Salvadoran population by the late eighteenth century.

Indigo production gave peasants a certain autonomy, whether they worked communal lands or their own, and limited the expansion of the estates by reducing the labor pool. These changes also affected Indian communities and peasants not involved directly in the indigo trade. Many Indian communities expanded economically and demographically during this period and gained in material well-being and autonomy—gains that were consolidated in the 1830–1880 period.

Indigo production and export in Central America had expanded greatly in the 1600s, supplanting cacao as the principal export, but declined toward the end of the century. The boom that began in the 1730s marked the beginning of an important economic and social change. Indigo brought profits to *hacendados* and small producers, tax revenues to the royal coffers, and cash income to Indian and Ladino laborers. At least half, perhaps two-thirds, of the indigo produced in colonial Central America during the eighteenth century came from small Ladino and Indian growers,[3] and 90 percent of the crop was grown and processed in the province of San Salvador.[4] The implications of this legacy, however, have not been well enough related to the development of the Salvadoran peasantry.[5]

Expanded indigo production encouraged the establishment of haciendas that also raised food and cattle, but small producers and Indian communities also responded to new demand for indigo. (The same applies to the colonial-era cattle trade, which was probably as important as indigo to the Indians.) The town of Chalchuapa in the modern department of Santa Ana, then mostly Indian, illustrates the links between the expanding indigo economy and other sectors. As a center for raising and selling livestock, Chalchuapa's cattle farmers provided food for hacienda laborers and skins for packaging the indigo.[6] As a result, many western and south-central towns, many controlled by Indian communities, specialized in small-scale cattle raising, a legacy that continued until the late nineteenth century.

In the eighteenth century, there was little competition for land except where dense peasant settlement coincided with estate expansion, such as around the cities of San Salvador and San Miguel.[7] In most other areas, especially where Indian communities did not title lands beyond the areas they occupied, extensive free lands were available throughout the century; the only limitation to their use was access to mule paths and roads.

Some successful large landowners and indigo producers began as tenants of Indian communities and eventually purchased or gained permanent control of their lands.[8] However, there were no economies of scale in indigo production, which permitted small producers to compete successfully in both producing and processing the dye. (Land dedicated to the indigo-producing weed for three months could be planted with corn the rest of the year.)[9] Their numbers increased over the century. Travelers who visited the region noted the growing of indigo "at every small settlement" across the province.[10] Observers estimated that between one-third to one-half of the crop was produced by *poquiteros* (smallholders). The more conservative estimate of one-third implies that at the height of colonial indigo production there were around 3,000 small-scale producers with an annual output of about 100 pounds. This figure is consistent with other data on the size of peasant *ejidos* (common lands held by municipalities) and communal holdings.

In 1768 Cortés y Larraz, bishop of Guatemala, who visited most towns in the region, commented on the large number of indigo and cattle haciendas, almost twice the number found in 1740. Of 540 haciendas, he found that about two-thirds grew indigo. But his description, together with other evidence, indicates that few could properly be called haciendas, given their size and the scale of their activities.[11] Ulloa, a colonial intendent who reported on the state of the province, also found haciendas to be small; frequently, the holdings of peasant Indian and Ladino communities and towns were larger.

The lack of an extensive internal market and a large economic motor such as silver mining or large-scale commercial agriculture, found elsewhere in Latin America, meant that most Spanish landholders in El Salvador were relatively poor, with little capital to invest; many were priests.[12] The lack of large-scale elite-controlled economic activity meant that these farmers lived most of the year on their lands outside the principal Spanish towns—Salvador, Santa Ana, San Vicente, Zacatecoluca, Sonsonate, and San Miguel. The decline in the revenue-producing Indian population limited the Spaniards' ability to accumulate wealth, especially after the decline of cacao production. What revenues they received from cattle, indigo, and sugar went to pay scarce and expensive laborers, high transport costs, and—more important—the merchant elite of Guatemala City, who controlled the export of the dye and imports of important products.[13] Many were actually quite impoverished, enjoying elite status only in relation to local standards.

A report prepared by the Real Consulado de Comercio de Guatemala (Merchants' Guild of Guatemala) for Antonio Larrazábal, deputy to the Spanish Cortes in 1811, described the poverty of the kingdom's *hacendados:* "Despite the vast lands that their haciendas include, in reality they are poor, because beside that their possessions have debts to the church *[capellanías]*, mortgages, and other encumbrances on them that are equivalent to their value; . . . they must go into debt to be able to work as they are accustomed to, rarely achieving the relief that happiness and well-being brings to man."[14] The largest and most productive estates were owned by Guatemala City merchants themselves—often after taking them over from indebted local proprietors. The Aycinena family, for example, owned some of the largest haciendas in the districts of Zacatecoluca and San Vicente. In addition, Ladino settlers from other provinces also held titled possessions and gained the status of local notables by serving in the militia, one of the few avenues for advancement outside of agriculture and manufacturing. Their farms, however, were never very productive, even if they covered large areas.

The income from indigo production, however, enabled hundreds of small producers, most of whom did not hire laborers but relied on family and community members, to acquire land and produce for the local market.[15] While 10 percent of indigo producers made tax payments, indicating the predominance of smaller farmers, few peasant producers appear in official records for a number of reasons. Many sold their crop unprocessed to larger producers who operated their own processing facilities *(obrajes)* and had access to the marketing networks required to export the dye.[16] In addition, it was easier for small producers to process and market their crops illegally without registering them with local authorities, thus avoiding taxes.[17]

The size of indigo producers varied significantly from one region to another. Most indigo haciendas were established around the cities of San Salvador, San Vicente, Zacatecoluca, and San Miguel. There were more than 200 *obrajes* surrounding San Salvador, and more near San Miguel.[18] Smaller producers tended to predominate in areas around Chalatenango, Tejutla, Sensuntepeque, and Santa Ana. Indigo was grown, however, in most populated areas. The regional and size breakdown of tithe payments (table 2.1) indicates the distribution of production, which reflected important demographic changes between 1740 and 1807.

As the Ladino population expanded and new areas on the borders of existing pueblos were colonized, new zones of indigo production were brought into cultivation by Ladino peasants. The regions of expanding indigo production before independence (San Miguel, Chalatenango, Cabañas, San Vicente) were also the regions of greatest demographic growth. (See appendix.) Among the principal regions of peasant indigo production were the northern districts of Chalatenango and Tejutla. Successful peasants and their communities were able to extend their titled

Table 2.1  Tithe Payments by Indigo Producers in 1804

|  | Small (<10) | | Medium (11–100) | | Large (100+) | |
|---|---|---|---|---|---|---|
|  | No. | (%) | No. | (%) | No. | (%) |
| Tejutla (Ch) | | | | | | |
| Tithe payers | 83 | (88) | 11 | (12) | 0 | ( 0) |
| Lbs. of tithe | 263 | (50) | 279 | (50) | 0 | ( 0) |
| Suchitoto (Ca) | | | | | | |
| Tithe payers | 32 | (55) | 24 | (41) | 2 | ( 4) |
| Lbs. of tithe | 176 | (18) | 534 | (54) | 272 | (28) |
| San Salvador (SS) | | | | | | |
| Tithe payers | 4 | (22) | 10 | (56) | 4 | (22) |
| Lbs. of tithe | 28 | ( 3) | 389 | (38) | 607 | (60) |
| San Vicente (SV) | | | | | | |
| Tithe payers | 4 | (16) | 11 | (44) | 11 | (44) |
| Lbs. of tithe | 25 | ( 1) | 450 | (19) | 1,922 | (79) |
| Zacatecoluca (LP) | | | | | | |
| Tithe payers | 0 | ( 0) | 2 | (25) | 6 | (75) |
| Lbs. of tithe | 0 | ( 0) | 151 | ( 8) | 1,815 | (91) |

*Sources:* Wortman, *Government and Society;* Rubio, *História del añil.*

lands to hundreds of *caballerías*. (A *caballería* was about 45 hectares.) Ladino peasant communities that called themselves workers' brother-hoods *(hermandades de labradores)* obtained title to very extensive lands in 1779, 1780, and 1782.[19]

Although the region had some medium-sized producers and a few haciendas, most of the crop was grown by peasants working communal lands.[20] The *Apuntamientos*—reports by the Central American represen-tative to the Spanish Cortes of 1811—described the 12,500 residents of Tejutla and Chalatenango, "the majority of whom are owners of small plots," as the most productive farmers in the kingdom, who despite the sterility and dryness of their lands outproduced all the haciendas, usually raising 150,000 pounds of indigo annually and over 225,000 in 1806.[21] Gutiérrez in 1807 listed the many hamlets in these districts and pointed to their specialization in indigo. This is not surprising, given that most towns, especially in the east and north, had no manufacturing or other nonagricultural enterprises.

Small producers often rented lands from *hacendados* or other land-owners, but the proportion of people living on haciendas has been exaggerated. Browning relied on Cortés y Larraz's estimate of 25–30 percent, but a more accurate (although incomplete) census of 1803, probably used by Gutiérrez in his report, states that in the entire Capitanía General of Central America, 13 percent of adult males were tenants. Gutiérrez himself reported 3,100 sharecroppers out of an adult male population of 58,000, that is, 5 percent.[22] Furthermore, as indicated by Cortés y Larraz's choice of the term *poblador* (settler) and other evidence, most hacienda residents were actually squatters who lived on haciendas but had no direct economic relationship with the owners. Others were tenants who paid a *terraje* (land-use) fee in cash or kind, but who usually did not provide labor services. Unlike the haciendas in other regions of colonial Spanish America, few had resident tenant workers who labored on the estate's productive enterprises.

Although indigo was not a very labor-intensive crop to grow, processing the plant did require significant labor during the eight-to-twelve-week season.[23] While Ladinos and Indians were increasing in population, large growers had difficulty getting field workers until new legislative policy imposed a labor tax on Indian communities in 1784. Although this law was constantly violated, the fact that growers had to resort to pressure to recruit workers indicates the autonomy of Indian communities when compared to other regions of Spanish America.[24] Wages were high and usually involved a large advance payment. The 1784 labor tax led to the recruitment of part of the adult male Indian population, who went to work on the farms and estates to fulfill their village quotas.

The 1784 labor legislation ordered the establishment of a town roster of one-fourth of a village's adult male population. According to a 1785 report, 3,280 Indian laborers from the provinces of San Salvador and Sonsonate worked on local estates. Another source estimated the male, tax-paying Indian population of Sonsonate and San Salvador at around 17,000.[25] Thus about 20 percent of all Indian men spent up to three months working on the 75 haciendas in the region (out of 400) that took advantage of the labor tax on Indian and Ladino communities. While only a handful of estates employed more than 100 workers, most were in the middle range, with 100–300 workweeks of forced Indian labor (roughly 15 to 30 workers) per farm. This means that the midsize haciendas employed about two-thirds of all the Indian laborers in the labor market.[26] In addition to forced Indian labor, an undetermined number of Ladino workers also worked during the indigo processing season.[27]

Land title records tell us much about eighteenth-century economic activities. Indian and Ladino peasant communities, as well as individuals, could purchase lands from the crown. (See table 2.2.) Pinto Soria mistakenly claims that *composiciones* (lands titled from the crown) unilaterally favored Spaniards and resulted in the loss of Indian lands. However, there were few well-established Indian lands in the early 1600s, when the native population had declined to a few thousand and many natives had been displaced to begin with.)[28] Most of the land claimed as *composiciones* was in indigo-producing regions, especially in sparsely settled areas (Chalatenango, San Miguel, and San Salvador). This data confirms that Salvadoran haciendas were not very large, since the mean for these *composiciones* was 855 hectares, an estimate that is distorted by the extremely large size of two peasant *composiciones* in Chalatenango of 3,555 and 4,365 hectares each. Excluding these two cases, the mean is 675 hectares. These claims were used mostly to establish new estates owned by individual landowners.

Table 2.2  Land Purchased from the Crown, 1748–1798
    (in *caballerías*)

|  | Sample Purchases | Total | (%) |
|---|---|---|---|
| San Salvador | 68, 2, 9, 12 | 91 | (13) |
| San Vicente | 4, 6, 19, 10, 9 | 48 | ( 7) |
| Chalatenango | 13, 79, 97, 31, 30, 34, 11, 13, 7, 5, 13 | 333 | (48) |
| San Miguel | 20, 57 | 77 | (11) |
| Sonsonate | 5, 30, 23 | 58 | ( 8) |
| Santa Ana | 14, 6, 4, 6, 9, 7 | 46 | ( 7) |
| Cuscatlán | 3, 3 | 6 | ( 1) |
| Ahuachapán | 7.5, 13 | 20.5 | ( 3) |
| La Libertad | 10 | 10 | ( 2) |
| Total purchases: | 36 | 689.5 | (100) |

*Source:* Solano, "Tierra."

*Note:* A *caballería* is approximately 45 hectares.

For two regions for which Cortés y Larraz provides details, the average hacienda in San Salvador (20 cases) enclosed about 1,012 hectares and in Chalatenango (12 cases) averaged 585 hectares, or 826 hectares for all cases—almost exactly as much as the average size of *composiciones* a few decades earlier. Eighteen community landholdings in Chalatenango averaged 400 hectares. This data helps to clarify the history of haciendas as a form of land tenure and as settlement and production centers. It confirms that haciendas, although relatively large, did not expand in size toward the end of the colonial period.[29] Haciendas were by no means the dominant social institution and at best a limited source of wealth.

## The Colonial Origins of Communal Landholding

El Salvador's system of common lands, which took shape in the colonial period, was based on medieval practices that were extended to Spanish America. (See map 2.) Under the law, the Spanish crown recognized the right of all towns to have enough land for their own subsistence. These lands were owned by municipal or ethnic bodies and could not be sold. Towns or communities could also purchase additional lands from the crown. These land use customs changed only gradually after independence. Most national governments did not challenge the legitimacy of municipal and peasant claims for free access to land, so this colonial legacy and its acceptance by republican governments provided a basis for community life and peasant production for most Salvadorans into the nineteenth century. Common lands were used for a wide range of economic activities, from large plots leased to wealthier peasants and investors for raising coffee or indigo to subsistence farming. Municipal and community landholding, as well as communal labor and irrigation systems, also influenced the formation of classes, communities, and ethnicity at the local level.

In the decades before independence, El Salvador's Indian pueblos and other communities dramatically expanded their landholdings. According to colonial Spanish law, every town, regardless of its ethnicity, could lay claim to 1,710 hectares of *ejidos*. Communities could survey and

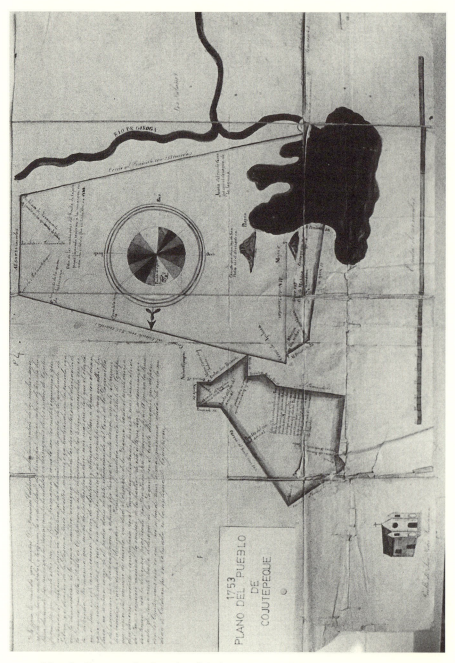

**Map 2. Community Lands of Cojutepeque, 1753**

purchase additional lands from the crown. Many Indian groups in the provinces of San Salvador and Sonsonate added lands to their *ejidos* in this way. However, claiming or expanding town lands was not an automatic process. Smaller communities, particularly in the northeast, often failed to seek titles for the full league of *ejidos* and seldom applied for additional *composiciones*.[30]

Communities were motivated to title lands for various reasons. In some cases they already used crown lands and were simply legalizing de facto possession. More frequently, however, communities expanded for political reasons. Control of land meant territory, and in the ethnically segmented polity of colonial El Salvador, ethnic competition became a search for control over land, regardless of the potential for its use. By claiming unused or peripheral lands, communities could create buffer zones against competing villages, ethnic groups, or landowners. This is apparent from the many colonial and nineteenth-century land documents and disputes between towns and between older Indian populations and new Ladino settlers. (See table 2.3.)

The ability to title new land depended on the political and cultural strength of a community.[31] Other factors included a community's ability to raise cash, the quality of its existing and new lands, and the presence of new settlers. Ladino *cofradías* (confraternities) were also given the right to title lands, a privilege usually reserved for Indian pueblos. Ladino *cofradías* also purchased haciendas and other privately owned lots. A few localities had both a Ladino and an Indian community.

The price paid for land in a *composición* was determined by combining the judgments of the crown's land surveyor with those of local witnesses, usually drawn from the community, about the value or usefulness of the land. Political factors also played a role. Indian communities were allowed to pay only half the assessed value of the land, while others had to pay in full. (Colonial land titles used in this section are listed in the appendix.)

Dozens of Indian and Ladino communities gained title to lands that ranged from a few *caballerías* to well over the 38 (1,710 hectares) to which they were entitled under colonial law. Table 2.3 lists the titles of village-owned lands (including *ejidos* and additional purchases), or most of the *ejidos* and *composiciones* titled in colonial Salvador. Some of the *ejidos* were less than the full 38 *caballerías* allowed by law. *Composi-*

Table 2.3  Confirmed Colonial-Era Titles to Lands Owned by Towns or Communities                          (in *caballerías*)

| Pueblo/Community | Year of Title | Haciendas/Plots | Ejidos | Composición |
|---|---|---|---|---|
| Guaymoco (Armenia) (So) | 1751 | | 3.5[a] | 10.5 |
| Jayaque (LL) | 1750 | one hacienda | | |
| Común de Ladinos de Guaymoco | 1750 | Santa Teresa | | |
| San Antonio del Monte (So) | 1753 | | 38 | |
| Juayua (So) | 1753–56 | | 38 | 61[b] |
| Dolores/Asunción Izalco (So) | 1753–79 | | 77 | 99 |
| Salcoatitán (So) | 1752? | | 26 | 12 ¼[c] |
| Común Ladinos Chalchuapa (SA) | 1755 | San Juan | 38 | 19 |
| | | Chiquito | 6 | |
| | | Guayavos | 21 | |
| Común de Pardos Santa Ana (SA) | 1729 | | 9.5 | 16 |
| Común Indios de Ataco (Ah) | 1751 | | 38 | 7.5 |
| Común Indios Nahuizalco (So) | 1777 | | 38 | 5 |
| Común Indios Nahuilingo (So) | 1778 | | 38 | 12 |
| Común Indios Ahuachapán (Ah) | 1751 | | 38 | 10 |
| Cofradía del Carmen (SA) | 1777 | | 18 | |
| "       " | | | 15.5 | |
| Huizúcar (LL) | 1774 | San Antonio Tepeagua | | |
| Comasagua (LL) | 1751 | | E | |
| Atiquizaya (Ah) | | | 76 | |
| Masahuat (So) | | | 50 | |
| San Pedro Pustla (Ah)[d] | 1737 | | 16.5 | |
| Común Ladinos Chalchuapa (SA) | 1829 | Canton Ayutepeque | | |
| "       "       " | 1826 | Santa Rosa & San José confirmed | | |
| | | Tierras del Arado, Rosario & Dolores | | |

Table 2.3  (continued)

| Pueblo/Community | Year of Title | Haciendas/Plots | Ejidos | Composición |
|---|---|---|---|---|
| Común Ladinos Chalchuapa (SA) | 1867 | Sitios Guachipilin, Sacamil confirmed | | |
| | | La Joya & Jocotillo (83 *cabs.*) confirmed | | |
| Común de Indios Atiquizaya (Ah) | 1883 | El Salitre confirmed | | |
| Común de Indios Nahuizalco (So) | ? | Los Trozos | | |
| San Bartolomé Perulapía (Cu) | 1805 | | 41–44 | |
| San Esteban (SV) | 1812 | Santa Catarina | | |
| Herm. Labradores Chalate. (Ch) | 1779 | | | 19 |
| Herm. Labradores Tejutla (Ch) | 1780 | | | 48 |
| Herm. Labradores Chalate. (Ch) | 1782 | | | 62 |
| Estanzuelas (Us) | ? | | E | |
| Perquin (Mo) | 1769 | | E | |
| Nejapa (SS) | 1806 | | 7 | |
| San Pedro Perulapan (Cu) | 1706 | | | 3.5 |
| San Juan Tepezontes (LP) | 1753–54 | | 24 | |
| Santa. María Ostuma (LP) | 1701/1755 | | | 32 |
| San Juan Opico (LL) | 1735–1742 | | | 10[a] |
| Santo Tómas (SS) | 1719 | | 11[a] | |
| Cacaopera (Mo) | 1724 | | 22[a] | |
| Ostuma (LP) | 1701 | | 4[a] | |
| Ostuma (LP) | 1701 | El Potrero | | |
| Santiago Texacuangos (SS) | 1660 | | 4+ | |
| "          " | 1736 | | | 3 |
| "          " | 1719 | | | 15 |
| "          " | 1807 | San Nicolás | | |
| Sensuntepeque/ Guacotecti (SV) | 1708 | | | 14 |
| Apastepeque (SV) | 1775 | | E | 14 |

Table 2.3  (continued)

| Pueblo/Community | Year of Title | Haciendas/Plots | Ejidos | Composición |
|---|---|---|---|---|
| Común Indios Cuscatancingo (SS) | 1749 | | | 4 2/5 |
| Soyapango (SS) | ? | | E | |
| Mejicanos (SS) | ? | | E | |
| Cojutepeque (Cu) | ? | | 20 | |
| San Sebastian (SV) | 1718 | | E | |
| San Pedro Nonualco (LP) | 1759 | | 6ª | |
| Santiago Nonualco (LP) | 1708 | | 38 | 5 |
| Santa Cruz Analquito (Cu) | ? | | 3 | |
| San Luis (LP) | ? | | 57 | |
| Texistepeque (SA) | ? | | 7 | |
| Tenancingo (Cu) | ? | | 5 | |
| Apaneca (AH) | ? | | 38 | |
| Estanzuelas (Us) | ? | | 33 | |
| Sensuntepeque (Ca) | ? | | 40 | |
| San Isidro (Mo) | ? | | 3 | |

*Sources:* See Note on Sources.

a. Possibly measured in "old" *caballerías* of 86 hectares.

b. Of which 12 ¼ were donated to Salcoatitán, in all likelihood.

c. Received as donation from Juayua.

d. Confirmed in 1880 with same extension of ejidos. E denotes the existence of *ejidos* of unspecified size.

*ciones* could range from a few *caballerías* to almost 100. The communities of the west and center were more interested in legalizing and extending land claims than those in other regions. Regions with the least *ejido* titling or the smallest *composiciones* were in the east and northeast, where Indian organization was weaker and where indigo haciendas had been largest and strongest. In general, Indian and Ladino communities were able to claim *ejido* land; there is little evidence of conflict over occupation of land with settlers or estates, except perhaps in the Indian towns surrounding San Salvador.[32] In the more densely populated region of San Salvador, Spanish-owned communal lands and haciendas were more likely to share boundaries rather than have extensive *baldíos* (unclaimed lands) between them, as elsewhere in the province.

## Commercial Agriculture and Indian Communities in the Late Colonial Period

Partly because of expanded commercial activity, at least compared with the other provinces of the kingdom of Guatemala, El Salvador has been depicted as a region of early ethnic and social homogenization, without strong urban polarities or regional inequalities, whose Indians tended to become ladinoized and deculturated.[33] The spread of the commercial economy promoted by indigo production, processing, and export is said to have encouraged these changes and the settlement of new regions and "dilution" of the Indian population.[34] This assessment is partially correct, but it simplifies the impact of the commercial economy, ignoring the wider processes involved in ethnic differentiation. While the Ladino population increased over the eighteenth century, Indian groups also persisted and in general demographic terms recovered after earlier declines. But many—perhaps most—Ladinos were not Indians torn from local communities. Most were immigrants from other provinces who were attracted to San Salvador by the region's economic success. These new settlers—many of them mulatto—often established themselves in Indian towns and contributed to the decline in ethnic cohesion and homogeneity in the eastern and northern regions of the province.[35]

Some scholars have attributed the demographic stagnation or decline of many Indian communities (a process that is rarely discussed as a *cultural* process of ladinoization) to the impact of the commercial economy.[36] Pinto Soria, for example, stresses the use of Indians in Spanish economic ventures as causing the Indian population to decline from around 200,000 to almost zero in the early colonial period.[37] Browning, while mentioning the impact of disease and disruption created by the conquest, also stresses the destructive effects of indigo haciendas on Indian communities. While there is indeed a correlation between hacienda-based colonial indigo production and the decline of Indian communities in these regions, the relation is not simply due to the exploitative or land-grabbing practices of haciendas.[38] Other processes were also involved; outside forces, such as immigration, contributed to the changes in the ethnic composition of San Salvador and Sonsonate. Internal elements also contributed to the decline in Indian predominance.[39] Colonial impositions, including taxes in kind and cash, and forced sales promoted the emigration of Indians, especially males, from their villages.[40] Resistance to these and other impositions caused demographic dispersal, in turn contributing to the deculturation of native or immigrant Indian groups. Opportunities in the Spanish cities and towns also promoted deculturation and ladinoization. Militia service offered upward mobility for male peasants, as shown by the significant number of militia officers who titled lands in the eighteenth century. According to Gálvez, the militia included almost all of San Salvador Province's *mestizos* and mulattos in 1740.[41]

All these factors indicate that the demands of the indigo economy alone could not have been responsible for the rise of Ladino population in the late colonial era. The economy itself, despite the linkages between cattle growing and indigo production, did not so much dissolve preexisting relations as promote new possibilities for action and mobility. This argument is confirmed by the extensive communal and ethnic autonomy of both Indians and Ladino peasant communities throughout El Salvador. Indeed, many elements of colonial society strengthened rather than weakened the ethnic corporate communities. By the late eighteenth century, a distinctive colonial institution—the Indian community—emerged side by side with an emerging Ladino peasantry with its own communal forms of land use and organization. As the Ladino population increased and some Indian towns became fully Ladino, many Indian communities grew and expanded their landholdings.

Western El Salvador provides examples of the success of both Indian and Ladino peasants in organizing communal forms of social organization and reproduction. At the end of the colonial period, western El Salvador had few large haciendas in production. Most productive "estates" were farms, often owned by poor Spanish and Ladino families, with little distinction in size or the value of their activities. Most were located in the arch of mountains and valleys between Ahuachapán, Chalchuapa, Santa Ana, and Opico. Sugar production was even more concentrated in contiguous parishes, between Santa Ana, Ahuachapán, and Chalchuapa. However, most enterprises were very limited in scale, and many were owned and run by peasant *cofradías* and communities rather than by individual Spanish or Ladino landowners. Indian and peasant autonomy, established early in the colonial period, was strengthened during the eighteenth century. Indian communities gained titles to more lands, and the hacienda economy remained limited to the coastal areas of Sonsonate and Ahuachapán and the northern parts of Santa Ana—regions of less dense Indian and peasant settlement. The peasant basis of settlement both on communal lands and elsewhere is evident. Cortés y Larraz noted that in the entire west, Santa Ana was the only locality where most of the Ladino population lived on haciendas, although probably as tenants or share-croppers rather than full-time laborers.

## Conclusion

The colonial inheritance of El Salvador included about 200 large and perhaps as many medium-sized haciendas, but their owners were never able to fully incorporate or subordinate a significant portion of the peas-antry. Most peasants, especially Indians, retained independent access to land in landholding communities or on various internal frontiers. While late colonial landowners and merchants received incentives and conces-sions from the state, especially the coerced wage labor of Indians, they were never able to displace peasant and community-based market pro-duction nor monopolize access to land. Peasants retained significant autonomy through the legal and paternalistic protection offered by the crown, combined with the limits to the power of isthmian elites and long-established commercial activities of many peasant communities. As the republican era began, the Ladino and Indian peasants of El Salvador controlled large areas through legal title. The hacienda system had not blocked their access to land or their ability to produce for subsistence and to participate in the commercial economy. This was an important starting point that would be reinforced after independence.

# 3   The Formation of Peasant Landholding Communities, 1820s–1870s

During the colonial period, landholding peasant communities were subjected to a series of colonial impositions that included coerced labor, forced sales, tribute payments, and other forms of coercive state-based extraction or market participation. After independence these long-standing colonial practices ended, and the power of the Salvadoran and Guatemalan elites that benefited from these policies weakened. After the 1810s, Indians in El Salvador no longer paid tribute or individual head taxes and could not be forced to work for wages. The new state had to build its incipient fiscal structures by creating liquor and tobacco monopolies that rarely provided reliable or expanding sources of revenue, or by taxing local trade in the major commercial centers. Merchants and landowners found themselves at a disadvantage without the structured networks and alliances of the colonial state that had supported their efforts to accumulate wealth. For peasants, independence meant relief from the external impositions of landowners and the state, but peasants did not necessarily withdraw from commercial networks and participation. An important part of the political economy of postcolonial El Salvador was the expansion of peasant control and acquisition of land and the extension of commercial participation. This chapter describes the expansion of peasant and community-held lands after independence. Between the

34

1820s and the 1870s, El Salvador became a stronghold of small-scale peasant producers with secure but complex (and often different) access to land.

## The Expansion of Common Lands After Independence

The use of common land in El Salvador changed little in the new independent Federal Republic. The new state did not, and probably could not, challenge the right of Indian or Ladino communities and municipalities to own and control land. Furthermore, between the 1820s and 1870s many communities acquired new lands through purchases or government concessions. During these years the Salvadoran legislature confirmed the (colonial-era) right of municipalities to own *ejidos* large enough to guarantee the subsistence of their residents. Later on, because of the collapse of the Central American Federation, civil wars, and political factionalism, no government could challenge the existence and extension of common lands. Political leaders who depended on popular backing used land-related policies to secure supporters or neutralize popular threats to government stability. Furthermore, the threat of peasant revolt and peasants' participation in armed movements facilitated the enlargement of holdings by municipalities, until peasant communities successfully competed with large private landowners for control over land.

By the mid-nineteenth century, a well-defined system had taken shape —one that gave the majority of rural Salvadorans access to land, as well as securing other resources and elements of community life. There were three types of peasant-held lands: individually owned or possessed plots, common lands held by municipalities and usually called *ejidos*, and lands held by either Ladino or Indian communities. This chapter focuses on how municipalities and ethnic communities, sometimes alone, sometimes in competition with each other, used, expanded, and negotiated over the resources they inherited from the colonial era.[1]

After independence, towns and communities needed to expand their lands because of demographic growth, and more of these lands were brought into cultivation. To expand their holdings, towns or communities could rely on the central government to grant them additional lands for their *ejidos* purchased from existing haciendas or granted from government-owned haciendas or public lands. Beginning in the 1830s and until 1862, the government was legally obligated to secure *ejido* lands for new municipalities.[2] At the very least, new towns received a portion of the *ejidos* of the town from which they had detached. An 1862 law ended the government's obligation to grant *ejidos* to new municipalities and forced new towns to purchase their own lands, although this law was not enforced after the overthrow of the Barrios government in 1863.[3] The number of new towns with their own *ejido* holdings created from settlements on private haciendas or state lands rose during the first half of the century and then more quickly after 1870. Nineteen new towns were established during the 1860s and 1870s, and of those, six were taken from the breakup of the large municipality of Cojutepeque after a major revolt in 1872. At least two others created municipal *ejidos* from properties held by local Indian communities.

Established towns also requested additional lands for their *ejidos*, usually arguing that their population had increased or that commercial agriculture had spurred the demand for land. Of the numerous requests, I found only one that was turned down by the government because this municipality had sufficient lands but had rented out too many of them to outsiders.[4] The ongoing expansion of *ejido* lands in new and established municipalities often resulted in significantly larger *ejido* holdings (see table 3.1). Nineteenth-century land grants or purchases ranged from just a few *caballerías* to more than 20 in many cases. Even municipalities with separate lands controlled by Indian or Ladino communities requested and received additional lands, either free or at relatively low prices. In some cases municipalities were able to purchase haciendas or large undeveloped lots privately, either with municipal funds or by raising subscriptions from residents. In 1860 the municipality of Apopa used funds from a local collection to purchase the hacienda "San Nicolás." They gathered 1,500 pesos toward lands costing 4,000, while the government donated 500 and gave the town six years to pay the rest. Contributors were charged half the normal rent for their *ejido* lands, although they complained that the lands belonged to them and they should not be charged at all.[5]

The Ladino-controlled village of Juayua and the city of San Vicente provide notable examples of the extension of *ejido* lands in two different

Table 3.1 Expansion and Confirmation of Common Lands, 1821–1880

| | | |
|---|---|---|
| San Vicente | 1842 | Hcda. Achchilco granted to *labradores* by govt. |
| Santa María | 1860 | From *baldío* 13.8 *cabs.* |
| Aguacaliente | 1861 | *Baldío* of El Cacao given by govt. |
| San Esteban | 1861 | $4,500 debt from purchase of hcda. San Esteban in 1831 canceled by govt. |
| Aguacayo | 1867 | *Baldío* of 11 *cabs.* ceded by govt. |
| Chinameca | 1860 | 69 *cabs.?* |
| Chinameca | 1867 | *Baldío* Coyolar at 20 pesos c/u 42 ⅜ *cabs.* |
| Guayabal | 1860 | Unspecified |
| Guayabal | 1867 | *Terreno* Tecomatepe 1.5 *cabs.* |
| San Matías Indian Community | 1888 | Ownership of hcda. Masajapa |
| S. Buenaventura | 1867 | Dueñas cedes *baldío* Palmital, paid cost of titling 10 *cabs.* |
| Opico | 1848 | Purchased ¼ of *baldío* of 8 *cabs.*; hcda. La Isla bought with local funds, $154 |
| Zacatecoluca | 1867 | Hcda. Los Reyes, 35 *cabs.*, purchased by govt. for $5,200 |
| Tonocatepeque | 1869 | Purchase of *terreno* Mistancingo |
| San Fernando | 1868 | Purchase of hcda. La Bobeda from S. Fran. Morázan, 12 *cabs.* for $1,200 |
| Apopa | 1860 | Local funds and govt. pay for hcda. S. Nicolás |
| Zacatecoluca | 1838? | Gift of ½ of hcda. Jalponguita, 13.5 *cabs.* |
| Jutiapa | 1859 | Terreno la Montaña given by Barrios, 9 *cabs.* |
| S. Miguel Jujutla | 1831 | Resurvey of *ejidos*, 33 *cabs.?* |
| Estanzuelas | 1864 | Resurvey of *ejidos*, 33 *cabs.* |
| Verapaz | 1840 | Purchase of hcda. San Francisco |
| Verapaz | 1872 | Hcda. Aquiquisquillo ceded by govt. |
| Tecapán | 1860–67 | Grant of part of *baldío*, 15 *cabs.* |
| Tecapán | 1847 | Grant of *terrenos* Bongos y Rillitos |
| Santa María Remedios | 1860–64 | Grant *baldíos* La Laguna and Mejicapa 18.5 *cabs.* |
| San Miguel | 1873 | *Baldíos* next to *ejidos* granted by Govt. |
| Nejapa | 1876 | Govt. purchase of 3 *cabs.* in hcda. El Angel |

Table 3.1 (continued)

| | | |
|---|---|---|
| San Lorenzo | 1830 | New Town, govt. granted *ejidos* |
| Tecapa (Alegría) | 1848 | Grant of *terreno* Chuchapuna by govt. |
| Santa Clara | 1859 | Granted La Laguna and part of Apastepeque's *ejidos* |
| Sensuntepeque | 1862 | *Ejidos* confirmed, 40 *cabs.* |
| San Isidro | 1862 | *Ejidos* confirmed, 3 *cabs.* |
| Estanzuelas | 1872 | Municipality owns hcda. Umaña |
| Usulután | 1866 | Bought from govt. @ 10 pesos, 6 *cabs.* |
| San Vicente | 1859 | Hcda. San Cristóbal purchased by govt. |
| San Vicente | 1843 | Hcda. Paras ceded by govt., sold $1,000 for schools |
| San Vicente | 1861 | Lands purchased for Apastepeque |
| El Triunfo | 1861 | *Baldío* in Tecapa given by govt., 20 *cabs.* |
| Santa Lucía | 1858 | New munic., 10 *cabs.*, later abolished and joined to Santa Ana, lands left for Indian community |
| Juayua | 1876 | Grant to municipality for *ejidos*, 20 *cabs.* |
| Sonzacate | 1848–67 | Nahuizalquillo plot bought by govt., 9 *cabs.* |
| Caluco | 1868–71 | *Baldíos* in *ejidos*, paid ¼ of value of 22 *cabs.* to claimant |
| San Pedro Pustla | 1871 | 25 *cabs.* confirmed as *ejidos* |
| Teotepeque | 1869 | *Baldío* Chiqulleca granted by govt. |
| Santa Tecla | 1854 | Hcda. Santa Tecla granted by govt., 55 *cabs.* |
| " " | ???? | Purchase of 8 *cabs.* |
| " " | 1856 | Part of *baldío* El Cimarrón by govt., 20 *cabs.* |
| La Libertad | 1847–54 | Part of *baldío* El Cimarrón by govt., 20 *cabs.* |
| Tacuba | 1874 | $400 in local funds to buy 8 *cabs.* in auction |
| Metapán | 1874 | *Terreno* Cara Sucia ceded by govt. |
| Acajutla | 1852 | Hcda. lands purchased by govt., 3 *cabs.* |
| Acajutla | 1871 | Govt. grant of 22 *cabs.* |
| Atiquizaya | 1870 | Govt. grant of 20 *cabs.* |

*Sources:* See Appendix.

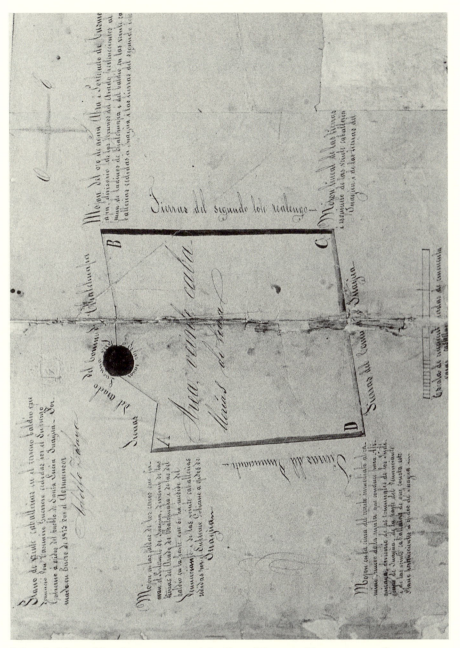

Map 3. Map of land grant to municipality of Juayua, Department of
Sonsonate, AGN, 1873

regions. Juayua, in the mountains of northern Sonsonate, was granted ownership in 1876 of an additional 900 hectares of *ejido* lands above and beyond the approximately 4,455 hectares it had titled during the colonial period. San Vicente was a small city in the central mountainous region that flourished during the eighteenth and early nineteenth centuries as an indigo-producing and artisanal center. San Vicente received the hacienda "Achichilco" in 1842 and the hacienda "San Cristóbal" in 1859 after the national government purchased it from its owner for 10,000 pesos.[6]

Land grants also extended into the 1870s by governments now characterized as "liberal." The best example is the town of San Rafael, founded in 1879. For this town, the national government purchased 1,890 hectares from Chinameca for 840 pesos, the same amount Chinameca had paid for the land decades earlier,[7] and 900 hectares were ceded to Atiquizaya in 1870.[8] Even after the abolition of *ejidos* in 1882, the government granted 4,500 hectares to Ahuachapán to be distributed and sold in small plots, together with its other lands.[9]

Between the 1830s and 1880s, Salvadoran governments did not pursue consistent or well-articulated land policies. A handful of laws from the Federation period (1824–1837), most of them used selectively by the regimes that enacted them and later ignored or reversed, reflected this instability. The Federation's attempts to use the sale of *baldío* (officially unclaimed) lands as a source of revenue were not successful. Only a few thousand pesos' worth of lands were sold during the Federation.[10] Later, the Salvadoran government intermittently offered incentives for the titling of *baldíos*. In 1844, for example, possessors (or those who worked) unclaimed lands could title them without going through the process of "denouncing" them as *baldíos*. If they did not possess the claimed lands, individuals had to make a moderate payment to the government, according to a 1835 law.[11]

In 1847 a new attempt was made to use unclaimed lands to pay the national debt. Local officials were ordered to make lists of local *baldíos* and lands with liens in favor of the state.[12] The available lands were to be sold at public auction, with three-fourths of the proceeds payable to the government in (probably devalued) bonds, and one-fourth payable in land or bonds to claimants, from which they had to pay for measuring and dividing the lands. However, the evidence shows that this legislation led to few claims on *baldíos;* the claiming of *baldíos* did not accelerate until after the 1860s.

An 1860 law affected a larger number of *baldío* claims. Claimants would no longer be able to demand part of the lands as payment for their services, since they always chose the best part of the lands for themselves. Thereafter they were paid in cash by the government, which would then sell the lands to the highest bidder. The government could also allocate the lands for *ejidos,* in which case claimants were paid in government bonds.[13] Later, an 1868 law specified that claimants of *baldíos* and excess lands within titled haciendas had to pay for surveys in advance and would be reimbursed only after the lands they "denounced" were sold by the government.

Other government efforts were aimed at controlling land transactions and titling. Before 1860 land titles were registered by individual notaries, but after that time three regional land registries were established under the Ministry of Justice. The General Treasury Court took over from the Land Court the task of resolving land disputes and selling government-owned lands. Many of the documents it inherited were damaged and unreadable. By 1872, however, it had copies of the titles to most of the country's haciendas.[14]

Individual use of *ejido* land by possessors was straightforward—once municipal permission was secured, individuals could fence in as much land as they could use and pay for without harming their neighbors. Town residents had up to three years (later reduced to two) to take possession and cultivate before the lands reverted to municipal control. Peasants and farmers constantly abused this condition by seeking to secure additional lands, either for speculation, future plantings, or crop rotation, although usually the extension of the plots was never very large.[15] However, because most municipalities had idle lands well into the nineteenth century, settlers apparently sought to colonize lands outside of the *ejidos* to avoid paying rent.[16]

Although most Salvadorans—excluding *hacendados*—could rent *ejido* lands, it is difficult to establish how frequently they did so. Demographic and land use data before the 1860s are hard to come by. Descriptions of the country in 1830–1850 show many people living in remote valleys and settlements, perhaps as settlers on untitled lands or unregulated municipal lands. But by 1855 U.S. diplomat Ephraim Squier noted, "Comparatively few of the people live outside of the numerous villages which dot over the state in every direction. The inhabitants of these towns have their little patches of ground at distances varying from one to five miles from their residences, and think little of traveling that distance in the morning to work them, returning at night."[17] Evidence suggests that by the 1850s, either as a result of state policies, demographic expansion, or local economic changes, dispersed settlers became more nucleated. This made access to and administration of municipal and community lands more important for an increasing number of peasants.[18]

The laws regulating municipalities determined how *ejidos* were organized and administered. Towns had to manage the funds and distribute the land according to a handful of laws or decrees established mostly by presidential fiat. For most of the nineteenth century, these laws were quite vague and usually not subject to enforcement, but population growth and the expansion of commercial agriculture gradually brought the towns under closer government regulation. Under these laws, municipalities had to rent lands to local residents who requested them and charge a small rental payment.[19] The law that regulated the use of common lands was expanded during the 1860s, when land acquisition increased markedly. In 1878 the government passed a law restricting the sale of rights to farms on *ejido* plots—an extensive practice throughout most of the country—including using these land rights as collateral for mortgages.[20] The sale of rights to *ejido* plots would be subject to a sales tax and municipal registration of the transaction. Other regulations established limits on the number of cattle a hacienda could have per *caballería* of grazing land, opened hacienda pastures to common use if they were unfenced, and set limits on the proximity of hacienda cattle to town *ejidos*.[21]

Although these laws were not necessarily enforced, they established parameters for the use of *ejido* lands. Most conflicts involving *ejidos* arose between municipalities over the boundaries of their lands or over claims to nearby *baldíos*.[22] Often the conflicts involved a town's *ejido* lands and those of a local or neighboring Indian or Ladino community (to be discussed later). The enforcement of land laws was irregular and could be affected by shifts in statewide political alliances. In 1835, for example, Chief of State Espinoza declared that all Indian communities could expel Ladinos from their lands and regain control of any lands previously rented or sold by town governments to Ladinos. But after attempting to support a large Indian revolt (see chapter 5), Espinoza was removed from power and his decrees were fully enacted in only a few localities. In the 1840s and 1850s, various administrations, especially under Dueñas, ensured the health of municipal *ejidos* by encouraging the acquisition and colonization of lands by small-scale producers and by offering state lands in small lots.[23]

President Barrios's attempts to maintain some social equality among the peasants and farmers in various parts of El Salvador provide another example of the relation between national governments and land policies. General Barrios took special interest in applying existing laws to the use of *ejido* lands and granted additional *ejido* lands to some municipalities. He also sent a special traveling commissioner with extraordinary powers to visit all of the Republic's towns. The officer's reports, some of which were published in the *Gaceta Oficial,* provide a detailed view of how *ejido* lands were used and the problems encountered by a centralizing, authoritarian government bent on enforcing a crude form of radical egalitarianism in the hopes of stimulating commercial production. Under Barrios's personal directive of favoring "one hundred against one," governors and the commissioner were ordered to ensure that municipalities did not allow the rental of lands to those who did not grow crops on their plots or who rented them out to third parties.[24]

Official ideology during the Barrios presidency—and probably earlier—was that *ejido* lands should be reserved for the working poor—the *proletarios*—of the pueblos rather than have them serve as a basis for speculation and enrichment by a few. This ideology underlay the government's efforts to stimulate the cultivation of export crops such as coffee on *ejido* lands. The national government found that Indian towns in La Libertad and San Salvador were especially lacking in their administration of community and *ejido* lands.[25] Carrying out these ideas depended on the availability of *ejido* lands. In the department of San Vicente, residents of some small towns with no *ejidos* were tenants on haciendas or rented plots from other municipalities.[26] A decree of February 18, 1860, prohibiting the rental of *ejido* lands to *hacendados* and merchants represented another attempt by Barrios to gain the support of peasant communities to tip the unstable balance of Salvadoran politics in his favor.[27]

The application of Barrios's policies in some towns meant taking plots away from many peasants with only marginally more land than they were entitled to. In 1863 in San Esteban, a small town in San Vicente, the departmental governor had redistributed one-third of the plots allocated by the municipality because they had more than .17 hectares of corn plantings. A total of 2.7 hectares of corn plantings were redistributed. Others who had rented out the lands they possessed lost all claim to them. In San Lorenzo the application of a similar measure led to the redistribution of about 2 hectares of corn plantings, and lands rented out to third parties were taken back. The governor reported that half the population in this relatively new town were paying high rents to other *ejidatarios* for lands to which they had rights as local residents.[28] In other cases, *hacendados* or speculators had amassed larger extensions of land for planting indigo or grazing cattle.[29] In towns where some plots within the *ejidos* had been privatized to favor those who had planted two-thirds of their land in export crops, the government forced the revocation of some titles when they discovered that their owners were not following regulations. In Villanueva and Ayagualo, for example, three plots of 16, 11, and 2 hectares were returned.[30] Although the peasants involved were small-scale producers with crops destined for the market, the purpose was to defend the coherence of municipal landholding. These disputes sometimes involved conflicts between Indians and Ladinos. In Apastepeque, for example, a peasant was awarded damage payments for the corn plantings he lost in the redistribution of *ejidos* ordered by Barrios.[31]

Barrios also ordered that *ejido* plots bordering on communal lands should not be used so as to avoid conflicts between towns and Indian communities. This supported an earlier (1848) law that ordered that lands that bordered on Indian community lands should be surveyed by a government-appointed surveyor.[32] In 1860 Barrios intervened in a legal dispute between the Indian community of Coatepeque (SA) and a claimant who attempted to title some lands known as *siete principes* (seven princes) as unclaimed land. The lands in question, about 2,745 hectares, apparently had been acquired by the local community from a convent. Basing his action on state laws that allowed the purchase of lands by corporate entities with "moderate compensation," Barrios allowed the community to title these extensive lands without payment.[33]

For the most part, however, Barrios was fighting the changes inflicted upon the peasantry by the expansion of commercial opportunities and demographic pressures—a peasantry whose resources in *ejidos*, communities, and unclaimed *baldíos* were substantial yet a potential source of instability. These efforts at rudimentary social equalization, which distinguished the Barrios regime from those that followed, were ineffective. First, most of the internal conflicts during these years arose in smaller towns without colonial origins and hence with smaller *ejido* or communal lands. Furthermore, the century-long growth of a peasant-based indigo and cattle economy had begun to put pressure on many villages and settlements with limited fertile lands, thus promoting differentiation within the peasantry.

Despite the efforts of the Barrios regime, few towns were interested in or prepared to manage their *ejidos* and the revenues derived from them. Peasants often resisted the charging of rents if they were not charged equally, if municipalities did not administer the funds appropriately, or if there were disputes over boundaries, titling, and ownership or possession of lands. In 1871, for example, some residents of Tecapa complained that the town was charging excessive *canon* (rent) for corn plantings. The town explained that rent had been charged inconsistently and unfairly and that many possessors considered themselves owners of large portions of land, to the exclusion of many members of the "proletarian class." Local officials called for a equitable redistribution of land to poorer peasants who would gladly pay rent.[34] This response sheds some light on the complexity of the conflicts that developed around the use of *ejido* lands. In this case, municipal officials tried to uphold the principles of equal access and proportional payment that Barrios had sought to establish, in opposition to the monopolization of *ejido* lands by a few richer peasants. Similarly, the peasants of San Esteban in 1861 refused to pay rent because the town lacked clear titles to its *ejidos*, which had come from a hacienda ceded by colonial authorities but was apparently not formally titled.[35]

## Landowning Ethnic Communities

Indian and Ladino communities present an even more diverse and complex picture. In many towns, all common lands inherited from the colonial period were considered to be part of the same unit; therefore, most considered any additional lands that had been titled in the colonial period to be part of their *ejidos*. However, many localities titled significant additional lands partly as a result of strong communal and ethnic organization. These towns were likely to be based on Indian and Ladino communities that survived into the nineteenth century and that claimed the *ejidos* or purchased lands as their own corporate property, even when the lands were recognized as part of the municipal *ejidos* by national law. For the most part, this meant that if a community had titled lands that were separate from the *ejidos*, they had undisputed possession.

Ladino communities that purchased lands within Spanish or Indian-controlled towns provide an important example of community landowning. Their properties were titled more clearly as their own property and rarely confused with municipal *ejidos*, making them more defensible from outside intrusion. With Indian communities, the distinction could be more complex. By the mid-nineteenth century, most Indian communities were formally distinct from the municipal administrations with whom they coexisted. In many cases, confusion or conflicts emerged over who had legitimate claim to any additional lands titled during the colonial period, in addition to the 38 *caballerías* of *ejidos* legitimated by colonial and republican law as necessary for any pueblo. In sparsely populated areas, Indians continued to use the lands without challenges; later in the century, as the Indian population expanded while ladinoization also advanced, conflicts emerged over borders and control of lands, and the government had to intervene in local disputes and clarify the competing claims.

In the 1860s problems arose over the administration of lands when many towns began to charge rental taxes and resurvey their *ejidos*. In 1866 the governor of Sonsonate, while not requesting the abolition of common lands, called for some sort of administrative supervision to account for income, bring new lands under cultivation, and expand commercial production. He explained that in some municipalities Indian communities were at odds with the town governments over whom they had a sort of practical veto power.[36] As a result, President Dueñas approved a decree in 1867 allowing towns to intervene in administering communal lands so as to control the income from renting such lands to outsiders.[37] Two years later, he established a law mandating the legal representation of all landholding communities in the country—officially recognized corporate entities were those in which more than twenty people held property together.[38] One intent of these laws was to open to agriculture the often extensive uncultivated lands held by Indian and other communities by clarifying who controlled these lands and which could be opened to use by others. In 1865 the governor of Sonsonate complained to President Dueñas that in Indian-controlled towns, Ladinos were excluded from renting lands or were charged high rents not charged to Indians.[39] Communities often held vast tracts of land in reserve, for crop rotation and to let plots lie fallow periodically, but excluded outsiders from using them. As towns defined their community-held lands and exercised a stronger role in community affairs, more land was brought into production.

As a result of the 1867 decree, Indian and Ladino communities were forced to choose an administrator and two assistants in elections supervised by the local town.[40] The administrator was to tend the books and report to the municipal council on community finances. These officials had to be bonded.[41] Also, communities now had to obtain the governor's approval before collecting rent, dues, or contributions from tenants to be used for legal procedures defending common lands. Communities could also elect a special ombudsman to represent their interests in court or before government officials.[42] Such representation reproduced aspects of Indian community organization from the colonial period that had fallen into disuse during the first fifty years of the Republic.[43] Because towns with a large majority of Indians were often more lax in their organization, this law was partly intended to regularize the administration of these lands. In 1867 the government ordered the town of Juayua to elect a mayor and *regidores* (council members). This once Indian community had lost its formal organization sometime between 1862 and 1867 when local Ladinos took control of the town.[44]

Regional officials perceived this law as a positive step. They claimed it brought more land into cultivation by clarifying the extension of *ejido* lands proper.[45] Other groups of peasants who had purchased lands or haciendas together were also affected by this law. For example, according to this law peasants in Atiquizaya who had gathered money in the late 1850s to purchase two large plots of land together (Salitre and El Rosario) had to form a community.[46] For most Indian communities, the new law legitimated their ownership of lands titled as *composiciones* during the colonial period—although the process was never automatic and usually led to new land surveys and disputes. This depended on a community's ability to organize a claim, show titles, pay for surveys, et cetera. However, most towns with distinct ethnic communities were also those with the largest eighteenth-century *composiciones* and were able to legitimate their claims to their lands and retitle them (see table 3.2). In some cases the lands considered to be the property of the Indian communities remained undivided *(pro indiviso)* from the *ejido* lands well into the nineteenth century and sometimes up to the time of their dissolution after 1880.

For the Ladino communities, property rights for most of their holdings were usually more clear, since their lands were always traced to purchases made as distinct corporate entities and were not confused with the claims of the municipalities themselves. In many cases both types of communities had purchased additional lands through the *cofradías* that they controlled, although *cofradías* appear to be mostly a Ladino institution in El Salvador.[47] An 1830 law, never systematically applied, called for the transfer of *cofradía* property to the government. A second law of 1832 prohibited the ownership of real estate by *manos muertas* (religious corporate bodies—literally, dead hands), allowing the privatization of individual plots on community lands owned by *cofradías*. But this law was applied selectively by a weak government, one that was promptly overthrown, and countermeasures were passed in 1835, again by a short-lived regime.[48] Most *cofradía* lands were actually in the hands of Indian and Ladino peasants, not the church—an institution that the weak Salvadoran governments of the 1830s were not willing to challenge.[49] However, these laws were cited a few times during the nineteenth century in attempts to dispossess communities and *cofradías* of their properties. Such attempts usually failed, both in 1867 and even as late as 1880, when community possession of lands was challenged by entrepreneurial farmers on this basis.[50] Furthermore, throughout the nineteenth century both Indian and Ladino communities purchased extensive additional large plots and haciendas from individual owners and the government.

The application of the 1867–1869 laws led to the formalization of new "communities" of Ladinos in places where none existed. The community of Ladinos of the hacienda "San Juan Masajapa" provides an example. A few dozen Ladino families collectively purchased the hacienda in the late 1840s or early 1850s. Eventually they organized an adminis-

## Table 3.2  Landed Indian and Ladino Communities, ca. 1880

| Ahuachapán | San Miguel |
|---|---|
| Ataco | Las Charcas (Positos) |
| Atiquizaya | Umaña |
| Ahuachapan | Santa Elena |
| Tacuba | San Miguel |

| Chalatenango | San Salvador |
|---|---|
| Chalatenango | Tonocatepeque |
| La Palma/San Ignacio | |
| San Miguel de Mercedes | Santa Ana |
| Las Vueltas | Comun de Ladinos del Volcan |
| Arcatao | La Laguna |
| Dulce Nombre de María | Comun de Ladinos de Chalchuapa |
| San Fco. Mercedes (Ladinos) | Coatepeque |
| Tejutla | |
| El Paraíso | San Vicente |
| Jocoatán (S. Fdo.) | Laguna de Santa Clara |
| | Tablón de Santo Domingo |
| Cuscatlán | Apastepeque |
| San Pedro Perulapan | |
| Suchitoto | Sonsonate |
| | Dolores Izalco |
| Cabañas | Asunción Izalco |
| Valle las Huertas, Ilobasco | Arménia |
| | Mejicanos |
| La Liberdad | Nahuizalco |
| San Matías | Juayua |
| Quezaltepeque | |
| Opico | Usulután |
| Balsam Coast Villages | Comun de Ladinos de Jucuapa |
| | San Buenaventura (Ladinos) |
| La Paz | |
| Santiago Nonualco | |
| Talpa | |

| Morazán | |
|---|---|
| Cacaopera | |
| Chilanga | |
| Guatijiaga | |

*Sources:* See Note on Sources.

tration, but the lack of any clear ethnic or collective solidarity was apparent when their lands were to be divided and privatized in 1882. The administrator and a few others who had served as assistants claimed all of the lands as their own and excluded at least thirty other people from the division. The legal case that resulted from this conflict lasted at least nine years.[51]

The identity and corporate organization of most of these communities before the 1869 law remains obscure. In some cases, property titles demonstrated a continuity from the corporate organization of the colonial period that was simply legitimated or recognized later by the government. In other cases legal recognition of possession rights based on ethnic identity strengthened or revived local solidarities that had weakened or disappeared. In Asunción Izalco—before the 1869 reorganization that established an administrator and two associates—the leader of the community was called *alcalde del común* (community mayor), indicating a clear continuity with colonial forms and a structure parallel to the local municipal council.[52] In Ataco, the governor reported,

> All the inhabitants are Indians and of old customs, and they want to do everything as when they were subjects of the king without minding the law, and according to their rules in order to become mayor or mayor's assistant they have to go through their rigorous schooling for what they call *oficiales* [using the old-fashioned terms] like the *alguacil* [marshal], *mayor de corte* [?], *alferez o sargento de milicias del rey y mayordomo común* [king's militia sargeant and community caretaker].[53]

This community obviously controlled the local municipal government but named its leaders according to colonial forms of Indian ritual and representation.

Furthermore, where Indian communities were based on ethnic identity, they were not formally recognized as a community if they did not own property, as in towns that had not purchased additional lands during the colonial period beyond the 38 *caballerías* of *ejidos*. However, in many places the Indians were able to control the town councils, in effect making themselves the legitimate local authorities who controlled the town's *ejidos* on the basis of ethnic solidarity. Ladinos had trouble securing access to lands in such towns. Where Indians were in the minority or were removed from control of the municipal council, the opposite occurred.[54]

Communities were not necessarily democratic, and communal affairs were generally controlled by a few old, wealthy men. Often elections were imposed by the national government and did not follow consistent procedures; few voted in the elections, and distribution of land reflected local hierarchies of class, prestige, age, and gender. The size of communal plots and demographic data indicate that Indian communities did not use all of their lands, that some Indians often had extensive farms and that communities frequently rented land to outsiders. While many Indians grew export or commercial crops on sizable plots of community land— especially sugar and coffee in the western departments—others eked out a minimum subsistence. Furthermore, there were strong pressures within Indian communities to concentrate surplus production through internal contributions and control of rental incomes.

The community of Mejicanos, or Mexicans, in the suburbs of the city of Sonsonate, provides an example of some of the internal workings of an Indian community. This small community was one of three founded by the Tlaxcalteca soldiers brought to the region by Alvarado in the sixteenth century and exempted from paying tribute and labor taxes.[55] This community held title to at least 225 hectares of arable land.[56] In 1853 it had only 290 members, of whom 191 were female. Given the size of its lands and the gender imbalance, it appears that men had left either to rent lands elsewhere or work on farms and haciendas—that is, to become Ladinos. Although most of the community's men were described as *jornaleros* (day laborers), it is clear from 1882 data that most families had plots within the common lands.[57] In its election for an administrator and two assistants in 1870, only forty-five men voted, while two years later only twenty-four voted.[58] Community members did not pay rent, but the community rented out lands to nonmembers at rates similar to those charged for *ejido* lands by municipalities. In 1878 the community —already significantly reduced in size—rented out five plots that ranged between 4 and 174 hectares to outsiders at relatively low cost, resulting in a yearly income of 69 pesos. This rental income was used to secure new titles to the community's lands.[59]

The strongest and wealthiest Indian communities in the west—probably in the entire country—were the two related communities of the Izalcos, Dolores and Asunción (discussed in chapter 8 in greater detail). In the colonial period, Izalco was the Indian cultural, demographic, and

economic center of the west. In 1870, both of Izalco's communities filed
a joint claim to all lands they had possessed as Indian communities during the nineteenth century, including the *ejidos* that had come under municipal control. Within the past fifty years, one of the town councils had
been taken over by the town's Ladinos, with whom the indigenous people
had a long tradition of conflict.[60] Community leaders pointed out that
the Ladino municipality did not hold the colonial titles to the lands;
from 1753 and earlier, these titles determined the extent of Izalco's two
"leagues" of *ejidos* and the additional 4,455 hectares given to the Indians
as a result of the land survey. For years the town had charged rent for
the use of any lands within the town limits. The Izalco Indians interpreted the 1869 decree that more clearly separated the *ejidos* from community lands as granting all the lands to them. They saw their titles as
proof that the king of Spain had given them the lands in 1753, stating
their case with a veiled threat of violence. This was a town that had already seen riots against the unwelcome Ladinos (and their roaming cattle
and control of the liquor monopoly) and at least one major revolt.

The Ladinos eloquently defended themselves by mobilizing the paternalistic discourse that interpreted independence and republican institutions as having liberated the Indians from colonial-era oppression:

> The worst part is that they want us to return to the year 1753, an era
> that they should forget, in order not to be like the Israelites who sighed
> for the food of Egypt. After independence from Spain (the glorious ac-
> complishment that without a doubt benefited Indians the most), the
> country received new institutions organizing municipalities and these
> were given *ejidos* so that they might subsist. Since then all towns have
> been in possession of their *ejidos*, from which they derive the rent pay-
> ments so necessary to cover their expenses.[61]

In the end, the governor of the department decided not to alter the existing usage of land until the Indians could resurvey and separate the
4,455 hectares purchased from the crown as a *composición* that would
then be recognized as communal lands. The Indian communities apparently agreed with this proposal, yet they also appealed to the "Supreme
Executive Power" for redress.

The largest and most important Ladino communities were in the departments of Chalatenango and Santa Ana. In Santa Ana the communities
of the Volcán and of the town of Chalchuapa were the most successful

and politically and economically autonomous peasant organizations. Chalchuapa's most important landholder by far was the Ladino community,[62] whose extensive land purchases were made in the late eighteenth and early nineteenth centuries.[63] By the 1870s Chalchuapa's Ladino community controlled at least 3,600 hectares of land, ranking among the largest landholding communities of El Salvador. On the basis of these lands the community turned Chalchuapa into an attractive and successful site of peasant and farmer agriculture. Unlike Indian communities, based in kinship, this Ladino community incorporated new members, although it recognized the predominance of a core of long-term resident families as well.[64] After 1860, pressure intensified to provide access to its extensive and uncultivated holdings to immigrant farmers and entrepreneurs living in nearby towns. A group of farmers from Santa Ana City—a leading center of coffee production and the region's principal commercial center—attempted unsuccessfully to manipulate the legal system for their benefit. The city's emerging coffee-growing sectors tried to show in court that part of the community's lands were actually owned by the state, thus subject to public use. For the Ladino community of Chalchuapa, the possibility that they would have to repurchase their lands (even at "moderate" prices) or that they might be sold at public auction constituted a major threat, so they mobilized their legal representatives and municipal authorities to defend their lands.

The community's response, combining legal and extralegal pressures, was to mount a successful legal defense while also petitioning government authorities to respect long-held land rights. The brief referred to the larger principle of communal landownership as practiced by many other Indian and Ladino communities throughout the country. In fact, their legal defense encouraged the Dueñas regime to clarify (and extend) the legal status of community landholding throughout the Republic.[65] Significantly, they partially couched their defense in terms of the same liberalism that would be used decades later to dissolve communal and municipal land tenure:

> With the fruit of their industrious labor they have been accumulating and gradually acquiring the lands which they now occupy in the name of the community and which they need *imperiosamente* [urgently] for their subsistence. . . . The lands of this community of said Ladinos, acquired with their own income and by the efforts of their industry, came to arouse the envy of some ill-intentioned men.[66]

Soon after, the mayor of Chalchuapa published a municipal decree stating that Chalchuapa would be willing to sell part of its communal lands toward the south in Las Joyas, Guachipilin, Zacamil, and Jocotillo—more than 1,340 hectares—to farmers from Santa Ana. The lands being offered for sale were those the Ladino community had bought earlier from the Indians.[67]

The Chalchuapans won their claim in court but had to permit portions of their substantial lands to be rented to outsiders. The commune declared a more open policy of rentals partly to offset the pressure from Santa Ana interests who opposed their having control over such extensive lands, but also to secure greater income for the community. The Chalchuapans explained that they had not wanted to lease lands for growing coffee and other "important" crops to those who were not local residents, but "they changed their minds, because they [were] fully convinced of the error in which they lived . . . offering their lands to all who would want to occupy them with coffee groves." In exchange, community administrators requested the end of all legal proceedings against their community, acknowledgment of the legality of their land titles, and increased local rental and tax revenues, to be used to repair the local church, pay the town schoolteacher, and expand the town's water supply system. Although community leaders reversed themselves out of fear of losing their lands, granting more open access to untilled land brought economic success over the next decade.[68]

The community of *pardos* of the Volcán of Santa Ana—also known as the "Plebeians of the Volcán"—provides a contrast to the community of Chalchuapa. (*Pardo* was a catch-all category that included *mestizos*, mulattos, and free blacks.)[69] The community, which in 1860 represented about half of the municipality's population, controlled lands on the slope of the Volcán de Santa Ana toward the city's southwestern suburbs.[70] Although the Ladino peasants and farmers managed to eke out a living on these lands, they did not have enough to expand their economic power like their neighbors in Chalchuapa. Their location within the fastest growing commercial and agricultural center of El Salvador also put greater limits to their autonomy. Nonetheless, the community of the Volcán—like the Indians of Izalco, Cojutepeque, and the Nonualcos—not only represented a successful case of local peasants and ethnic groups defending their interests, but also became a political and military factor of national importance.

Unlike the Ladinos of Chalchuapa, the Volcaneños came to be known, feared, and despised for their aggressive defense of their lands and their participation in many factional political battles of the elite. In 1867 their local enemies in the city of Santa Ana tried to keep them from clarifying the titles to their lands. Their complaint to the Supremo Poder Ejecutivo (President's Office) explained that although the departmental governor was against them, "most of the inhabitants are united in supporting their legitimate rights to the land and titles that they are trying to take away from us because of the defection of a few from the same plebeian whose foolishness is exploited by outsiders to the community who are very interested in gaining control of our property."[71] They asked for the "governor's paternal hand" to protect them, but also mentioned the potential for violence. The president sternly ordered the governor not to interfere with the titling of their lands and held him responsible for protecting the lives of the community leaders. Nonetheless, the Volcaneños revolted against local authorities in 1870 and against the national government a few months later (see chapter 5).

This same community was accused by the Indian community of Coatepeque, a town to the southeast, of dispossessing them of part of their lands.[72] A few years later, in 1871, the community complained to the new government of Santiago González—whom they helped bring to power—that ex-president Dueñas had taken their titles, which they now demanded. The eighteenth-century titles included their purchase of one hacienda—the same one (or portions thereof) claimed by the Indians of Coatepeque—and their payment of a *composición* for additional lands totaling 1,125 hectares.[73]

In general, ethnic communities had more conflicts with town authorities than with haciendas. In Atiquizaya, for example, the mayor imprisoned Indian leaders in 1851 when they requested the titles to their lands. As elsewhere, this colonial title included both the standard 38 *caballerías* of *ejidos* and the additional lands purchased by the dominant indigenous community. The Indians needed the title to resolve a dispute not with their municipality but with the nearby Ladino community of Chalchuapa.[74]

In the western departments, conflicts between Ladinos and Indians were common, usually over control of *ejido* lands and the use of common lands near the town center for cattle grazing. In 1854 the government ordered new elections in Nahuizalco after the Ladinos apparently stole the town elections from the Indian community, and in the second election the Indian community regained control.[75] At stake was keeping the cattle of Ladino peasants off the *ejidos*. Eighteen years later, the municipality was still controlled by Indians when they negotiated with the national government to resume payment of a local head tax of 2 reales on all members of the Indian commune known as "tribute." The tax had been abolished in 1868 in exchange for Indian payment of the rent *canon* because the size of lands controlled by Indians made it less costly to pay the head tax than the quitrent. (The legal basis for any head tax on Indians had been abolished early in the republican period.)[76]

As late as 1878, the municipality of Armenia in Sonsonate had not separated its *ejido* lands from those claimed by the town's Indian community. After an 1873 survey, a representative of the General Treasury Court recommended that all lands be put under town control since they had not been held by individuals but by the entire town. Later, when Indian communities were abolished, Armenia's Indian commune began to sell lands that the town now considered part of the *ejidos*, leading to a major conflict.[77] Similarly, in 1862, the Indian community of Juayua complained that the municipality wanted to take part of their lands "to distribute them to the Ladinos who request them for coffee or because they want to pay a *canon* as if they were *ejidos*." The complaint went on: "To date community lands and municipal *ejidos* are undivided, and [the town] desires to separate its lands in order to avoid claims against their rightful owners."[78]

Disputes over land with neighboring haciendas were rarer than between communities and towns. When they occurred, their outcome was never certain, since communities, towns, and haciendas sometimes had unclear boundaries, and both landowners and authorities feared violence from community members.[79] The strength of the communal and municipal forms of land tenure is illustrated by the town of Texistepeque, in Santa Ana. When a nearby *hacendado* encroached upon its lands, the town made plans to buy the hacienda.[80]

## Ethnicity and Ethnic Relations

Besides questions relating to land and agriculture, ethnicity and ethnic conflict were fundamental to the political economy of peasants' lives and relations with other social groups. Despite the challenges, demands, and exploitation imposed by the colonial restructuring of native life in the sixteenth century,[81] an Indian, community-based culture emerged and was institutionalized both by Spanish policies and indigenous practices and identities. These communities maintained some economic autonomy by retaining control over lands and agricultural enterprises. Indians protected their autonomy by resisting the demands of the colonial state and the church, partly by continuing to control important resources.[82] The colonial provinces of San Salvador and Sonsonate retained this character even after the commercial and demographic revitalization that occurred after 1700. In 1732 colonial authorities attempted to revive the production of cacao, which was still in Indian hands.[83]

The definition of Indian ethnicity after independence is a complex issue. While dress, language, and appearance were central markers of Indianness, other factors played an important role. Expectations as to the proper behavior for an Indian also played a role in self-imposed and externally imposed definitions. Indian ethnicity was usually associated with participation in local communal organizations, so most Indian identities were tied to a specific locality and/or corporate organization. But many areas with significant numbers of Indians had no formally organized community, even before the abolition of communal lands. In other areas, national legislation and policies regarding land use affected the creation and formalization of many ethnic associations, giving them more coherence than they originally had. Furthermore, many of the officially recognized ethnic communities were not Indian at all, but based on the loosely defined oppositional category of Ladino.[84]

Nineteenth-century definitions of ethnicity were fluid in a country where Indians were not always distinguished by dress or language. In Cojutepeque the local governor complained that when local administrators tried to charge rents to common land tenants, many Ladinos suddenly declared themselves Indians to avoid payment.[85] Ethnic definitions were flexible and relative throughout the century, tied as they were to allegiance to corporate organization and self-identity rather than appearance or language. Officials could ascribe different degrees of "Indianness" to different localities, depending on the openness of specific groups to the outside world. Indianness, in its purest form, was constructed both by outside observers and by community leaders in their public discourse, as a self-enclosed, defensive, ancestral, and pure (therefore naive and innocent) way of being. As a result, the dominant attitude toward Indians and Indianness in nineteenth-century El Salvador was not a rigid form of racism but a "benign" paternalism that constantly made excuses for the behavior of Indians based on their ancestral oppression and their "natural" naiveté and blind obedience to their leaders.

Commercial expansion after the 1860s set in motion certain contradictory processes that led to the increasing ladinoization of sectors within the Indian population. Peasants were often defined as Ladinos simply because they farmed commercially.[86] Yet many people who continued to be associated with formal Indian communities participated in the market, while Ladinos, by circular reasoning, were not perceived as Indians because they sold their products. Migrants detached from their original communities were thus seen as Ladinos, while residents of entire localities slowly lost their Indian character and forms of association and solidarity. In some regions observers from the local elite perceived this transition as one from subsistence agriculture to export production, despite many examples of Indians participating in regional and even export markets. In both Ahuachapán and La Paz, for example, many Indians and their families produced sugar and sugar-related products. In Cojutepeque this transition was seen as a change from "corn and beans" agriculture to raising sugar cane, coffee, and tobacco.[87] Often this meant very little in terms of dress or language, but was more closely tied to the rental of *ejido* lands and the loss of access to communally controlled lands.

All these factors affected perceptions of Indian ethnicity, although when local officials were asked to identify Indians, local categories and usages were more likely to play a role in the creation of demographic and other information. In the early nineteenth century, officials paid little heed to Indians as a category, even though political events were closely determined by the alignment of various Indian communities. Later the ethnic composition of the population received more attention, and government statistics aimed to reflect these divisions. What an Indian was varied dramatically from place to place.

By 1913 Juayua appeared mostly Ladino to the governor, mostly because the town's Indians dressed like Ladinos. Some of Salcoatitán's residents were described as "natives who are assimilating in dress to the Ladinos." Similarly, the Indians of Armenia dressed as Ladinos and were "already significantly mixed." Some balsam-producing towns that had been entirely Indian at midcentury had changed significantly by the twentieth century. Ishuatan, for example, was composed of mostly Ladino immigrants attracted by the balsam trade. The town's remaining Indians had left the town's center and moved to a suburb. Indians had almost entirely lost control of balsam gathering and trade.

Cuisnahuat, Santo Domingo, Nahuilingo, San Antonio del Monte, and Sonzacate, however, continued to be mostly composed of Nahua-speaking Indians, and most property was in Indian hands. However, officials noted that many of them were "assimilating." Izalco, the region's largest municipality, was still significantly Indian, although it was run by "many and important Ladino families that have managed to dominate the Indian masses, since for many years the local authorities are Ladino, which accounts for [the town's] flowering progress." Indians still observed their religious and communal rituals and had a mayor whom they followed "as much in religion as in politics."[88] Indian ethnicity and community, attached as it was to communal organization and locality, were affected by changes in land tenure, politics, and agriculture. While the Indian population remained fairly constant, Indian identity became more fluid and open-ended because of the decline of communal identity and organization. Thus increasing numbers of people classified as Indian were not part of any formal corporate body.

The most important feature of Indian demographics in nineteenth-century El Salvador (including the years of the privatization of community lands, 1880–1910) was the relative stability of the population officially classified as Indian, both in local and national statistics. Because there are no reliable figures for the 1820–1850s, estimates made by travelers and observers are our only source. In 1837 Galindo estimated the Indian population at 25 percent; Scherzer commented in 1857 that the "pure" Indian population was increasing, while *mestizos* were becoming more like Indians.[89] By 1901 the Indian population was officially 33 percent, but in 1913 Domville-Fife estimated that 40 percent of the population was Indian.[90] (See table 3.3.)

Table 3.3  Population Classified as Indian, 1880–1901   (in percent)

|              | 1880 | 1883 | 1889 | 1892 | 1901 |
|--------------|------|------|------|------|------|
| Ahuachapán   | 33   | —    | —    | 46[a] | 50  |
| Sonsonate    | 55   | —    | —    | —    | 50   |
| La Paz       | 54   | —    | —    | —    | 50   |
| Cuscatlán    | 53   | —    | —    | —    | 50   |
| San Salvador | 55   | 50   | —    | —    | 37   |
| Morazán      | 32   | —    | —    | —    | 25   |
| La Libertad  | 22   | 29   | 22   | —    | 20   |
| Cabañas      | 0    | —    | —    | —    | 14   |
| La Unión     | 14   | —    | —    | —    | 10   |
| Usulután     | 7    | —    | —    | —    | 9    |
| Chalatenango | 10   | —    | —    | —    | 7    |
| San Vicente  | 8    | —    | —    | —    | 4    |
| Santa Ana    | 5    | —    | —    | —    | 2    |
| San Miguel   | 3    | —    | —    | —    | 1    |
| Average      | 24   | 27[a] | —   | —    | 33   |

Sources: "Salvador," *Monthly Bulletin of the Bureau of American Republics,* March 1902, 634; Jiménez, *Memoria,* 8–9; Mora, *Memoria . . . (1883),* 154, 161, 165; Larreynaga, *Memoria,* 75; *Diario Oficial* 1 (March 1881): 10:51, 210; Informe que el señor Gobernador del Departamento de Ahuachapán dirige al Ministro de Gobernación, AGN-CM-MG, 1892.
  a. Births only.

Official demographic data for the 1910s and 1920s confirm Halle's observation (in 1936) that the percentage of Indians, either officially or self-identified, had remained somewhat stable for fifty years. This was especially true for the west and center (which had larger concentrations of people identified as Indians), excluding Santa Ana and San Vicente, but less true of eastern departments like San Miguel and La Unión.[91] In the north and east, mostly Ladino since the early nineteenth century, Indian population declined, at least between 1880 and 1900. Statistics are difficult to come by, and most local censuses did not distinguish between Indians and Ladinos, perhaps because of the homogeneity of most small towns in the center and west. The 1853 census of the Barrio de Mexicanos in Sonsonate City, for example, did not mention that this was the city's Indian community.[92]

Birth and death data from western departments also suggest the stability of the Indian population in the early 1880s.[93] In 1800 the population of Sonsonate and Ahuchapán was 66 percent Indian; in 1857 Scherzer found that about half of the residents of Ahuachapán City were Indians who spoke only Spanish.[94] But again we find diversity: while Thompson mentions the propensity of some western Indians to wear shoes, stockings, trousers, and petticoats as a sign of their progressiveness, Montgomery commented on "the aborigines in all their original simplicity, and their adherence to the languages and habits of their ancestors, even while living in the vicinity of large populous towns."[95]

There is no single way to define Indian ethnicity in El Salvador. More than anything, Indian identity was tied to local origin and a shared communal tradition (perhaps defunct), and thus Indian ethnic identity was heterogenous and fragmented. In this fundamental way, Indian identity was a colonial creation, both as a result of the subjugation of a population administered as a "native" people to be taxed and forced to work, but also of categories of classification that continued after independence. By the mid-nineteenth century, more than any other force, controlling and defending lands and other resources, and the belief that Indians were rightfully entitled to these resources as a colonial prerogative, provided a basis for local Indian organization and identity.

ETHNIC CONFLICT

Throughout the nineteenth century, ethnic difference and competition underlay most cases of violence or legal conflict, especially those involving municipal power, land, irrigation, and taxes. In localities with more rigid political blocks, Indians and Ladinos competed for power, often violently. Antagonists often formed alliances with national movements or factions. In most places, the Indian population was usually organized around a distinct community with its own internal organization, lands, and identity. The typical conflict was between an Indian population that resisted a growing or upwardly mobile Ladino population's attempts to gain control over town resources and authority. The town of Nahuizalco, which remained overwhelmingly Indian into the twentieth century, provides a late example. A 1913 report explained that the Indian and Ladino populations were extremely at odds and blamed Ladinos for the prostitution of Indian women. Indians avoided the town schools because they did not like to mix with the Ladinos.[96] In effect, most questions involving land, municipal authority, or agriculture were distorted by the tension created by ethnic identity and conflict. This often divided the peasantry over local issues of land and power, although as the century passed alliances between Indians and Ladinos were more likely when it came to national political movements.

Stereotyped or racist perceptions of Indians were common among Ladino officials. Indians were perceived as having no interest in accumulating wealth: "[They] only have things of little value, having corn and beans, they have no other needs."[97] Local agriculture was perceived as backward: "This sector has advanced little, because those who are in it are confident of the fertility of the land, barely use the machete, hand sickle, and a bad type of plow."[98] One Ladino department governor did not like the practice of shifting subsistence plantings from one place to another, which he saw as characteristic of Indian agriculture. He also complained that the Indian communities of Sonsonate and Ahuachapán wasted their substantial resources on dances, drinking, and festivities.[99]

Ladino officials in Sonsonate perceived the Indians' communal organization in most towns in Sonsonate as an obstacle to the development of agriculture. In 1865 the governor observed:

> Large parts of the town lands are unused because the Indians keep new settlers from cultivating them, because of the noticeable lack of unity between them and the Ladinos, either [the Ladinos] subdue [the Indians] when they become more numerous, putting upon them many onerous charges, or, when the Ladinos are few, they make the Indians worry that they will damage them; . . . but there is also another reason—when municipalities are composed only of aborigines they don't charge rent except to Ladinos, who also try to elude payment. These problems impede the progress of all of these towns, holding back agriculture and producing a scarcity of [municipal] revenue. The laborer who knows he has to pay for the land makes an effort to make it produce, forgetting the habit of abandoning each year and changing the location of his corn and bean plantings, destroying the jungles where he needs to get wood. The governor believes that giving control of land to the municipal council, legitimate representative of the peoples *[pueblos]* will lead to the advancement of agriculture.[100]

Echoing the sentiment of local officials, investors, and farmers, the report blamed communal land tenure for conflicts between the town and the Indian community:

[They] are almost always over lands, and the municipality tries to impose work on the Indians without pay. If the municipality needs to rent lands for grazing, it forces the workers to abandon their crops . . . but the governor believes these evils are due to the fact that the Indians don't pay rent for their land and as a result the municipal council has no revenues, forcing them to demand contributions in labor.[101]

A few years later, the Dueñas regime passed two important laws regulating the use and administration of lands claimed by communities.

Most observers of El Salvador, however, have relied on rigid definitions of ethnicity and Indians, while also allowing their sympathies for indigenous peoples to obscure their understanding of Indian-Ladino relations. While the rigid categories of the colonial era gave way to more fluid forms in the nineteenth century, the racism of Ladino and white economic elites hardened in the early twentieth century. Indian identity became equated with the behavior of quarrelsome Indian communities in the 1910s and 1920s that allied themselves with the pseudo-populist and communist movements of this period. Indian ethnicity, by 1932, was associated not only with rigid, hierarchical, and formal associations like the well-known communities of Izalco, Juayua, and Nahuizalco, but also perceived as a threat to everything held dear by the commercial and political elite: export agriculture and political stability.

## Peasant and Elite Use of Municipal and Community Lands

One of the most important aspects of peasants' and farmers' use of municipal lands was the charging of rent. Most national governments took some interest in securing a stable basis for municipal finances. Although *canon* payments were obligatory, few towns collected them with any regularity until the 1860s, when improvements in the organization of the national state and the increasing importance of commerce encouraged the collection of both municipal taxes in general and *ejido* rental payments. Rent was generally low, relative to the productive value of the land. For example, in 1876 one *fanega* (1.5 bushels) of corn cost about 1 peso,[102] while in Zacatecoluca that amount of corn could be produced on one *manzana* (.67 hectare) two or three times a year; a plot of this size could provide a cash income of about 16 reales, while costing only 1 or 2 reales to rent. In most areas it cost 1 peso to rent .67 hectare of land suitable for coffee, while this size planting could generate an income of between 20 and 50 pesos. However, in frontier places like Turin (Ah), coffee land in need of clearing was a bargain at 2 reales per .67 hectare in 1879.[103]

Rent taxes varied, but in many places they were an important source of municipal revenue. In 1852 Santiago Nonualco's *canon* income of 21 pesos was 9 percent of its total revenues, while neighboring San Juan Nonualco's 49 pesos was 40 percent of its income. By 1861 this town's rent payments constituted 65 percent of its revenue. In Suchitoto in 1862, rent payments were 10 percent of its revenues, while Zacatecoluca received virtually no rent income during these years.[104] Although rent payments remained low during the entire life of the *ejido* system, other local taxes were even more precarious, especially in towns without established merchant firms. Other revenues (slaughterhouse taxes, market taxes, fines, commercial taxes) were usually small. In small towns with little economic activity and where residents paid their other taxes in labor rather than cash, the *canon,* while not large, provided the most important income.[105] However, *ejido* taxes could rarely provide a stable base for new public works or extraordinary expenses; and they were reduced in periods of crop failure or plagues.[106] Often tenants did not pay the *canon* at all, claiming poverty.[107] In some towns, rent charges could lead to substantial conflicts.

Zacatecoluca, capital of La Paz in the south-central region, had trouble with its *ejidos.* In 1868 a large group of tenants refused to pay rent, claiming that they had a legal and moral right to ownership and should not be charged to use the *ejidos.* They based their claim on having contributed a few hundred pesos for an 1850 survey. Most requests of this type went through official channels, either the courts or administrative review. The Zacatecolucan peasants identified themselves as a distinct community with its own history, legitimacy, and rights, calling themselves a laborers' guild with a corporate identity similar to that of the Ladinos of Chalchuapa and the Volcán de Santa Ana. The lands in question, specified as one-quarter of the city's *ejidos,* were likely from an eighteenth-century *composición* that remained undivided and was confused with the *ejidos* proper.

The peasants' petition used language that emphasized the historical legitimacy of peasant access to land but also recognized the state's authority:

> We the individuals who appear today as the majority of the community of this city . . . making use of the rights granted us by the law . . . [protest] that having seen the poster posted in the streets of this city imposing one real for each *manzana* of land that we the community of laborers possess in the *ejidos* . . . that this new tax weighs upon us because most of us are poor and produce only subsistence products; . . . we have nothing against the decisions of the municipality if they seek to raise funds without taxing all the poor people *[la jeneralidad de la indijencia]* . . . because if we work to support our families it is by sacrificing part of our production to those who lend us money. . . . As a result we tell you that since time immemorial, since our first fathers we had this imposition placed by the Spanish government called tribute to benefit all the peoples of Central America since Christopher Colombus discovered these provinces . . . and it because of this that we think the *ejidos* have been paid for, not only with our treasures, but also with the blood of the backs of our past fathers, without any authority helping these peasants *[labradores]*. . . . To you, respectable municipal body, we ask and beg to be considerate of us and lift this tax because it will damage our miserable families and we have no source of income that will produce enough to pay this tax; . . . it is justice that we seek. . . . October 8, 1867[108]

The Ministry of the Interior denied the request, noting that the town had the right to charge for *ejido* use and that in other towns even Indian communities had paid to separate their lands from the *ejidos*.

A similar conflict in the town of Osicala illustrates the profound ethnic divisions and conflicts that erupted over the use of common lands. In this case the entire local tax structure, the only taxes that affected the peasantry directly, was at issue in a dispute in which three Ladino farmers complained that the town's Indians charged them rent for lands under municipal jurisdiction, when they themselves paid no rent and no local taxes. To make things worse, the Indian-controlled town had doubled their rent. The Ladinos called on the government to enforce the republican principles of equality and destroy what they termed an "odious feudalism" that divided the town into unequal ethnic groups and was "condemned by our constituitive laws."[109]

The Indian-controlled town government replied by citing both colonial and republican history to defend the land tax. Indians were entitled not to pay rent because in 1845 they contributed 700 pesos to settle a land dispute with nearby Guacotecti. The income from those lands was to go to the town in lieu of the Indians' *beneficiencia* (beneficence) taxes. The increased taxes for Ladinos was justified by their recent improvements to the land and expanded production. Moreover, the Indians had been given the land by the king of Spain, whereas the Ladinos, who had been there only since the 1790s, were still considered outsiders. The Indian community defended the principle of ethnic separation and community rights established in the colonial era:

> The claim that the Indians be forced by this government to pay rent for their plantings is not just because the indigenous peoples received the *ejido* from the king, our lord (may God protect him), as is shown by the title we keep and in that era it was given only to Indians and there is not a single document that shows that they were given to the Ladinos; because for more than seventy years Ladinos have settled here from different parts and now they are a significant number, and although by law we cannot deny any citizen a place or residence, this has hurt us . . . for which reason their petition should not be heard.[110]

This dispute reflects the tensions created by the selective preservation of colonial-era practices and the Republic's failure to abolish caste privileges. Ladinos who settled in Indian-controlled towns faced an uphill battle, especially if they claimed lands considered part of the town's colonial inheritance. But as the century progressed the greater commercial involvement by both Ladinos and Indians, and (after the 1870s) the state's increased ability to intervene more firmly in local land matters, facilitated Ladino access to land in towns formerly controlled by Indian communities. Yet in many sparsely populated regions Ladinos settled and claimed land without challenge, continuing the pattern of Ladino settlement that expanded dramatically in the eighteenth century.

Traditionally, *ejido* tenants had to live in a town to use its lands, but after 1875 a new law allowed towns with free lands to rent them to outsiders.[111] *Ejido* plots were usually rented by males, although a few women appeared as tenants.[112] The size of *ejido* plots varied from small corn plantings to a few hectares. In the town of Turín, peasants rented plots of 3–6 hectares.[113] Some towns rented out other exploitation rights, such as rights to extract balsam from unclaimed trees or to take wood from local forests.[114]

In the 1860s, more *ejido* lands were brought into cultivation as part of the concurrent expansion of sugar, coffee, indigo, and cotton by both small-scale peasants and commercial farmers.[115] This was not a sudden "land grab" by wealthy speculators, but a result of the developing differentiation of local peasants and farmers and the increased agricultural production by merchants who became involved in export-oriented crops.[116] Farming for export on *ejido* lands was greatest in the villages surrounding the cities of San Salvador, Santa Tecla, Sonsonate, San Vicente, and Santa Ana. Some towns offered incentives for planting export crops. In Sonsonate in 1879, for example, those who planted one-third of their *ejido* plots with export crops would pay 2 reales in rent instead of 3. Town or agricultural committees offered free coffee tree plantings to all peasants and farmers, a practice that expanded during the century.[117] Merchants, artisan shop owners, teachers, community leaders, commercial farmers, and many peasants planted for export.

Wealthier peasants or members of the local elite might hold 40 or more hectares of *ejido* land. Entrepreneurs could sell or rent their possession rights but could not transfer ownership. In 1864, for example, one entrepreneur offered to sell possession rights to a cleared farm in the *ejidos* of Juayua with lands suitable for growing coffee and sugar cane.[118] Indigo farmers also had a long tradition of renting community or municipal lands.

Santa Tecla (Nueva San Salvador) provides the best example of elite access to *ejido* lands for commercial purposes.[119] This town was founded on a hacienda purchased by the Republic as the site of a new capital after an earthquake destroyed much of San Salvador in 1854. Instead, it became a rapidly expanding internal agricultural frontier that opened its lands to both capitalist speculators and peasants. Nueva San Salvador quickly came to have one of the most dynamic coffee economies in the country. In addition to the lands of the hacienda "Santa Tecla," which the new town received as its *ejidos*, it was granted part of the unclaimed "Cimarrón" in 1856, while additional lands were purchased later.[120] This gave it a total of about 5,580 hectares in *ejidos*, probably the largest in the nation. Because of its location and the significant number of landowners and merchants who moved there from San Salvador, distribution of

lands in Santa Tecla soon became a profitable business for land speculators and coffee producers alike.[121]

Santa Tecla's *ejidos* were so extensive, that the allocation of its lands
was a slow process, taking over thirty years. By 1883, 3,832 hectares
had been distributed, although more was held in reserve for new settlers.[122] The use of the city's *ejidos* for export crops brought with it a
higher rent—probably the highest in the country.[123] Many of these lands
were no doubt claimed by speculators and settlers who did not have
possession rights and did not use them productively. In 1867 the governor of La Libertad complained:

> In this town . . . often many people with municipal lands do not culti-
> vate them except a small part and don't even fence them for lack of re-
> sources; while other people with means for important agricultural work
> ask for them in vain and can't get them because the possessors do not
> want to sell them or ask large sums for them, causing in this way great
> damage to agriculture, and thus to the country's wealth.[124]

The minister of the interior responded by defining the limits to the possession of *ejido* plots, especially under the provision of an 1847 law and
others that called for planting coffee and other export products within
*ejidos*.

The trend reported by the governor, however, reflected both commercial pressure on municipal control of the land and resistance to the loss
of access by small producers. These problems, however, did not limit the
expansion of the city's landholding population, since it still had available lands. In 1870 the municipality threatened to expel local farmers
and speculators who had begun to cultivate land in the outlying sections
that were reserved for new settlers. Some of the farmers actually in possession of these lands petitioned the interior minister for protection. He
decided that their plantings could remain until the lands were needed
for new settlers—a ruling that respected the formal use of these lands as
*ejidos* but also aided their illegal appropriation by farmers who had already been allotted plots and were interested in gaining private control
in order to open a market in land.[125] Santa Tecla's economic success is
reflected in its demographic expansion. From a population of 1,500
people in 1857, the town expanded to 3,100 in 1868, 9,400 by 1883
and 15,000 at the end of the century. This accelerated expansion also

promoted investment and settlement in the rest of the department of La Libertad.[126]

A similar problem emerged for settlers and entrepreneurs over the control of plots distributed when the city was founded. Given the wording of the decrees and the aspirations of the recipients, *ejido* grants in Nueva San Salvador came to be considered private property. In 1862 Barrios acted to prevent the municipality from continuing to distribute its common lands to speculators and reversed part of the distribution and other transactions.[127] In this confrontation with Barrios, some local farmers were forced to return the excessive lands they had taken. (This was a major element in the formation of anti-Barrios sentiment and the realignment of the Santa Tecla and Santa Ana elite in support of Dueñas. In a communique issued after Barrios was expelled from the country, Dueñas cited his violation of private property rights as one reason for his demise.) However, a later ruling in 1878 gave tenants virtual ownership of their lands.[128] In 1880, just two years before the 1882 law that abolished the *ejidos* nationally, a special provision was made by the government allowing for the sale of these lands to their possessors.[129]

## Conclusion

Salvadoran systems of land use were an important element in the country's economic and social development. The forms of land use and organization in nineteenth-century El Salvador reflected the preeminently peasant organization of agriculture and the economic needs and political influence of this sector. Both the state and enterprising landowners recognized and had to accommodate to the tradition and practice of the nation's peasantry. An early twentieth-century historian summarized this balance: "Most of the citizens were owners. The state supported their destinies and gave land at low prices, so they would cultivate them and for their own homes, which in synthesis is to give all their own homeland *[patria]*, or the symbol of their homeland; . . . patriotism is the sentiment and fear of a threat to their well-being . . . which derives from the multiplicity of smallholders that populate the land."[130]

In the nineteenth century municipal and community-controlled lands expanded at the expense of haciendas and state lands. Peasant-run municipalities could easily manage local resources as long as demographic or commercial pressures did not strain local political, social, and ethnic relations. Before the 1880s most peasant communities had enough lands to allow for significant subsistence and commercial production by peasants, farmers, and entrepreneurs. But after midcentury, municipal control over extensive and often unused lands began to come under contradictory pressures. The principle of equal peasant access to land was challenged by emerging differentiation among local peasants, the increasing use of *ejido* lands by upwardly mobile peasants, farmers, merchants, and entrepreneurs, and the secure possession needed by those who invested in permanent tree crops such as coffee, cacao, and rubber.

By the 1860s the administration and use of municipal and common lands had already led to tension because of the early effects of commercial agriculture within peasant communities. The administration of common lands, both by municipalities and ethnic communities, was never egalitarian. Even the most equitable and cohesive communities and municipalities were characterized by contradictions and hierarchies of power. Internal differentiation had already led to significant conflicts among peasants and farmers and added to the persistent ethnic tensions between Indian and Ladino peasants. Participation in commercial networks reinforced and intensified these internal hierarchies. Because of the importance of political factors in local peasant reproduction, even when peasants were in the ascendant and prospering earlier in the century, common land tenure and use both contained and encouraged deep inequities in access to land and markets. The survival and transformation of this system recognized the peasants' claims to subsistence but also limited their development. The uncertainty and arbitrariness that could accompany municipal control of such an important resource put strains on the institution—especially in a few key localities—and eventually contributed to its dissolution.

# 4 The Peasantry and Commercial Agriculture, 1830s–1880s

Between 1820 and 1880, El Salvador became a stronghold of peasant producers organized around the resources provided by municipalities or ethnic communities. This chapter examines rural society and peasant social structure in selected parts of the country, especially in the west. Archival sources provide a valuable perspective into many of the critical processes that shaped El Salvador's agrarian history during this period. Peasants organized in communities or town governments with their own local and ethnic identity, or relied on these bodies to secure their subsistence and market-oriented production.[1] Few could survive without them. But peasant communities were not egalitarian utopias, either. The deepening connections between peasant producers and regional and export markets also brought tensions and competition.

## Peasants, Haciendas and Indigo After Independence

Large producers of indigo, the principal commercial crop of colonial Salvador, faced a new set of obstacles after independence that contributed to the decline of estate-based indigo production after the 1810s. The systemwide crisis of the Spanish Empire that began in 1808 and continued until 1822 and the civil wars of the Central American Federation caused a breakdown in the hacienda-based indigo economy by disrupting markets and trade routes.[2] Added to this were increasing problems with recruiting workers, because independence brought an end to forced Indian labor. Conflicts with Guatemala also weakened or destroyed the mercantile ties between producers and merchants, while many Guatemalan *hacendados* themselves lost access to their lands. Indian revolts in Guatemala and in many regions of El Salvador during the 1830s contributed to the decline of the haciendas, many of which remained unused or harbored independent settlers at least until the 1860s. Small-scale producers were able to hold on to their traditional markets in South America, while access to European trade declined.[3]

After a decline associated with the independence-era economic crisis, indigo production returned to its highest level (equal to that of 1790–1791) as early as 1830. Evidence of this growth contradicts views that stress the generalized economic decline of the Republic after independence and during the conflict-ridden Federation years. However, production levels were not based on an expanded hacienda-based economy, but rather on the success of smaller cultivators.[4] By 1860 the indigo economy had doubled its output of 1830 and went on to a boom led by the high prices of the 1860s and early 1870s. Furthermore, despite drastic price declines after the 1880s, indigo continued to be a very important crop in the early twentieth century in regions where the land was not suitable for other crops. By 1872—the high point in indigo production —about 32,000 hectares of land were dedicated to indigo. By comparison, in 1880 coffee occupied around 10,000 hectares, and other important export products like tobacco and sugar occupied similar areas.

After independence the elite-controlled hacienda economy experienced a protracted crisis.[5] Between the 1820s and the 1870s, many haciendas lay abandoned for lack of investment. Estates were also confiscated and destroyed as a result of political and military conflicts in the 1830s. (Most overthrown presidents lost their estates and properties.)[6] Hacienda lands were either settled or purchased by peasant communities such as those of the San Vicente and La Paz regions, significant indigo-producing areas in the late eighteenth century.[7] In La Paz a report identified various haciendas "that used to produce indigo," while in San Vicente four haciendas were advertised for sale in one year alone. Travelers Robert

Dunlop and John Baily commented on this decline between 1830 and 1850. According to Baily, "Few parts of Central America have suffered more from the devastating effects of civil discord. Broad tracts of land have been thrown out of cultivation; some valuable estates have been almost ruined, many entirely so."[8] In the 1850s a hacienda owner in Zacatecoluca had to request government help in recruiting outsiders to come to his hacienda as settlers or tenants.[9] In San Vicente a governor's report in 1864 mentioned the decline in indigo for lack of capital and investors, noting unused lands and farms.[10] Esteban Castro, writing about San Vicente in the 1870s, also observed the decline of local haciendas. He attributed it to fluctuations in the international price of indigo and the "ruinous system of advances" whereby producers, including larger producers, secured loans from merchants by promising their future crops and putting up their lands as collateral—forcing them to pay interest rates as high as 30 percent.[11] In 1885 a report written for the U.S. consul also noted the many abandoned estates throughout the country.[12]

Other former indigo haciendas owned by Guatemalan families since the end of the colonial period were sold after midcentury. The marquis of Aycinena had owned 16 indigo estates in San Salvador, all of which were expropriated in the 1820s; some were restored to him in 1830 but were found abandoned or destroyed. As late as the 1860s, the Aycinena family was still seeking to regain some of its lost properties.[13] In 1870 the hacienda "Nuestra Señora de la Concepción Ramírez" in Tecoluca (SV) was sold to a Salvadoran by the Aycinena family for 20,000 pesos, but the purchaser had no cash to pay the 1,000-peso *alcabala* tax to the Salvadoran government. In 1871 a Ladino merchant who was also a militia colonel in San Vicente had been ceded portions of four different haciendas worth 6,000 pesos by debtors, but could not pay the 5 percent government *alcabala* tax to transfer the titles.[14]

The many estates offered for sale, some of which came under state ownership after it assumed all church-owned mortgages, provide further evidence of the decline of haciendas. (An early Federation-period law laid the basis for the state's control of many idle properties sold at auction later in the century or the debts transfered to new owners or possessors.) The hacienda "Guadalupe" (SV), for example, was sold by the General Treasury Court in 1873 because of a *capellanía* (debt to the church).[15] The abandoned hacienda had been settled by a dozen peasant families.[16] In 1876 another observer noted that many of La Paz's 31 indigo haciendas were still abandoned.[17] Furthermore, many settlements established as municipalities had begun in former haciendas either possessed, purchased, rented or (in some cases) received as donations by peasants.[18] The town of Sesori was founded within the hacienda "Espíritu Santo," San Luis de la Reina on the hacienda "El Ostucal," and Guayabal in the hacienda "San José." The municipality of Carolina was also founded in 1883 on a hacienda purchased by the government.[19]

By midcentury many of the country's haciendas were subdivided for peasant, municipal, or investment purposes—a trend similar to that elsewhere in Latin America, especially Mexico.[20] Even the most productive and valuable haciendas, such as those in La Paz owned by Guatemala's most prominent family, the Aycinenas, lay unrecovered by their owners for decades. By the beginning of the twentieth century they had been turned into small farms by local peasants.[21] In 1859 the government purchased the hacienda "San Cristobal" in San Vicente—portions of which had already been rented out to local farmers—from the Barros family of Guatemala for 10,000 pesos. The lands were to be distributed "in the most equitable manner" among San Vicente peasants and farmers.[22] In 1864 the Mortgage Registry of San Miguel registered mortgages on portions of haciendas or large plots within haciendas by individual owners more often than entire haciendas.[23]

Besides the subdivision of haciendas in transactions involving landowners or merchants, some haciendas came to form part of municipal lands, Indian communities, or were simply purchased by groups of peasants. The cattle and indigo-producing hacienda "San Juan Buenavista," in La Libertad, was originally composed of 2,250 hectares and titled as a purchase from the crown in 1628. After a series of eighteenth-century expansions and divisions, it was subdivided by inheritance, sale, and forfeiture that reduced the estate to around one-eighth its original size.[24] The haciendas "El Angel" and "San Juan Masajapa" were purchased by Ladinos from San Matías and Opico.[25] The hacienda "Las Salinas" in Sonsonate came to be owned by a group of farmers, the hacienda "Los Trozos" was owned by residents of Nahuizalco in Sonsonate, and the hacienda "Santa Catarina" was ceded by the government to the town of San Esteban.[26]

Until the 1860s the price of land remained relatively stable, and it was not easy to find buyers for the many estates offered for sale. For the most part, large haciendas, like the one measured in Sesori in 1845 owned by a local priest and composed of 3,870 hectares, remained uncultivated and served only as a source of marginal income from free-roaming cattle and as a guarantee for loans or debts.[27] Even as late as 1877 the church had difficulty selling the *terreno* "Los Reyes" of 1,575 hectares in La Paz for 5,200 pesos at public auction. There was not a single bidder.[28]

The increased production of indigo in the 1830s was based on the work of peasants and small-scale farmers, while hacienda production declined. These changes meant that indigo production increased in regions of communal peasant or tenant settlement. Chalatenango, Cuscatlán, and Cabañas increased their share of indigo production between the early 1800s and 1852 (see table 4.1), while older, hacienda-based regions of San Salvador, Santa Ana, San Vicente, and La Paz lost their standing. The stagnation of the haciendas in the central and south-central regions also contributed to a demographic shift over the century. Former indigo-producing regions whose economies had not recovered began to lose population to the western departments where sugar and coffee production were expanding, and to other departments where peasant-based indigo and cattle production were still important.[29]

Table 4.1  Regional Distribution of Indigo Production, 1786–1890 (in percent)

| | 1786–1806 | 1803 | 1804 | 1852 | 1859 | 1860 | 1876 | 1880 | 1883 | 1890 |
|---|---|---|---|---|---|---|---|---|---|---|
| Santa Ana | 9 | 1 | 5 | 1 | 2 | 4 | 2 | — | — | — |
| San Salvador | | | | | | | | | | |
| La Liberdad | 10 | 14 | 9 | 5 | 4 | 3 | 3 | 4 | — | — |
| La Paz | 6 | 13 | 9 | 2 | 2 | 1 | 4 | — | 2 | — |
| Cuscatlán | 4 | 2 | 6 | 15 | 11 | 11 | 7 | — | — | — |
| Chalatenango | 13 | 13 | 6 | 17 | 22 | 22 | 17 | 31 | 25 | — |
| Cabanas | 8 | 14 | 11 | 22 | 12 | 19 | 29 | — | 20 | — |
| San Vicente | 20 | 17 | 25 | 15 | 11 | 11 | 10 | — | — | — |
| Usulután | — | — | 1 | — | — | — | 3 | — | — | — |
| San Miguel | 19[a] | 12 | 25 | 25 | 37 | 28 | 26 | 32 | — | — |
| Morazán | — | 13 | 3 | — | — | — | 1 | — | — | 14 |
| La Unión | 1 | — | — | — | — | — | 3 | — | — | — |

*Sources:* See Note on Sources.

a. Probably includes data from Morazán and La Unión.

Generally, the production and marketing of indigo was a risky venture for both *hacendado* and merchant, and was usually based on extensive debt for lack of liquid capital. While all producers suffered from fluctuations in the price of indigo or market disruptions caused by war or competition during the nineteenth century, small farmers and peasants could more easily survive these difficulties. Even if they temporarily ceased production, they could rely on household and communal labor to produce and process their crop.[30] Furthermore, those who could grow their own food were less dependent on the income from indigo. The large commercial fairs and myriad individual transactions led to the barter of indigo for imported manufactured products, overcoming the dependence on centralized marketing of the colonial period. Small-scale indigo production was also aided by the abolition of the colonial *montepío* (government-sponsored bank) in 1827. Since the 1780s the bank had controlled indigo prices and made loans to larger producers from a special tax paid by all producers, but it was plagued by difficulties, notably its dominance by large producers and a high rate of default on loans. An 1816 government report questioned the utility of the bank for smaller producers because it excluded them from borrowing while taxing their production.[31]

Some decades after independence, the Salvadoran government provided incentives to indigo producers, but the larger estate-based sector never fully recovered. At various times between the 1830s and 1850s the government supported a *montepío* of indigo growers, but it did not help larger producers. Producers and processors paid a tax to regional tax offices, but there is no evidence on how the system was administered or how long it lasted.[32] Other laws at midcentury offered exemptions from military service and municipal taxes to workers and farmers involved in indigo production.

Even after the relative decline in indigo prices and exports that began in the 1880s, indigo continued to be important to El Salvador's economy. Peasant producers and small farmers continued to dominate indigo production well after its decline as the major export crop. While prices fluctuated somewhat throughout the century, smaller producers who did not have to monetize their labor costs and with access to cheap land could weather these fluctuations relatively well. Many peasants continued to produce indigo on a very limited scale and sold the unprocessed crop to larger producers or merchants who controlled processing facilities in otherwise unused haciendas, such as those in San Vicente.[33] New regions of colonization were incorporated into the indigo economy even as prices declined.[34]

## Commercial Agriculture and Social Structure in Western El Salvador, 1830s–1880s

Western El Salvador includes three distinct ecological zones (see map 4): (1) the north, along the Guatemalan border, Chalatenango, and northern San Salvador, including the mountainous portions of the Santa Ana; (2) the south, a mountainous area with high plains marked by the triangle formed by the towns of Santa Ana, Tacuba, and Santa Tecla; (3) the southwest, comprising the southern portions of Ahuachapán, Sonsonate, and La Libertad, low-lying lands, valleys, and hilly coastal lands. During the colonial period portions of Ahuachapán and all of Sonsonate composed a separate province that was incorporated into the Republic soon after independence. Santa Ana—part of the province of San Salvador—was composed of the parishes of Metapán, Santa Ana, Texistepeque, and Chalchuapa. At independence, these three formed the department of Sonsonate. In 1855 most of the municipalities of modern-day Ahuachapán were incorporated into the newly formed department of Santa Ana. The lands that formed the town of Nueva San Salvador in 1855 and towns to the southeast and northwest were part of San Salvador after independence. They were later grouped into a separate, sparsely populated department in 1865. Finally, in 1869 the department of Ahuachapán was made from portions of Santa Ana and Sonsonate.

Western El Salvador combined strong elements from both the colonial-era hacienda-based economy and the community-based peasantry. Nineteenth-century records tell us much about the use of *ejido,* communal, and other lands. The areas around the cities of Santa Ana, Metapán, Ahuachapán, and Sonsonate included many haciendas and *chacras* (suburban farms) of city dwellers, while the many Indian and Ladino villages provide diverse examples of peasant life. Further, the west played an important role in the developing coffee economy that began in the 1860s and accelerated somewhat in the 1880s. The mostly unoccupied and un-

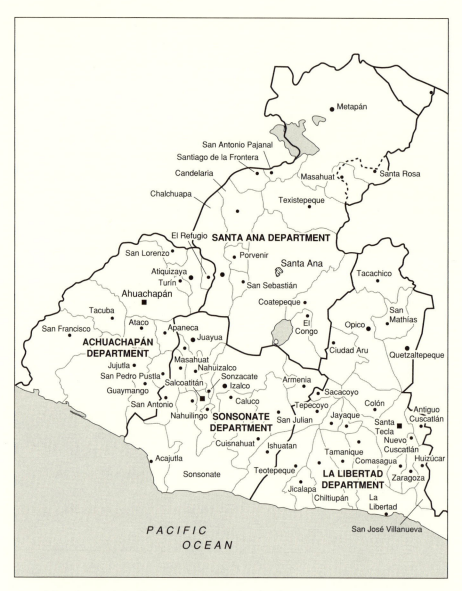

**Map 4. Municipalities of Western El Salvador**

cultivated areas surrounding Santa Ana, Chalchuapa, Coatepeque, and
the Indian villages between Sonsonate City and Ahuachapán City saw a
rapid expansion in coffee production and are still important today. In
addition, major political movements of the nineteenth and early twentieth centuries had their origins in the cities of Santa Ana and Santa Tecla,

or in smaller regional towns. Masses of peasants from western villages participated in revolts and protests—including the major revolt of 1932 —and in the less dramatic system of patronage and incorporation by national and regional political movements.

### ECONOMIC CONDITIONS, CA. 1850

Between 1824 and the 1850s El Salvador's commercial and agricultural progress was tempered by wars, but also by the relative weakness of the national state and its elite.[35] War-related disruptions contributed to the relative stagnation of many long-distance commercial activities, especially elite-owned enterprises. However, a relative improvement was noted with the first Dueñas administration in 1852–1854, especially outside the estate sector. According to Carl Scherzer, a contemporary observer, under Dueñas "the culture of indigo revived, and the markets of San Miguel were once more pretty numerously frequented by foreign traders; but still there was no real confidence in the stability of the government, and no faith in the duration of peace. Capitalists remained anxious and uneasy; the government could procure no loan; in the larger indigo plantations, formerly doing such profitable business, there was a complete stagnation."[36] Baily agreed:

> In all respects [El Salvador] is an important district, and, from natural resources as well as position, capable of being rendered most flourishing; but owing to the civil discords which have so generally and continually afflicted the country, from one extremity to the other, during a long series of years, it has suffered numerous checks to its prosperity; its commerce has been greatly diminished, and its agriculture has sustained immense injury.[37]

But even at this point, before the expansion of the 1860s and the introduction of coffee, observers viewed El Salvador as a potential economic dynamo. In 1855 a diplomat and businessman described El Salvador as a country with "few large tracts held by single individuals . . . a circumstance favorable to the general industry, which contrasts creditably with that of the other states; . . . in respect to industry, general intelligence and all the requisites of good order, its people are entitled to first rank in Central America."[38] Other travelers similarly emphasized the great industriousness and activity of Salvadorans—a description echoed by foreign travelers and local ideologues for the next century. A few years before E. G. Squier, the Dutch traveler Jacobo Haefkens stated that because of their economic well-being and market participation, El Salvador's Indians were the most "civilized" in Central America.[39]

Unfortunately, there are no systematic descriptive accounts between the late eighteenth century and the 1850s, and the documentary record is also weak. The best available sources are for western El Salvador and are provided by foreign travelers such as those quoted above and a handful of late colonial and early republican documents saved from deteriorating archives in the cities of Sonsonate and Ahuachapán. Nonetheless, the picture of western El Salvador that emerges is of a region more "Indian" than the rest of the country, where the communal institutions consolidated during the eighteenth century provided the basis for an Indian and Ladino peasantry divided into three sectors: (1) peasants who cultivated the more remote lands for their own subsistence and who did not participate in local or regional markets; (2) a greater number of Indians and Ladino peasants based on community and municipal lands who farmed for their own subsistence but also sold their products in the food, coffee, sugar, and cattle markets; (3) a smaller sector—usually Indian— that specialized in manufacturing such as palm leaf crafts or scarves, or in processing activities such as producing sugar and collecting balsam. Although these divisions were clear-cut at the end of the colonial period, by midcentury the most significant group was the second, with most peasants, both Indian and Ladino, producing corn and sugar for local consumption.[40]

At least since the eighteenth century the western departments supported a number of complementary economic activities. The coastal plains of Sonsonate and Ahuachapán developed cattle ranches (*sitios*, *potreros*) and small-scale sugar farms and mills.[41] Production of corn, beans, and other food for subsistence and local markets had always been a mainstay of the local peasantry and some of the haciendas. Producing products for export such as indigo and sugar was compatible with the seasonal requirements of raising food. Balsam trees provided the principal income to the Indian villages of the balsam coast. The extensive cattle and dairy haciendas and iron ventures of Metapán also had roots in the late colonial period. Indigo was also a significant crop for these northern haciendas and other farms around the cities of Santa Ana and Sonsonate.

According to reports gathered around 1858–1860, villages developed differently because of a combination of inherited colonial features and ecological factors. Texistepeque (SA), for example, did not prosper because its *ejido* lands were small and of poor quality. It had 315 hectares of "broken land" that were not attractive either for subsistence or commercial crops. Furthermore, these *ejidos* were surrounded by private haciendas and farms, limiting the expansion of community-based peasant agriculture. Other villages faced additional limitations. One village, while having extensive small-scale sugar production using hand-driven sugar mills, still had most of its men at work "in other people's labors." Some predominantly Indian towns specialized in crafts and manufactures and rented their lands for cattle grazing or farming to outsiders.[42]

Cities and towns with more diversified economic activities, usually involving cattle and sugar, such as Ahuachapán, Sonsonate, Santa Ana, and Chalchuapa, had a larger percentage of artisans and/or *jornaleros* (day laborers). However, most of those classified as *jornaleros* were not excluded from renting *ejido* lands or having access to the lands of Indian communities. Indeed, the governor of Sonsonate generalized in 1865 that all of the department's inhabitants were farmers.[43] Indians from places like Izalco worked on the haciendas and farms of Sonsonate, even when their own communities controlled large areas.[44] Working for wages formed part of a strategy based on communal or domestic organization of labor but did not preclude access to land.

In general terms, the smallest and more isolated western villages were subsistence-oriented but never entirely detached from market activities. The Indians of the balsam coast, a secluded and economically autonomous region, had a very different form of communal property. Theirs was a communally based economy organized around the allocation of balsam trees, rather than land.[45] From their small villages, accessible only by footpaths, they controlled the coastal balsam trees and sold their product to creole and Ladino merchants. Despite their insertion into mercantile networks linking them to the export sector, outsiders perceived the extraction of balsam as a subsistence activity, geared to communal reproduction rather than individual accumulation.[46] The governor commented that the Indians of Cuisnahuat relied entirely on the income from balsam: "Since the product of balsam satisfies their needs, in their lands you can't find one head of cattle and only very small grain plantings."[47]

The economy of western El Salvador was based mostly on peasants' and farmers' access to common (municipal and community) lands. For the most part, residents of western El Salvador were small-scale producers, of whom a small but significant percentage worked for wages on a seasonal basis. By the end of the century, they formed—together with immigrants from other departments and from Guatemala—a slowly growing class of seasonal laborers. The Indian (and some Ladino) communities of the west were very successful at securing and extending their common lands at a time when hacienda production was not very important and involved mostly cattle production rather than agriculture. Most villages had lands and did not closely regulate the use of common lands until the 1860s, though some villages where Indian communes controlled all of the lands or the renting of plots for cattle grazing made efforts to exclude Ladinos. Some villages charged rent only to Ladinos, others to all who used the land (especially where Indian community cohesion was weak), while still others entirely ignored the regulations on the administration of communal and *ejido* lands. The difference between these two types of lands was not always clear before the 1860s, and a variety of in situ solutions were found that depended on the interaction of local forces and national policies. The 1859 *Estadística* commented that most lands in Sonsonate were poorly administered, and an 1866 report by the local governor of Ahuachapán complained that most municipal lands were not well divided or rented.[48] Villages had not only reserve lands, which were used as communal grazing grounds, but also in most cases substantial forests that provided firewood and housing materials, some explicitly preserved for those purposes.

The village of San Pedro Pustla shows how an Indian town combined manufacturing with agriculture. In 1830 the residents were mostly hat makers (58 percent of adult men) with smaller groups of *labradores* (small farmers, 14 percent) and *jornaleros* (13 percent). Most of the hat makers tended to be young unmarried men, while the farmers and laborers tended to be older and married.[49] Fifteen years later, the town still produced mostly hats in about the same quantity for about the same price. Agricultural production (coffee, corn, sugar, and rice worth 10,000 pesos) supplemented the income from crafts.[50] By 1860 San Pedro had 240 households, with the great majority of the men (293 of 342) still hat makers. Using materials grown within the town's *ejidos*, the hat makers manufactured about 350,000 hats each year, mostly for export, receiving a sizable income of around 35,000 pesos in 1858 and 24,000 pesos in 1862. The hats were sold at one real each.[51]

While most of San Pedro's inhabitants tilled small farms on the town's Indian-controlled lands, the municipality allocated some lands to outsiders or Ladino settlers. These were rented mostly by residents of the city of Ahuachapán. By the 1880s most of the town's farmers were Ladino immigrants from other departments who came to rent most of the town's usable lands. They also developed this town's first coffee farms. Most areas were planted with coffee, plantains, and some cane, and the rest with grains. The town had begun to charge rent to local Indian residents a few years before 1880 at 2 reales per 100 *tareas* (4.35 hectares), plus an additional charge of 5 pesos on the sale of possession rights over *ejido* plots. Income from the sale of *ejido* plots was 100 pesos in 1878, indicating that 20 plots (or 8 percent of the total of 257) had exchanged hands —an active market in possession and use rights.

Table 4.2 presents the distribution of land use in San Pedro in 1878. The 12 plots that ranged between 22 and 66 hectares were probably used for cattle grazing. The smallest plots, 26 percent of the total, averaged 1.5 hectares. The largest group, 40 percent of the town's units, averaged around 10 hectares. These plots were closer in size to the national average for privatized *ejido* plots in the mid-1880s and demonstrate that, even including community and town lands rented to Ladinos, most farms were small and peasant-based. The total land in use (1,804 hectares) was a large share of San Pedro's total lands. (The town originally had only 1,620 hectares of *ejidos* in 1860, including a *composición* of 742 hectares from the eighteenth century, but in the early 1870s they added more lands.)[52] Clearly by 1880 the town was using all of its *ejido* land. Conflicts with a nearby community indicates that it too had reached a similar limit. As was typical for this region, there was little competition for land between large outside landowners and the *ejido*-based peasants, although development "from the inside" had caused San Pedro to use up its internal frontier by the early 1880s.

Salcoatitán provides another example of the complex use of *ejido* lands. In 1859 the town was a small settlement of poor laborers or servants, Spanish-speaking Indians who planted mostly staple crops and small plots of coffee and cane. It had no haciendas or farms in its juris-

Table 4.2  Distribution of *Ejido* Lands in San Pedro Pustla, 1878

| Plot Size (hectares) | No. of Plots | (%) | Total Hectares | (%) |
|---|---|---|---|---|
| 1–2.2 | 66 | (26) | 93.0 | (5) |
| 2.3–4.4 | 75 | (29) | 281.7 | (16) |
| 4.5–21.7 | 104 | (40) | 973.3 | (54) |
| 21.8–43.5 | 9 | (4) | 265.7 | (15) |
| 43.6–60.9 | 3 | (1) | 190.4 | (11) |
| Total | 257 | (100) | 1,804.1 | (100) |

*Source:* "Testimonio del censo estadistico que se paga a las municipalidades del pueblo de San Pedro Pustla," AGN-CG-AH, 1880.

diction, which did not extend beyond its own *ejidos*. Its lands, although not irrigated, were fertile, and local crops were sold in the city of Sonsonate. It had 150 households and an adult population of 324, of whom 143 were men—123 described as *jornaleros* and 23 as *labradores*. There were only three artisans in the town. Most of the men described as day laborers were not landless workers but rented small *ejido* plots in the 1850s.

However, by the 1860s about half of the town's *jornaleros* had no plots in the town's *ejidos* despite the availability of land.[53] Around this time— 1862—Salcoatitán had developed two modest sugar cane farms, with 2.87 hectares of plantings, and about 70 hectares of coffee within its *ejidos*.[54] As in San Pedro, most plots were smaller than 22 hectares, although a few very large ones took up 46 percent of the town's lands. The development of modest but successful enterprises in sugar, cattle, and coffee in the town's *ejidos* between the 1850s and 1860s had important repercussions. More of the plots were under 100 *tareas* (43.5 hectares) than in San Pedro, reflecting the early emergence of a layer of landless, land-poor, and probably immigrant workers in this town. Similarly, ten farms came to rent more than half of the town's land. (See table 4.3.)

The municipality of Ataco, in Ahuachapán, provides further evidence on how local peasants and farmers used *ejido* lands, but also shows how a significant number of landholding peasants also began working seasonally on *ejido*-based commercial farms. In 1859 it had 1,072 people and was the third most populous municipality in the department. It did not have any haciendas or cattle ranches, and one source commented that "all the lands that are of significant extension are dedicated only to sub-

Table 4.3  Distribution of *Ejido* Lands in Salcoatitán, 1868

| Plot Size (hectares) | No. of Plots | (%) | Total Hectares | (%) |
|---|---|---|---|---|
| 1–2.2 | 35 | (38) | 41.1 | (6) |
| 2.3–4.4 | 24 | (26) | 67.0 | (10) |
| 4.5–21.7 | 24 | (26) | 189.0 | (29) |
| 21.8–43.5 | 7 | ( 8) | 177.7 | (28) |
| 43.6–60 | 3 | ( 3) | 165.9 | (26) |
| Total | 93 | (100) | 640.7 | (101)[a] |

Source: "Cuadro de los terrenos acotados y distribuidos en Salcoatitán," 29 May 1868, AGN-CA-SO.

a. Total exceeds 100 percent because of rounding.

Table 4.4  Distribution of *Ejido* Lands in Ataco, 1880

| Plot Size (hectares) | No. of Plots | (%) | Total Hectares | (%) |
|---|---|---|---|---|
| 1–2 | 95 | (24) | 135 | (5) |
| 2–4 | 86 | (22) | 288 | (10) |
| 4–20 | 192 | (50) | 1,737 | (61) |
| 20–40 | 11 | (3) | 341 | (12) |
| 40–60 | 6 | (2) | 380 | (12) |
| Total | 390 | (101)[a] | 2,881 | (100) |

Source: "Copia autorizada que forma el alcalde municipal de Ataco del catastro en que constan los nombres de los poseedores de terreno ejidal, las tareas y canon anual que pagan," 23 January 1880, AGN-CG-AH.

Note: Table excludes data on the 68 plots rented out to residents of Atiquizaya, a nearby town.

a. Total exceeds 100 percent because of rounding.

sistence production *[labranzas]* and are in the most part grazing lands." It did have, however, two large coffee farms in its *ejidos* owned by Quirino Escalón and Teodoro Moreno, governor of the department of Santa Ana. By 1876 Ataco was the largest coffee-producing municipality in the district (later department) of Ahuachapán, with an output of 8,000 quintales, more than Ahuachapán City itself. It also produced the largest quantity of corn in the department.[55] Table 4.4 presents the distribution of *ejido* plots in this town on the eve of their privatization.

Ataco probably had no more than 400 households in 1878, corresponding to the number of *ejido* plots. However, in addition to the *ejidos*, the town's Indian community also had separate lands which they considered their property and reserved for their members. Factors other than access to land must account for the emerging social differentiation within villages like Ataco, since a large percentage of its population were listed as *jornaleros* who worked seasonally for wages. An 1888 military census listed 77 *jornaleros* (65 percent) out of a total of 120 men between age fifteen and fifty. Another 42 (35 percent) were listed as farmers.[56] From the number of plots in this town's *ejidos*, it appears that most people called *jornaleros* had access to lands, probably the smaller plots.

Occupations in villages with Indian communities, such as Izalco, Juayua, and Nahuizalco in Ahuachapán, tended to be more homogeneous. (See table 4.5.) Before 1860 most residents are listed as *labradores* or craft workers, but within these communities the organization of economic and social life remains a mystery. The administration, division, and allocation of *ejido* and/or communal lands was a complex matter, af-

Table 4.5  Male Occupations in Selected Western Towns, 1859
(in percent)

| | Farmers & Peasants | Laborers | Artisans & Small Tradesmen | Craft Workers |
|---|---|---|---|---|
| Izalco | 65 | 16 | 14 | — |
| Juayua[a] | 96 | — | 4 | — |
| Santo Domingo | 97 | — | 3 | — |
| Armenia | 78 | — | 22 | — |
| Cacaluta | 97 | — | 3 | — |
| San Pedro Pustla | 7 | — | 7 | 85 |
| Ahuachapán | 25 | 53[b] | 21 | — |
| Atiquzaya[c] | 34 | 56 | 10 | — |
| Coatepeque | 96 | — | 3 | — |
| Chalchuapa | 29 | 60 | 11 | — |
| Texistepeque | 78 | 12 | 10 | — |
| Metapán | 95 | — | 5 | — |

*Sources:* "Padron general en que se contienen todas las familias de ambos secsos en Nahuizalco," 23 February 1835, AGN-CA-SO; "Padron del pueblo de Sta. Lucia Juayua que contiene mil quinentas treinta y cuatro havitantes," 1830, AGN-CA-SO; "Libro que contiene la calificación de todos los ciudadanos de esta jurisdicción," 15 November 1874, AGN-CG-AH.

a. In 1830, 99 percent were *labradores* (small-scale farmers or peasants) in Juayua.

b. Includes both *mozos de campo* (farm workers) and *jornaleros* (day laborers).

c. In 1874, Atiquizaya's electoral lists included 970 men of which 13 percent were *agricultores* (farmers) 54 percent *labradores*, 12 percent were *jornaleros*, 6 percent artisans, and 1.4 percent merchants.

fected by local factors and traditions, policies and laws of various regimes, and interactions with neighboring areas.

Major conflicts in this region were usually between towns and communities, typically over the occupation of one village's lands by settlers from another. The communes of Izalco and Nahuizalco, for example, feuded over land limits throughout the nineteenth century.[57] Similar conflicts existed between the communes of Coatepeque and the *volcaneños* of Santa Ana. Ethnic divisions within villages sometimes also amplified class conflicts.

The western economy was closely connected to that of southeastern Guatemala, with a continual flow of crafts and manufactures, food products, and seasonal and permanent migrations between them. Craft exports to Guatemala, for example, came from as far as Tenancingo in the department of Cuscatlán.[58] These ties from the colonial period became important again as the economies of the west diversified and expanded.[59] In 1854 the Salvadoran government prohibited the export of grains to Guatemala to avoid a possible scarcity.[60] According to statistics gathered by the governor of Santa Ana, 7 percent of the value of the department's imports in 1859 (including Ahuachapán, 10,550 pesos' worth of imports, out of a total of 153,500 pesos) came from other Central American states, mostly Guatemala. In the 1850s Herrán and others noted that much of Guatemala's export and import trade was conducted by way of Sonsonate. Similarly, in the 1860s and early 1870s Laferrière noted the trading and money economy that linked Santa Ana to Guatemala. In 1880 only .5 percent of the country's regulated imports came from other Central American republics, since there was little control of land-based trade until the twentieth century.[61] The increased economic activity attracted migrants from elsewhere in Central America toward the end of the century.[62]

Regional wars, especially during the Federation years, disrupted the Indian communities from which soldiers were recruited. The war against William Walker in Nicaragua also burdened the peasant population and the larger economy. Soldiers were recruited to serve in the thousand-strong units sent from El Salvador between 1856 and 1857. Officials raised forced taxes and new local taxes (with much difficulty) to finance the campaign, burdening local merchants and peasants.[63] Returning troops spread a cholera epidemic throughout much of the country in

1857. In the department of Sonsonate alone, 2,399 people (mostly Indians) had died of cholera by 8 August 1857.[64] These difficulties hampered the Salvadoran economy.

### URBAN CENTERS AND THEIR ENVIRONS
### IN WESTERN EL SALVADOR

For most of the colonial period and well into the nineteenth century, the city of Sonsonate was the region's most important urban center, although it declined in the eighteenth century as the cacao trade diminished.[65] The opening of the ports of Peru and Chile—major consumers of Salvadoran indigo and other products—also contributed to this decline. Products from within the Spanish Empire no longer received preferential treatment in these ports, although indigo exports to Peru and Chile continued throughout the nineteenth century.[66] Population declined in the city and on surrounding haciendas and farms. In 1790 the city had 3,400 inhabitants, but in 1858 it had only 3,100, less than other municipalities with extensive communal lands and few haciendas.[67] Travelers in the early 1800s commented on the city's decline.[68]

Owners of haciendas and farms surrounding Sonsonate bartered their products for imported goods, which they then sold to the local population. The most successful landed enterprises were operated by a handful of foreigners attracted by the cheapness and productivity of the land.[69] The region's haciendas and farms exported rum, sugar, horses, cattle, indigo, and tobacco and satisfied the local elite's need for imported products. According to Haefkens, no single merchant in El Salvador could purchase an entire shipment of foreign products, so most were sold in small quantities.[70] Another traveler noted the "mixed blood" and dark-skinned appearance of Sonsonate's creole elite, which reduced their status within the national hierarchy.[71] As late as 1857, Scherzer reported, city notables depended on their farms outside the city: "Almost every tolerably opulent inhabitant of Sonsonate possesses [a farm], where he cultivates all kinds of nutritious plants and fruits, and passes most of the dry season." They required little attention, he observed, since "in most of the *fincas* I did not see more than three or four laborers at work, and those men live entirely on vegetables, in simple huts made of reeds and palm leaves."[72]

Sonsonate's economy was obviously linked to the larger agrarian econ-

Table 4.6  Occupations of Men and Women in Sonsonate City,
1853–1865

|  | 1853 | | 1860 | | 1865 | |
|---|---|---|---|---|---|---|
|  | N | (%) | N | (%) | N | (%) |
| **Men** | | | | | | |
| Day laborers | 255 | (27) | 146 | (20) | 240 | (32) |
| Agriculturists | 109 | (12) | 124 | (17) | 132 | (17) |
| Artisans/tradesmen | 435 | (46) | 323 | (44) | 303 | (41) |
| Servants | 91 | (10) | 60 | ( 8) | — | — |
| Professionals | 14 | ( 2) | 17 | ( 2) | — | — |
| Retail tradesmen | 41 | ( 4) | 48 | ( 7) | 47 | (6) |
| Small-scale farmers | — | — | — | — | 12 | (2) |
| Total men | 945 | (100) | 718 | (100) | 734 | (100) |
| **Women** | | | | | | |
| Servants | 252 | (25) | 256 | (20) | 106 | ( 9) |
| Artisans/tradeswomen | 621 | (63) | 819 | (65) | 677 | (58) |
| "Female occupations" | — | — | — | — | 124 | (11) |
| Midwives | 4 | (<1) | 8 | (<1) | — | — |
| Farmers | — | — | — | — | 3 | (<1) |
| Merchants | — | — | 52 | ( 4) | 79 | ( 7) |
| Hacienda owners | — | — | 2 | (<1) | — | — |
| Food preparers | — | — | 128 | (10) | 177 | (15) |
| Prostitutes | 98 | (10) | — | — | — | — |
| Total women | 975 | (100) | 1,265 | (100) | 1,166 | (100) |

*Sources:* Scherzer, *Travels*, 1857; Ipiña, "Estadística"; "Resultados del Censo de Sonsonate," 17 June 1865, AGN-CA-SO.

omy (see table 4.6). Much of its population consisted of independent or apprentice artisans and tradesmen, some of whom processed cattle and farm products. In 1865 Sonsonate City had 15 large haciendas, most of them along the extensive coastal plain, covering 29,925 hectares (an average of 1,995 hectares each).[73] In the communally based peasant economy of the west, however, the size of these estates made little difference to the peasants, since they were located in low-lying coastal areas of sparse settlement on lands suitable for cattle grazing and perhaps sugar cane and cotton. The mostly cattle and horse economy of these haciendas required little labor. (See table 4.7.)

Sonsonate experienced a commercial revival after the 1850s, with a

Table 4.7  Commercial Farms and Estates in Sonsonate and
          Ahuachapán in 1866

|  | Sugar | Coffee | Food | Grazing | Mixed Haciendas | Cattle | Indigo |
|---|---|---|---|---|---|---|---|
| Sonsonate | 15 | — | 151 | 17 | 4 | 11 | — |
| Nahuizalco | 3 | — | 20 | 807 | — | — | — |
| Santo Domingo | — | — | 41 | 3 | — | — | — |
| Nahuilngo | 1 | — | 100 | 20 | — | 2 | — |
| Sonzacate | 6 | — | 89 | 227 | — | — | — |
| San Antonio | 1 | — | — | 70 | — | — | — |
| Izalco | 8 | — | 200 | 382 | 1 | 2 | — |
| Armenia | 5 | — | — | 210 | — | — | 3 |
| San Julián | — | — | — | 68 | — | — | — |
| Ishuatán | — | — | — | 13 | — | — | — |
| Cuisnahuat | — | — | — | 22 | — | — | — |
| Caluco | — | — | 50 | 156 | — | — | — |
| Juayua | 2 | 89 | 80 | 123 | 1 | — | — |
| Masahuat | — | 4 | — | 50 | — | — | — |
| Salcoatitán | 1 | 12 | — | 101 | — | — | — |
| Guaimango | 17 | 11 | — | 72 | — | 2 | — |
| San Pedro Pustla | — | — | 12 | 2 | — | — | — |
| Apaneca | — | 33 | — | 304 | — | — | — |
| Jujutla | — | — | 10 | — | — | — | — |
| Total | 59 | 149 | 753 | 2,647 | 6 | 17 | 3 |

*Source:* Ipiña, "Estadística."

brief cotton boom during the U.S. civil war. This expansion of cotton production, while demonstrating a quick response to market incentives, also depended on high market prices.[74] High prices were needed to off-set the high transport and labor costs that made the region's farmers and *hacendados* weak and vulnerable.[75] According to a report from the 1860s, most of the country's cotton was grown by Indians.[76] In 1850, Baily noted the use of cotton for home textile production.[77]

Nonetheless, a few investors profited from the demand for cotton and sugar through most of the 1850s and 1860s by importing a few steam-driven mills. The owners of the haciendas "Bebedero" and "Los Lagartos," for example, purchased new sugar mills in 1861.[78] Other economic activities expanded, in part stimulated by growth in the production and export of coffee and liquor and a steady increase in population.[79] The town of Caluco invited settlers in 1864, offering incentives such as exemption from serving on the municipal council and access to adequate lands.[80] However, despite recent changes the governor of the department noted in 1862 that the region's resources, including its diversity of climate, accessible seaports, and extensive lands and forests, remained unexploited.[81]

The regions around Santa Ana and Metapán, mostly Ladino northern districts, were involved in the indigo trade and raising cattle for export to Guatemala and Honduras. Data for the 1860s indicate that they were also large producers of grain and wheat. Santa Ana City had never been a trading center, housing only a few dozen Spaniards at the end of the colonial era. In the early nineteenth century the city developed very slowly, but by midcentury it was the west's most populous municipality, with a thriving commercial economy. After 1850, Santa Ana's economic importance grew when many of the surrounding hacienda and common lands were turned into centers for coffee production. But the region had diverse economic activities that included cattle raising, sugar and food production, and an enlarged import trade as well. Santa Ana also participated in the brief cotton boom of the mid-1860s.[82]

In 1860 Santa Ana had only seven haciendas and forty-six sugar farms with milling machinery. Its incipient coffee economy, while among the three largest in the country, was still not large enough to dominate the economic landscape—its sugar and corn crops together were valued at more than ten times the value of its coffee production.[83] As an official report described it: "Among the neighbors of this city the spirit of enterprise has risen, and they are investing large sums in new plantings of cane and sugar . . . which will soon produce abundant fruits for export."[84] Santa Ana's urban artisans, professionals, and entrepreneurs had begun to plant coffee and other export products in nearby lands. The agricultural frontier exceeded the limits of the town's *ejidos* and began to influence neighboring economies. Increased production led to a faster claiming of *baldíos* and contributed to the early privatization of Indian community lands in both Santa Ana and Chalchuapa.[85] However, the lack of cheap and stable labor was a continuing problem until the early twentieth century.[86] In 1864 the governor complained that workers received too much in cash advances from farmers and often never fulfilled their obligations: "Regarding laborers, here there is the damaging custom of paying them ahead of time *[habilitar]* with large sums, and one individual commits himself to various bosses, and even though this is punished, this practice does not end; . . . it could be remedied only by prohibiting the use of advance payments."[87] Two years later the complaint was repeated and tied to the perennial lack of liquid capital.[88]

Workers in Santa Ana followed diverse occupations, as in Sonsonate, but more men and women worked as *jornaleros*. (See table 4.8.) Despite the tendency toward a wage labor economy, by 1879 more than half of the city's males were considered independent producers or landowners. A similar number of men were *jornaleros,* although they, too, might have had access to land in other towns, in the *ejidos,* or on haciendas. Curiously, the number of landowners and farmers more than quadrupled over twenty years.

The census of 1879 classes a large percentage of women as *jornaleras* —seasonal farm workers. Women farm workers are rare in nineteenth-century occupational data. Since the data was gathered during the coffee-picking season (December), the influx of women was probably temporary. This explains the fact that in the census females exceeded males by about 2,000.[89] Also important is the large percentage of women working as artisans or in manufacturing. Only the city of San Vicente had similar numbers of artisans, although they were mostly males.[90] Clearly Santa Ana's more advanced commercial economy had begun to mobilize female wage labor in a new way.

Santa Tecla (Nueva San Salvador) in the department of La Libertad experienced a similar expansion in commercial agriculture. Founded as an alternative to the capital of San Salvador when it was damaged in 1855, the city expanded quickly, attracting wealthy speculators, professionals, and many peasants. It soon became the epicenter for the expansion of coffee production into the new and sparsely settled department. (The government considered settling Europeans in this region, but all attempts at attracting Europeans or even Chinese laborers failed.)[91] In addition to coffee, cane growing and sugar manufacturing also expanded: in one year alone, five new steam-driven mills were installed.[92] One hacienda put up for sale in 1864 comprised "five and a half *caballerías* of fenced land . . . 14,000 feet of coffee, of which 10,000 are in production, two grazing fields, as much cane, 80 heads of cattle, one coffee mill, two houses."[93] The expansion of commercial farming that began in the late 1850s was an impetus for the transformation of communal and

Table 4.8 Occupations in Santa Ana City, 1859–1879

| | 1859 | | 1867 | | 1879 | |
|---|---|---|---|---|---|---|
| | N | (%) | N | (%) | N | (%) |
| **Men** | | | | | | |
| Agriculturists/small-scale farmers | 940 | (34) | 1,340 | (35) | 4,419 | (51) |
| Professionals | 14 | (.5) | 22 | (.5) | 38 | (.5) |
| Artisans/tradesmen | 423 | (15) | 349 | ( 9) | 415 | ( 5) |
| Day laborers | 1,206 | (43) | 1,984 | (52) | 3,600 | (42) |
| *Hacendados* | — | — | 12 | (.3) | — | — |
| Handicapped persons | 80 | ( 3) | — | — | — | — |
| Servants | 79 | ( 3) | 78 | ( 2) | — | — |
| Merchants | 37 | ( 1) | 39 | ( 1) | 160 | ( 2) |
| Total men listed | 2,779 | | 3,824 | | 8,632 | |
| | | | | | | |
| **Women** | | | | | | |
| Artisans/tradeswomen | 1,493 | (30) | 1,487 | (47) | 1,406 | (22) |
| Servants | 138 | ( 3) | 149 | ( 5) | — | — |
| Nannies | 32 | ( 1) | — | — | — | — |
| Merchants | 89 | ( 1) | — | — | — | — |
| Shopkeepers/market workers | 1,516 | (31) | 10 | (.2) | — | — |
| Food preparers | 1,782 | (36) | 1,505 | (48) | 2,589 | (40) |
| Day laborers | 2,355 | (37) | — | — | — | — |
| Total women listed | 4,961 | | 3,141 | | 6,449 | |

*Sources:* López, *Estadística; El Constitucional,* 6 June 1867; "Censo de Población de La Ciudad de Santa Ana," 1879, AGN-CM-SA.

*Note:* The totals for 1879 are 8,841 adult men and 17,652 adult women, although occupational data is not available for all people in the census. This includes thousands of naturalized immigrant Guatemalan women.

*ejido* lands in the 1870s and 1880s. By then the government was seeking to diversify Salvadoran exports because of fluctuations in indigo and coffee prices. A more complex agrarian economy, which included subsistence peasants, small export producers, and elite and urban investors in agriculture, blossomed during these years, leading to changes in the social structure and ethnic relations of peasants over the following decades.

Table 4.9 presents the Interior Ministry's 1882 data on agricultural enterprises. Although the data are incomplete, they probably cover the larger enterprises owned by elite and urban groups, but not many small-scale producers. Nonetheless, the fact that this census found roughly

Table 4.9  Commercial Farms in Western Departments, 1882

| Department | Gen. Farms | Cattle Hcds | Coffee Farms | Sugar Farms | Pasture Farms | Food Farms | Plantain Farms | Indigo Hcdas. | Sugar Mills |
|---|---|---|---|---|---|---|---|---|---|
| Sonsonate | 670 | 24 | 416 | 43 | 254 | 0 | 0 | 0 | 8 |
| Ahuachapán | 85 | 13 | 1,048 | 54 | 10 | 11 | 19 | 0 | 4 |
| Santa Ana | 428 | 63 | 1,588 | 118 | 200 | 0 | 46 | 51 | 23 |
| La Libertad | 27 | 69 | 232 | 83 | 149 | 99 | 14 | 5 | 54 |
| National Total | 1,893 | 452 | 4,358 | 1,993 | 994 | 342 | 2,964 | 748 | 2,455 |

*Source:* Mora, *Memoria . . . (1883),* 141.

6,000 commercial agricultural units in a region with only about 25,000
households indicates the proliferation of small-scale productive units.
From the total heads of households, we must eliminate those in urban
occupations, especially artisans, residents of balsam coast villages (not
included in the census), and others not likely to hold agricultural property. At a rough estimate, there was one unit for every three heads of
household, suggesting that at this stage agricultural ownership was better distributed than in later decades.

PEASANT CAPITALISM

The municipality of Chalchuapa, northwest of San Salvador and adjacent to Santa Ana, provides an example of successful peasant-based
commercial agriculture. Chalchuapa was a cattle and hog-raising center
throughout the colonial period. In the late colonial period Chalchuapa
was important because of its strategic location between Salvadoran cities
and Guatemala. (It was a battlefield during nineteenth-century cross-
border and factional confrontations.)[94] While it did not produce colonial El Salvador's principal export (indigo), it benefited indirectly from
expanded indigo production.[95] In the eighteenth century the town's
Ladino and Indian communities began to enlarge their holdings by purchasing lands from the Spanish crown.[96] By the early nineteenth century,
its population was growing fast: from about 600 people in 1740 to
2,200 in 1760, 3,000 in 1807, and 4,600 in the 1860s. Population estimates between the 1860s and 1870s ranged between 5,000 and 9,000
inhabitants, overwhelmingly Ladino.[97] By 1910 Chalchuapa's popula-

tion had expanded to over 20,000, and in 1916 was estimated at nearly 30,000.[98] This increase took place despite the loss of various neighborhoods and haciendas that were separated into smaller municipalities in the 1880s.

A boom in the local economy allowed dozens of Ladinos to form new coffee and sugar farms. In 1867, before the further opening of their lands to Santanecos, the Ladino peasants were reported to have "great coffee groves, food plantings, sugar cane fields; . . . everybody worked, and even the poorest people had their plantings of coffee." Chalchuapa was said to provide a model for the country's development, one based on government support for poor producers who struggled to keep their lands while expanding their participation in commercial agriculture.[99]

Over the next twenty years (the 1870s and 1880s), Chalchuapa became one of the most commercially successful municipalities in Santa Ana and an important center of coffee production. With only about 2 percent of all the productive coffee trees in the country in 1859, by 1876 it was producing a third of the department's coffee. In 1862 it produced about 14 percent of the sugar in the departments of Santa Ana and Ahuachapán, but by 1876 it produced 28 percent. It also enlarged its production of cattle and hogs.[100] By 1883 Chalchuapa held 44 percent of all the coffee trees in the department of Santa Ana.[101] This required approximately 2,500 hectares of land planted in coffee—the second largest extension for any town after Santa Ana.

Sixty percent of Chalchuapa's residents were classified as *jornaleros* in 1859, the highest for the western region outside of Santa Ana City, and in 1868 this percentage had increased to 62 percent.[102] Although, as elsewhere, men classified as *jornaleros* still had access to *ejido* or community lands, their relative predominance shows the greater development of commercial agriculture in Chalchuapa and the resulting trend toward proletarianization. Chalchuapa's commercial success had a mixed effect: while it provided wage work for many residents, it did not detach them from the land, creating instead a hierarchy of producers in which only a few were fully marginalized as full-time wage workers.

By the 1890s Chalchuapa's character had changed significantly since the 1860s. In the minister of the interior's 1893 report, it was described as having much commerce, especially with Guatemala, from where they buy large amounts of grains and basic subsistence items, especially during the coffee harvesting season, this being the main source of wealth of all this region; . . . [there is] a shortage of the labor required to give it a greater push and to regulate wages; there is a need to enforce the fulfillment of labor contracts contracted by day laborers or farm workers with more severe measures than currently, because otherwise, this situation will lead to the demoralization of the working class and the state of agriculture will inevitably suffer.[103]

The report also pointed out the significant profits made from coffee, tobacco, sugar, and grains, while noting a decline in cattle raising. Although it made a brief comeback, stock raising never became as important as it once was.[104] This description exposes most strikingly the transition from a focus on community and land acquisition to questions of labor discipline and wages. The town's social structure also reflected the expanded role of commercial agriculture. While the number of *jornaleros* (988) had increased by 1898, so had the number of modest landowners (499) and artisans (230).[105] In 1910 small and medium-sized producers still had an important role in the town.

### PEASANT AGRICULTURE IN CENTRAL EL SALVADOR

By 1858 Cuscatlán and Cabañas, two departments that produced a large amount of indigo during the colonial period, had increased their share of total production. This increase was reflected in demographic expansion in the nineteenth century. After midcentury, however, the regions of Chalatenango, Cabañas, and San Miguel came to dominate indigo production and held the largest fairs.[106] Smaller producers evidently rented lands on haciendas for indigo production in San Miguel. Cotton farms also appeared in San Miguel in the 1860s, while they also grew enough wheat to perhaps feed the entire country.[107]

In the northern reaches of the department of Cuscatlán—around Suchitoto—there were 24 indigo and cattle haciendas and an additional 110 midsize farms and ranches.[108] This hilly, dry, sandy region was better suited to growing indigo than food products. In the late colonial and early republican period, the Indians of this region died off due to cholera or became Ladino, joining the ranks of Ladino immigrants attracted by the indigo economy.[109] An 1856 census described most men in the department of Cuscatlán as *jornaleros* (5,763), while a significant number were small farmers (1,803).

However, despite the presence of large haciendas, most men in the Suchitoto district were *labradores* (small-scale producers) (1,672 or 80 percent)—most involved in indigo production—while only 432 (20 percent) were considered *jornaleros*. In Cinquera most people produced indigo on a small scale, as did many in San Pedro Perulapán, Jutiapa, and Ilobasco. In Jutiapa alone there were 60 working *obrajes* (one for every 10 heads of household) in addition to abandoned ones.[110] The town of Guayabal was unusual in that most of its residents were tenants on haciendas, renting from *hacendados* unable to organize a plantation system. The region's specialization in indigo required extensive imports of food and other products, spurring the peasants of surrounding regions (Sonsonate, Santa Ana, and elsewhere) to supply Cuscatlán markets.[111] Many small shops, agriculture, and active trade with nearby settlements gave Cuscatlán the appearance of "solid prosperity."[112]

Cojutepeque provides further evidence of the autonomy of peasants and artisans in the nineteenth century. As the center of a regional commercial network, the city consolidated its common lands by clarifying and extending its titled holdings in the late 1700s. Local peasants did not have to compete with haciendas, for there were none of importance. In the 1760s only one hacienda or farm in the municipality benefited from the labor draft from Indian communities—and it was among the smaller ones in San Salvador Province. The department as a whole contained 3–5 percent of the province's larger farms and haciendas, and only a few private (noncommunity) *composiciones* titled in the eighteenth century—only two encompassing 270 hectares, or 1 percent of the total for the province.[113]

In the eighteenth century Cojutepeque's economy was based on grain and sugar production, the latter exported throughout the province. Local producers sold food to travelers on the Camino Real.[114] The economy did not change much in the nineteenth century, consisting of many *chacras* that raised coffee as well as food products and sugar cane. (On his way to Cojutepeque, Haefkens noted many small farms, each with its own animal-powered mill.)[115] In 1859 government officials described it as having no haciendas but many *hatos y chacras* (ranches and suburban farms). Most farms just outside the city grew coffee, using animal- or water-driven mills and wood rollers for processing.[116] Tobacco production expanded by midcentury, especially around San Vicente and Cojutepeque, as well as exports of cigars, indigo, coffee, sugar, cattle, products, and crafts.[117] Food production was so generalized as to not be considered a "speculative business" except during shortages in Honduras when demand for exports raised the price of grains in Cojutepeque and helped local residents accumulate cash.[118]

With economic success, the region's population expanded dramatically. In 1740 Cojutepeque had only 330 Indians, the same as in the 1570s.[119] From around 2,500 residents in the 1790s, it expanded to 8,000 around 1830 and to 11,000 by 1853.[120] By the 1870s the city's rate of expansion declined to just below the national average. At midcentury more than half of the population was Indian, although with the expansion of commercial agriculture came ladinoization.[121] Many saw this transition as a change from Indians engaged in "corn-and-beans" agriculture to farmers and artisans producing sugar cane, coffee, and tobacco. This opinion ignored the many examples of Indians participating in regional and even export markets, including commercial cattle production, but it revealed a trend.[122]

Small producers—both independent peasants and tenants—predominated in the eastern and central regions. Even commercial fairs included many poor merchants trading on a very small scale, contributing to a great temporary inflow of population during the major fairs.[123] Of special importance was the annual fair in the city of San Miguel, said to attract more trade than the entire rest of the country.[124] Thus, expanding commercial opportunities began to differentiate between subsistence peasants and those capable of participating more widely in the production of export and commercial products. New local and foreign demand for indigo, sugar, hides, tobacco, manufactures, coffee, and other products stimulated these changes.

Often, *ejido* lands were rented for crop production, but sometimes the rewards were enjoyed only by the municipality and a few farmers. In Guacotecti, for example, most of the lands were rented to outsiders from Sensuntepeque. This contributed to the impoverishment of the Indians, now in an increasingly marginalized minority. According to a governor's report,

The *ejidos* are monopolized by 19 prominent Indian individuals of the *principales* of Sensuntepeque in amounts more or less large without measure and for which the rent they pay in general has been arbitrary to the point where one of these owners who possesses . . . about thirty *medios* of plantings, paid the *censo* [tax] of various years with a book he gave to the municipality.[125]

However, despite accusations of monopoly, the amount of land or crops involved were not large. The *principales* mentioned in the document appear to have been peasants or small farmers themselves, given the scale of their productions (the largest planting amounting to far less than a hectare).

Even San Vicente, where hacienda-based agricultural production declined throughout most of the century, remained an important trading and artisanal center. Small producers and farmers had also dominated the production of tobacco in Istepeque since colonial times—although tobacco production there declined toward the end of the century. Their products supported the extensive manufacture of cigars and cigarettes by women in San Vicente City and in other major cities.[126]

San Vicente began as a settlement in the 1600s when colonial authorities separated whites and mulattos from the indigenous population. The town residents were given 225 hectares of lands as *ejidos*.[127] In the decades before independence, San Vicente City and its environs became a principal center for the indigo trade. Guatemalan and Salvadoran investors developed important haciendas along the San Vicente–La Paz axis. Residents San Vicente owned haciendas in the region, especially in the coastal areas of La Paz.[128] At the peak of hacienda-based indigo production, these haciendas attracted settlers and laborers and the region had the most hacienda residents in the province.[129] There were also a significant number of small-scale peasant producers, many based on the common lands of indigenous communities.[130] By the early eighteenth century, San Vicente was a classic Spanish city with a landholding and official aristocracy, and a laboring class of mulattos and other *castas* (persons of mixed blood), many of whom served in the militia.[131] By the nineteenth century San Vicente was one of the largest cities in El Salvador, with 8,000 people.[132]

In the 1860s regional trade involved significant indigo sales and the import of cheese and cattle from Nicaragua and Honduras.[133] Indigo, agricultural products, and imported and domestic manufactured items were sold in fairs. Not until the 1890s did large-scale merchant investors enter the export trade, and even then fairs continued to be important for local commerce despite the decline in indigo as the main export. Significantly, for most of the eighteenth century the region's main fair was based in Apastepeque, an Indian town, but was moved to San Vicente in 1827.[134]

There were two kinds of haciendas in the region: larger ones, which in San Vicente tended to be to the east and away from population centers, and in La Paz along the coast, also removed from the mostly Indian towns. Smaller haciendas were more closely integrated into the local economy and often bordered on the common lands of communities and towns. San Vicente City and its environs have been thought to be a hacienda-controlled area by the time of independence, with weak peasant and Indian communities; however, much evidence points to the predominance of midsize farms instead of larger properties.

As a result of its agricultural successes, manufacturing expanded in San Vicente City. By 1870 the city with 10,000 inhabitants compared with other important commercial centers like Santa Ana. It produced textiles, cigars, sugar products, and leather products. As in Santa Ana and Sonsonate, its large number of artisans and workers included many females.[135] It also benefited from the short-lived cotton-planting boom of the mid- 1860s. By the 1870s most of its lands were dedicated to indigo (810 hectares), pasture (900 hectares), and corn (1,125 hectares)—but it still held much uncultivated land. There were also 110 important indigo mills, 17 sugar mills, and many smaller ones.[136]

In the early 1870s profits from indigo and tobacco production slowed. Indigo producers incurred debts at high rates of interest. Price declines also affected industry, although smaller producers generally remained in production. Coffee was being praised as a good substitute for indigo. One observer commented that the lands on the volcano, then used only for pasture or vegetables, could be turned into coffee groves. By 1880 he noted the changes already in process—mostly the privatization of *ejidos* —and that San Vicente was developing a new economic sector based on its unexploited resources. The region had an abundance of land but needed capital. Around 1900 substantial amounts of indigo were still produced and sold in the local fairs, despite a drop in price and locust damage. Manufacturing also remained vibrant, with textiles from San Vicente and San Estéban being exported to Guatemala and Honduras at "good prices."[137]

At the turn of the century, Istepeque was the country's major producer of tobacco, still based on small-scale production. Guadalupe also produced tobacco, while coffee had begun to expand.[138] San Lorenzo, San Ildefonso, Apastepeque, and San Estéban produced grains and coffee and sugar in small plots. By 1914 the department of San Vicente still had 40 indigo-producing haciendas and 44 with cattle. Apastepeque continued its specialization in cattle with 12 herds and many small-scale owners. The capital still retained a significant portion of its artisanal manufacturing with 50 looms, 7 tanneries, and 15 shoemaking shops. The region's best lands were in Tecoluca, owned by residents of San Vicente and held largely in haciendas (14,175 hectares) producing mostly cattle and grains. Tepetitán, on the other hand, reflected the long-term predominance of peasant agriculture. It contained only one hacienda of 450 hectares and two small coffee farms.[139]

Nearby Zacatecoluca, with 3,500–5,000 inhabitants divided among 800 households in 1858, also had a dynamic and diverse commercial economy.[140] The great majority (64 percent) of the town's men were peasants *(labradores)*, but the town's sizable artisanal sector (34 percent of men) included weavers, shoemakers, tailors, carpenters, blacksmiths, and masons. The overwhelming majority of the town's employed women listed mostly artisanal or manufacturing occupations—probably in tobacco and textiles. The town had been a regional center of indigo and cattle production since the colonial period. However, by the mid-nineteenth century the hacienda-based indigo economy had virtually collapsed and most indigo haciendas lay abandoned. Nonetheless, the city maintained a vibrant regional economy based on peasant and artisanal production, which had become the backbone of the local economy.[141]

Local and foreign markets for sugar production in Ahuachapán, Santa Ana, Metapán, and Cojutepeque also stimulated economic activity. Sugar mills were usually animal- or water-driven, with rollers built of wood rather than metal. There were very few large producers until the 1860s, when some investors began to import English-made steam mills, but they relied on small-scale growers for much of their cane. Later in the century commercial cane farms expanded, but the industry could not compete with the technical advancements of other countries. El Salvador thus did not become a major exporter, even though trade with California in liquor and sugar increased.[142] Yet small-scale sugar production provided a livelihood for thousands, especially in Cojutepeque, where as early as the later eighteenth century small producers and millers dotted the surrounding valleys.[143] San Pedro Nonualco, for example, with 2,000 people, had 1,059 sugar or plantain farms and 100 sugar mills.[144] Santa María Ostuma produced tobacco on lands purchased by its Indian community.[145]

Cattle raising was extensive throughout the entire country, especially in the east and northeast, and most farmers had cattle as a form of safe investment. Even on the haciendas, herds were never large. In the late nineteenth century, authorities complained that farmers preferred to spend their resources on a few cattle rather than raising "new" export crops. A few eastern towns, both Indian and Ladino, specialized in small-scale subsistence cattle raising, grazing their cattle on rent-free communal lands.[146] Indians from the villages near San Salvador, especially women, supplied the city markets.[147] These villages, with land grants from the eighteenth century or earlier, had a long communal land tradition of subsistence farming and local market production.

Small producers in Indian and Ladino communities, independent *labradores,* squatters, and peasant tenants began to respond to new market opportunities, the decline of the haciendas, state incentives, and elite economic demands after the 1860s. The dynamic peasant and small-producer economy competed effectively with the haciendas, which were beginning to suffer from rising labor costs, a lack of capital, and other problems. Between 1800 and 1880 the Salvadoran peasantry expanded in size and complexity, gaining greater control over landed and other agricultural resources, and deepening its participation in diverse and complex local, regional, national, isthmian and international markets.[148] The peasantry also began to differentiate along ethnic, class, and regional lines but without threatening the survival of any one layer.

Not only peasants but also an expanding sector of commercial farmers developed who possessed or rented common lands owned by ethnic communities or towns. More peasants began to supplement their subsistence agriculture with seasonal wage labor. Different kinds of producers began to emerge. Many peasants continued to maintain their ethnic communal ties held over from the late colonial period while responding to new forces.

## 5    Peasant Politics, Revolt, and
the Formation of the State

Throughout the nineteenth century, peasants and artisans struggled for power and significantly influenced the formation of the Salvadoran nation-state. By so doing, peasants and artisans also shaped their local social and economic conditions, gaining or maintaining local or regional autonomy and using their political clout to defend local resources. As a result, they limited the social and economic power of local elites and the power of national elites to shape the nation.[1] Popular protest and mobilization ranged from local revolts or riots to participation in regional or national political and military alliances involving elite-led factionalism. (I prefer the term *factionalism* because it includes other processes not included in most usages of the term *caudillismo*.) Peasant mobilization was a formidable force in nineteenth-century El Salvador.[2]

Scholars have turned with new interest to the political and economic autonomy of Latin American peasants during the half century after independence.[3] Many continue to frame peasant politics in the context of the *nation*, albeit in new forms or conceptions of it.[4] However, instead of seeing the nation and the national state as central to discussions of peasant politics, this chapter will focus on the polity and state as the locus of peasant political mobilization where national formations and ideologies are weak. Further, this chapter will clarify the links between political mobilizations and local peasant life to uncover connections between local and national processes and clarify the discontinuity and decentered character of the political history of this period.

## State Formation and Popular Contestation, 1832–1849

As part of the so-called Central American Federation (Provincias Unidas), El Salvador belonged to a larger entity, held together mostly by the actions of a fragmented, small, and mostly unsuccessful political-military faction led first by Manuel José Arce and then Francisco Morazán. After the final and tumultuous breakdown of the Federation in 1839, El Salvador continued to be tied by political struggles and formal alliances to Guatemala and Honduras, even after declaring itself an independent republic in 1847. Between the 1840s and the 1890s, the Salvadoran state moved in fits and starts toward a centralized, consolidated system.

One result of independence in Central America was the loss of the mediating role of local Spanish and Ladino elites in the state's political relations with Indian and other peasant communities. In the colonial era, the urban elite in cities like San Salvador, San Miguel, Sonsonate, and San Salvador formed political alliances with peasant communities and helped to resolve their conflicts and claims. However, during the process of independence (1811–1821), in which Indian, Ladino, and mulatto peasants and artisans were integral actors, local elites—creoles and *peninsulares*—became divided and weakened, and regional means of social control were dissolved.[5] Officials of the newly independent state could not sustain the delicate ethnic balancing act of their colonial predecessors, so both Ladinos and Indians now faced new social and economic relations no longer mediated by colonial institutions.

After the 1830s many communities mounted antitax revolts that drew them into larger political struggles or into defending the country from invasions. In 1832 uprisings throughout the Federated States of El Salvador and Guatemala inaugurated a surge in popular revolts and political instability that continued for a half century. These popular mobilizations began when El Salvador's head of state, Mariano Prado, tried to enforce a series of unpopular laws imposing new head taxes, public works laws, and limits on community landholding. Riots in the mostly Indian neighborhoods of San Salvador ultimately led to larger revolts and conspiracies.

The government imposed a direct head tax of 8 reales in 1832, arguing that independence had ruined the entrepreneurial class and the costs of running the new state should be shared by all.[6] In addition, the government ordered all adult men to contribute two days' labor a year for public works. Opposition to these unpopular measures began in San Salvador and spread throughout the state. In Izalco a group of Indians revolted and raided the city of Sonsonate. Other revolts followed in Zacatecoluca, Santiago Nonualco, San Vicente, and San Miguel, and the Legislative Assembly moved the capital from Cojutepeque to San Salvador.[7]

These revolts had a clearly political character. In the city of San Miguel, local authorities were vigorously attacked. Government troops sent to repress this rebellion incited a second, larger revolt in which the local garrison was attacked twice and looting and killing spread throughout the city.[8] Residents from Usulután and Chinameca joined in.[9] The governor, the mayor, and other notables were shot. Fresh troops sent from La Unión failed to take the city; then a new attack by Colonel Benites brought it under government control. The city was placed under martial law and although most leaders managed to escape, those captured were tried by military courts.[10] In Chalatenango City, a priest led Indians in similar uprisings in January 1833. In nearby Tejutla the mayor and municipal secretary were killed. These revolts were also suppressed by government troops.

A new uprising in San Salvador forced Chief of State Prado out of office. As a result of these revolts, the National Assembly eliminated the hated taxes. The new chief of state, Joaquín San Martín, then decreed an amnesty, but more than opposition to new taxes was at stake.[11] A much larger uprising began in La Paz in February 1833 when Indian hacienda workers rebelled. Historians have emphasized that these results were caused by the low wages and cruel treatment they received at the hands of their white employers.[12] The leader of this revolt, Anastasio Aquino, enraged by the beatings suffered by his brother, stole from white landowners and systematically distributed their wealth among the poor. Aquino's goal of killing the region's *hacendados*, especially those in Zacatecoluca, the nearby Spanish city, are well known.[13]

Yet while complaints over the agrarian social and economic abuses or privileges of Spanish landowners undoubtedly contributed to the revolt, these motivations have been overstated. Indian communities were mobilized at a time when both *hacendados* and political elites were weakened and the haciendas of La Paz were in decline. Most agrarian conflicts in this region were between Indian and peasant communities and Ladino merchants in the towns. Indian opposition to the legitimacy of white and Ladino political and military authority was key to their mobilization. However, Aquino's movement did not unite the region's Indian communities entirely, and he did not recruit in the adjacent rival town of San Pedro Nonualco, which suffered under his control. The Indians of Santiago Nonualco had long-standing land rivalries with San Pedro. Aquino's followers even attacked Ladino laborers on one hacienda.[14]

One factor in the Aquino revolt of 1833 was opposition to military conscription.[15] Peasants and artisans battled government recruitment teams, captured weapons, and attacked the local garrison. The movement then extended to the Indian towns of San Juan Nonualco, Zacatecoluca, and San Sebastian Analco.[16] Aquino emerged as a rebel leader when he reportedly established "order" among the recruits.[17] A first attempt to suppress the Nonualco rebellion failed. The governor and commander of San Vicente, Juan José Guzmán, bested the Indians in two encounters before being defeated.[18] As a result, Aquino and at least 2,000 followers sacked the Hispanic city of San Vicente, forcing Guzmán to retreat, then continued toward the haciendas north of the city, killing notables and their families along the way.[19] In Tepetitán Aquino had the archives burned and issued a series of laws.[20] From there they marched to Olocuilta for further recruitment on their way to San Salvador. The movement was defeated on February 14 when new troops from San Salvador forced Aquino to retreat to his native town and finally defeated and captured him, but only after major battles involving 3,000–5000 rebel Indians and 8,000 government troops.[21] This defeat was followed by harsh measures against the local population, including massive executions. After some months in prison, Aquino was executed—his head put in a cage for public display.[22]

Despite the changes in government in early 1833 and the suppression of the revolts of December 1832–February 1833, discontent continued. A dispute between Federation president (and dictator) Morazán and Salvadoran chief of state San Martín led to the latter's ouster in mid-1833 and the confiscation of his seven properties in Sonsonate. (Similar measures affected the properties of Presidents Malespín, Campos, Dueñas, Barrios, Zaldívar, and Ezeta.) According to U.S. State Department sources, this involved San Martín's alliance with Indian communities opposed to Morazán.[23] As a result of the political struggle at the top, civil war broke out, leading to an important uprising in San Miguel. Morazán was forced to move the Federation government to Sonsonate. Civil and military conflict involving Federation, state, and local forces continued in 1833–1834, contributing to the political chaos caused by attempts to maintain the Federation despite popular opposition.[24] A year later, another crisis began when a new coalition of indigenous communities and political factions organized to overthrow the Federation government, demonstrating yet again the intertwining of ethnic with economic issues and the ties between local and national politics.

In 1835 President Morazán removed General Nicolás Espinoza as chief of state after only a few months in power.[25] Espinoza was accused of conspiring with the Indians of the central region and their allies in Guatemala to overthrow the Federation and establish an Indian republic. He had managed to tap into deeply felt ethnic resentments of the Indians in an attempt to gain their support. Their goal was to destroy the Federation in both El Salvador and Guatemala and to forge a stronger, more centralized state while establishing an ethnic-based alliance with the Indians of Los Altos, Chiquimula, and Quezaltenango in the state of Guatemala. Despite its failure, this movement helps to explain how the ethnic identity and political autonomy of local peasant communities contributed to regional political movements. It also shows the relation between local and statewide processes of state formation, which included peasants, notables, and military and factional leaders.[26] In many ways this movement anticipated Carrera's successful Indian-peasant alliance against Morazán and the Federation government in Guatemala.[27] The movement certainly laid bare the weaknesses of the Salvadoran state and its federal umbrella by exposing the narrowness of Morazán's power as well as that of other Ladino state builders.

The Espinoza-led conspiracy also reveals how tenuous was the power of early republican leaders and how indigenous groups perceived the emerging Federation state as a white or Ladino imposition. The Indians of central El Salvador justified the rebellion with two arguments based on the same principle: legitimate rule over land. First, Indians did not want

Ladinos and whites to use any lands in their towns. This was not an agrarian conflict over productive land, nor did it involve reduced peasant access to land; instead, it rejected any non-Indian's claim to control land. Charges of "slavery" in rebel leaflets did not refer to actual labor practices or the impoverishment of Indian communities. The claims were political, aimed at weakening the Ladinos' control over land and their representation in town governments. Second, President Morazán was accused of selling Central American territory to the English—a charge that resonated among the Salvadoran Indians. This claim referred to deals made with British companies to cut trees along the Caribbean coasts of Honduras and Guatemala.[28] Indigenous communities clearly had strong notions of political sovereignty and legitimacy at a time when the character of the new nation-state was still not defined.

It is not clear why Espinoza had conspired with these indigenous communities. The prosecutor found his conduct "at all times as strange as inexplicable . . . [revealing] in the short time of his rule the secrets of his soul."[29] The problem was not that Espinoza had conspired to overthrow the Federation but that he had allied himself with Indian militias. Espinoza's own ethnic identity is a mystery (he had presented himself as an Indian by referring to the color and perhaps texture of his hair), although in all likelihood he considered himself a Ladino. The U.S. chargé d'affaires in Central America, Charles G. De Witt, referred to him as an Indian—a "cunning and well-educated" one at that.[30]

Espinoza's alliance with the Indians began in April 1835 (during his brief tenure in office) when he signed a decree that forced Ladinos to be tenants of Indian communities and nullified any previous land purchases made by Ladino farmers or peasants.[31] Ladinos could own only the crops they grew and were obligated to pay a *canon* (rental fee) to the communities. Lands lost by communities through lease or debt had to be returned. Ladinos who refused to pay rent would have to return their lands and be compensated only for the value of their crops. (At this time, land legislation did not yet distinguish between municipal *ejidos* and community lands; following colonial tradition, towns controlled by Indian communities usually claimed all lands as theirs.) This decree meant that Indian communities had legal sanction to expel Ladinos from their towns. Furthermore, it added credence to the idea that Ladinos had no place within an Indian polity.[32] In the words of one Ladino, the Indians "claim that the land has been theirs since the first humans settled in Central America . . . that the lands of America can only be owned by them, as owners and lords since before and after the Spanish Conquest."[33]

After this decree the crisis proceeded at two distinct levels. The first involved the familiar actors of nineteenth-century political history: presidents, *jefes*, assemblies, generals, ministers. In this sphere Espinoza sought to gain supporters in the federal and state assemblies, but when he failed, he was forced to quit his post. While he did garner the support of important local notables, including some assemblymen, many state officials remained opposed to him, including his second in command, who alerted Morazán to the impending catastrophe. After his ouster, Espinoza continued to foment rebellion from afar.

The attempt to "stupidly divide the society into classes in order to destroy the social order" was the less visible second component of the crisis.[34] This involved the Indian communities of central El Salvador, who spent a number of months organizing for a large-scale confrontation with the Federation government. Federation authorities feared, with great justification, that this revolt was more threatening than the Aquino revolt of 1833. For one thing, the scale was larger—this time up to 10,000 Indians were thought to support the movement. This sentiment was shared by the U.S. chargé d'affaires in Guatemala: "The aboriginals outnumber other classes, and would naturally rally under his banner."[35] Furthermore, the Indians had white and Ladino allies who supplied them weapons and other resources. These same connections facilitated communications with supporters outside the central region in Chalatenango and Sonsonate, and outside the state in Honduras and Guatemala.

At the center of this conspiracy were the central region Indian communities. The alliance centered on Cojutepeque and included Indians from the towns of Apastepeque, Ilobasco, Guatijiagua, San Pedro Perulapán, Sensuntepeque, Santiago Nonualco, San Pedro Nonualco, San Miguel, and the Indian *barrios* of San Salvador and Tenancingo. The Indian communities organized spies and agents, circulated letters and posters, and eventually mobilized a 500–700-man militia led by Indians who held various municipal and state-level posts.[36] With Espinoza's support, the "invincible battalion" even infiltrated the Federation's only Salvadoran garrison located in the nearby Hispanic city of San Vicente.[37]

In this mobilization, the indigenous communities of El Salvador articu-

lated a pan-Indian identity that cut across the many obstacles that separated Indian communities. The movement also established contacts with
"los negros" of Sonsonate, in all likelihood the community of *pardos* of
the Volcán de Santa Ana (then part of the department of Sonsonate).
This was another peasant community that mobilized repeatedly during
the nineteenth century, often in alliance with Guatemalan regimes. There
were also contacts with Indian communities in Guatemala. Some Salvadoran participants evidently worked with "the oppressed peoples
of Verapaz, Quesaltenango, Totonicapan, and Solola" (in Guatemala).
Guillermo Quintanilla, a local judge in Zacatecoluca who ran a munitions
workshop for the rebels, later became an officer in Carrera's Guatemalan
army. The U.S. chargé d'affaires thought that Espinoza also had factional supporters in Mexico who "were prepared to cooperate with him
at all hazards."[38]

The movement also recruited from the local militias. Espinoza had encouraged the Indian communities to participate in local elections so that
they could expel Ladinos from local government. Their goal, an attempt
to "unite in solidarity those of their caste," represented an attempt to
break the hold over state making and legitimacy that Ladinos and whites
had maintained since independence. But what at the state level became
mostly a failed revolt at the local level was open conflict between Ladinos and Indians. In at least two towns, Indians attacked Ladinos and destroyed their crops and houses. In another town, Ladinos slept in the
fields for fear of Indian attacks in the night.[39]

Indian leaders from Cojutepeque clearly stated one of the driving conceptions of their movement: "You want to know what we fight for? We
tell you that it is our beloved freedom that we have upheld, since the beginning when Aquino raised it."[40] Ethnic solidarity, however, was not
absolute. Some Indian municipalities rejected the movement and warned
the government of the threat: "Even though we are Indian we obey and
respect the laws, and we know that there can be no division among the
castes, since we are all Central Americans; and hence in our town there
is no alteration of public order, we are tranquil, all of us working in our
workshops."[41]

After Espinoza was forced out and Federation troops were sent to El
Salvador to pacify the insurgent regions, the conspirators were offered
an amnesty in which they could exchange their weapons for cash or face

jail terms. The offer of amnesty reflected the government's inability to enforce its terms. After some confrontations, the principal military leader of the movement, Atanasio Flores, and his Indian militias surrendered to a general sent to chase them out of the hills.[42]

This movement raises the question of whether Indian communities were manipulated by white or Ladino leaders or whether they were bound by alliances of convenience. While no one can say how these coalitions would have turned out if the Indians had won, the participation of non-indigenous elites does not diminish the importance of the movement. Both indigenous communities and white or Ladino politicians appeared flexible in seeking allies. Throughout the century, Indian communities pursued such alliances, but not with the blind passion or personal loyalty that has often been attributed to them. Instead, Indians sought allies that would enable them to protect local resources and their political autonomy, holding the factional politics of Ladino and white political-military leaders hostage to their support.[43]

The Indian communities of El Salvador extended their political claims to demand new forms of autonomy, aiming to reconstruct the emerging Federation in terms more consistent with their desires. But their failure in this pursuit did not mean that they became inactive; the events of the early national period were only a prelude to new forms of mobilization. The Indians and peasants of the central region continued to struggle for control and to define the state and its relations with Guatemala. Between 1835 and the early 1850s, local factional and military leaders positioned themselves (often in alliance with external forces) to control the incipient national state; meanwhile, local communities continued to mobilize, holding a sort of veto power over any claimant to national power.

In 1837 the peasants of the Volcán de Santa Ana revolted against local and Federation authorities with the support of Guatemala's General Carrera. As part of this movement, 4,000 Indians from the recently pacified department of Cuscatlán, claiming that Ladinos had poisoned their water and caused a cholera epidemic, invaded the city center in May 1837. They captured and tortured the prison master and killed a government doctor who had been sent to contain the epidemic. With peasants from nearby Zacatecoluca, they attacked the garrison of this city, looting and killing city residents. A few days later they attacked the San Vicente garrison but were defeated by troops, assisted by city residents.

Other Indian villages rose up in May 1837, motivated by priests protesting civil marriage laws and the cholera epidemic.[44]

Federation President Morazán sent additional troops from San Salvador to help control the region. After two days in Cojutepeque, they moved on to Ilobasco, where Indians had raided houses and killed a number of people. Eventually, this uprising was also suppressed and all prisoners executed.[45] As in the 1835 events, peasant communities of western and central El Salvador mobilized in alliance with communities from nearby Guatemala—this time triggered by an outbreak of cholera in the region.[46] (Woodward links these revolts to the power of village priests to mobilize peasants against the liberal, anticlerical state, leading to major upheavals in 1837 throughout Guatemala and El Salvador.)[47] Although these upheavals failed to bring about a change of regime, they led to the eventual defeat of Morazán's liberal faction by conservatives allied to Carrera in Guatemala.

Following a major popular revolt in San Salvador in September 1838, Carrera again attacked the cities of Santa Ana and Ahuachapán on October 28, withdrawing to Guatemala after the raid.[48] He received support from the region's Indians and left weapons behind for his supporters. In 1839 and 1841 the peasants of the Volcán of Santa Ana revolted again but were defeated each time by government troops.[49] A similar revolt took place in Santiago Nonualco on December 10, 1840, but was quickly repressed. Government troops destroyed houses and the church, killing many people and forcing others to flee to the hills and surrounding haciendas. All of these movements were connected to larger political turmoil about which little is known.[50]

Popular uprisings and alliance building continued virtually without interruption in the 1840s. In 1842 civil war broke out again as opposition to President Lindo grew. An attack on the garrison by residents of San Salvador's poor neighborhoods contributed to Lindo's removal. City notables were also implicated, including General Quintanilla, one of Morazán's generals who began his career as a leader of the Volcán community. These uprisings were in support of Central American unity, something which Lindo opposed, and were organized by Morazán supporters.[51] General Carrera sent Aquilino San Martín from Guatemala to the border region in 1842. In 1843 he advanced to the Volcán de Santa Ana to recruit followers. Once again the *volcaneño* community mobilized, and national political turmoil allowed them to defend their own interests by attacking local landowners with whom they had disputes.[52] On October 8, 1843, the partisans of the Volcán rose up again with Guatemalan arms. They were defeated in Santa Ana City by the local commander.[53] Other protests broke out between 1844 and 1848 against President Malespín in Santiago Nonualco, Cojutepeque, San Vicente, Sensuntepeque, and San Salvador, and violence erupted involving the Indians of Santiago Nonualco and San Pedro Nonualco.

Given the weakness of the central state and national identity, in which authority and legitimacy rested on a fragile balance of regional, ethnic, factional, and community alliances, political stability was an elusive goal. Order depended on shifting alliances between communities and Ladino factional leaders, most of them military men. Any leader's attempts to build a stable regime faced great challenges, given his inability to control local communities and the lack of a professional military and strong state institutions. Throughout most of the century, political turmoil enabled local communities to protect their interests and maintain their autonomy. As we have seen, grass-roots communities, especially Indian groups, defended their rights to land, control of town governments, and autonomy from other political forces, including the state itself.

## Persistent Mobilization: The Indian Faction of Cojutepeque, 1863–1872

In the 1850s political violence in El Salvador subsided, especially the popular and specifically Indian mobilizations of the previous decades. But the recent activism established a tradition of contestation and collective action. An example was the Indian community of Cojutepeque.[54] A contemporary observer commented, "These are in the majority *indígenas,* robust, and well shaped, extremely bellicose, rustic, and tenacious: so all political parties believe themselves to have a great ally if these aborigines serve among them. On the other hand, they are very religious, dedicated to hard work, and friends of peace."[55] These were the same Indians who served in the Salvadoran armies sent to defeat William Walker in Nicaragua during this decade.

The 1860s inaugurated a new period of national and isthmian turmoil. After the defeat of invading Guatemalan forces at Coatepeque in 1863, Salvadoran President Gerardo Barrios began to prepare for a new invasion from Guatemala and an attack on Nicaragua by increasing military recruitment. He sent his most trusted officer, General Bracamonte, governor and commander of San Vicente, to recruit soldiers, but Bracamonte met opposition (led by militia officers themselves) in the Indian neighborhoods of Cojutepeque. On June 30, government troops and recruiters exchanged fire with residents; the next day there was again bloodshed, and captured government officers were executed. (White or Ladino city notables, however, supported Barrios and opposed Carrera's intervention.)[56] The Indians chose José María Rivas, a Ladino farmer with military experience (perhaps with Indian blood), as their commander,[57] giving him no choice: "Either you lead or we'll cut you down with our machetes."[58] Rivas reluctantly organized his forces and seized weapons from the local garrison.[59]

Faced with organized resistance, Barrios appealed to the patriotism of the Indians of Cojutepeque—his government was at war with Guatemalan forces—and asked them to desist.[60] His public statement read:

> Various measures of leniency have been offered to you so that you will return to order, but far from that, each day you commit more murders and new crimes, maintaining yourselves in a constant rebellion, and this conduct is more criminal when the attention of the government is on the defense of the motherland. Under these circumstances I declare to you, that if in three days you have not surrendered your weapons and the two or three leaders who have disrupted the obedience and submission you owe the government, all of those who are found gathered or armed will be executed *[pasado por las armas]* and your fields and houses destroyed. The same will happen to all of those who join the enemy forces. There is no middle position in submitting to the government; only death that all traitors and rebels deserve. There is still time for you to return to your duties. Reason calls out for this, and so does your self interest and public convenience; but if you continue obsessed—Tremble! A severe punishment is near. I can still open my arms to you as a father and receive you like children. Take advantage of the opportunity.[61]

Barrios's appeal to patriotism did not impress the Indians of Cojutepeque, whose ethnic and political alliances, while built upon a local identity, transcended national boundaries. Rivas's Indian militias continued their war, and government troops from San Salvador were unable to defeat them. Gen. Indalecio Cordero, commander of the government forces, reached an agreement with Rivas (probably without President Barrios's sanction), naming him governor of Cuscatlán and allowing him to keep his people armed. On July 4, as Rivas approached Cojutepeque with his troops, local Indians, taking advantage of their victory, rioted in the town center. They burned government buildings, attacked the liquor monopoly, and freed prisoners from the jail. They were eventually stopped by the town priest. Rivas then entered the city, apparently without knowledge of the riot, and established order.

A few days later, 800 soldiers led by Gen. Eusebio Bracamonte attacked and defeated Rivas, now lacking weapons and ammunition, and executed twenty of Rivas's supporters. On July 7, Rivas took Cojutepeque again after Bracamonte left for San Vicente to put down yet another peasant uprising. On July 16, Bracamonte attacked again, defeating Rivas after heavy fighting. Meanwhile, General Cerna—one of Carrera's officers—invaded from Honduras with 1,000 Guatemalan troops and approached the city. Cerna was received by a crowd of 10,000—probably all the Indians in the entire department.[62] In Cojutepeque, Cerna organized the locals and took forced loans from the town's elite. He left the city with 4,000 men, mostly machete-wielding peasants who had joined his forces. On their way to San Salvador, Barrios was overthrown by Guatemalan troops, aided by many of his own officers, and Francisco Dueñas was made president. After the coup, José María Rivas remained governor of Cuscatlán.

A Guatemalan officer described the obvious alliance between Carrera's government and local forces in these events:

> [Cojutepeque] was one of the most notable supporters because of its enthusiasm for the new order of things, but Barrios wanting to avenge himself sent an expedition under General Bracamonte that committed excesses and violations of various types. The indignant population, exasperated, resolved to avoid similar incursions, rose in mass, organizing a battalion of 400 men, but as they lacked weapons and good officers, they went to Santa Ana to get them. There General Carrera gave them as much as they needed.[63]

The Indians of Cojutepeque were able to determine the fate of national regimes that did not respect their local autonomy by allying themselves with other factions within or outside the Salvadoran state. This power, feared by national leaders, also gave them much local autonomy. The alliance between Rivas and the Indians of Cojutepeque lasted over thirty years and served as the basis for the political and military autonomy of the central region. This did not lead to the creation of a national state based on the power of peasants and artisans, but it did strengthen a political order forced to rely on local communities whose power often rested on peasant militias. One observer commented, "In [Rivas's] headquarters in Cojutepeque you rarely see soldiers; [the peasants] were all allowed to continue in their agricultural work and keep their weapons in their own houses, with the understanding that upon hearing the sound of a cannon in the town they would present themselves to their leader."[64] The armed mobilization of peasants was the basis of Cojutepeque's autonomy.

In the first years of his rule, President Dueñas tried unsuccessfully to disarm the Indian faction of Cojutepeque; according to De Belot, it was "powerful and armed" and "posed a threat to the government."[65] On December 26, 1868, 200 Indian rioters assaulted the garrison but were dispersed. One observer linked the revolt to a conflict over a religious image. They disapproved of placing a figure of the city's patron saint in the city church for safety; they wished to control the icon.[66] But this explanation does not account for the attack on the garrison, which suggests a political motivation.[67]

In 1870 Rivas went into exile in Honduras after his brother was killed by another peasant-based faction in Santa Ana, apparently in a clash over the Dueñas regime. He took all the soldiers from the local garrison with him, including some artisans and peasant supporters. From Honduras, his faction joined Gen. Santiago González in his efforts to oust Dueñas, but this time Cojutepeque's Indians did not follow him. Nonetheless, González took power on April 12, 1871, aided by various other Indian and peasant factions, including the *volcaneño* peasant militias of Santa Ana whose revolt contributed significantly to Dueñas's defeat. But just as the *volcaneños* were coming to support the new regime, the Indians of the department of Cuscatlán began to mobilize against it.

As Dueñas's government was being overthrown, one of his generals who was returning from a campaign in Honduras disbanded his troops in Sensuntepeque, and the Cojutepeque Indians seized their weapons. Mobilizing independently of Rivas, they rose in opposition to the new regime. On April 27, 1871, President González's commander for the central region battled and defeated 400–1,000 Indians from Cojutepeque. Generals Barrientos and Salignac, who had news of the Indian mobilization, also went to confront them.[68] President González traveled to Cojutepeque and ordered the Indians to surrender; those who resisted were shot. Rivas then quit his post with Gonzalez's government and temporarily retired to private life.[69]

But the Indians of Cojutepeque were prepared for further mobilizations. On July 10, 1871, government troops defeated an invading column of 500 Indians; then on July 22 more Indians, including the militiamen of Talpetate Valley, joined the movement.[70] Eventually it was dispersed and many leaders were beaten to death. Others, both male and female, were taken to prisons in San Salvador.[71] Six months later, twenty-one participants were granted amnesty because of the "natural simplicity of their character."[72] As a result of the upheaval, security measures were enacted throughout the central region. The mayor of Santiago Nonualco —the site of similar disturbances often connected to Cojutepeque—took preventive measures to preempt further trouble.[73] Police were ordered to detain strangers even if they had a good conduct pass ("certificación de buena conducta") and to look out for army deserters or suspicious people with weapons.[74] The government increased its control over the region while meeting local demands for political autonomy. Cojutepeque was divided into six new towns (San Cristobal, El Carmen, Monte de San Juan, Santa Cruz, and La Candelaria), each retaining a portion of the original communal lands and assigned judges, police commissioners, and teachers.[75]

Observers give differing accounts of the motivations behind the revolt. Laferrière stated that the Indians desired to return Cojutepeque to its former status as national capital and center of state power (the city had served as capital in the 1830s and 1850s). They hated Barrios because he transferred the capital to San Salvador.[76] For Bancroft, the revolt was part of a larger uprising also taking place in El Salvador's major cities "with ramifications in Guatemala" aimed at destroying the new "liberal" regime.[77] Local officials also saw the revolt in these terms—as an attempt to steal from and kill "the best-known liberals."[78]

These are the extremes defining the interpretations of this kind of movement: as the result of either a narrow localism or an equally narrow allegiance to liberal or conservative elite-led factions. But the mobilizations of the Indians of Cojutepeque and their allies were more complex. For one thing, they formed national and extranational alliances strongly associated with ethnic solidarity and ethnic-based notions of sovereignty. Following the Cojutepeque rebellion, on August 12, 1872, the Indians of Izalco revolted.[79] Ideological motivations are not sufficient to explain their actions. Even though the Indians of Cuscatlán had developed an alliance with Guatemala under conservative rulers, Indian factions developed links to Guatemalan liberals that became apparent in a series of revolts in 1885. The Cojutepeques began as allies of conservative Guatemalan governments and mobilized against Presidents Gerardo Barrios and Santiago González (perceived as liberals), but they also resisted Dueñas (touted as a conservative) and supported Guatemala's liberal President Barrios in 1885 when he invaded El Salvador to overthrow the repressive and "liberal" Zaldívar regime.[80] Moreover, Rivas later became a leader—still backed by peasant militias—of what was deemed a radical liberal faction.[81] This faction, later led by Prudencio Alfaro and Rivas's nephew, provided a bridge between the popular radical liberalism of the 1880s and the populist clientelism of the 1920s.[82]

## Land, Liberals, and Peasant Revolt

After the confrontations of the 1860s, which involved mostly the central region, another threat to state authority emerged among the *volcañenos* of Santa Ana. They also had a long tradition of rebellion going back to the eighteenth century and had engaged in the conflicts of the 1830s and 1840s.[83] In August 1870 the *volcaneños* rose up in a land dispute. Led by Silverio Carranza, the community's administrator, 200 peasants marched into Santa Ana City. The peasants used as their mediator Juan Barbarena, a white surveyor who had been measuring their lands to separate them from the municipal *ejidos*. The governor ordered Carranza to withdraw his people and asked to meet with him, but Carranza refused. Barbarena convinced the *volcaneños* to return home, promising to write to the president on their behalf.

The national government sent Dr. Rafael Zaldívar to negotiate with the *volcaneños*.[84] With the help of a local priest, an agreement was reached between the rebels and the city on August 30, 1870.[85] Yet in December hundreds of *volcaneños* armed with machetes, pistols, and shotguns burned the municipal building, roamed the streets drinking, burning, and looting. Local priests tried unsuccessfully to contain them. They mortally wounded the military commander, Gen. Francisco Rivas (brother of José María Rivas), in an attack on the garrison in which they freed the prisoners, and they killed two ex-mayors and ransacked the farms of at least one of them.

The *volcaneño* peasants held the city for three days, withdrawing only when troops from San Salvador under Gen. Tomás Martínez approached the city. (Martínez was the former president of Nicaragua who delivered Gerardo Barrios to Dueñas to be executed.)[86] More than 400 "noncombatants" surrendered.[87] On August 6 President Dueñas decreed an amnesty, giving those implicated in the revolt who were not leaders or guilty of murder three days to surrender their weapons; those who resisted would be declared enemies of the state and tried by military tribunals. Dueñas promised that the *volcaneños* would cease to be a threat once and for all, intending to give them "an exemplary punishment."[88] Many leaders were put on trial, and Nicolás Lemus was executed for killing local landowner and ex-mayor Rafael Paz. Many surrendered, and more than 800 *volcaneños*, most of them not participants in the violence, "presented themselves" to General Martínez.[89] Martínez promised "to disappear the remaining few" by "pacifying" the Volcán.[90] His troops raided the area, destroyed the houses of the *volcaneños,* and took more prisoners.[91] Those captured were tried and many were shot.[92] On Martínez's return to San Salvador, his troops were received with a parade and festivities.[93]

A long-standing dispute over land but also a sense of ethnic and cultural hostility toward Santa Ana's commercial and political elite were the motivations for the revolt of the *volcaneño* community. Even local officials acknowledged, "For many years there has been a deadly rivalry between the inhabitants of the Volcán de Santa Ana and those of the city, beginning with a conflict over lands and past hostilities between both factions."[94] The rivalry had been revived by the survey of the borders between the hacienda "Comecayo" and the communal lands of the *volcaneños*. Francisco Arcia, one of the men murdered in the revolt, had claimed lands that bordered on the *volcaneño* community's lands in 1867, probably by declaring them part of the municipal *ejidos*. The lands he took very likely belonged to the community but constituted only a small portion of the community's lands. Peasants who occupied these lands complained that he had tried to charge them rent, and national authorities had sided with Arcia. Moreover, his family controlled the municipal and judicial posts in Santa Ana, allowing the peasants no local recourse.[95] The hostility against the Santa Ana elite was reflected in the attack on Rafael Paz's farm and house, causing extensive losses to his property, coffee and sugar stocks, and equipment valued at more than 10,000 pesos.[96] Paz was a forty-year-old merchant with a small inherited fortune who with "great effort" had turned himself into a proprietor *(propietario)*, in the words of his obituary. He had served as mayor of Santa Ana and had held other municipal positions.[97]

Government sources insisted that the events were of purely local relevance and had no "political character." However, this revolt, despite its strong local motivations, occurred just as the Dueñas government was being threatened by Salvadoran exiles in Guatemala and Honduras. A few months later, the *volcaneños* mobilized again to support González's attempt to take power in April 1871.[98] (He was also supported by many prosperous landowners and entrepreneurs from western El Salvador.)[99] After Dueñas's overthrow, criminal charges were filed against him for his actions in Santa Ana, specifically for ordering the burning of more than 400 *volcaneño* farms.[100] In November 1872 the new mayor of Santa Ana reported that more than one hundred families from the Volcán had requested lots so they could "come down to live in the town." He distributed small parcels of land in the town.[101]

The new government also repaid the *volcaneños* for helping to defeat Dueñas by recognizing their de facto possession of lands that were claimed by a local landowning family—probably part of the land over which they had revolted. When this family sued the government years later for compensation, a prominent liberal intellectual and lifelong state administrator, Rafael Reyes, defended the *volcaneños* and the municipal authorities who had allowed them to remain in possession of the disputed lands: "The Indians *[sic]* who have occupied these lands have given important services, starting with their overthrow of the government of Sr.

Dueñas in Santa Ana on the celebrated tenth of April 1871. They had to be rewarded." He explained that the peasants took these lands thinking that they belonged to ex-President Rafael Campos—an ally of Dueñas in exile whose properties were expropriated as a result of the change in government.[102]

Local revolts did not necessarily become connected to national politics. In smaller or more marginal localities, Indian and peasant communities quarreled over purely local issues. Usually the conflict was between Ladinos and Indians, although questions of land and municipal power were often at the root. In the small western highland town of Juayua, a conflict over land and local power erupted into violence. In 1867 the Indian community of Juayua had lost the power to administer the lands they possessed to the municipal council (which had Indian members but was dominated by Ladinos). In 1872 they disputed the results of a local election that gave full control over the municipality to Ladino officials.[103] Increasing tensions led members of the indigenous community to attack the municipal building on March 1, 1873, killing a number of Ladino officials and farmers in their own homes.[104] After the revolt the governor visited the town and held a joint meeting with Indians and Ladinos to discuss the cause of the conflicts. The Indians complained that they had lost lands in a survey to separate the municipal *ejido* from their community lands. Another source of tension was Ladino control of a *baldío* which the Indian community either claimed or hoped to acquire. An accord was reached and signed: the Ladinos disavowed revenge and the Indians agreed to stop threatening them with violence.

Ladino officials claimed that the Indians desired to exterminate all Ladinos, merely using defense of their land as an excuse for violence. Ladino farms had been acquired legally, but the Indians wanted all the land for themselves. The Ladino-controlled municipality sent a petition with three pages of signatures asking the president to abolish landholding communities and to send additional troops for the local garrison. Juayua's mayor, an upwardly mobile Ladino landowner, also banned all Indian meetings because, he claimed, they led to drunkenness.[105] The failure of the revolt signaled the political and even demographic decline of Juayua's indigenous community. Ladinos already constituted one-third of the town's population, and by the end of the century they controlled most of the town's lands and resources and municipal offices.

## Peasant Mobilization and National Politics, 1880s–1900

The relative tranquility of the 1872–1885 period was marked—at the national level—by the emergence of new, perhaps more peaceful forms of political participation. These included liberal clubs, expanded suffrage, representative and/or constitutional assemblies, and improved connections between the central state and local systems of repression, cooptation, and patronage. The transfer of presidential power, however, was still characterized by violence and the intervention of Guatemalan and Honduran political or military factions. In 1876 Guatemalan forces replaced President González with Rafael Zaldívar, who ruled between 1876 and 1885. Zaldívar has been usually presented as a liberal, but like most political leaders of the period, he was not consistent. Zaldívar had served as President Dueñas's strongest ally. He was imposed as president in 1876 as a compromise—he did not come to power with the support of liberal organizations or activists.[106] Despite years of stability and economic growth, by the mid-1880s Zaldívar's relationship with Guatemala and local liberal supporters had soured.

The turmoil pervading Salvadoran politics in the mid-1880s was partially related to Zaldívar's attempt to get himself reelected after he had promised free elections. Although these events are usually understood as the result of Guatemalan interference, internal forces were more important this time. One factor was Zaldívar's open opposition to the candidacy of Rafael Ayala, who had extensive popular urban support, especially among liberal artisans and professionals.[107] When Zaldívar responded with repression, the opposition went to Guatemala and Honduras and organized an uprising against him with Guatemalan support.[108]

On April 1, 1885, President Barrios of Guatemala attacked El Salvador, aiming to overthrow Zaldívar's government after he failed to enact Barrios's decree calling for unification of the Central American republics. His massive forces took Chalchuapa and Santa Ana, with the support of 500 (mostly Indian) Salvadoran peasants and artisans from the Volcán de Santa Ana, Izalco, Nahuizalco, Chalchuapa, and Atiquizaya. Prominent "liberals" and landowners such as Gen. Francisco Menéndez (a wealthy sugar and coffee planter from Ahuchapán), Rafael Meza, Rosa Pacas, and Manuel Pacas supported his movement. Initially Zaldívar characterized these revolts as mere "riots," but the U.S. consul in El Salvador thought the events justified requesting the presence of a U.S. man-of-war off the Salvadoran coast.[109]

As part of the movement against Zaldívar, the Indians of Santiago Nonualco, with other forces from the region, attacked the Zacatecoluca garrison. A local *hacendado* brought "his people" to help them but withdrew his support when the violence got out of hand. But other local issues were involved, as Ladino store owners in Santiago Nonualco were also attacked. Workers on a local hacienda owned by Zaldívar revolted but were repressed violently.[110] Troops from Zacatecoluca retook the town and rounded up men, shooting them in the town plaza, and townspeople fled to surrounding villages. After the defeat of Zaldívar, Menéndez rewarded the Indians of Santiago Nonualco by granting them an extensive *baldío* suitable for coffee cultivation that was distributed among the town residents.[111] In other localities, local political conflicts, often ethnic in nature, erupted as opposing factions took advantage of the breakdown of the national state to settle disputes or to enhance their position by allying themselves with the emerging victors at the national level.[112]

In Cojutepeque, José María Rivas (leader of the indigenous movement of the 1860s who had returned as departmental governor) renounced Zaldívar's rule and his short-lived successor, General Figueroa. He left for Suchitoto with 300 men, including many Indian recruits. After marching through various towns, he called on the region's Indians to rise up and attack the city, which they took on June 11, 1885. On June 18 President Figueroa quit and recognized the provisional government of Francisco Menéndez.[113] Rivas then marched with 3,000 Indian troops armed with machetes and rifles to San Salvador, defeating various government detachments along the way. He entered the city with General Menéndez, and both were received by popular ovation.[114]

Most observers, including the U.S. consul, attributed Menéndez's victory to the peasant and artisan militias, especially those led by Rivas. After this mobilization, most observers expected Rivas to become the new president—a likely outcome, given the extreme opposition to Menéndez among the elite of San Salvador and Nueva San Salvador, and Rivas's strong alliance with the most important Indian communities in the department of Cuscatlan. According to the U.S. consul, there was "no power in the Republic to resist him." He was "perhaps the best soldier in the Republic" with "ten thousand Indians about him, devoted to him personally."[115] Menéndez managed to retain presidential power and removed Rivas from his command. Menéndez awarded Rivas 10,000 pesos, citing his modest means,[116] but Rivas refused the money and donated it to public education.[117]

Rivas's alliance with Menéndez was short-lived. In December 1889, President Menéndez had to send 500 troops from San Salvador to fight yet another Cojutepeque-based revolt led by Rivas. Menéndez had attempted to remove Rivas from his power base as governor of Cuscatlán after Rivas disapproved of Menéndez's choice of successor. When Rivas captured the new governor as he tried to assume his position, Menéndez sent Gen. Carlos Ezeta (who would later overthrow Menéndez and whom Rivas himself later betrayed after a brief alliance) to combat Rivas's forces.[118] Rivas prepared to resist, but his Indian militias were not well enough equipped and were forced out of the city. Again, Rivas had armed and relied upon what Menéndez government officials called "popular and ignorant mobs" *(populosas e ignorantes turbas)*.[119] After the defeat, prisoners were executed and a fierce wave of repression was unleashed against the residents of Cojutepeque. While occupying the city, the new governor, Gen. Melecio Marcial, replaced his Indian militia from Nahuizalco with professional soldiers, or *veteranos*, after the Indians went on a rampage. After other battles in the north, Rivas was forced to leave for Honduras.[120] However, despite the increased repression throughout the region, an irregular resistance force led by Rivas's nephew, Manuel Rivas, continued to harass government troops in the first months of 1890.[121] In one confrontation he led ninety Indians from San Pedro Perulapán against government forces.[122]

When Menéndez was overthrown by his own officers in June 1890, General Ezeta emerged as the victor and declared himself provisional president. During the transition Guatemalan forces attacked the new regime, forcing Ezeta to ask Rivas to return from Honduras to form an army. In Cojutepeque thousands of people received him, and a public celebration was held in his honor. Rivas quickly formed an army of over 1,000 men (which later swelled to 1,500), marched to San Salvador to equip his forces, and from there proceeded to the border to fight the invading Guatemalan troops.[123] They marched to the nearby city of Santa Tecla, only to turn against Ezeta's new government the following day, calling for a return to proper constitutional succession. Rivas had no problem convincing his fighters of his change of heart—an opposing commander noted how Rivas's forces, most of whom were from Cuscatlán, were more faithful to him than to the republic.[124] After they defeated the San Salvador garrison in heavy fighting, fresh Ezetista troops retook the city with a fierce bombardment that killed hundreds of civilians. Rivas's army was disbanded and Rivas himself captured and executed.

Throughout his last campaigns, Rivas's support came not only from the peasants and artisans of Cojutepeque, but also from liberal intellectuals and students in San Salvador who opposed Menéndez and supported Ezeta's provisional government. (Like all his predecessors, Menéndez fell out of favor with liberal groups.) In addition to acclaiming Rivas, newspaper supplements gave "vivas" to the *"indígenas of Cuscatlán,"* without whom Rivas would have had no power. An 1890 leaflet published by a student group referred to Rivas as the savior of the people's freedom.[125]

How autonomous were the Indian peasants and communities in their mobilizations? Outsiders saw Rivas as the caudillo of the local Indian faction. While Rivas at first was perceived as a draftee of the Cojutepeque Indian community and faction, by the early 1890s he was the leader of the faction who on one occasion referred to his Indian military escort, presumably his higher-level militia officers, as *"inditos"* (little Indians).[126] As with many caudillo-based movements, both the factional leader and the peasant communities that supported him had something to gain. For Rivas, peasant support was his only vehicle toward national power. For the Cojutepeques, acting as the arbiters of national politics was a source of strength and a guarantee of local autonomy. Although after the early 1890s the Indians of Cojutepeque never again mobilized as they had earlier, factional leaders and members of José María Rivas's family continued to fight regimes they considered tyrannical or antiliberal. Prudencio Alfaro, Rivas's nephew and one of his recruits against Menéndez, led successful movements against Ezeta and later against President Escalón.

Another important elite-led confrontation, one held dear by later generations of the western elite, was the revolt launched from Santa Ana against the government of General Ezeta in 1894. The Ezeta regime was defeated in the west, but—despite the claims of liberal mythology—the opposition movement actually began in the east when antigovernment activists invaded from Honduras, making their original declaration in

Concepción de Oriente.[127] Why the western elite should risk life and property to overthrow an established military government is unclear, but
popular participation was fundamental to the outcome of this nationally
glorified event. Western opposition to Carlos Ezeta had begun as early
as 1890 when Sonsonate's representatives in the National Assembly opposed his presidential nomination. Another reason may have been the
forced loans, some as high as 20,000 pesos, demanded by his regime
from the region's wealthy investors.[128] The famed "Group of 44" from
Santa Ana included important landowners and entrepreneurs from at
least two western departments.[129] This movement also enlisted troops,
militiamen, and other supporters from western towns, including 150
volunteers from Izalco and Nahuizalco.[130] Peasants from the Volcán de
Santa Ana also participated, confronting the Ezetista troops from San
Salvador with machetes and forcing them to retreat.[131] Altogether, 2,000
peasants and artisans were recruited. The battle occurred in Armenia,
where the rebels triumphed.[132]

The last major political transition in which peasants and soldiers in
local militias mobilized, as they had throughout the nineteenth century,
was General Regalado's coming to power in 1898.[133] While there were
stirrings in the western departments, especially Izalco, the greatest
consequences of this transition were felt in the central and eastern departments.[134] A professional military, the containment of conflicts and
divisions among the civilian political elite, the stability brought by land
privatization, which in turn reduced the coherence of Indian communities, contributed to the decline of popular mobilizations after the 1890s.

## Conclusion: Peasant Communities, Liberalism and State Formation

El Salvador did not have a strong centralized national state until the
1880s, and even then it was torn by instability and fragmentation.[135] If
a national state is one that can mobilize fiscal, military, administrative
and ideological resources consistently within a defined national territory
to suppress challenges to the status quo, most Salvadoran governments
were inadequate on many fronts, relying usually on shifting and insecure
alliances, resources, and personnel. This does not mean that the central

state was unable to accomplish any of its goals before the 1880s, but that state power was strongly mediated by local power and ineffective without it. The power of the national state could be legitimized only by speaking in the name of local sources of sovereignty and authority. Furthermore—and this point is crucial to the analysis of the above cases—the reliance on local and fragmentary power centers prevented national power holders from instituting any conception of *nation* during most of the nineteenth century. In fact, most "national" political struggles turned on other issues: Central American unity, liberalism, community or ethnic affiliation, and regional competition. They rarely mobilized any ideology other than loyalty to a common polity that ruled over the *patria*.

Between 1820 and the 1880s, national politics were determined by contradictory and conflicted sources of power. Outside of the small and unstable military factions, the pueblos and ethnic communities were the strongest power base and, according to nineteenth-century liberal doctrine, the only sources of legitimate rule. (Salvadoran landowners had little political power because of the weakness of haciendas, while priests probably did not act as agents of the church when they were involved in politics.)[136] It is this strong communal and municipal autonomy, inherited from the colonial era, reinforced through the liberalism of the early republic, and sustained by the economic autonomy of peasant and artisans throughout the century, that explains the weakness of the "national" and contributes to the instability and diffuseness of state formation in El Salvador between the 1820s and the 1880s. The formation of a central state was also weakened by the absence of discursive and political practices centered on the concept of nation.[137] The absence or diffuseness of this concept distinguishes the Central American cases from others in Latin America.[138] The Salvadoran polity between the 1820s and the 1880s was built on a republican compromise: state-level political elites sought to represent the pueblos, but ultimate sovereignty resided in the legitimate corporate bodies of the pueblos. Most political conflicts of this period must be understood in the context of the tension between the project of forming a central state and protecting local sources of power and sovereignty.[139]

One fact that contriubted to the Indians' relative autonomy as participants in national politics, but could also lead to their subordination, was that political leaders relied on Indian communities for both regular and irregular military recruitment. As we have seen, throughout the nineteenth century Indian militias played important roles in the factional battles over national power and the larger wars with Honduras and Guatemala.[140] All male peasants and artisans were forced to serve in the government militias, which met every Sunday for drills. For example, in Izalco the patriots' corps *(cuerpo de patriotas)* in 1890 included four sections, each with two squads of fifteen men. Until the 1880s the central state continued to rely on citizen-militias—a system rooted in the country's radical liberalism since the mid-nineteenth century—instead of building a large professional standing army.[141]

Even in the professional army Indian draftees abounded. Not until the 1890s was a large, permanent, and well-equipped military force assembled, and even then it was subject to the politics of its leading factions and their struggles with civilian liberals. Throughout the nineteenth century most permanent armies that presidents managed to recruit were destroyed or disbanded in internal conflicts or in wars with Guatemala and Honduras. In the 1890s (when Ezeta was defeated in 1894, for example) Salvadoran army units broke into factions that ended up fighting each other as often as they disbanded in disarray and desertion. At midcentury, the country had only a few hundred professional soldiers and could not secure foreign trainers.[142] The Ezeta government managed to reopen the military school in the 1890s and raised troop levels to 3,400 men, plus a top-heavy structure of over 1,000 officers. Again, during the 1898 change in government, military units were disrupted by fighting. El Salvador relied on the use of citizen-militias into the twentieth century.[143] So while forced recruitment was a hardship that sometimes pitted members of the same family against each other, it also gave the Indian communities a very powerful weapon. The constant participation of militia members in both local revolts and larger regional mobilizations is all too clear from the cases discussed above. Military recruitment itself was a source of conflict. Peasants and artisans usually resisted by fleeing to the hills, but sometimes resistance itself led to violence.[144]

While the tradition of peasant and especially Indian contestation and mobilization that has been presented here certainly gave these social sectors the power to negotiate aspects of their lives, in the long run it did not yield an institutionalized integration of the forces and interests that peasants and Indians represented. The process of state formation in the nineteenth century involved two parallel and contradictory models of popular participation. The first was competitive elections—citizens' rights to participate in political life through sovereign local entities—the pueblos. (The generally liberal constitutions of the Federation and of independent El Salvador offered the vote to most adult males in local and national elections that took place more often than previously believed in the nineteenth century.)[145] The other model, militaristic and authoritarian, reflected the factional struggles of the period that manipulated or simply disregarded the rights of the people. Military officials and their constant efforts to undermine each other by any means led to a closed and self-serving process that empowered only those who attained presidential power and contributed to the long-term subordination of other political forces.

Despite the participation of peasants in defining and negotiating matters of substance throughout the nineteenth century, by the beginning of the twentieth the social differentiation promoted by the emerging capitalist economy and the constantly changing administrative and repressive abilities of the state marginalized the peasants and closed off any possibility that they could become a legitimate political force.[146] Even in the nineteenth century their participation depended on the vagaries of factional conflict and in a way perpetuated political unrest. The ultimate winner was the state itself—the central, national state that continued to be reproduced by El Salvador's complex mixture of liberal-democratic, authoritarian, and patronage politics.

Without a doubt, peasants took advantage of moments of war or conflict—especially around 1885 and 1886—to resolve local disputes or conflicts over land or other matters.[148] National conflicts also intensified local competition for municipal power.[149] Other national changes such as land-related legislation were also linked to contentious mobilizations. However, traditional interpretations of the role of land issues in nineteenth-century revolts—based on land scarcity and appropriation of the lands of Indian subsistence farmers by commercially driven landlords—do not go far enough. Land-related disputes also crossed over into other conflicts between ethnic groups and struggles for control of local government.

While issues relating to land and other local resources explain some of the causes of these revolts and mobilizations, conflict between agrarian interests or ethnic groups provides only part of the explanation. Furthermore, the classic understanding of these revolts (at least those of the 1880s and 1890s) as the result of the expansion of coffee and the wholesale appropriation of western Indian lands is misleading. Existing interests might have come under attack but were not completely expropriated. Furthermore, most agrarian issues and interests intersected with ethnic and political competition and conflict. (For example, the activism of a priest in San Miguel triggered a violent outburst that was initially motivated by conflict between a landowner and local authorities and market vendors, but expanded quickly into a major class-based and ethnic confrontation aimed at the city's entire merchant class and official elite.)[149] These conflicts also involved ties to larger factional leaders at the state level. The Indians and other peasants of the Cojutepeque region, the Nonualco region, Santa Ana, and Izalco-Nahuizalco were particularly adept at maintaining their mobilizations over decades and of cementing strong but flexible and temporary alliances with national leaders and factions of diverse ideological bent.

# 6 Coffee and Its Impact on Labor, Land, and Class Formation, 1850–1910

The growth of the coffee economy in the nineteenth century and the wealth generated by coffee exports produced a new elite class while also benefiting countless peasants, farmers, and merchants.[1] By the late 1880s, income from the export of coffee surpassed that of indigo. Coffee's share of total exports, negligible in the 1850s, rose to 99 percent by the 1920s. A new prosperous elite could import products from abroad and gained in power. By the 1960s, landownership and wealth were extremely unequally distributed in El Salvador, driven by the power of the country's agro-export elite. The success of this class has led to the assumption that the character and impact of the coffee economy had always been the issue. During the ideologically polarized 1980s, many attributed El Salvador's authoritarian politics and oligarchic social structure to the control of land or coffee production by the country's elite. But this is misleading; El Salvador had a heterogeneous economy and social structure well into the twentieth century. In the nineteenth century, exports and local economic activities and products other than coffee were crucially important to thousands of people, while the immediate impact of coffee growing on land use and labor directly affected at most a large minority. Further, the expansion of coffee created varied landholding patterns and different labor and class relations from region to region.[2]

The development of the coffee economy from 1850 to 1920 had its own distinct character and a different impact on land and labor from developments later in the twentieth century.[3] Raising coffee allowed new growers and merchants to consolidate their standing by investing in other enterprises and to buy land, but it did not quickly create an oligarchy. Furthermore, the expansion of coffee production did not disrupt the existence of the landed peasantry that provided most of the seasonal labor. Coffee farms were rarely the large-scale plantations mentioned so often in the literature, and in many areas peasant plots and modest farms predominated over larger farms and haciendas.

Coffee developed slowly between the 1850s and 1870s, with production concentrated in a few areas. During this period, peasants and entrepreneurs established small farms, either in the suburbs of emerging population centers (Santa Ana, Nueva San Salvador) or on lands rented from towns or ethnic communities. From the early 1870s to the early 1890s, coffee production expanded throughout the three regions with suitable conditions, but mostly at higher altitudes on previously unused lands. Especially after 1880, coffee trees were planted on idle community and *ejido* plots, as well as hacienda lands and state-owned *baldíos*. From the mid-1890s to 1918, coffee went through a series of production crises and prices more or less stagnated. Small plots were consolidated into larger farms, with fewer new plantings. After the end of World War I, coffee acreage nearly doubled within ten years as cultivation expanded into the valleys.

Coffee exports in Central America began in Costa Rica and expanded within a decade or two to Guatemala, Nicaragua, and El Salvador.[4] (See table 6.1.) Costa Rica's success provided an important, if not easily copied, model to landowners and enterprising peasants elsewhere in the Isthmus. (President Barrios's interest in coffee has been attributed to a trip he made with Federation President Morazán to Costa Rica in the early 1840s.)[5] Local and national government administrators encouraged the planting of coffee as early as the 1840s, but there were no dramatic increases in investment until the late 1860s.[6] Coffee plantings began in the suburbs of Nueva San Salvador, Santa Ana, and Ahuachapán, and in towns in the departments of Ahuachapán and Sonsonate, all in western El Salvador. By 1854 samples of coffee from a hacienda in Sonsonate owned by José Campo were exhibited in London.[7] However, production

Table 6.1  Coffee Production and Export, 1860–1918

|      | Production (quintales) | Exports (quintales) | Land in Use (hectares) |
|------|------------------------|---------------------|------------------------|
| 1860 | 11,000                 | —                   | 850                    |
| 1876 | 100,000[a]             | —                   | 7,700                  |
| 1877 | 146,330                | —                   | 11,300                 |
| 1880 | 200,000                | 166,000             | 15,400                 |
| 1881 | —                      | 200,000             | —                      |
| 1885 | 300,000                | —                   | 23,100                 |
| 1890 | 600,000                | —                   | 46,200                 |
| 1891 | 575,000                | —                   | 44,200                 |
| 1893 | 600,000                | —                   | 46,200                 |
| 1895 | —                      | 431,230             | —                      |
| 1896 | —                      | 252,937             | —                      |
| 1901 | 556,000                | 437,326             | 42,000                 |
| 1902 | 400,000                | —                   | 30,800                 |
| 1905 | 775,000                | 620,391             | 60,000                 |
| 1910 | 772,000                | 618,347             | 59,000                 |
| 1916 | 988,674                | 777,326             | 61,000                 |
| 1920 | 1,026,715              | 817,108             | 73,000                 |
| 1924 | 1,304,347              | 1,061,065           | 80,000                 |
| 1929 | 1,413,492              | 1,017,021           | 98,000                 |
| 1932 | 1,357,321              | 862,065             | 97,000                 |

*Sources:* El Salvador, *Anuario Estadístico;* Montis, *Informe documentado;* Lever, *Central America; Diario Oficial,* 19 February 1878, p. 170.
   a. Estimate.

increases also spurred local consumption, so surpluses for export were not large until the 1860s.[8]

The modest expansion of production continued in the 1860s,[9] but the country was not a major producer before the 1870s.[10] Tens of thousands of trees were planted by pioneering investors and peasants but had still not come into production. The 2 million trees in production in 1867 in the entire west took up only 1,400 hectares. Farms were generally small. A well-known pioneer's farm in Sonsacate, with 17,000 trees, had 13 hectares in production. Most early coffee farms were formed within *ejidos* of a few western towns.[11] In the small Indian town of Masahuat, for example, five of its twenty tenants on its communal lands produced coffee, an activity compatible with basket weaving and subsistence farming.[12] In Izalco, a town with extensive community and *ejido* lands and well-established commercial agriculture, a few thousand coffee trees were planted in its *ejidos* and Indian-controlled lands and were tended by many growers.[13] By 1860, other regions had begun to grow coffee, such as the town of San Pedro Nonualco in the department of La Paz. This town was characterized by small-scale peasant agriculture and had no haciendas or large farms.[14] Cojutepeque also had many small farms that combined coffee with growing food and sugar cane. There is evidence of coffee plantings by Indians in Cojutepeque as early as 1857.[15]

Coffee production and new plantings expanded significantly in the 1870s and 1880s, then entered an unstable period between 1890 and 1905 in both production and prices. While production recovered somewhat between 1900 and 1910, land use remained relatively stable, hovering around 60,000 hectares.[16] The coffee economy stagnated again because of declining trade with Europe caused by World War I.

In Usulután in 1921—after a few years of increased production—California, Berlín, Alegría, Santiago de María, and Jucuapa were all depressed. Prices were too low to get sufficient advances from merchants, and farmers could not pay workers to pick the beans. Investment declined, and the farmers were not even weeding their coffee farms. The region's crop was only 100,000 *quintales* in 1921, half of what it had been in 1908.[17]

The expansion of coffee production had a limited impact on how land was used. While less than 20,000 hectares was dedicated to coffee production in 1880, by 1896 the figure was 50,000 hectares. (Some 2,000 hectares had been abandoned because of land exhaustion.)[18] Between the late 1890s and 1918, expansion slowed. To put these numbers in perspective, in 1880 coffee covered as much land as indigo had in 1860. However, this represented a still modest extension of land. Three large *baldíos* claimed and settled in the 1880s and 1890s covered more than twice this much land. Further, a dozen or so municipalities accounted for the great majority of production, minimizing the impact of the crop throughout the rest of the nation. Thus the land devoted to coffee during these years grew out of previous patterns of use, slowly incorporating forested areas on state lands, *ejidos*, and haciendas.

After 1870, increased demand and higher prices, as well as better transport facilities and processing technology, convinced El Salvador's farmers and entrepreneurs that export agriculture was the key to the nation's future.[19] The government promoted not only coffee production and exports, but also other kinds of commercial agriculture. *Almácigos* (tree nurseries) were formed for free distribution in the mid-1870s and extended in the 1880s.[20] The local agricultural boards *(juntas de agricultura)* created by the national government in the 1880s supplied tens of thousands of free coffee trees to farmers and peasants to encourage production and reduce startup costs.

Municipalities sought to benefit from increased coffee production to finance public works and education.[21] But many peasants, both Indian and Ladino, resisted the inducements to produce coffee for several reasons. One discouraging factor, especially for smaller farmers, was the decline in coffee prices that occurred just as the country's common lands were being privatized and coffee planting actively promoted.[22] Furthermore, few peasants occupied lands suitable for coffee production. Ladino government officials often explained the resistance of peasants to new crops as the Indians' reluctance to depart from traditional ways.[23] But many Indians who had participated more extensively in the commercial economy or had left their communities—especially after the abolition of landholding communities in 1882—were likely to be identified as Ladinos. However, resistance to new crops went beyond the small producers.[24]

Coffee succeeded in the 1870s and 1880s because startup costs were low or subsidized, especially for established peasants and farmers. The per-unit cost of establishing a larger plantation was higher for commercial investors who had to secure and clear land, plant trees that did not render a product for at least five years, and pay workers to maintain the plantings, all of these requiring a cash investment.[25] Between the 1860s and 1890s, land was available and privatized *ejidos* and *baldíos* provided new low-cost frontiers. While recruiting enough labor was always a problem for larger farmers and *hacendados,* startup costs were small, since most wages were paid only during picking season. Generally speaking, establishing a farm was a safe speculation if it did not involve large amounts of borrowed capital or did not risk one's subsistence. If coffee prices dropped too low to cover labor costs, growers could always avoid the three largest expenditures: paying workers during picking season (which was not a problem for peasant producers), processing, and transport. However, production costs were higher in El Salvador than in most other coffee-producing nations over most of the century (mostly because of higher capital and labor costs), although proximity to seaports helped keep transport costs down. One source reported that El Salvador paid $26 in production costs for each ton it exported, while other countries paid $6–10.[26]

In a still-open agrarian frontier, land was cheap compared to the cost of credit and other expenses. Credit networks were crucial to the coffee economy, and credit and capital were always problematic for larger commercial producers.[27] An 1883 article referred to the "enormous sacrifices" made by coffee producers who sometimes had to sell their crop ahead of time for only 5 pesos per *quintal* (100 pounds), well below the actual price at the time of export.[28] A political divide arose between coffee producers and what were termed "usurious" capitalists, and some called for the establishment of an agricultural bank.

The role of merchants and lenders is clear from the great number of coffee producers who had debts. Before the abolition of common lands, hundreds of farmers and peasants had mortgaged their possession rights to their small *ejido* plots that produced small amounts of coffee. In La Libertad many *fincas* were mortgaged in 1882 to a handful of people, including Salvador Sol and Asención García. The amounts of coffee involved in a sample of these transactions was 12–36 *quintales*.[29] This implies that these producers had 1–5 hectares in production, the typical farm size for *ejidos*. In western towns, myriad small loans and sales involving coffee were registered locally.[30]

Production methods changed very little over the century, except in processing, which increased the value of the bean and reduced the cost of transportation.[31] Five pounds of ripe beans became two pounds after the hulls were removed, and after further processing became only one pound of coffee *("oro")* ready for export.[32] But despite technological advances in large enterprises (which relied on hydraulic and later electric power), most producers relied on simple milling machinery using animal power.[33] Local entrepreneurs devised simple devices for minimal processing.[34] However, by 1884 there were only 27 full-scale *beneficios* (processing mills) in the country, anticipating the great concentration of processing and marketing to come in the early twentieth century.[35]

By 1900, coffee processing and export were very concentrated. For the more than 500 producers in Santa Ana City alone, plus hundreds of others in nearby towns, there were 10 to 20 processors, most of whom were also exporters. Processing in Nueva San Salvador was even more concentrated; in 1915 Nueva San Salvador had only four *beneficios*, owned by Herbert Fryer, Baruch y Commercial, Rafael Guirola, and Fernando Cañas.[36]

Investors set up large milling and processing facilities to prepare beans raised by other growers for export. Using external sources of credit, they could control the trade by combining profits from production, processing, and export. They also served as bankers to myriad small producers. Yet although the export trade came to be controlled by a few merchants, this did not rule out the participation of many smaller traders. In 1895, Meardi and Company, also one of the largest coffee producers and processors, controlled 23 percent of the export trade from El Triunfo and 31 percent from La Unión. Another handful of exporters (none approaching the volume handled by Meardi) controlled another 40–50 percent of the total. Some relatively large exporters were not producers at all (such as Goubad), while others (Cohn and Dreyfus) were apparently involved in processing and exporting but not in coffee growing.

## The Local Political Economy of Coffee

Coffee growing began and expanded most rapidly in the west (Santa Ana, Ahuachapán, Sonsonate, La Libertad). Production began soon after in central El Salvador (La Paz, San Salvador, San Vicente), but expansion was slow until the 1880s. At this time, production took off in the east (San Miguel, Usulután), reaching important levels by the 1890s. (See table 6.2.) In the far west, coffee expanded from central Santa Ana to nearby Chalchuapa and Coatepeque, then into a few lower-lying municipalities of Izalco, Ahuachapán City, Nahuizalco, Salcoatitan, Armenia, and then into the large expanses of unclaimed land further west in Ahuachapán. At the same time, coffee spread from Nueva San Salvador west and south, forming a distinct pattern of expansion in the lower hills of southern La Libertad and eastern Sonsonate. Because of these regional variations, coffee expanded differently in various regions. Solutions to problems in growing, processing, and marketing varied according to regional conditions and reflected preexisting land and labor use patterns.

Table 6.2  Coffee Production, 1876, and Commercial Farms,
1876 and 1882

| | Quintales Produced, 1876 | No. of Farms | |
|---|---|---|---|
| | | 1876 | 1882 |
| Santa Ana | 31,811 | — | 1,588 |
| Ahuachapán | 20,029[a] | 148 | 1,048 |
| La Libertad | 12,495[b] | 24 | 232 |
| Sonsonate | — | — | 416 |
| San Vicente | — | — | 46 |
| San Salvador | 9,832 | — | 361 |
| Cuscatlán | 1,451 | — | 16 |
| Cabañas | 68 | — | 24 |
| La Paz | 406 | — | 82 |
| Usulután | 939 | — | 425 |
| Chalatenango | — | — | 29 |
| La Unión | — | — | 14 |
| Morazán | — | — | 47 |
| Total | 81,375 | — | 4,344 |

*Sources:* González, *Lecciones;* Mora, *Memoria . . . (1883),* 141.

*Note:* The term *commercial farm* is distinguished from the larger commercially oriented farms that were more likely to be counted in official statistics than small peasant plots and coffee holdings.

  a. Average of 135 *quintales* per farm.
  b. Average of 520 *quintales* per farm.

Coffee production was accompanied by a diversity of local social relations. The western departments were the earliest producers and have
retained their importance to this day, with the department of Santa Ana
as the leader. In the 1860s it had the greatest number of farms and experienced the fastest growth rate. In 1876 it was already producing around
32,000 *quintales* (about a third of the country's production), of which
20,000 came from the suburbs of Santa Ana City and another 10,000
from the municipality of Chalchuapa.[37] (See table 6.3.) In 1881 the department produced about 175,000 *quintales*—more than a third of the
country's total output, and a fourfold increase in just five years. By 1881
the department had 500 coffee farms (a dramatic increase from 214
in 1868) with 14 million trees in production and another 18 million
planted.[38] Relatively speaking, the department's coffee farms were larger
than elsewhere, averaging 30 hectares, with 60,000 trees that produced
about 250 *quintales* per farm.

Table 6.3  Coffee Production in the Department of Santa Ana,
1860–1915 (in *quintales*)

| | |
|---|---|
| 1860 | 2,000 |
| 1876 | 31,800 |
| 1877 | 55,000 |
| 1878 | 85,000 |
| 1879 | 130,000 |
| 1880 | 145,000 |
| 1881 | 175,000 |
| 1915 | 186,000 |

*Sources: El Constitucional,* 31 December 1876, p. 787. *Diario Oficial,* 11 May 1882, p. 546; Gobernador de Santa Ana, "Datos."

Santa Ana City had the most coffee trees in the department (3,500,000, or 52 percent); Chalchuapa had 3,000,000 trees (44 percent), and Coatepeque had a mere 203,700 trees in production (3 percent), although it would become the department's expanding coffee frontier in the early twentieth century. Each town had about half a million additional trees planted but not yet in production. Total land with productive coffee trees in 1883 ranged from 2,900 hectares in Santa Ana City, 2,500 in Chalchuapa, and 180 in Coatepeque.[39]

Starting in the 1860s, coffee was grown in Santa Ana City on commercial farms owned by urban capitalist investors that hired seasonal laborers. The city became an economic engine with many enterprises that benefited from the expanding commercial opportunities brought by coffee production. The entire department's rural properties were valued at around 200 pesos per *caballería,* while its entire agricultural industry was valued at 8 million pesos.[40] But even in this city of advanced development, the governor considered property to be extensively divided.[41] Between 1868 and 1915, the number of farms in the municipality almost tripled, from 214 to 580. They were not large; in 1912 some 500 coffee farms produced 80,000 *quintales* of coffee—an average of 160 *quintales* and 15 hectares each. The 1914–1915 coffee crop was about 100,000 *quintales,* produced by 580 farms (172 *quintales* average per unit). (In the municipality of Nuena San Salvador, by contrast, the largest farms accounted for more than half of all production.) Most had been formed by the first wave of entrepreneurs who began their farms on municipal *ejidos* and privatized them after the early 1880s.[42] By the 1910s larger producers had expanded by consolidating smaller units, many of which also raised other crops, including sugar (11,000 *quintales*) and grains.[43]

The town of Chalchuapa had both Indian and Ladino communities that controlled substantial extensions of land. In the pre-1880 period, the Ladino community rented communal lands to outsiders for coffee production, both peasant producers and investors from Santa Ana City. In 1867 a local official reported that "even the poorest" had a nursery with coffee trees. A boom in the local economy allowed many Ladinos to form new coffee and sugar farms. In 1867, before the Ladino community began to rent more of their lands to farmers and entrepreneurs from Santa Ana, the Ladino peasants were reported to have "great coffee groves, food plantings, sugar cane fields; . . . everybody worked, and even the poorest people had their plantings of coffee." Chalchuapa, this author thought, was a model for the country's development: government support for the efforts of poor producers to keep their lands while moving into commercial agriculture.[44]

By the 1890s, an inadequate labor supply was perceived as the major local obstacle to further development of the crop in Chalchuapa.[45] However, significant profits were made from coffee, tobacco, sugar, and grains, with a decline in cattle raising.[46] Over the next twenty years, Chalchuapa became one of the most commercially successful municipalities in Santa Ana and an important center of coffee production nationally. (See chapter 4.)[47] However, in 1910 smaller producers still had an important role in this municipality. The largest farms produced more than one-fourth of the total in 1910, while the remainder was produced on hundreds of smaller farms.[48] In Santa Ana City, by contrast, a few large farms accounted *for more than half* of all production.[49]

Another major producer in Santa Ana department was Coatepeque. While it initially lagged behind Santa Ana and Chalchuapa, by 1900 Coatepeque had grown in importance, mostly through the settlement of unclaimed lands and the purchase of *ejido* and communal plots by outside entrepreneurs. Haciendas were also brought into production, which made Coatepeque the expanding frontier of the department. A desire to gain access to Coatepeque's Indian community lands was an important reason why local entrepreneurs supported the abolition of such communities. However, most of Coatepeque's Indian peasants were able to gain title to the lands they possessed. In 1893 most residents—including many

Indians who had privatized their plots in 1881—raised coffee because of recent, if short-lived, price increases.[50] Few of the farms in Coatequepe were large until after 1900. But some smallholders lost their plots through debt or sale.[51] Even as late as 1916, if we exclude the municipality's ten haciendas (some of which had been subdivided by 1900), the largest coffee farms had an average of 55 hectares in production.[52] By then Coatepeque, with at least 161 medium-size and larger growers, produced 12,000 *quintales* of coffee (75 *quintales* per unit). As late as 1931 two-thirds of Coatepeque's coffee farms were less than 17 hectares.[53] But coffee did not eliminate other products such as sugar, processed in many small iron and wooden sugar mills. By 1915 Coatepeque produced 19,000 *quintales* of sugar, and many of its farms, especially haciendas, combined coffee with cattle raising.[54]

The expansion of commercial agriculture in Coatepeque and its role as Santa Ana's expanding frontier led to the development of all of its lands by the 1910s. (See table 6.4.) Significant *baldíos* and older haciendas were purchased by wealthy entrepreneurs from Santa Ana City. A large *baldío* surrounding Lake Coatepeque was converted into coffee farms and vacation homes for the city's elite.[55] This led to conflicts with Coatepeque's Indian community, which claimed some of the unused lands, but while they probably lost land, most Indians continued as small-scale producers after the expansion of coffee growing and land privatization. The community lost a few *caballerías* not to the expansion of coffee but to the Ladino community of the Volcán de Santa Ana in 1872. The community, which had the government's favor after helping to bring Santiago González to power, were allowed to keep the disputed lands.[56]

Coffee production advanced slowly in the department of Ahuachapán. Peasants in Ahuachapán City, including many Indians, were among the earliest coffee producers, and many smallholders grew coffee into the twentieth century.[57] From the 1860s until the 1890s, most of the department was considered too remote,[58] and coffee lagged behind other products, such as construction goods.[59] In 1900 most people in the department were considered farmers, and most produced coffee.[60] In 1876 Ataco was the department's largest coffee producer, with 8,000 *quintales*, and Ahuachapán City and Atiquizaya produced 5,000 *quintales* each. Elsewhere coffee production was significantly less.

The expansion of coffee in Ahuchapán was based on unused munic-

Table 6.4 Coffee Production in the Department of Santa Ana,
1876 and 1915

| | 1876 | 1915 | | |
|---|---|---|---|---|
| | Quintales Produced | Quintales Produced | No. of Farms | Average Quintales per Farm |
| Santa Ana | 20,000 | 100,000 | 580 | 172 |
| Texistepeque | 15 | 52,770 | — | — |
| Coatepeque | — | 12,000 | 161 | 75 |
| Chalchuapa | 10,149[a] | 10,000 | — | — |
| San Sebastián | — | 10,000 | >9 | — |
| Metapán | 235 | 748 | 200 | 4 |
| El Porvenir | — | 428 | 2 | 114 |
| Masahuat | — | 40 | — | — |
| Total | | 185,986 | | |

*Source: Gaceta,* 31 December 1876; 787; Gobernador de Santa Ana, "Datos para el Anuario Americano," 2 December 1916, AGN-CM-MG.

   a. In 1876 Chalchuapa encompassed San Sebastián and El Porvenir.

ipal lands but especially on state-owned *baldíos.* Apaneca started early with 33 farms in 1866 and by 1912 about two-thirds of its 250 square kilometers were covered by coffee trees, and total production was 15,000 *quintales.* San Pedro Pustla had no haciendas but many important farms. Its six largest commercial farms ranged between 18 and 41 hectares in 1912. Tacuba, a large municipality that had been settled like a frontier by peasants and commercial entrepreneurs alike in 1880–1900 boasted some large farms formed on *baldíos.* Most of the land in Tacuba's coffee farms and its one large colonial-era hacienda (2,250 hectares) were idle, allowing for substantial future expansion and production of other crops. The town of Turín produced less coffee, mainly in small plots. It expanded only in the 1920s, also on *baldíos.*[61]

In the west, the department of La Libertad and eastern Sonsonate (mostly unused mountainous areas to the south and west of San Salvador City) became zones of rapid coffee expansion. In 1865 La Libertad was described as a forest frontier with fifty underutilized large haciendas, most of which raised cattle, with small, isolated Indian communities involved in balsam collection, small-scale farming, and cattle raising. Few had any contact with outside political factions or fought in the political conflicts of the postcolonial era. The *ejido* and communal land systems were never extensive. In part because of its frontier aspect, by 1876 coffee production in La Libertad was experiencing the fastest growth outside of Santa Ana City, and surpassed the latter by the turn of the century. This was especially true of towns outside Nueva San Salvador, which had begun to expand much earlier. In 1900 the department was described as having a few large farms and many small ones. Farms on the hills of Tepecoyo, Jayaque, Comasagua, Cuscatlán, and Quezaltepeque were already raising the bean.[62] In towns like Tepecoyo, Indian peasants controlled 4,500 hectares of *ejidos* and community lands but cultivated very small portions, relying instead on income from balsam. They rarely used their higher-altitude lands, many of which were sold by the municipality to outside investors. By 1910 it had surpassed Nueva San Salvador in tree plantings.

Nueva San Salvador started off with a very large tract of land that allowed for at least forty years of continuous settlement. Other lands from a nearby *baldío* were added soon after, expanding its frontier. The founding of the city of Santa Tecla (later Nueva San Salvador) led to the creation of the department of La Libertad, created in 1865, which had previously been part of San Salvador. The coffee economy of Nueva San Salvador expanded outward, transforming the surrounding forest into coffee farms. In 1865 the municipality produced 2,056 *quintales* of coffee.[63] By 1882 the municipality had 2 million trees in production. Dr. Gallardo, a prominent landowner and coffee producer, owned a farm that produced 1,100 *quintales* of finished, processed coffee. Nueva San Salvador produced 30,000–35,000 *quintales*, with more farms being developed. Farms employed 2,000 men and 2,000–3,000 women and children at harvest time. Workers came from nearby San Salvador City, making Nueva San Salvador a principal center of the wage economy.[64]

Coffee exports in Nueva San Salvador also spurred the aquisition of *ejido* plots by commercial investors who incorporated them into well-capitalized enterprises. (See table 6.5.) Angel Guirola, a wealthy entrepreneur who owned the best house in the city, titled a total of 495 hectares distributed among ten plots. He purchased some of the plots, while others were directly allocated to him by the city.[65] Guirola's large and modern processing plant could process 7,000–8,000 *quintales* from Guirola's own farms in two months.[66] Guirola employed 50 women who worked on the terrace selecting beans, with his two European-educated daugh-

Table 6.5  Coffee Production in Nueva San Salvador, 1885

|  | No. of Trees | No. of Coffee Farms | Land in Coffee (hectares) | Average Farm Size (hectares) |
|---|---|---|---|---|
| Suburbs | 1,902,000 | 33 | 1,221 | 37 |
| Limón | 260,000 | 5 | 185 | 37 |
| City | 50,000 | —[b] | — | — |
| Various[a] | 1,230,000 | 18 | 820[c] | 45.5 |
| Matazano | 21,600 | 3 | 18.5 | 3.7 |
| Los Amates | 800 | 1 | 5.2 | 5.2 |
| Granadillos | 2,500 | 1 | 10.6 | 10.6 |
| Callejón | 7,000 | 49 | 6 | .12 |
| Total | 3,473,900 | >110 | >2,266 | 13 |

*Source:* Alcalde de Nueva San Salvador, "Informe especial de agricultura," 30 January 1885, AMNSS.

a. In Sacazil, La Laguna, Ayagualo, Victoria, and Ateos. Data are not complete.
b. "In small plots."
c. Estimate.

ters supervising the work. They also served as "housekeepers, accountants, treasurers and bookkeepers," also processing the payroll for their father's 12 or 14 farms. The technician who installed Guirola's equipment set up another *beneficio* at his own expense to process coffee raised by more than a hundred small-scale local producers.[67] But even in a place like Nueva San Salvador, coffee did not displace other products such as cattle, corn, and sugar cane, which were still produced extensively.[68]

In 1885 Nueva San Salvador produced a crop worth 350,000 pesos of 35,739 *quintales* (12 percent of the national crop) with a high productivity of 1 pound per tree. The average farm had 32,000 trees (about 13.5 hectares, or 320 *quintales* of production), with a net revenue of 3,200 pesos. In the three principal neighborhoods with coffee production, the average suburban farm had 52,000–68,000 trees in production, or 37 hectares of productive trees per farm. But even in this city of larger producers, in the districts where peasants lived there were many small plantings. Most peasants who worked seasonally *(jornaleros)* also owned their own small plots with a few hundred trees. At 5 pesos per quintal for unprocessed beans, these few hundred trees could bring smallholders as much income as they could earn in wages in a year. By 1898 they were 50 percent of the city's male taxpayers. (The tax structure provided

an incentive for peasants with land to declare themselves *jornaleros*.)
The rest were professionals, farmers, or artisans.[69]

In 1910 Nueva San Salvador's total coffee production was around
15,000 *quintales*, over half of which was produced by the four largest
producers—Angel Guirola (3,500 *quintales*), Rafael Guirola Duke (3,000
*quintales*), Félix Dardano (2,000 *quintales*) and Mr. Sounder (1,200)—
whose properties covered 310, 270, 180, and 105 hectares, respectively
—the biggest coffee farms in the country. The next largest group of producers farmed 20–30 hectares, as in the 1880s.[70] By 1916 Nueva San
Salvador's production had increased to 20,000 *quintales*, of which Dár-
dano's portion increased (through new plantings and purchase of more
farms) to 7,000 *quintales*.[71] A small, extremely wealthy oligarchy controlled all aspects of production during a period of deflated prices and
sagging exports. But these wealthy entrepreneurs (who were also processors and exporters) still coexisted with smaller producers.

Of the western departments, Sonsonate produced the least, yet coffee
became one of the most important local crops. In 1866 the department
produced 5,000 *quintales*—one-third as much as the department of Santa
Ana. Within a few decades, production had expanded somewhat but
Sonsonate had fallen behind. Nonetheless, the towns of northwestern
Sonsonate formed part of the nucleus of coffee production centered in
Santa Ana City. Its highland municipalities were ideal for coffee and were
closer to the port of Acajutla. Coffee was first grown at higher altitudes
and in sparsely settled municipalities that shared the highlands with the
department of Santa Ana, such as Juayua, Salcoatitán, Nahuizalco,
Izalco, and Masahuat. Juayua had 89 coffee-producing farms, with one
in every five families growing coffee. Similarly, Izalco had 200 farms,
and one in every eight households had coffee plantings on their farms.
All of Salcoatitán's farms were relatively small, producing around 5,000
*quintales* total, or an average of 25 *quintales* each—the equivalent of
about 1.7 hectares of coffee trees on each farm.[72]

Juayua (El Progreso) and Salcoatitán were by far the largest producers before 1900, with 73 percent of the department's crop (see table 6.6).
The expansion of coffee was so successful that local producers attempted
to add a spur to the Sonsonate-Acajutla rail line in 1897.[73] In Salcoatitán
and Juayua, places that did not have many haciendas, commercial coffee
farms were formed by local Ladino entrepreneurs on rented *ejido* lands.

Table 6.6  Coffee Production in Sonsonate, 1893

| | No. of Farms | Quintales Produced | | Hectares in Production | |
|---|---|---|---|---|---|
| | | Total | Average | Total | Average |
| Juayua | 100[a] | 10,000 | 100 | 875 | 8.8 |
| Salcoatitán | 300 | 6,000 | 20 | 525 | 1.8 |
| Izalco | 195 | 3,000 | 15 | 263 | 1.4 |
| Nahuizalco | 62 | 1,000 | 16 | 88 | 1.4 |
| Masahuat | 14 | 1,000 | 71 | 88 | 6.3 |
| San Julían | 10 | 300 | 30 | 26 | 2.6 |
| Armenia | 23 | 300 | 21 | 26 | 1.9 |
| Sonsonate | — | 150 | — | 13 | — |
| Cuisnahuat | 15 | — | — | — | — |
| Santo Domingo | —[b] | 200 | — | — | — |
| Total | 719 | 21,950 | 31 | 1,904 | 2.7 |

*Sources:* El Salvador, *Memoria;* "Informe de comercio y agricultura del Distrito de Sonsonate," 1893, AGN-CM-SO.
   a. Plus additional smaller units.
   b. All small farms.


Juayua had been producing coffee since the 1860s. Farms had also been planted in municipal *ejidos*. In 1893 Juayua had about 100 commercial coffee farms that produced 10,000 *quintales,* including coffee grown on two colonial-era haciendas: "Los Naranjos" (1,800 hectares) and "San Luis" (900 hectares).[74] By 1910 Juayua produced 30,000 *quintales* of coffee, and in 1913 1,675 hectares were planted with coffee trees. However, most farms were relatively small and averaged only a few dozen *quintales.*[75]

Similarly, most of Salcoatitan's farms originated in *ejidos*. In 1868, for example, one of the founders of the Salaverría family, which became very wealthy in the twentieth century, rented plots totaling 89 hectares. Two other large users of *ejido* lands in this town were Amelia Kerferd (with 61 hectares) and Tomás Sandoval (with 46 hectares). The rest of the plots were smaller than 15 hectares.[76] Only later, in the 1920s, would these producers create large farms by consolidating adjoining lots through purchase or foreclosure. Francisco Salaverría's "San Francisco" (38 hectares) had been formed in the town's *ejidos* and was titled in 1882, then expanded in 1889.[77] Coffee had attracted many Ladino settlers, mostly from the department of Ahuachapán.[78] In 1893 Salcoatitan produced 6,000 *quintales* on 300 farms of all sizes. The largest and most valuable were owned by the Angulo, Alfaro, Salaverría, and Castillo families. By 1900 all of the town's lands were occupied and few forested tracts were left.[79] According to a 1908 report, all residents produced some coffee,[80] and food had to be imported from other towns because this town could no longer feed itself.[81]

In the 1890s, even smaller localities with less desirable lands began to expand production. While in 1892 Armenia produced only small amounts of coffee on 23 farms (300 *quintales*), by 1895 it had 42 coffee farms that by 1908 produced 1,400 *quintales*.[82] Five large commercial farms, ranging between 30 and 135 hectares, produced 150–300 *quintales* each.[83] In this region peasants continued to have access to land, so commercial investors found it difficult to recruit sufficient labor.[84] By 1910 production had increased, especially in Armenia's haciendas. Some of these estates, owned by landowners from Izalco and Sonsonate City, had their own rail stations and produced a variety of other products.[85] Nonetheless, the town had 36 small and midsize farms with an output that was dwarfed by that of the town's two largest producers. In 1892 Indian peasants in Masahuat produced 1,000 *quintales* of coffee on 14 farms.[86] In this town most coffee was produced by small-scale producers.[87]

In Nahuizalco the principal commercial farms were dedicated to sugar production and cattle and most of its Indian residents were still involved in crafts and raising grains. However, they also kept small plantings of coffee, although a handful of Indians and Ladinos had larger plantings on a few hectares.[88] The governor commented in 1913, "One circumstance that most favors the development and well-being of this locality, is the way in which landed property is divided; there each inhabitant owns a piece of land where he plants his crops." Nonetheless, the prevalence of smallholdings did not mean that the residents of Nahuizalco did not participate in the labor market: the town also provided many seasonal laborers (men, women, and even children) who worked in the farms and haciendas of Sonsonate, Santa Ana, and Ahuachapán.[89]

The central region is defined by the triangle formed by the cities of San Vicente, San Salvador, and La Paz and includes the departments of San Salvador, San Vicente, and Cojutepeque. Coffee did not advance quickly in the department of San Salvador. However, the slopes of the volcano, shared by municipalities in La Libertad and San Salvador, served as a northern frontier to the expansion of coffee from Nueva San Salvador. In the department of San Vicente, there was little enthusiasm for coffee in the 1870s. In 1878, San Vicente City produced only 67 *quintales*.[90] By the early 1890s output was still small; observers noted its potential, but the problem of getting the beans to port made it much less profitable than in other regions. The roads were adequate, but transport and labor costs were high. A railway connecting the region to port would not be available for another three decades. The initial impetus to the development of coffee after the 1890s came from the claiming and settlement of the *baldío* of the Volcán, which began in the 1870s but accelerated in the 1890s when dozens of properties were titled.

Coffee expanded just as slowly in towns that shared the volcano slope with the city of San Vicente. This slow pace developed despite a larger trend that stimulated tobacco growing and the production of cigars, textiles, and other manufactures for export to Guatemala and Honduras at good prices.[91] Still, around 1892, parts of the department still had "immense virgin forests" which were looked upon as a coffee frontier.[92] Municipalities like Istepeque, Tepetitan, San Lorenzo, San Esteban, and Apastepeque produced small amounts of coffee on small peasant farms. Only Guadalupe had large commercial farms that produced more than 500 *quintales*.[93]

By the turn of the twentieth century, coffee was the principal product of many municipalities in the south-central department of La Paz, including the capital, Zacatecoluca (see table 6.7). Production in La Paz began in the 1850s but did not become significant until 1890. Coffee production expanded first in the northern reaches of the department of La Paz.[94] In 1882 the entire department had 1,280,000 feet of trees on midsize farms, significantly less than the west.[95] Zacatecoluca came to produce most of the department's coffee on elite-owned commercial farms.[96] Coffee did not develop extensively in the department of Cuscatlán because its lands were not suitable. However, there was some small-scale production ranging between 20 and 400 *quintales* per town. Peasants and small-scale farmers also produced other products like indigo, cattle, sugar, tobacco, and grains.[97]

Despite a slow start, the eastern region of El Salvador was producing significant amounts of coffee by the late 1880s. However, this expansion reflected a faster, frontierlike expansion into forested lands, including

Table 6.7  Coffee Production in the Department of La Paz, 1894

|  | Quintales Produced | Hectares in Production |
|---|---|---|
| Zacatecoluca | 18,000 | 1,575 |
| San Pedro Nonualco | 10,000 | 875 |
| Santa María Ostuma | 3,000 | 262 |
| San Juan Tepesontes | 3,000 | 262 |
| San Miguel Tepesontes | 2,000 | 175 |
| San Emigdio | 800 | 70 |
| San Pedro Masahuat | 500 | 44 |
| Paraíso de Osorio | 500 | 44 |
| Santiago Nonualco | 300 | 26 |
| Analco | 200 | 18 |
| La Ceiba | 200 | 18 |
| Jerusalén | 150 | 13 |
| San Juan | 100 | 9 |
| Chinameca | 50 | 5 |
| Total | 38,800 | 3,395 |

Source: Alfaro, *Memoria,* 127.

many privatized *baldíos*. In the department of Usulutan, the towns of Santa Elena, Jucuapa, Santiago de María, Alegría, Berlín, Tecapan, and San Agustín were suited to coffee production. Most investors and farmers were settlers from elsewhere. In the 1890s coffee was considered a great source of wealth, as farms had expanded and multiplied.[98] The *ejido* system provided the initial basis for the formation of farms by peasants and entrepreneurs, but soon new lands were brought into cultivation.[99] The expansion into *baldíos* provided the impetus for creating new municipalities like Berlín and California—the two largest producers by the twentieth century.

Coffee production converted a relatively backward and thinly populated region into a major commercial center. Most farms established in the 1890s were on cleared forest land; there is little evidence of the conversion of *ejido* and communal lands to coffee production in this period. Entrepreneurs from outside such as the Canessa, Araujo, Sol, and Schonemberg families invested in the region. Production increased dramatically, from 20,000 *quintales* in 1892 to more than 200,000 in 1908 and 300,000 in 1916 (about 30 percent of the national crop).[100]

By 1909 the economies of Santiago de María (8,000 *quintales*), Berlín

Table 6.8  Coffee Production in the Department of Usulután, 1894

|  | Quintales Produced | Value of Crop (in pesos) | Hectares in Production |
|---|---|---|---|
| Santiago de María | 8,000 | 240,000 | 700 |
| Berlín | 5,000 | 100,000 | 438 |
| Alegría | 4,400 | 96,800 | 385 |
| Tecapán | 1,500 | 30,000 | 131 |
| Jucuapa | 1,500 | 34,500 | 131 |
| Santa Elena | 150 | 3,000 | 13 |
| Mercedes | 50 | 1,000 | 4 |
| San Agustín | 50 | 1,000 | 4 |
| El Triunfo | 20 | 400 | 2 |
| Jucuarán | 6 | 150 | .5 |
| San Buenaventura | 3 | 69 | .5 |
| Total | 20,679 | 506,919 | 1,809 |

Source: El Salvador, Memoria, 72.

(5,000 quintales), and Alegría (4,400 quintales) depended entirely on coffee production and processing (see table 6.8). These towns produced as much coffee as the older western municipalities, excluding the three largest producers (Santa Ana City, Chalchuapa, and Nueva San Salvador), but they were expanding while the older municipalities remained stable.[101] Cultivation in Santiago de María, where new farms were established in the 1880s with 3 million trees in nurseries, was managed by commercial entrepreneurs instead of peasants or farmers.[102] As early as 1882 most of the municipality's production was concentrated in larger farms with 50,000–100,000 trees. But even here there were at least 35 small-scale producers with less than 5,000 trees each and another 10 with less than 15 hectares.[103] By the 1890s, the structure of production was even more diversified, with 100 large farms and more than 200 smaller ones.[104] Tecapán began production after Santiago de María. Most of its farms were small, producing less than 100 quintales in 1882. One-quarter of all productive trees were found on very small farms (with less than 1,000 trees) that produced 13 percent of the department's crop.

In 1883 the northeastern department of Morazán had only 100,982 linear feet of trees.[105] Production was still low in 1890, at 245 quintales.[106] Around 1910 only the towns of Lolotiquillo, Chilanga, Jocaitique, Arambala, and San Fernando produced coffee.[107] The Volcán de Osicala (Cerro Cacahuatique) provided unused lands that were not divided during the abolition of *ejidos*. In 1893 farmers had been buying lots and forming "large and beautiful coffee farms,"[108] but in 1909 coffee farms were still small-scale.[109] The department of Morazán continued to specialize in crafts, mining, indigo, grains, sugar, and henequen. Coffee had begun to expand in the department of San Miguel in 1865.[110] Most production was concentrated in two regions: the slopes of the San Miguel volcano and Chinameca.[111] In 1884 the municipality of San Miguel had 19 farms with a total of about 122 hectares in use. The region had 463,000 trees in nurseries, of which 70,000 were reserved for distribution among San Miguel's peasants and farmers and a third of these earmarked for the town's poor.[112]

## Labor

The expansion of coffee production and the larger commercial economy and the privatization of land between the 1860s and the early twentieth century did not lead to the proletarianization of most Salvadoran peasants. However, expanding agro-exports provided seasonal employment to an increasing number of poorer peasants and landless workers, while also affording women of various classes an opportunity to earn income. During these years landlessness increased slowly, then accelerated after the 1910s when the agricultural frontiers were closed, although not only as a result of the expansion of coffee.

Most coffee production workers were not only seasonal and migratory but also—from the commercial farmers' and plantation owners' viewpoint—unreliable. This was true for the entire country. As late as the 1970s large segments of the population of eastern towns traveled to the coffee-growing regions in search of temporary work.[113] Many observers noted the restless mobility of wage workers. The U.S. consul attributed El Salvador's inability to compete in the world sugar market to the uncertainty and high cost of labor.[114] Most workers—even miners—were apt to return to their subsistence plots after only a few weeks of wage work. In 1882 the director of the government-run "model *finca*" in San Vicente complained, "You can't count on having the same workers for more than two weeks; and it is well known that a permanent worker works harder and better than recent arrivals. . . . This mobility seems innate to them, and does not allow them to take an interest in what they do, nor is it possible to create good projects from them." Military conflicts also affected the availability of labor. Because of a war in 1871, male workers either were drafted or disappeared to avoid conscription.[115] Reports published abroad in 1893 cited the difficulty of securing sufficient workers during picking season and transport costs as the chief obstacles to coffee enterprises.[116] This behavior may indicate workers' resistance to employers' demands. Laboring seasonally for wages was only one of many survival strategies for peasant families with small plots of land; peasants could not leave their own crops for too long.

The department of Santa Ana, the most "capitalist" of coffee regions, provides the best evidence on the sources of labor in the production of coffee. In 1859 officials complained of the lack of labor and the high wages and advances required to attract workers. One coffee grower called for the import of machinery to reduce production costs. Santa Ana employed 5,000 men and women in the 1859 coffee season, or roughly half of the department's total adult population, although even in this early stage laborers migrated from other departments.[117] Many also cut and processed sugar cane, as sugar production took place at the same time as coffee was picked. Complaints about labor costs and shortages continued in the 1880s. In 1880 the governor of the department called for foreign immigrants and a rural police to help solve the labor problem.[118] An 1882 article in the *Boletín de Agricultura* summarized the many complaints over the absence of workers and the loss of cash advances by farmers and *hacendados*,[119] since workers would take a salary advance and disappear.[120]

Before 1900 Santa Ana's coffee economy relied extensively on seasonal migrants from Guatemala and to a lesser extent other regions of El Salvador. Many were women who worked hard for "good" wages. (Female coffee workers had earned "high salaries" as early as 1860.) Laferrière, who visited a large farm during picking season in 1877, found 80–100 women being housed and fed there.[121] An 1879 census for Santa Ana, collected at the beginning of the picking season, listed 15,749 men and 27,960 women, a dramatic gender difference explained by the seasonal immigration of women. Of these, 4,715 were "naturalized" women, while 3,600 were listed as Guatemalans; only 3,711 men were "naturalized," and 881 were from Guatemala.[122] (Similarly, in Sonsonate City the number of women workers, especially in food preparation and artisanal employment, increased, while the number of males declined. Guatemalans, especially women, flocked to other towns in the department of Santa Ana. In 1910, 80 percent of the residents of the town of Candelaria came from Guatemala.[123]

In Nueva San Salvador, the country's second coffee-producing municipality, women earned 15 cents a day, plus two meals, sorting beans at a *beneficio* owned by the Dueñas family.[124] Generally, wages ranged from 25 to 50 cents per day, plus two meals, although these wages were often paid by the task. Most workers, however, received premiums or advances. One employer complained that a woman who had been given an advance of 20 pesos had never shown up for work, and that he was then forced to hire others at 25 cents per box. At these rates, coffee pickers could make 50–75 cents per day.[125]

By the 1910s the western departments had more or less sufficient labor. Several factors could affect the labor supply, such as crop damage caused by insects that forced peasants to seek wage jobs, the closing of agrarian frontiers, and other commercial fluctuations. Competition from small manufacturing workshops, mining, sugar production, and road and rail building, which often paid higher wages, also limited the availability of labor.[126] Public works projects, in particular, tended to pay higher wages. The demands of the commercial economy, however, did not lead to a rapid creation of a large landless rural proletariat. Only regions with more dense capitalist agriculture like Santa Ana City, Nueva San Salvador, and in parts of the municipalities of Sonsonate, San Vicente, and San Miguel developed permanent nuclei of wage workers, mostly after 1900. In the mid-1920s, when the coffee economy and the larger commercial economy had begun to alter dramatically, a visitor observed:

> The bulk of the labor of the picking season . . . comes from the small landowners and their families. These independent Salvadoreans, if they are coffee raisers, finish their own picking first, and then go with their wives and children to work on one of the big *fincas* nearby, where they have worked, perhaps, through every picking season for generations. There they join volunteers who have come from the town, and also, another class like themselves, small farmers who raise other crops than coffee but who come to work on the *fincas* through the picking season.[127]

By the early 1920s this picture had changed dramatically with the expansion of a distinct class of landless workers that roamed the countryside in search of work. After the market crisis in coffee production in 1921, many workers in eastern El Salvador had to emigrate to find work. According to the governor of Usulután, they arrived "in squadrons" in the lowlands, and some even left for Honduras.[128]

An important source of information are the labor registries that listed the names of workers and employers. Laws requiring the keeping of these books were almost universally ignored until the early twentieth century. Santa Ana, one of the few towns to keep such books, began to use the *Libros Inscripción de Jornaleros* in 1908. In Santa Ana, farms and haciendas of all types employed 5–30 workers, typically less than 15. Because wage advances were customary throughout El Salvador, some workers collected more than one advance and moved from farm to farm.[129] In 1882 Izalco officials complained that local towns did not keep the registers because employers would not report the names of whom they hired and how much they were paid. This reflects the relative bargaining power of workers and their ability to play off one employer against another. Employers negotiated directly with the laborers and accepted the practice of (sometimes forfeited) wage advances as a necessary cost.[130]

The increased use of seasonal laborers spurred the creation of larger and more efficient policing institutions, but they had little success until after 1900.[131] While laws regulating labor contracts, debts, and other legal aspects of labor were in effect in the 1880s and 1890s, they were usually based on decrees from the 1840s and 1850s and reflected a continuation of established practices, not a sudden surge of labor repression connected to the privatization of lands. For example, a decree of April 14, 1841, established that all individuals without any known property had to prove they were employed by means of a document provided by their employer or else be deemed vagrants.[132]

Measures to control laborers were directed mainly at settling disputes between indebted workers and their creditors.[133] A short-lived system of rural judges intended to deal only with agrarian and labor matters was instituted in the early 1880s but was abolished under pressure after the overthrow of President Zaldívar.[134] While governors, mayors, and the courts always boasted of their efforts to bring "debtors" to "justice" and to curb abuses of the advance-payment system, the national state rarely intervened in recruitment or hiring for commercial ventures. The state's function regarding peasant workers was to prod local authorities to secure labor to build and maintain the roads. Workers were paid directly by the departmental governors or worked off their local taxes with two days' labor a year.[135] After the 1880s, workers could either pay or work out their tax, and many preferred to pay cash.[136] Some mayors would send those who had registered as *jornaleros,* despite having "their own work," to work on the farms of local officials.[137] Laborers were not kept or rehired if they accumulated too large a debt to an employer. In 1897 the administrator of the hacienda "Chilata" "dismissed" 10 absent workers for owing amounts that ranged from 5 to 13 pesos.[138]

Much-touted efforts to establish rural or mounted police forces in areas of denser seasonal labor use generally failed in the late nineteenth century. In 1890 San Salvador's farmers requested the governor's help in forming a rural police that would protect their valuable coffee crop, but the resources were lacking.[139] Not until the creation of the National Guard in 1913 was there an effective rural police force. Yet most of the efforts of local police forces were aimed at avoiding thefts, especially from coffee farms during picking season, and settling the myriad conflicts caused by drunkenness. Police arrests for drunken behavior far outnumbered arrests for labor debts (a few dozen per year in any one department). The governor of Usulután reported in 1900 that because of the agglomeration of people on the coffee farms during picking season, more police were necessary to protect travelers and farmers and to prosecute criminals. (Even drinking water became scarce in Santiago de María because of the thousands of immigrant workers who arrived during coffee season.[140]

In 1900, the governor of Ahuachapán reported 20 trials against debt-breakers *(quebradores)* in the entire department. In 1915, officials arrested 122 as vagrants, which was a different offense and was usually related to drunkenness. The majority of labor-related cases were over debts and wages, and did not involve coercion of workers into wage work. Some workers, especially during Zaldivar's rule (1876–1885), were sent to work on public works or on private farms, but there was no systematic effort to force propertyless workers or poor peasants to work for wages nationwide. In Izalco, one of the largest towns in the west, only three people were tried for wage debts in 1900,[141] and in Juayua 28 workers were arrested and accused of evading their labor debts.[142] There is no evidence of a state-enforced system of labor coercion or mobilization in this period.

Sometimes wealthy coffee farmers requested that national guardsmen or police should be stationed on their farms during the coffee season. The usual fears were the theft of coffee beans and violence. In one case the request was rejected, since a National Guard post had been established in the town, and its agents could patrol the farm.[143] It was not until the early twentieth century that police forces were deployed and expanded.[144]

## Conclusion: Land and Class Formation

How the coffee economy affected the formation and transformation of social groups in El Salvador is a much-debated issue. By 1915 the wealthiest families known as the "fourteen" (whatever their actual number might have been) were well established socially and economically, but not without the participation of many other elite sectors and family groups. However, the idea that these families achieved high status merely because they owned land or controlled coffee production is not entirely accurate. Many investors who were mainly merchants also played a role. The small group of exporters and processors came to control the country's most important source of income at the points where it was most profitable and secure (processing, export, and credit), allowing for diverse forms of social organization at the production level.

Coffee producers were of many types and grew coffee in a wide variety of settings. The small growers, once in the majority, gradually saw their share of total production decline. By the beginning of the twentieth century, better-capitalized entrepreneurs began to consolidate smaller farms and to develop underused haciendas, especially those with highland areas suitable for coffee. There were differences even among the peasant producers who originated in the communal or *ejido* land systems. By the twentieth century, a handful of entrepreneurs, Indian and Ladino, had become far more prominent and wealthy than the many other local producers from whom they began to profit through laws and marketing. In some regions a "farmer" type of land use predominated, with larger plots and more commercial ties, that usually involved petty merchants, professionals, teachers, artisans, and so on. These farms hired a few workers for wages, although the owners did their own work and also raised other crops such as corn or sugar.

In 1884 the economy of El Salvador was described in this way:

> Wealth is well distributed and there is no concentration of wealth in one individual or family, as you see in other parts; but you don't have too many cases of extreme poverty either. . . . From the profuse division of wealth comes the proportional or relative distribution of land . . . There are only a few owners of large extensions of land, and even fewer of those who dispose of large amounts of capital to dedicate to agriculture.[145]

Clearly, there were strong obstacles to an extreme concentration of wealth by any entrepreneurial group or class. Referring specifically to coffee production, this author noted that the intense competition for lands resulted in a lack of concentration: "You almost don't have large enterprises, having only a few farms that exceed one or two hundred thousand feet of coffee trees." Most coffee was produced by the many coffee plantings under 20,000 feet of trees, and all producers relied on merchants who used coffee to pay off their debts for imports. The author blamed the relative poverty of producers on their dependence upon merchants to process their beans and recommended that producers organize and invest in their own departmental processing facilities.[146]

In 1897, Lambert de Sainte-Croix also commented on the structure of land tenure in El Salvador:

> It is a strange thing, property here is very divided, and one does not find, as in Mexico or in Guatemala, the type of farms that enrich only one family. Everyone is a small owner in Salvador, and the least Indian has his little coffee plantation; this explains the difficulty one has in finding workers for the harvest. The largest properties give no more than 200,000 to 300,000 kilos; in Guatemala, there are properties, like that of Chocola, which is in the hands of Germans, that produce 3,500,000 kilos per year. However, some owners in Salvador possess several properties of 300,000 kilos, which makes for a large revenue.[147]

The larger farms of 2,000–3,000 *quintales* cited by Lambert had between 186 and 280 hectares in production. Certainly the vast majority of Salvadoran farms were smaller than this, but they could be highly profitable. Lambert also noted that Ladinos and Indian peasants were small-scale coffee producers, which partially contributed to the shortage of labor faced by larger producers when picking season arrived. Another traveler provided a similar vision: "The secret of the Salvadorian's relative happiness and content I found on my ride across the country, when I passed plot after plot of coffee ground as large as village squares, each owned and worked by some peasant proprietor."[148] The success of El Salvador's coffee industry before the twentieth century could not have occurred without the existence of a peasantry capable of reproducing itself outside of the coffee sector. Coffee expanded because the bean could be produced by independent peasants and farmers who, with others, could also provide the required seasonal labor.

Commercial entrepreneurs also had various origins. Many merchants first invested in coffee by loaning money to producers, then came to own farms themselves. Other urban professionals such as doctors, teachers, or lawyers saw coffee raising as a lucrative investment. This is one reason why Santa Ana's and Nueva San Salvador's coffee lands had urban nuclei. In 1882 one farmer wrote:

> Until very recently, agriculture in El Salvador seemed to be the exclusive patrimony of simple and poor people; the inhabitants of the cities looked upon it with disdain and only sought careers with the military and in commerce. Fathers educated their children to make them doctors, lawyers, or priests; agriculture was not attractive to young people . . . who would not distance themselves from places where revolutions were plotted. And agriculture, the source of the country's wealth . . . could not develop; . . . but in the last few years we have seen with great pleasure that the pattern is different; it has passed on to the hands of more educated entrepreneurs *who are usually merchants who know how to . . . make their enterprises prosper.*[149]

In 1883 Guzmán confirmed these views, stating that most people with capital were dedicated to commerce, while few invested in haciendas except for cattle raising. (Lands suitable for cattle were much more concentrated in ownership than any other type of land.)[150] However, during much of the nineteenth century, farmers were generally recognized as being at the mercy of wealthy merchant creditors. While these entrepreneurs controlled an increasing percentage of coffee exports and later processing as well, small-to-medium producers continued to be linked to these tightening networks of debt and marketing. This led many defenders of agrarian progressivism to call for the formation of state-supported banks to free farmers and peasants from this burden.

A wealthy and powerful coffee-based elite did emerge from the changes of these decades. However, their investments were diverse and usually combined production with processing and marketing. Borghi B. Daglio and Company was one of the country's largest exporters by 1915, when it exported more than 50,000 *quintales* of coffee, or about 5 percent of the total national coffee crop. The company also owned *beneficios* in four cities; Daglio himself served as Italian consul. Another group, Rafael Alvarez and Sons, owned fourteen coffee farms with a total of 3,200 hectares, of which 900 were planted in coffee and produced 13,000 *quintales* annually. They also exported 50,000 *quintales* under three different brands, and their properties were valued at $700,000. Like many other wealthy entrepreneurs, by the 1930s Rafael Alvarez had also become involved in industrial production.[151] Mauricio Meardi, another wealthy investor, owned four *beneficios* in Usulután and also owned large plantations in this department. By 1895 Meardi controlled one-quarter to one-third of all the exports from La Unión and El Triunfo.[152] Although he was listed as a merchant living in San Salvador, his company was one of the largest merchant firms in eastern El Salvador.[153]

In some cases, entrepreneurs who began as small-scale commercial farmers within *ejidos* and who later privatized their farms could also turn to local commerce as they expanded their economic interests. Their families included professionals and military officials who invested in agriculture. The Salaverría family of Sonsonate provides an example. Family members were involved in coffee production very early in Salcoatitán and Juayua. By the early twentieth century, they owned the region's principal coffee farms and *beneficios,* as well as other properties. They served as mayors, governors, and military officers, and owned small shops in the city of Sonsonate.[154] However, the Meardis were unusual because most immigrant merchants rarely participated in production during this period. In 1914 a Salvadoran author referred to immigrants who became wealthy merchants (with names like Bloom, Baruch, Dreyfus Schwab, Dreyfus

May, Borghi Daglio, Bang, Palomo, and Goldtree Liebes) as foreigners *(extranjeros)*.[155]

Other products besides coffee, such as sugar and cattle, were also important in the rise of an agricultural bourgeoisie. Investment in noncoffee activities had an equally strong impact on the rural political economy. Sugar enterprises were very profitable, for example. Signatures to a published letter from the country's sugar producers, refiners, liquor distillers, and exporters regarding export taxes reads like a who's-who of the Santa Ana and Nueva San Salvador entrpreneurial elite.[156] Large-scale producers and investors often made profitable investments by buying large, often underused haciendas in regions with different ecological conditions. Their forest lands could be slowly brought into production, while money could be made from the sale of balsam, cattle, horses, indigo, and food products. This trend also promoted the subdivision of haciendas, a process that began in the 1860s and accelerated in the 1880s as the demand for land increased.[157] In 1910 many haciendas still had extensive virgin forests that made expansion possible, as well as providing one-time profits from the sale of wood products. These trends led to the incorporation of lands in central departments such as La Paz, San Vicente, La Libertad, and San Salvador.

The families that emerged as the wealthiest and most powerful by the twentieth century had all developed extremely diversified patterns of investment. For example, Gerardo Barrios had significant interests in mining and trade; Santiago González invested in mining; Duke invested in electrification, port building, and government bonds. In 1925 the principal officers and local investors of the Salvador Railway were Angel Guirola, Herbert de Sola, Recaredo Gallardo, Eugenio Araujo, and Eduardo Guirola.[158] Typically, the largest landowners owned large coffee farms, extensive cattle haciendas with lands in reserve, balsam and sugar farms, sugar milling and refining facilities, and so forth. Yet even though some very large coffee-producing units were organized on existing haciendas, privatized common lands, or newly settled *baldíos,* most commercial farms were not very large before 1900. Furthermore, the strength of this emerging agrarian bourgeoisie did not preclude the existence of peasant and farmer forms of production that maintained a continuity with previous patterns, both within and outside the common land system.

The greatest impact of the elite on other social sectors came through their control of credit, processing, and exporting—not on monopolization of the land. In retrospect, it was not the production of coffee as a crop that had the greatest social impact on El Salvador's rural landscape, but the power it gave to a relatively small, extremely dynamic elite to amass wealth that could be reinvested in more coffee-related activities and other enterprises. By the turn of the century, a distinct layer of the Salvadoran elite had taken shape—a financial elite, perhaps the only sector worthy of the term *oligarchy* at this time—that had moved beyond investment in production and trade to banking and speculation in commodities, government bonds, and loans.

# 7 The Privatization of Land and the Transition to a Freeholding Peasantry, 1881–1912

This chapter asks the question: was the privatization of community and municipal lands that began in 1878 initiated and manipulated by a self-serving coffee oligarchy, or was it the result of more complex interactions between other sectors of Salvadoran society? How were lands divided and titled? And what did this transition mean for the tens of thousands of peasants, farmers, and entrepreneurs who possessed these kinds of lands? Many have understood this process as part of the enactment of liberal reforms promoted from the top by modernizing elites. Historians persistently portray privatization as an elite-controlled process, and in most accounts coffee is the principal motivation. For most, these reforms placed El Salvador's land and labor firmly in the grip of market forces, a result of state policies intended to benefit a small elite of capitalist entrepreneurs chiefly involved in coffee production. In this view, privatization brought the increasing impoverishment and proletarianization of Salvadoran peasants.[1]

This chapter reinterprets the privatization of common lands in the context of larger changes in the Salvadoran state, society, and agriculture. The move to privatize lands had multiple origins and motivations; it was not meant to destroy peasant landholding but to consolidate it and direct it toward the commercial economy. Similarly, the results of privatization were complex and led to the titling of land by peasants, farmers, and urban entrepreneurs alike.

Turning the nation's common lands into the private property of individual landholders ranks among the most important events in Salvadoran history. Thousands of plots previously held and administered by communities and towns came into private hands. Peasants, farmers, and entrepreneurs gained title to plots that they could now sell or mortgage with greater ease, and which they could administer without going through municipal authorities or community administrators.

The abolition of earlier forms of land tenure and administration radically altered the power of corporate bodies such as towns and ethnic communities. Having lost their primary role and the source of local solidarity and coherence, Indian and Ladino communities had to search for new ways to maintain their identity and formal organization. Yet the privatization of common lands also resolved many tensions and pressures that had been developing among peasant producers and farmers, bringing new conflicts and contradictions, some of which are still part of El Salvador's agrarian landscape today.

## *Liberalism and the Origins of Land Reform*

The abolition and privatization of communal lands had important precedents. During the nineteenth century the Salvadoran state enacted various measures to privatize unclaimed public lands or to grant ownership titles to *ejidatarios* who planted permanent commercial crops. In one municipality that was dissolved because of its size, *ejidos* were distributed and sold to possessors.[2] Revenues from the sale went toward repayment of the national debt. In cases like this, the motives were practical rather than ideological and did not entail a rejection of the concept of common lands itself. Other steps toward privatization were intended to promote export products such as coffee. On various occasions, the state offered incentives to farmers and peasants interested in planting new commercial crops by offering them titles to the *ejido* or *baldío* lands they tilled.

After 1870, however, growing problems with *ejido* use and the increasing commercialization and density of settlement led many to question the wisdom of relying on a common land system as the mainstay for peasants and commercial farmers. This concern was linked to the promotion and diversification of agricultural export products. Although *ejidos* and communal lands continued to exist in the 1870s, there were some early proposals to abolish the system. The pressure first emerged regarding communal lands controlled or used by Indian communities, not *ejidos*. From Opico in 1872 there was a local (presumably Ladino) request to abolish the 1869 law that had institutionalized the Indian and Ladino communities. This quickly led to threats of violence by Indians, causing the town's mayor to request additional troops.[3] As usual, Ladinos and whites of all classes saw the Indians as privileged, inefficient, and quarrelsome, and regarded their control over lands as inequitable and antirepublican—an extension of "caste" privileges from the colonial period into the late nineteenth century. These claims had some merit, at least as they clashed with the popular republican ideal (among Ladinos and whites at least) of the right of all citizens to possess the basic means of subsistence and formal equality; late nineteenth-century liberalism popularly equated the ideal citizen with the landowning farmer. Control of often extensive lands by a gradually diminishing Indian population certainly appeared as a privilege to outsiders who did not have access to rent-free lands.

An emerging rural middle class consisting of commercial farmers, upwardly mobile peasants, and merchants provided the core of opposition to the *ejido* system. Their voices were reflected in various articles published in the *Boletín de Agricultura* in the year preceding the abolition of *ejidos* and contributed to growing opposition to the system. The lead article of the journal's second issue attacked *ejidos* as wasteful:

> The quantity of lands known as *ejidos*, which by law have no particular owners, since their possessors cannot consider them as their own, deprives farmers of the benefits of cultivating their own property, defrauding both the state and the individual. . . . What reason is there for the continued existence of these *ejidos*? A rich and extensive source of prosperity will be opened to the Nation when with a direct and unconditional law they are reduced to individual property, all the more since they include excellent farmlands that will be more productive if the owner tills them with his own labor. We have observed in our towns the custom of giving neighbors these *ejidos* for a given rent, using the proceeds for municipal expenses, but collection of these rents is always trouble-

some and inexact and thus does not even fulfill this purpose. . . . The towns that have more *ejidos* have been the least industrious, because their residents, due to the uncertainty mentioned above, remain happy with plantings of little importance and enough produce to fulfill their needs, which is as far as their aspirations go. With private ownership of the land, . . . a great number of new families, taking their produce, arts, and knowledge everywhere, will improve the town morally and materially: something that cannot be accomplished under the *ejido* system, since it is well known that the aborigines of the towns have little interest in new settlers, a circumstance that has caused them to stagnate since the conquest.[4]

The author called on the National Assembly to abolish the *ejido* system. The following month another article had a more concrete goal: "The adjudication of the *ejidos* or their free and proportional distribution among the neighbors of each locality will increase the number of owners and farmers, with a clear benefit to society."[5] Another writer asserted that despite the changes since the 1860s El Salvador still lacked an agricultural industry. He also linked the changes in land tenure to an important aspect of Salvadoran class structure:

It has been only a few years since capitalists began to look at coffee [1860]. In no part of the republic do you have real estates . . . dedicated to exploiting the soil. Except for the cattle haciendas, which require some capital for their purchase, . . . most who own some capital dedicate it to commerce, because [farming] demands hard work and special knowledge. Raising cattle is very lucrative, and this had led to the concentration of land in the hands of a few owners. But what constitutes a real and heavy burden on national agriculture, in a country as small as ours, is that misunderstood distribution of lands that the state had conceded to the municipalities and certain Indian communities; . . . with the new law . . . we have fixed this problem, dividing property into useful portions that will benefit agriculture. . . . Progress becomes general, the country advances, the towns extend their prosperity, and there is a great incentive to replace crops of little importance with exportable ones.[6]

The author goes on to discuss other problems that hindered the development of national agriculture such as the lack of sufficient labor and credit.

The privatization laws were written by Teodoro Moreno, a senator from Santa Ana, a former governor of the department, and now president of the National Assembly. Of all the officials associated with state administration and coffee production, he was the most knowledgeable.[7] The year the decrees abolishing the *ejidos* were passed, Moreno stated in his closing speech to the Assembly:

> The *ejidos* . . . were created to protect the sons of this virgin land from the ambitions of the conquerors. Today . . . there are no conquerors, there are no social differences recognized in law. Science, on the other hand, rejects the removal of territorial property as damaging, and the *ejidos* do not produce anything for the nation and less for their possessors. It was then necessary to put those lands on the common market.[8]

The minister of the interior and development concurred in this analysis of the impediments established by municipal landholding:

> The system of *ejidos* is also a cause of the backwardness, principally in those towns which, following tradition, insist on not renting them permanently, renting them only, and often for no charge, to local residents who use them only for one season. This, besides making income insecure and transitory, maintains the spirit of localism, provokes animosities between neighboring towns which tend to invade each other's lands.[9]

The minister presented the law abolishing *ejidos* to the National Assembly a few weeks later.

The government justified the abolition of landowning communities by explaining that extensive lands they controlled went unused and that great inequalities had developed in the administration of these lands.[10] Community landholding and its associated structures retarded the development of national agriculture by keeping land out of cultivation and discouraging peasants and farmers from raising long-term crops such as coffee, rubber, and cacao. Conflicts among community members and with outsiders were a threat to public order. To a great extent, this assessment was true. Both for noncommunity tenants or investors wanting access to community lands, but also for many aspiring commercial farmers within communities, communal control of land was a problem.

Because more and more peasants were producing for the market, the distribution of unused lands was a contentious matter. They were either acquired by wealthy community members or allowed to remain idle. In many municipalities, Indian or Ladino communities owned the best lands and often refused to allow peasants or farmers from other towns to use them.[11] In 1882 the minister of the interior celebrated the legislation:

> The suppression of this anti-economic institution, which kept large portions of land in the hands of a few people and which the system of administration regularly rendered unproductive, with negative consequences for public wealth, has had positive results. Most of these communities have been abolished, with only a few left whose partition has been delayed for various reasons—especially the resistance to reforms, even the most beneficial ones, occasioned by routine and custom.[12]

National policies had consistently pointed in the direction of privatization. In the late 1870s, various local and national decisions allowed for the privatization of *ejido* lands that were cultivated with valuable crops, but these measures had a very limited regional impact.[13] A foreign businessman observed of the trend toward privatization:

> One of the factors that brakes the development of agriculture is the attachment of lands by the municipalities, since it is a fact, confirmed by experience and elevated to the level of economic science, that lands produce more for the owner than to those who cultivate them with a precarious right of possession. If those lands were reduced to individual property, without the loss of municipal revenues, agriculture would be enlarged in a way we cannot yet measure. Two systems could be followed for reaching this goal: either authorize the municipalities to sell their lands to current possessors, or cede them freely to each individual in lots.[14]

Even many who were deeply involved in *ejido* use began to oppose the common land system, for two reasons: the growing differentiation among the peasantry and the long-established participation of commercial entrepreneurs in the *ejido* system. These pressures on the common land system increased in periods of economic expansion, so that the *ejidos* were perceived as a primary cause of the backwardness of agriculture in general. Newspaper articles in 1874 advanced progressive ideas, such as a public bank, subsidies to artisans' societies and schools, and research trips to Cuba and other places to investigate new methods of producing sugar and tobacco.[15]

More concretely, commercial agriculture was hampered by an arbitrary and unpredictable system of land use that did not provide secure control over land. Most Ladino government officials saw the system as blocking the peasants' ability to become entrepreneurs. They believed that working common lands made much of the peasantry, especially Indian peasants, economically conservative; moreover, the system contributed to protracted disputes within and among municipalities and communities. As in certain parts of Europe, common ownership of land was an obstacle to the creation of a fully market-integrated peasantry and farmer class. There was little incentive to bring more land into production when significant commercial production was already based on the use of *ejidos*. It was also hoped that the privatization of common lands would allow for freer access to credit. If more lands were claimed and used, especially in western El Salvador, the common land system threatened the further development of commercial agriculture. Under the current system, a creditor who claimed farms offered as collateral would gain only possession rights or ownership of "improvements" in case of default. This claim could also be contested.

## Export Promotion Policies and Land Reform

Discussions about the benefits of privatizing the municipal and community lands were part of larger debates about expanding agricultural production. In the late 1870s and early 1880s, liberal intellectuals had promoted the idea that the state should offer larger incentives to expand and diversify agriculture. Books like *Lecciones* and *Apuntamientos*, published in 1876 and 1883, respectively, provided a overview of the country's regions and agricultural practices with detailed information on traditional and new products, including production methods, types of soils, et cetera.[16] Ladino and white intellectuals, farmers, and political actors agreed on the need to modernize both the institutions that provided a basis for agriculture as well as the primitive techniques that were still widespread. To this effect, the government sponsored publications like the *Boletín de Agricultura,* begun in 1881 and published by the Central Agricultural Board, which reported on products, techniques, and the state of agriculture throughout the republic. The government also opened new experimental agricultural schools that trained farm supervisors.

The government established a national statistics office. Data gathering, which had begun decades earlier, was streamlined in the 1880s and 1890s, but depended on information provided by local officials. It was not until the twentieth century that the statistics office and local administrations had sufficient resources to collect systematic and reliable agricultural and demographic data. Progressive administrators in commercially developed areas often took it upon themselves to gather statistical information. The municipalities of Nueva San Salvador and the governor of Santa Ana were among the first to include detailed economic data in their reports.[17] A national land registry and bank were proposed as well. The land registry was established, but not the bank.[18]

For many years various regimes had tried to encourage the development of exports by offering incentives to producers, such as lowering *canon* payments on *ejidos* or similar devices. In 1879, for example, the municipality of Sonsonate decided that its scant 90 hectares of *ejidos* should be used for cacao, rubber, and vanilla. Possessors of lands would have to plant one-third of their lands with any of these crops or face an increase in rent. The extra income from the rent would be used to plant new commercial crops. The municipality requested that farmers create *almácigos*, which it would then purchase at 25 pesos per 1,000 cacao trees or 10 pesos per 7,000 rubber trees.[19] In some municipalities, however, *canon* taxes were raised for those who planted export crops. These measures were effective in only a few municipalities such as Santa Tecla where the distribution of *ejidos* was closely tied to the production of coffee and sugar. The privatization of common lands occurred along with a flurry of similar measures, usually at the request of a few municipalities, such as offering easier terms to privatize possessed lands or to purchase additional lands when they would be used for export or commercial products.

Although boards or *juntas* had tried to promote agriculture before the 1880s, they had met with little success. However, the Central Agricultural Board, created around 1880, expanded quickly and developed local chapters.[20] Local boards, led by farmers interested in improving their technical skills, supervised experimentation with seeds and crops appropriate for local conditions and purchased small plots for nurseries. They also distributed seeds and trees among all classes of producers. Their limited revenues came from local and national taxes and sometimes from the sale and titling of *ejido* lands. There seems to have been little participation by peasants, except as recipients of trees and seeds. A problem throughout the century was that farmers and investors tended to pull back quickly at the first sign of fluctuation in the price of their product. They were of necessity fairly conservative.[21]

Export products slowly became more diversified, although coffee and indigo accounted for most of the total value of exports. New products were added, such as woods, rubber, and cacao. Cattle grazing was also expanding and spurred the incorporation of the extensive unclaimed lands that were titled and divided in the last decades of the century.[22] Even in departments with substantial irrigation such as Sonsonate, more lands were used for cattle grazing because of the relative scarcity of labor and other factors; most farmers and *hacendados* in Sonsonate were involved in raising cattle to some extent.[23] But political factors curtailed these efforts at promoting agriculture. Because of regional and internal conflicts or other fiscal problems in the 1880s and 1890s, wealthy farmers and merchants had to make forced loans to the state. The most notable examples are from the Ezeta administration, but this also occurred under Presidents Campos, Barrios, and Zaldívar.[24] Some of the assigned amounts were very large. Such uncertainty, not to mention war damage itself, limited agrarian expansion.

## Legislation and Its Application

Proposals to abolish both *ejidos* and community lands were presented to the National Assembly by the minister of the interior and development. A Senate commission told delegates to rewrite the draft law and apply it only to communities.[25] The government approved the law drafted by Teodoro Moreno on February 12, 1881, and a few days later the Senate approved it without changes.[26] A year later the Ministry of the Interior submitted a law to abolish municipal *ejido* lands, and it passed in February 1882.[27] The law gave possessors of *ejido* plots four years to pay the equivalent of six *canon* payments. This amount was small, since in most places *canon* rents was generally low (around 2–4 reales per 4.3 hectares of land per year). At 2 reales per 100 *tareas*, a representative plot of 13 hectares cost 30 pesos.[28] Many peasants paid the amount in full upon receiving their title. Local mayors issued the titles and admin-

istered the process. Additional legislation covered exceptions, postpone-
ments, and specific local problems. Provisions in the original decrees that
allowed excess and unused *ejido* lands to be sold at public auction were
changed (apparently as a result of popular pressure) by a September 13,
1882, decree that allowed municipalities to distribute undivided lands to
"those individuals who, because of their effort and honesty, were worthy
of having full ownership over their lands."[29] This was perceived as a
measure that would guarantee equity, since payment for the lands would
be a token amount.

Ten years later, a new law essentially repeated the terms of the 1881
law. The Ezeta government decree of April 24, 1891, acknowledged that
many community lands had not been partitioned. Interestingly, one of
the national assemblymen who signed this decree was a nonresident tenant of communal lands in Izalco and had not paid rent since the early
1880s, while attempting to title the lands.[30] Many communities had not
carried out the mandated division and titling, or they had begun the
process but later reversed or abandoned it. This was partially due to
local resistance, but it was also a result of tremendous conflicts among
communities themselves, given changing regimes and the impact of regional wars (discussed in chapter 8). The decree stated that since the abolition of *ejidos* had "multiplied" the value of lands and ended conflicts
over land allocations, abolishing communities would have the same effect. Governors were to proceed with the distribution according to the
1882 rules abolishing *ejidos*. The revenue from the lands was to be distributed among all community members, and the local municipalities
were to pursue and resolve all pending judicial disputes over community
lands. The decree allowed six months for the partitioning, after which
time the state would take over the remaining lands.

After ten years of conflicts and delays, the decrees of the 1890s increased the role of the national state in the partition process. The 1891
decree was followed by more specific guidelines for partitioning communal lands. Communal archives were to be integrated into the municipal archives and all titles given to the governors. Governors would also
name the surveyors who would survey and map all existing lots and
form suitable lists. Governors were to ensure a fair and unbiased survey
and to resolve disputes. They would also provide titles to each community member for a 25-cent fee. Possessors would have to pay 1.875 pesos

for each *manzana* (.67 hectare) they titled. This corresponded to the six *canon* payments of 31.5 cents for each *manzana,* which had been required by the original 1881 law. These could be paid in four yearly installments plus an additional charge based on interest rate of 9 percent. Claimants would also pay a 5 percent tax to the municipality. All remaining lands would then be sold publicly, with revenues from the sales and titling distributed equally among all community members after expenses had been covered. The law that privatized the *ejidos* called for the preservation of forests if they had not been apportioned.[31]

Subsequent legislation was intended to give any possessor of lands that had been nationalized because they had gone untitled (whether unclaimed land, former *ejido* land, or communal land) first right to a title even if the lands were "denounced" by someone else. These ordinances were generally carried out, with some outstanding exceptions when force or manipulation of the judicial-administrative process led to illegal expulsions and appropriations.

After 1891 some municipalities requested that lands that had not been titled according to earlier decrees should be distributed. Most of these requests were not approved. Instead, the government decreed that these lands were to be sold at a price established by two appraisers, one of whom would be named by the claimants. Although the result was the same, the price could sometimes be higher than if they had been titled in the early 1880s.[32]

Throughout the 1880s and 1890s, the privatization process faced a series of obstacles. Despite the need to follow systematic procedures, local authorities often interpreted the law as they wished, excluding clauses they thought contravened local practices or seemed inconvenient. Local governors oversaw the process in an irregular fashion. Sometimes important documents or record books disappeared from archives, as in 1895 when the new governor of Santa Ana found that the books that registered the yearly installment payments were missing. In this case, *ejidatarios* had to prove they had paid all installments before having their titles returned.[33] A similar problem emerged when a group of peasants from the abolished community of the Volcán de Santa Ana requested the distribution of undivided lands. Although it was generally known that the titles had been deposited in the governor's archive when the community divided its lands, the documents were not found.[34] Nonetheless, most peasant farmers from the region were able to claim their plots by virtue of their membership in the *volcaneño* community. Many, however, lost their lands through debt or sale in the early twentieth century.[35]

## Stages in the Privatization of Ejidos *and Communities*

Although the government intended to regularize and simplify the land tenure system when it abolished *ejidos* and community lands, the outcome was somewhat different. Legislation before 1880 had clarified distinctions in the use and administration of such lands both nationally and locally, but on-the-ground conflicts and disputes still continued, especially where the use of land had not yet raised the issue of undefined boundaries. Other complications emerged when municipalities or communities attempted to divide or sell unused lands, parts of which might have come into peasants' possession after the privatization decrees. In addition, as the division and sale reached the borders of these territories, myriad disputes emerged over the location of markers and the interpretation of colonial titles. This increased the need for surveys and judicial or administrative resolutions.

The process of titling was open to manipulation and corrupt practices by municipal authorities, especially in towns with large portions of unused lands or where checks on their power were weak. However, the process was closely watched by national officials and complaints were usually listened to. The government wished to curb abuses in land distribution. In the city of La Unión, for example, the mayor had been given title to a whole valley, well beyond the 34 hectares he possessed. In this case a complaint was sent to the minister of the interior, and the mayor's title was revoked and the official was fired. The empty lands were distributed among the town's poor.[36] In San Julián the mayor was fined for giving illegal titles to persons who were not the actual possessors.[37]

The national government and local authorities attempted to secure sufficient lands for poor peasants, often allowing smaller payments and the distribution of small plots of unused lands to those who could not pay. In some places plots were limited to 3 hectares and, as elsewhere, the land was granted under the condition that one-quarter would be used for "permanent" commercial crops. In some municipalities the total amount of land distributed in this way was significant. The municipality of Usulután had requested permission in 1882 to sell to the poor 1,800 hectares "not [yet] surveyed or fenced" in plots of 5 hectares and without payment, and larger plots of 5–20 hectares at 3 reales per hectare. San Rafael distributed 540 hectares in a similar manner, and Guaymango, San Alejo, Santiago Texacuangos, Jicalapa, and San Isidro, among others, followed suit. In Jiquilisco 2,700 unused hectares were distributed in plots of 10.7 hectares at 1 peso for each .7 hectare, with four years to pay.[38]

The division and privatization of community lands, although speedy in some places, was generally a twenty-five-year-long, conflict-ridden process in places were local tradition or community resistance slowed the reformation of established practices (see chapter 8).[39] The claiming and titling of relatively large tracts of unused lands within *ejidos* or communities continued into the 1890s. In Tacuba, for example, many claims were made for its extensive unused lands during this period. In 1890, nine years after the initial decrees, the Ministry of the Interior reported that the *ejidos* of Chinameca, Santiago de María, Nejapa, Comacarán, Santa Elena, Gaucotecti, San Buenaventura, Nueva Concepción, Tamanique, El Rosarío, Cacahuatique, Suchitoto, San Alejo, and Armenia had been fully sold.[40]

Various ministers of the interior reported throughout the 1880s that the division of local lands had been completed, but once new legislation was passed that allowed for easy titling or simply restating existing provisions, a plethora of new requests for titles and claims for untitled lands emerged. The 1890s decrees that provided for reabolishing communities and extended the time period allowed for the sale of remaining *ejido* plots had this effect.[41] This was particularly true of community lands that were possessed by community members but controlled by towns. Some border disputes extended into the twentieth century.

In the early twentieth century, some lands were surveyed that had been measured and divided but never titled. In 1901, for example, surveyors were sent to measure the Montaña de Quezalapa, portions of the Volcán de Santa Ana, and San Miguel de Mercedes.[42] As late as 1912, a group of Coatepeque Indians requested the division and titling of 765 hectares on the hacienda "San José de las Flores," which the community had "bought from the king of Spain and was titled during the Zaldívar administration." The community's title was held by the General Treasury

Court, which decided that the request was not covered by the terms of a recent decree. However, the Supreme Court ruled otherwise, allowing for the division of the lands by the Interior Ministry.[43]

## The Privatization of Municipal *Ejidos*

Municipally owned *ejidos* constituted at least half of El Salvador's common lands. The rental of *ejidos* had intensified in the late 1860s and 1870s, clarifying many boundary issues, and as a result municipal authorities were prepared to administer the privatization. Compared to the ethnic communities, the privatization of *ejidos* was generally straightforward. By 1884 the Interior Ministry reported that most *ejido* lands had been divided among private owners and recommended that the income from further land sales come under national control.[44] Still, privatization was not simple, involving the participation of peasants, urban speculators, local politicians, army officers, and town artisans, who all benefited. Even those who later became wealthy entrepreneurs claimed some relatively small plots. Alfredo Schlesinger, a wealthy entrepreneur, requested title to 4 hectares in Santa Ana, while Juan Mathé Sol received title to 2.7 hectares in El Progreso. These plots were probably contiguous to or near farms they already owned, possessed, or rented.[45] Large-scale farmers were interested in consolidating smaller plots, including those purchased from peasants or titled as their own *ejido* plots.

The cost of plots was determined by the rental payments owed by the possessor. This provision of the law created some problems in places that had never charged rent. In Lislique (LU) residents contributed money to cover local needs instead of paying rent. The president had to make a special provision, which allowed them to pay 3 pesos per *manzana* in four annual payments. In Nueva Esparta (Ch), no rent was paid. The plots were valued at approximately 1 peso per *manzana*, and tended to be roughly twice as large (15.3 hectares) as the average *ejido* plot in western towns.[46] This also meant that the cost of acquiring land was not uniform and reflected previous customs rather than market conditions. In places where the municipality had received land as gifts from individuals, as in Armenia, *ejidatarios* refused to pay the six *canon* payments in order to receive their titles. Other municipalities requested that the payments for titling *ejido* plots be waived for poor peasants. Uluzuapa was granted permission in 1882 to sell the lands for 12 reales per *manzana* after the municipality requested they be titled at no cost due to poverty and the lack of rent payments. In Cuscatancingo *ejidatarios* were allowed to purchase land at 2 reales per *manzana*, since they had not been paying rent. In the first few years of the division, dozens of municipalities were granted reductions in the cost of *ejido* lands or an extended payment period. In some places, *ejidatarios* with coffee trees received special concessions, such as a lower sales tax on the titling. Many requests for extensions were granted.[47]

There were also differences between places with unused lands and those that had partitioned all their lands. In 1882 San Miguel de Mercedes (Ch) could find only 12 unused plots good for corn and indigo, and these averaged around 17 hectares. In the city of Chalatenango, the governor found only three empty plots to sell at auction after distribution of the *ejidos*. They were 7.5, 3.5, and 23 hectares in size and good only for cattle and indigo.[48] Some municipalities without enough *ejidos* to provide lots for all residents were often granted additional lands by the government. In 1882 the town of Opico (LL) was given an additional 270 hectares of land to distribute to people without *ejidos* or who were not *comuneros*.[49] A few municipalities, such as Nueva San Salvador and San Pedro Nonualco, asked to keep certain lands as reserve since they protected water sources.[50]

The process of claiming and titling lands often led to conflicts, some of which were reported in the official newspaper. In 1882 residents of Usulutan complained that four people had purchased all the lands left over from the division of *ejidos*, while others remained poor. They asked the government to take back the lands and sell them to the town's poor. A recent decree that allowed for more time for the distribution of *ejidos* also called for the sale of excess land to as many hardworking and needy people as possible. Government officials said that more time was needed because of the flood of requests for titles and because some had not yet requested their titles out of ignorance or negligence. The sale of leftover lands was also postponed to encourage the claims of existing possessors.[51]

The General Statistics Office, established in 1882, was supposed to receive monthly reports from all mayors on their distribution of titles. The office reported that after the initial nine months, mayors ceased to

Table 7.1  Partial Results of the Privatization of Ejidos,
March–December 1882

| Department | No. of Titles | Area (in manzanas) | Average Area | Revenues (in pesos) |
|---|---|---|---|---|
| La Libertad | — | 37,469 | — | 65,000 |
| Ahuachapán | 1,089 | 4,373 | 4 | 13,684 |
| La Paz | 166 | 461 | 2.8 | — |
| Cuscatlán | 339 | 10,056 | 29.7 | 1,796 |
| Cabañas | 878 | 2,911 | 3.3 | 7,787 |
| San Miguel | 406 | 3,125 | 7.7 | 2,834 |
| Morazán | 197 | 1,058 | 5.4 | 190 |
| Usulután | 1,566 | 6,779 | 4.3 | 2,617 |
| La Unión | 62 | 706 | 11.4 | 213 |
| Total | 4,703 | 66,938 | 6.3 | 94,121 |

*Source: Boletín de Agricultura* 2 (1 February 1884): 52.

report the titles, and they had been unable to follow how many titles were granted after the various extensions for titling *ejido* lands.[52] Although incomplete, the data in table 7.1 provide some indication of how the titling proceeded. The three departments with the largest extension of titled *ejido* lands—La Libertad, Ahuachapán, and Usulután—were the most closely related to the expansion of coffee in the 1880s. Titled plots outside of these coffee-producing departments were larger. In Cuscatlán, San Miguel, and La Unión, the average plot was much larger than elsewhere. Plots in these departments averaged 2.4 hectares per title and were valued at 1.5 pesos per hectare. Altogether, the average farm was about 6 hectares, a typical size for a modest farm providing both subsistence and some commercial production.

In the department of Santa Ana, almost 8,700 hectares had been distributed by 1883, This was ten times the number in San Vicente, a department of comparable size (see tables 7.2 and 7.3). As in San Vicente, the data for Santa Ana do not include the extensive Indian and Ladino community lands of Coatepeque, Chalchuapa, and Santa Ana, nor is it possible to determine clearly the number of titles issued in each municipality.

In La Libertad, one of the few departments for which a report on the partition of *ejidos* was issued in the first year, some 37,500 hectares of land worth 64,494 pesos were distributed (see table 7.4), but the report

Table 7.2  Division of *Ejidos* in the Department of San Vicente,1882

|  | No. of Titles | Size (in hectares) | Hectares per Title | Price (in pesos) |
|---|---|---|---|---|
| Apastepeque | 247 | 637 | 3.0 | 1,542 |
| San Cayetano | 73 | 290 | 3.8 | 574 |
| Tepetitán | 46 | 136 | 2.8 | 259 |
| Verapaz | 114 | 373 | 3.1 | 1,184 |
| Tecoluca | 30 | 71 | 2.3 | 151 |
| Guadalupe | 144 | 582 | 3.9 | 157 |
| San Esteban | 160 | 262 | 1.6 | 582 |
| San Lorenzo | 195 | 244 | 1.2 | 1,288 |
| Santa Clara | 47 | 72 | 1.5 | 302 |
| Total | 1,056 | 2,667 | 2.5 | 6,039 |

*Source:* Mora, *Memoria,* 54.

*Note:* This tables excludes the extensive *ejidos* of San Vicente City, as well as the communal lands of Apastepeque and other municipalities with Indian communities.

Table 7.3  Division of *Ejidos* in the Department of Santa Ana, 1883

| Municipality | Hectares Sold | Plots Possessed Without Title |
|---|---|---|
| Santa Ana | 1,694 | 213 |
| Chalchuapa | 1,752 | 155 |
| Coatepeque | 1,305 | 149 |
| Texistepeque | 3,535 | 111 |
| Metapán | 508 | — |
| Santiago | 210 | — |
| Masahuat | 106 | 68 |
| Total | 9,110 | 696 |

*Source:* Mora, *Memoria . . . (1883),* 57.

does not state how many received these lands, nor did it include three Indian communities (Opico, Quezaltepeque, and Masajapa).[53] While, predictably, the municipality of Nueva San Salvador had thousands of hectares of land titled, other municipalities, some with only a few hundred inhabitants, had similar amounts of lands privatized (see table 7.5).

A special problem emerged in some balsam coast villages where, as in Teotepeque, Indians claimed possession rights over trees while not owning or claiming the land. The solution, one that would surely lead to conflict, gave ownership of the land to one person but allowed for open

Table 7.4  Division of *Ejidos* in Department of La Liberdad, 1882

|  | No. of Hectares | Cost (pesos) | Free Hectares | Down Payment (in pesos) | Debt |
|---|---|---|---|---|---|
| Nueva San Salvador | 3,832 | 9,429 | — | 4,543 | 4,876 |
| Nuevo Cuscatlán | 622 | 1,861 | — | 1,060 | 800 |
| Zaragoza | 1,469 | 3,216 | — | 2,302 | 914 |
| San José | 2,936 | 2,153 | — | 1,675 | 478 |
| Huizucar | 2,251 | 3,055 | — | 2,235 | 819 |
| La Libertad | 1,531 | 4,367 | 42 | 529 | 3,837 |
| Comasagua | 3,321 | 6,016 | — | 2,129 | 3,887 |
| Chiltiupan | 3,949 | 5,373 | — | 1,552 | 3,820 |
| Jicalapa | 2,644 | 2,294 | — | 342 | 1,951 |
| Teotepeque | 3,590 | 4,039 | — | 810 | 3,229 |
| Tepecoyo | 1,369 | 3,076 | — | 1,518 | 1,557 |
| Zacacoyo | 481 | 1,086 | — | 392 | 694 |
| Jayaque | 1,551 | 2,935 | — | 769 | 2,165 |
| Talnique | 1,193 | 2,736 | — | 814 | 1,922 |
| Tamanique | 2,752 | 3,185 | 23 | 558 | 2,627 |
| Opico | 728 | 1,710 | — | 1,700 | 10 |
| Quezaltepeque | 2081 | 6,398 | 125 | 2,974 | 3,423 |
| Tacachico | 637 | 1,559 | — | 350 | 1,209 |
| Total | 37,469 | 64,494 | 190 | 26,269 | 38,225 |

*Source:* Mora, *Memoria*, 38.

*Note:* The data for Tacachico, Jayaque, and Jicalapa are not complete.

Table 7.5  Purchase of Sample *Ejido* Plots Titled In Nueva San Salvador, 1882–1884

| Size of Plot (in hectares) | Paid in Installments | Paid in Full | Total Plots Titled |
|---|---|---|---|
| .1–5 | 0 | 22 | 22 |
| 6–10 | 1 | 11 | 12 |
| 11–25 | 9 | 8 | 17 |
| 26–76 | 13 | 4 | 17 |
| Sample total | 23 | 22 | 45 |
| Average size (in hectares) | 31.4 | 9.4 | 20 |

*Source:* "Libro compuesto de 96 fojas . . . en que se notan los titulos de propiedad de terrenos ejidales estendidos por esta alcaldia," 1882, AMN-SS.

access to those who possessed the trees; anyone who destroyed the balsam trees would be fined.[54]

Generally, when there were conflicts over claims, those who could prove actual use and possession over a series of years were usually granted a title. In some places where the unused lands were to be divided among poorer "neighbors," conditions were attached, such as the requirement to plant sugar, balsam, or cacao, as occurred in Panchimalco, Atiquizaya, Yucaiquin, and Intipuca in 1882. In Conchagua all *ejido* plots were titled with the stipulation that one-quarter of their capacity would be used for "long-term" plantings. The *ejidos* of Santa Ana had been entirely divided and *ejidatarios* who had received owners' cards were allowed to title their plots according to the new law.[55]

In most departments, especially in the west and center, entrepreneurs and landowners had for decades had access to portions of the *ejido* lands through possession rights or rentals, in the case of communal lands. Privatization allowed them to establish permanent farms at relatively low prices. Furthermore, the process of claiming, titling, and counterclaiming was complex and confusing, so that *hacendados* and farmers sometimes possessed and titled lands illegally. In other cases, haciendas with long-term conflicts with bordering *ejidos* or communities found it easier to maintain their claims. However, local authorities were not automatically predisposed to favor powerful landowners. They had, after all, a long tradition of defending and extending local claims to common lands. Instead of distant wealthy landowners, they were more likely to favor local residents who had farms or haciendas in the municipality and also participated in local life, perhaps with relatives in local administration.

Claims against *hacendados* were made often. In 1873 the national government gave the municipality of Tepetitan lands in the nearby *baldío* of the Volcán de San Vicente. Local *hacendados* enclosed these lands, and the town did not have documents to prove its claim, which were thought to have been lost in the National Palace fire that destroyed most of the government archives in 1891. Two *hacendados*, Domingo Velasco and Guillermo Cárcamo, took possession of a portion of these lands, while others in the town had none. The municipality asked the governor to give them possession in light of an 1859 decree that ceded the lands and a court order of 1873 that gave them possession.[56]

More often conflicts occurred when town administrators discovered as their *ejidos* were being divided that the borders were poorly defined or overlapped with claims of their neighbors. Such conflicts, as when the representatives of Cuisnahuat and Caluco contested some 225 hectares, led to the examination of whatever colonial or early nineteenth-century documentation each side could bring to bear in its favor. The prevailing interpretation, however, was usually that provided by the governor or the ministry. The governor favored Cuisnahuat, mostly because its people had possessed the lands for decades. When the ministry ordered a survey, surprisingly the lands were found to be within neither town's *ejidos*. The possessors from Cuisnahuat who requested the titling were thus in a precarious situation, since they now had to claim their lands as *baldío* and risked a conflict with nearby haciendas.[57] A similar order from 1886 sought to resolve disputes between Ishuatan, Teotepeque, and Cuisnahuat.[58]

The result of the privatization was less than favorable for some peasants in Guacotecti where local farmers and peasants produced subsistence products and indigo. But they lacked room for expansion. They used to have enough, but, according to the local governor, "the law that abolished the *ejidos*, apparently so beneficial in its results [elsewhere], reduced them to misery, since property, which constitutes the life for the proletarian classes, ended up in the hands of a few that are not even from this town. You can feel the need that these inhabitants have for land to improve their conditions."[59] However, besides the loss of access to land, the decline in the price of indigo also contributed to the region's economic problems.

The privatization of the *ejidos* posed new challenges and opportunities for municipalities. Revenues from the sale of *ejidos*, as well as from the auction of unused portions, either wholesale or in small plots, were usually allotted for municipal use, sometimes for education, but more often for the local agricultural boards.[60] Most smaller towns had relied on rent income from their *ejidos* to cover local expenses, and the sale of *ejidos* would cutail this source of funds.[61] But rent collection had always been erratic and open to favoritism. Eventually, *ejido* income was replaced by various local taxes on production. While the income from the sale of lands was to go to the towns, partition and titling also involved additional expenses. Income from the sales also varied widely. In Chalatenango, where the distribution of *ejidos* went smoothly, income from sales in one district amounted to $4,400 and $388 in another.[62]

In 1896, after almost fifteen years of privatizing *ejido* plots, municipalities were ordered to make lists of the former *ejido* and communal (now national) lands that remained undivided or untitled. The results varied greatly from one place to another. Small municipalities like Guaimango had few lands left. The 42 plots they reported ranged from 1 to 80 hectares.[63] Many places did not comply with this request at all, either due to neglect or simply because they lacked lands. But in some localities substantial lands remained, though probably of the worst quality.

## Baldios *and the Frontier Aspect of the Reform*

Even before the abolition of common lands, the government had begun to encourage the sale of national *baldíos* to promote agriculture and provide good selling terms. In the late 1870s some occupied national lands were systematically privatized—divided into small plots for peasant purchase. One example is the *baldío* Achapuco in Ahuachapán, which was divided in 1874 among 38 individuals. The plots were small, though relatively cheap, at an average cost of 15 pesos.[64] In the 1880s and 1890s, municipalities and the national government also distributed, sold, and titled massive quantities of other available lands outside the *ejidos*. The privatization of *ejidos* also prompted towns to claim adjacent *baldíos* to divide among their residents or to sell. This eventually resolved various ambiguities over possession rights, including lands that were thought to be communal but were eventually titled and distributed as *ejidos* because they had been abandoned.[65] Other unclaimed lands were "denounced" by towns, which sold them and claimed all or part of the revenue. In essence, towns could sell or distribute all undisputed unclaimed lands with proper permission. Sometimes the process was carried out by governors, who then distributed the land. (See table 7.6.)

As with the *ejidos*, farmers and merchants pressed for the sale of *baldíos*. A lead article in the *Boletín de Agricultura* for 1884 called for the distribution of the country's extensive *baldíos* "conveniently and equally among the working classes of our people, under generous conditions, that will allow each possessor to pay the price of his lot in in-

Table 7.6  Purchase of "Denounced" Plots in Baldío Cara Sucia, 1891

| Claimant | Size (in hectares) | Cost (in pesos) |
|---|---|---|
| F. Billeti | 270 | — |
| L. Padilla | 405 | — |
| L. Padilla | 90 | — |
| A. Magaña | 135 | — |
| Salvador Sol | 1,260 | — |
| Onofre Durán | 270 | — |
| J. Aguirre | unknown | — |
| B. Orosco | 1,395 | — |
| M. Prado | 90 | — |
| E. Cardona | 30 | — |
| Ignacio Márcial | 270 | 400 |
| Silverio López | 90 | — |
| José María Monzón | 103.5 | — |
| Ing. Adolfo Zalaya | 1215 | 1,364 |
| Bonifacia Menéndez | 765 | 650 |
| Francisco Aguirre | 765 | 650 |
| Higinio Valdivieso | 342 | 444 |
| Sucesión Menéndez | 765 | 650 |
| Domingo Tobar | 495 | 550 |
| Francisco Fitelli | 270 | — |
| Rodolofo Magaña | 135 | — |
| Pedro Vázquez | 45 | 66 |
| Mariano Prado | 90 | 133 |
| Bonifacio Mendoza | 270 | — |
| Federico Prado | 450 | 333 |
| Federico Prado | 630 | 1,283 |
| Benito Orozco | 1665 | — |
| Salvador Sol | 1260 | — |

*Sources:* "Cuadro que manifiesta las cantidades en efectivo . . . ," 25 February 1992, AGN-CM-MH; "Cuadro No. 1 de las causa civiles fenecidas en el Juzgado General de Hacienda," 25 February 1892, AGN-CM-MH.

stalments or with part of his crops." The author praised the abolition of *ejidos* and communities, and outlined the goal as to "increase the number of proprietors; which will only increase the number of defenders of the homeland, [the homeland] of truly independent men, of dignified and honest men, loyal supporters of our institutions."[66]

Claiming *baldíos* was still going on actively at the turn of the century (see table 7.7). In 1882 the treasury minister reported that the national government owned *baldíos* of about 15,000 hectares worth $22,000 pesos.[67] However, identifying and claiming *baldíos* was always a continuing process, especially in regions of less intense use where haciendas had never established clear borders or where legal action had held up the partition. The General Treasury Court was responsible for handling claims to *baldíos* and land claims. Many *baldíos* were large, although there is little evidence that they remained whole once brought into production. They seem to have been fairly evenly distributed throughout the republic. Some of them were possessed and used by peasants, farmers, or even their claimants. Existing possessors had first claim, while claimants to *baldíos* still recovered benefits such as income from the sale of plots.

The desire to promote agriculture and create a class of enterprising commercial farmers led to the grant of large tracts of land to possessors, new grantees, and speculators. The best example was the Volcán de San Vicente, where coffee cultivation had begun in the 1880s on its forested slopes by municipalities in the department of San Vicente and La Paz that shared access to its lands. In August 1889 the national government granted San Vicente the "*baldío* del Volcán." Their lands on the cone of the volcano would be surveyed and sold in lots or granted to those who had already begun to settle the land. However, in 1892 a report claimed that despite the suitability of these lands for coffee production, the lands had still not been divided and titled, although portions had been claimed by some people who did not cultivate them. Another decree that year announced that the lands would be sold to possessors. The intent of the decree was to protect the settlers who were planting coffee from speculators and arbitrary claimants.[68]

These lands, considered among the best in the country, extended over three-fourths of the volcano's cone. They were to be sold at 100 pesos per *caballería,* a reference price that had been used for decades (and a generous one, considering the high quality of the land). Income from the sales would go toward the department of San Vicente's educational budget.[69] Some of the farms titled in 1893 in the Volcán were of 7, 8.6, 24, 18.6, and 55.3 hectares.[70] Other sources listed 23 plots in both departments (San Vicente and La Paz). The size ranged from 7 to 173 hectares (an average of 35 hectares), sufficient for a modest coffee farm.[71]

As usual, there was some confusion with this process. The town of

Table 7.7  Purchase of "Denounced" *Baldíos*, 1899

| Claimant | Location | Size of Plot (in hectares) |
| --- | --- | --- |
| n.a. | Acajutla | n.a. |
| Chaparrón | Aguacaliente | 540 |
| n.a. | Ahuachapán | 135–180 |
| Cara Sucia | Ahuachapán | 31,050 |
| Santa Rosa Tierra Blanca | Candelaria | 450 |
| El Brujo | Citalá | 4,500 |
| n.a. | Cojutepeque | 45 |
| n.a. | Colon | 1 |
| Planes de Tazulá | Cuisnahuat | 135–180 |
| Dolores | Dolores | 90 |
| El Tabacal | Juicilico | 765 |
| Tabacal | Jiquilisco | 135 |
| Tabacal y Hermita | Jiquilisco | 1,350 |
| Shumapán | La Palma | 270 |
| La Paterna | La Palma | n.a. |
| Pilar de Zarazosa | La Unión | 225 |
| n.a. | Metapán | 90 |
| Las Aradas | Metapán | 2,700 |
| Forera del Naranjo | Metapán | 135 |
| El Naranjo | Metapán | 90 |
| Malpais y excesos | Metapán | 135 |
| Capishul | Metapán | 90 |
| Colina de NSS | Nueva San Salvador | .3 |
| Malpais | Quezaltepeque | 1,350 |
| n.a. | San Agustín | 180 |
| n.a. | San Pablo Tacachico | 445–490 |
| El Boquerón del Volcán | San Salvador | n.a. |
| Las Anonas | Santa Ana | n.a. |
| n.a. | Santa Ana/Chalatenango | 180–225 |
| Chaparrón, Marimbas, 7 Cerros | Santa Ana | 90 |
| n.a. | Santa Ana | 22 |
| Salinas La Herradura | Santiago Nonualco | 180 |
| n.a. | Santiago Nonualco | 1,755 |
| n.a. | Sensuntepeque | n.a. |
| Sitio de la Peña | Tecapán | n.a. |
| Volcán de San Vicente | Tecoluca, Guadalupe, Zac. | n.a. |
| n.a. | Tepetitán | 270 |
| n.a. | Volcán de San Salvador | 2,250 |

*Source:* "Estado de los juicios pendientes en el Tribunal de Hacienda," 1899, AGN-CM-MG.

Guadalupe had to ask the Ministry of the Interior if the decree that allowed for the titling of plots in the Volcán applied to communal lands that also happened to be there. They asked it be extended to these lands so that current occupants could claim their titles.[72] Verapaz also asked for about 200 hectares (4 or 5 *caballerías*) of lands in the Volcán for its residents, but the request was temporarily rejected because of pending legal battles.[73]

In many places additional lands were distributed. In Atiquizaya 267 hectares were parceled out to the poorer residents who lacked money or land in 1882–1883. Dozens of other plots, some very large, were distributed in this fashion. This practice was approved by a decree that allowed municipalities to allocate land to the poor instead of selling them at public auction. In 1886 the government granted Ahuachapán a *baldío* of 4,500 hectares that was to be sold in plots. The municipality had to pay only 700 pesos for the measurement.[74] Another *baldío* in Ahuachapán was sold in plots in 1894. Its 15 plots ranged from 2 to 122 hectares and averaged around 34 hectares.[75] Other *baldíos* and *ejidos* were offered for sale. In Jucuarán (Us), 33 hectares were to be sold whole or in parts. A bid was registered by Simon Montes and Gerbasio Zelaya of 10,200 pesos for all of the land. The single possessor of these lands made no offer, despite having priority; instead, he protested the proceedings. The sale to the bidders was authorized and improvements by the occupant would be paid for. In the *ejidos* of Yayantique, 360 hectares were sold to the possessors and the rest auctioned off.[76] Lands "denounced" as a *baldío* in La Palma (Ch) of 2,700 hectares were measured by Barbarena. The governor asked the minister to allow the lands to be sold and the revenue put to public use. Towns where remaining *ejido* lands were sold to possessors in lots or at auction in 1889 were Santiago de María (450 hectares), Tamanique (150 hectares), Nueva Concepción (180 hectares), Suchitoto (100 hectares), Santiago and San Pedro Nonualco (107 hectares), and San Buenaventura (450 hectares).[77]

In another case, the government ceded a *baldío* to the municipality of Santiago in Santa Ana, which had to pay for a survey. One peso was collected from 168 peasants who were to benefit from the distribution, but the measure was never carried out. The haciendas on both sides discovered that they shared a border and thus there was no *baldío* between them.[78] Also, during the survey of the border between San Pedro Ostuma and Santiago Nonualco in the department of La Paz, a *baldío* of more than 180 hectares was discovered and divided equally between the towns for distribution to local residents "as equitably as possible."[79] In some cases, the government distributed haciendas to peasant possessors who were able to purchase small plots. The hacienda "Santa Ana" in Chapeltique was distributed and sold in this manner, while its idle lands were sold at public auction.[80]

Where *ejido* lands were not of sufficient quality or where farmers and peasants had not been interested in settling, larger plots were sold. This occurred in Acajutla where lands were suitable only for cattle raising and where most local residents where either fishermen or port workers.[81] In 1894, for example, the governor of Sonsonate received approval for the sale of 630 hectares of undistributed *ejidos* to General Miguel Batres for $7,500.[82] In Tacuba, lands that had been purchased in 1874 with funds from a local subscription but had not been administered as a community were sold as *ejidos*—these 360 hectares had never been used by anyone.[83] Numerous claims of all sizes were made in this small town with a mostly Indian population, In 1891 a claim was made for 135 hectares by a group of 18 men. As in most cases where there were no counterclaims or opposed possessors, the claim was granted. Between 1891 and 1893 claims of 45, 90, 135, 270, and 450 hectares were approved to individuals in the *ejidos* of Tacuba.[84] Many of these claims were in Loma Larga, a large plot of about 2,700 hectares that was owned by the municipality as *ejidos* but never fully distributed.[85] In some cases groups of individuals claimed joint possession, as in 1895 when 15 men requested that some lands they used should be divided and titled to them. Only portions of the lands were used to raise grains, fruits, sugar cane, and coffee. The surveyor sent to measure the lands had to settle a dispute between "these Indians," since some wanted to claim more than others would agree to: "Some wanted to leave others without land." At least these peasants could afford to leave part of their lands fallow.[86] Large portions of the lands in Loma Larga were not sold until the twentieth century when the municipality of Ahuachapán requested the remaining 1,350 hectares be sold to raise money for a new market building. According to the town, only a few poor people and one farmer interested in purchasing a portion were in possession.[87] These might have been the same peasants whose plots were surveyed and titled in 1905. The plots ranged from a few hectares to 450 hectares, with an average of 107 hectares. Of the forty-three plots surveyed, counterclaims were established on nine by previous possessors.[88]

The *baldío* Cara Sucia in the department of Ahuachapán was perhaps the largest *baldío* ever claimed—31,500 hectares—more land than was devoted to the entire coffee economy at that time. Although claims in this region had begun in 1876, the bulk of its lands were divided among claimants, possessors, and towns in the late 1890s.[89] Ahuachapán City alone received 4,500 hectares from this *baldío* to distribute among its residents.[90] A government surveyor named Zimmerman measured portions of this *baldío,* including those possessed by peasants and farmers in Tacuba in 1896 (see the appendix). Portions of Cara Sucia were distributed without cost to many "invalids" in 1896. Of the 63 plots distributed in this fashion, 21 people received 22 hectares, while other plots ranged between 7 and 20 hectares.[91] Claims continued into the 1890s; 34 peasants requested a survey and titled their lands in 1897.[92] However, in a trend that would accentuate in the twentieth century, other large plots in these extensive *baldíos* were titled to speculators and entrepreneurs. Table 7.8 lists some of the claimants, some from the families of leading merchants and entrepreneurs. The titled claims ranged from 90 to 1,665 hectares, at an average price of $1 per hectare, well below the general market price and also below the $6.70 per hectare suggested by surveyors in 1892.[93] However, speculators and claimants of these *baldíos* quickly moved to offer their lands for sale on the open market at significantly increased prices. For example, plots totaling 45 hectares purchased by Federico Prado at prices averaged .65 pesos per hectare were offered for sale at prices ranging from 2–3 pesos per hectare—and this before the titling process had concluded.[94] While fewer *baldíos* were available after 1900, some important claims took place in the twentieth century. In Nueva San Salvador, despite heavy settlement and agricultural development of the previous decades, in 1900 the municipality identified a *baldío* worth $50,000–60,000.[95]

Table 7.8  Selected Purchasers of *Ejido* Plots Titled in Nueva San Salvador, 1882–1884

| Name | Age | Occupation | No. of Hectares Purchased | Cost (in pesos) |
|---|---|---|---|---|
| Jesús Gochez | 25 | farmer | 50 | 62 |
| José Maria Pineda | 38 | farmer | 32 | 7 |
| Victoriano Cuellar | 50 | farmer | 33 | 49 |
| Juan Belloso | 27 | farmer | 8 | 12 |
| Mateo Cámpos | 38 | farmer | 9 | 13 |
| Rufino Portillo | 50 | farmer | 1.5 | 2 |
| Alejandro Cabrera | 65 | farmer | 9 | 13 |
| Manuel Alas | 36 | farmer | 14.5 | 21 |
| Daniel Brizuela | 35 | farmer | 21 | 31 |
| Marcelo Surio | 30 | farmer | 3 | 4 |
| Asención García | 64 | farmer | 73 | 132 |
| Enrique Hölter | 66 | farmer | 48.5 | 82 |
| Maximo Romero | 49 | farmer | 12 | 18 |
| Teodoro Montano | 36 | farmer | 1 | 1 |
| Cristoval Mencia | 50 | farmer | 2.5 | 3 |
| José Luz Rodiseo | 40 | farmer | 84 | 126 |
| Secundino Arias | 25 | farmer | 4 | 6 |
| Santiago Campos | 29 | farmer | 50 | 75 |
| Onesifo Luna | 49 | farmer | 12 | 18 |
| Rafael Rodríguez | 48 | farmer | 43 | ? |
| Cermina Cabrera | 35 | household worker | 4.5 | 6 |
| Bonifacia Tirón | 26 | household worker | 6 | 9 |
| Alejandra Mulato | 30 | household worker | 3 | 4 |
| Josefa Alas | 33 | household worker | 173 | 308 |
| Mumela Rojas | 70 | household worker | 11 | 16 |
| Gen. Agatón Solarzano | 45 | military | 10 | 15 |
| Macedónia Durán | 35 | "of her sex" | 8.5 | 12 |

*Source:* "Testimonios de los titulos que expedio la Alcaldía Municipal de Nueva San Salvador desde 1882 hasta 1884," BGA.

## Privatization and Peasants, Farmers, and the Elite

Although the government's intentions were never fully clear and we have few records of how the legislation to privatize common lands was drawn up, the goal was to create a class of peasant farmers and entrepreneurs that would advance the country's agricultural development, especially its export sector. The result, however, was more mixed and contradictory than anyone had intended. The result was a massive transfer of ownership rights, for the most part to peasants and small-scale farmers but also to the emerging entrepreneurial elite—notably by the auction or sale of unused tracts of land to commercial investors, *hacendados*, and speculators. In some respects, privatization locked peasants into the historic socioeconomic patterns (and the physical limits) of the *ejido*/communal system. The division institutionalized and rigidified a decidedly flawed system, since it was based on the use of land for subsistence farming in a period when commercial agriculture was expanding and competition for resources was increasing. Although the privatization of common lands clearly facilitated the titling of *baldío* lands possessed by peasants, the fact that most privatized plots were created from what had been municipal or community land made them different from "frontier" settlements that typically could establish larger claims.

In Armenia, a town of 5,500 inhabitants in 1895, at least 321 individuals received titles when the *ejidos* were distributed.[96] Most claims, however, had been processed earlier. In 1887, for example, $1,500 worth of lands were titled by this town. At around 5 pesos per *manzana*, this equaled approximately 200 hectares of land (an estimate based on the 5 percent sales tax on the titling of *ejido* plots.)[97] Although Armenia's lands had come under municipal control earlier, they were still distributed as communal lands to their Indian possessors. Therefore the total number who received titles was larger than indicated by the titling of *ejidos* plots.

The division of *ejidos* was much influenced by the character of the local economy. In Nueva San Salvador, the development of local agriculture by an emerging national elite was evident in the results of privatization. In this municipality with extensive and fertile *ejidos* suitable for coffee growing, plots were much larger than elsewhere, but there was a large range of sizes. Most of the recipients of titles were listed as agriculturists. In Nueva San Salvador, most plots were paid outright at the time of purchase—although, interestingly, prominent entrepreneurs such as Enrique Hölter, a construction engineer, took advantage of terms that allowed them to pay over four years at 9 percent interest (commercial interest rates ranged from 12 to 24 percent).[98]

In Sonsonate City, a similar sample of 28 *ejido* titles revealed a range of 1–16 hectares, with an average plot of 3.7 hectares. The value of the plots ranged from .5 to 6 pesos per *manzana*. This data show that in municipalities such as Sonsonate, where *ejidos* were very small and the local economy had been dominated by private farms and haciendas since the colonial period, the titling of *ejidos* was mostly a peasant affair.[99]

The national government attempted to take an inventory of former communal lands in 1896 and requested municipal surveys. Some of the results provide a window into local land use. In Tacuba (Ah) where extensive *baldíos* were titled in these years, the 1896 survey found 205 plots. Some were without titles, some had incomplete titles, and some were unused. Table 7.9 shows that 25 percent were smaller than 1.3 hectares, 55 percent were 1.3–8 hectares, and the remaining 20 percent 45 hectares.[100] In Atiquizaya all *ejido* lands had been titled earlier, so the 1896 survey included only titled plots. Two-thirds of the plots distributed in the town of Atiquizaya (Ah) were small, 1–3 hectares. Only a few exceeded 14 hectares. These were smaller than those in other municipalities during the privatization process. However, it was one of the more densely populated towns in the department, second only to Ahuachapán City. This distribution, while certainly allowing most Atiquizeños access to land, also seriously constrained their ability to provide land for the next generation.

In Chilanga, a small town, more than 200 people received lots in 1882. Also, 342 lots were surveyed in 1896, although whether these overlapped with the 200 lots titled earlier is unclear. Most of these had cane farms with wooden mills, grains, and fruit trees. However, there were complaints that in 1882 the lots had been given out in an arbitrary fashion to some nonpossessors who were still unable to expel the possessors. The plots titled ranged from 1 to 4 hectares, while most were of 2 hectares.[101]

## Conclusion

The pressure of increased commercialization of agriculture in the 1880s forced the state move to resolve the contradictions and dilemmas created by the country's common land system. But even the privatization process

Table 7.9 Privatized *Ejido* Plots in Atiquizaya, 1896

| Plot Size (in hectares) | No. of Plots | (%) |
|---|---|---|
| 1–3.5 | 392 | (67) |
| 4.2–7.0 | 133 | (23) |
| 7.7–14.0 | 47 | ( 8) |
| 14.7+ | 16 | ( 3) |
| Total | 588 | (101) |

*Source:* "Minuta de las tierras ejidales tituladas, Atiquizaya," 1896, AGN-CM-MG.

that followed was held hostage to earlier practices and expectations. Privatization laid the groundwork for the creation of sizable classes of peasants and small-scale farmers, while also giving the agrarian elite an unprecedented opportunity to turn land into capital. While it is impossible to calculate exactly how much land was privatized, it is safe to assume that *ejidos* and community lands composed about a third of the country's land mass and a higher proportion of its arable land. *Baldíos* probably covered about 25 percent of the country's land. The remnants of the few hundred colonial-era estates, which saw a revival in these years, held another 25 percent of the land already in private hands.[102]

Privatization carried on some of the limitations, contradictions, and inequalities of the *ejido* and community land systems as they had developed over the nineteenth century, while creating new problems. Peasants and farmers were usually able to title the lands they possessed or cultivated, but if they did not claim additional idle lands, the chance that their heirs could remain landowning peasants was diminished. This meant that over the next generations opportunities for land acquisition would be constrained. Peasant producers and their families were locked into a landholding pattern that was intended to be flexible and allow for expansion with use, but by the turn of the century, population growth in many municipalities, even those with communal lands in addition to the *ejidos*, limited their ability to acquire more land. Of course, the process was subject to great regional variations, but idle lands tended to be inferior. Thus while the process created a peasantry with clear control over their lands, it also opened the door for the eventual impoverishment of many others and certainly the potential for proletarianization or landlessness.[103]

Peasants and farmers who did not establish claims to *baldíos*, *ejidos*, or community lands had to become tenants, squatters, or full-time wage workers. Furthermore, the extensive claims on *baldíos*, leading to the establishment of many midsize farms, and the activation of colonial haciendas prevented the expansion of the peasantry. *Ejido* and communal plots were generally not large, and while many municipalities had other lands available for claiming, others, especially near the major cities, had few lands left.

# 8 The Abolition of Ethnic Communities and Lands, 1881–1912

The privatization of community lands, especially in the west, reveals the complex interaction between peasant agency, state policies, land tenure, ethnic conflict, and agrarian capitalism triggered by the partition. The partition of these communities involved political and cultural factors that were often extraneous to the abolition of *ejidos* and led to delays and internal and external conflicts. It took more than twenty years to settle most issues connected with the privatization of community lands, but by the early 1900s most communities had been dissolved and their lands transferred to individual property holders.

Just as the state had supervised important aspects of the lives of communities since at least the 1860s and had decreed their abolition in 1881, it played an important mediating role in the partition. This added to its legitimacy and influence, especially in communities that had been involved in the political or military upheavals of the nineteenth century. In many cases, courts, governors, and other government officials made decisions and managed petitions and conflicts among the many parties involved. However, the often violent and conflict-ridden character of the state itself contributed to the confusion over the partition. In addition to examining the division of community lands, this chapter also notes important differences between the privatization of communities and of *ejidos*. Finally, it discusses the role of ethnicity and local context in establishing individual (mostly Indian) landowning in the context of expanding agrarian capitalism.

The Ministry of the Interior claimed in 1883 that most ethnic landowning communities had privatized their lands within a year of the 1881 decree.[1] Some communities did divide their lands quickly and without major problems. The Ladino peasant community of Umaña in Mercedes (Us), a former hacienda, did so in 1882 without much trouble. The Indians of Coatepeque (SA) also divided most of their lands among possessors very quickly, forming clear rosters of the owners, their farms, and how much they contributed to the cost of the partition.[2] However, many communities took much longer to partition their lands, especially those with extensive unused land or in which local ethnic and political competitions complicated the process.

In truth, few communities privatized their land effortlessly. Despite the fact that *comuneros* were supposed to receive their land free of payment, communities had to organize and pay for the cost of the surveys and any legal actions necessary to clarify titles or boundaries. In Chalatenango, for example, the community of La Palma had to pay 400 pesos for a survey of its extensive communal lands.[3] A year after the decree, the governor of Sonsonate reported that none of its communities had carried out the partition. In Izalco surveyors wanted too much money for the operation.[4] In Juayua confusion over rights and boundaries led to great resistance. In this town, the lands of the Indian community had been administered by the municipality since 1875. The mayor was to divide and title the lands, but the Indians threatened to revolt and the president suspended the partition. Similar problems emerged in Nahuizalco. Both towns had experienced Indian revolts against local Ladinos in the 1870s as a result of conflicts over control of lands not clearly defined as communal or municipal, and over control of municipal government.[5]

The many years of interaction between national land policies and on-the-ground solutions created a diverse and complex quiltwork of land use patterns and political alliances that made the process of abolition of ethnic communities more protracted and conflicted. Unlike the municipal *ejidos*, community lands were to be divided at first by an outside partition judge, but this position was quickly abolished because of opposition. Instead, partitioners named or elected by communities themselves would carry out the partition. In some cases, town officials played a role either as allies or antagonists of Indian communities. Sometimes municipal authorities completed the process begun by the communities. In most places, community structures and internal divisions influenced the process.

The partition of community lands was generally more conflicted than the abolition of municipal *ejidos,* which had been rented by individuals of varied social background and were usually better administered by the towns. Furthermore, few towns had extensive unclaimed lands, reducing the potential for conflict over their sale. For the ethnic communities, however, privatization brought conflicts with neighboring communities or *hacendados* who could claim or enclose unused lands; with tenants who were not community members but could claim control over their lands; and with town officials over borders or other matters. Defending community interests against outsiders grew more difficult as those interests were being disaggregated. But most disputes were vented and resolved through official channels, although there was always a threat of political and even military repercussions.[6] Outright violence was rare, but the potential for violence and repression cut across all land transactions involving communities.

Compared to the privatization of *ejidos*, the distribution of communal lands was more open to arbitrary and corrupt practices, since the communities themselves had extensive autonomy in carrying out the partition. Usually those in charge not only were community members but also had been elected or selected by their own leaders. But internal conflicts did arise. Some larger communities experienced serious problems, with their partitioners constantly challenged by internal factions, and they often had idle lands not possessed by anyone before the partition began, which added more confusion. In smaller municipalities with less political influence or visibility, authorities or elites found it easier to attempt to manipulate the process for the benefit of a few. Charges of mismanagement of communal funds from collections or from the sale of portions of the lands ostensibly to raise cash for the expenses associated with the survey and partition were raised in both of Izalco Indian communities and in the small community of Mejicanos in Sonsonate City. (See map 5.) In 1884, for example, many members complained to the mayor that the partition judge had embezzled hundreds of pesos.[7]

Some communities, most of them Ladino, had partitioned their lands

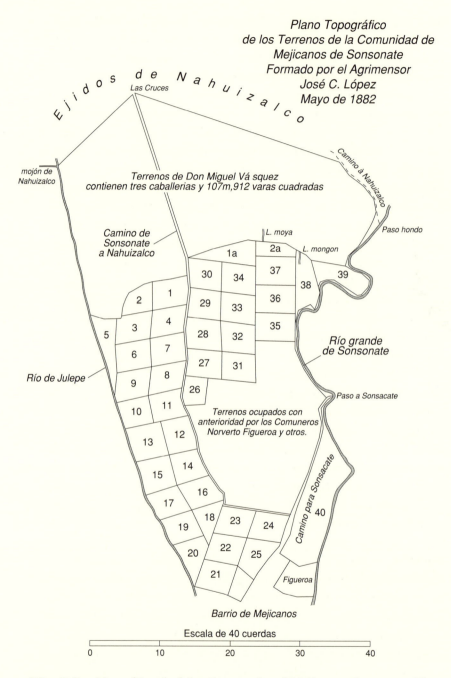

Plano Topográfico
de los Terrenos de la Comunidad de
Mejicanos de Sonsonate
Formado por el Agrimensor
José C. López
Mayo de 1882

Ejidos de Nahuizalco

Las Cruces

Camino a Nahuizalco

mojón de
Nahuizalco

Terrenos de Don Miguel Vásquez
contienen tres caballerias y 107m,912 varas cuadradas

Camino de
Sonsonate
a Nahuizalco

L. moya

Paso hondo

1a    2a    L. mongon

30    34    37

38    39

2    1    29    33    36

5    3    4    28    32    35

6    7    27    31    Río grande
de Sonsonate

9    8    26

Río de Julepe

10    11    Terrenos ocupados con
anterioridad por los Comuneros
Norverto Figueroa y otros.

Paso a Sonsacate

13    12

15    14

17    16

18    23    24    40

19    Camino para Sonsacate

20    22    25

21    Figueroa

Barrio de Mejicanos

Escala de 40 cuerdas

0    10    20    30    40

**Map 5. Partition of Land of the Community of Mejicanos, Sonsonate City**

before the 1880s, allowing members to hold their farms as virtual private property. In Santa Ana the Ladino community of the Volcán and the Indian community of Santa Lucia of Santa Ana had already privatized and titled their lands. Similarly, in San Vicente the communities of La Laguna de Santa Clara and Santo Domingo had already divided their lands but had not issued titles. In yet other towns, Indian communities had become Ladino and allowed their lands to be integrated with the municipal *ejidos*. In most towns in La Paz, lands that had previously been considered communal had by 1880 come under municipal control without any overt conflict or resistance and were thus divided as *ejidos* by municipal authorities.[8]

Many communities held extensive lands that included large unused plots. Because of Chalatenango's large eighteenth-century *composiciones,* communities like those of La Palma–San Ignacio controlled 3,060 hectares but did not use them all.[9] In this case, *comuneros* received larger plots and had a greater chance of acquiring land than municipal tenants. Where community lands were not so extensive, communal plots were relatively small. In Ataco, for example, each *comunero* received about 5.3 hectares.[10]

In Usulután, communities were no longer considered Indian but rather Ladino, and unlike lands in western Ladino communities, their lands were administered by the town. In Santa Elena, where a local peasant community had purchased a hacienda, officials could not decide whether it was *ejido* or community land. If the latter, community members would not have to pay for their plots but would have to pay to survey and title them. Members of the Ladino community of San Ignacio encountered additional difficulties. Two different administrators claimed the right to control the partition—a dispute that found its way into the *Diario Oficial.* The dividing line between the communal hacienda and the town's *ejidos* had never been clear, further complicating the process. Together they covered at least 1,800 hectares. Other confusions arose where community residents had purchased additional lands at an earlier time but the lands were administered by municipal authorities in conjunction with the community.[11]

Myriad other problems arose. The three Indian communities of the department of Morazán claimed that they could not afford to pay a surveyor. This problem, combined with border disputes, kept them from dividing their lands in 1882. Conflicts also emerged between Indian communities and the church over control of lands formally owned by *cofradías* but administered by the communities. In Ahuachapán City, even though the local community had divided its lands by 1882, a tract remained in dispute with the church. In El Rosario, 225 hectares of land purchased by a *cofradía* in the eighteenth century that had come under municipal control after independence were put up for sale by the church. The municipality sued and received half of the proceeds.[12]

Following a law of 1867, lands that had been purchased collectively by groups of peasants were legally considered communities and thus subject to the partition law. The hacienda "Ajuluco" in Tenancingo—1,012 hectares—was owned by eleven people. In 1891 they petitioned for a new title so they could partition the land. (The original title had been lost in the National Palace fire).[13] For lands that had been purchased by an Indian community, the partition was open to greater confusion, usually because of the lack of clear titles or border disputes. The Indians of Nahuizalco in Sonsonate, for example, had purchased portions of the hacienda "Los Trozos" and had to pressure the government to classify it as community land.[14] A similar problem emerged in Chapeltique where the Cofradía de la Virgen owned the hacienda "Santa Ana" and rented it to tenants. In this case, since the ownership of land by "dead hands" and *cofradías* had been illegal since the 1830s, the land was ordered auctioned in lots with preference to the tenants, and the *cofradía* lost all claim to the land but recovered the income from the sale.[15]

## The Partition of Community Lands in Chalatenango

The department of Chalatenango provides an important example of how communities with a long history could become conflicted and fragmented in their attempts to divide their lands. Chalatenango's once extensive community holdings had been subdivided as new towns were formed, each breaking off some of the original communal lands. The new towns then made further distinctions on the basis of local usage as to which lands were to be treated as *ejidos* and which communal, sometimes without clarifying borders. Yet these problems did not always stall the process or lead to conflict. In El Paraíso, Otton Fischer oversaw a survey and partition that went smoothly, while in Dulce Nombre community members settled the partition themselves.[16] However, in 1886 the governor of Chalatenango reported increasing resistance to the partition of communal lands in both Chalatenango City and Tejutla. While some peasants supported the partition, most were opposed and they lived "in constant conflict because of this law." In Tejutla the conflict was not merely over the allocation of lands but resistance to the abolition of the community itself. *Comuneros* continued to hold meetings and elect officials, in open opposition to the abolition law.[17] By 1898 they still had not divided their lands and were still at odds with Ladino peasants and farmers.[18] In a similar process, the Ladino community of Chalatenango asked the governor to intervene and redistribute with more equity some lands purchased by the community in 1865 and divided in 1891 because some had taken more than their share.[19]

Similarly, in Chalatenango City the Indian community did not divide its approximately 600 hectares as ordered by official decrees in 1881. Ten years after the initial decree, it still had not carried out the process. New attempts in 1891 led the Interior Ministry to warn the local governor to be careful "because this kind of operation always brings disorders that must be avoided."[20] Additional problems emerged in 1892 when the leaders of the indigenous community of Chalatenango requested that the 585 hectares they had possessed "since time immemorial" (of which only about 250 were useful for agriculture) should not be divided at all, since they could be productive only through communal, not private, use. They explained, "Carrying out the partition of the commons as is ordered by the recent law . . . will only help a few and damage the largest part of those of us who compose this community, because we are more than 300 and the best lands would be kept by 20 or 30 and this is very prejudicial to the community in general; . . . we work all the good lands in common . . . which is why we ask you allow us to keep this plot the way we own it and work it."[21] In another request, they asked the National Assembly to order the return of lands allegedly taken from them.[22] Evidently, Chalatenango's Indian communards where not ready to give up their strongly entrenched traditions.

In 1895 the community's assistant mayor divided the lands without major complaints. The government approved the partition and said it would distribute titles to all according to the decree that again ordered the privatization and distribution of community-held lands. Then many *comuneros* began to sell their lots to Ladinos, and the purchasers requested titles. Only about one-tenth retained their lands. Everything was ready—they only needed the governor to give the titles. Then two or three *comuneros* who opposed selling lots to Ladinos complained and asked for a new survey. The president's office suspended the partition. Further requests in 1897 and 1898 indicated serious divisions within the community. Some 80 (mostly male) community members had secured a reversal of the 1895 distribution from the Interior Ministry, but it was never enacted. This group asked for a new surveyor and demanded that no titles be issued according to the old allocation. In response, the governor suggesting that lands from unused plots still owned by the community be distributed to the authors of the complaint.

The mayor of Chalatenango agreed, claiming that the opposition to the partition was not valid because many who had received plots had sold them and tacitly accepted the results. Of 197 plots, 167 were sold by their owners between 1894 and 1897. Both new purchasers and those with unsold plots needed titles, and the town needed the title fees (of 3 pesos per *manzana*). Moreover, a new survey would be difficult and costly; local food prices had increased, since few plots were being tilled. Since 1881 community members had been in continuous conflict over the partition of their lands, while purchasers were afraid that they would lose their plots in a new survey. The mayor reminded the ministry that when the extinction of *ejidos* was ordered in 1882, the Indian community

> illegally requested from the government two lots of about [135 hectares], alleging that they were communal and not ejidal. . . . [President] Zaldívar, to avoid trouble, agreed to let them have them. The *comuneros* who now condemn the partition kept the best of these lands for themselves. The municipal council had to return 2,000 pesos that they had received for the sale of the lots, and even though they could have challenged the decision by presenting the land titles, they refrained from doing so in order to keep the peace with neighbors who were claiming that the government was trying to take away the Indians' lands.[23]

According to the mayor, many signatures on the complaints were forged. But the municipality supported the titling because it would resolve lingering local divisions, "removing in this way forever the source of discord that since time immemorial has existed between members of the community and has damaged the proletarian class."[24]

Not discouraged by such opposition, one smaller faction within the community tried again in 1899, after a change in the national government. They celebrated the new administration for being "progressive and liberal" and for restoring constitutional rule, then proceeded to blame the previous administration for damages. The governor was asked to investigate whether the petitioners had been members of the community at all. He responded, "They are not possessors of community lands because some are dependent sons and their fathers received their portion and some of the wives of the same *comuneros* also received their lots; . . . others sold their lots . . . and others are not possessors because they have no rights." The next step in the administrative review process involved a judgment by the National government's *abogado consultor* (general counsel). He decided that the 1897 decree ordering the titling according to the existing partition should be carried out.[25] However, some avowed members of the community still persisted, clarifying their claim to the ministry and president in this way:

> The signers below, members proper of the community of Indians of Chalatenango, confronted by injustice, claim the attention of the excellent president and his ministers, so that manipulation and injustice do not prevail, as they intend to do by despoiling us of our lands. We have always based ourselves on the decree of April 5, 1897, which asked for the reform of the arbitrary partition practiced by Assistant Pérez, a partition that left 60 *comuneros* without any land. Today, the general counsel orders that the partition be carried out as established by this law. And such is the inequity: each comunero was supposed to receive 4 *manazanas*, yet we have been excluded despite being legitimate owners, as we can prove with the titles we are presenting to you; . . . and some by intrigue and manipulation have managed to take 100, 60, 40, and 30 *manzanas*, leaving us without any land. Much noise has been made by the holders of our land that they will be damaged by our claims; . . . this is what they have wanted; although supported by [Governor] General Duarte who is hostile and opposed to the people and protects our enemies. If there is justice they will have to return the lands that they have taken, as we are the legitimate owners as our titles show; . . . we ask you name an agricultural engineer of science and conscience *[de ciencia y conciencia]* to practice the division and stop the scandal that we are complaining about.[26]

This eloquent petition carried 90 signatures. In his response, the mayor explained that the principal issue was the claim that the lands in question were communal when in fact the municipality considered them part of the *ejidos*. The governor then asked the ministry to investigate whether a trial or other procedure had ever established the character of the lands.[27]

While sources are lacking to trace this conflict in its entirety, clearly one reason the community delayed the partition for so long was not that they opposed the concept of private property but they knew the immense obstacles and fault lines that would impede the process, including perhaps that many would benefit unequally. In Chalatenango City, internal factionalism coincided with a dispute between the community and the town to produce a protracted conflict that apparently led to the exclusion of many *comuneros* from the partition.

## Privatization and External Conflicts

In a few documented cases, local authorities used violence to claim land without judicial or other government consent. Settlers on the hacienda "Masajapa," formed in the early eighteenth century, had been using the land as if theirs for decades. In 1859 Matilde Najarro denounced the lands as a *baldío* and with local assistance formed a community. Members spent much money to have the lands titled and President Barrios gave them ownership. However, their lawyer manipulated the titling of the land in his favor. In 1860, when a judge called a meeting of 200 community members to deliver the title, they discovered that the title listed only their lawyer, Artiaga, and a few other *comuneros* of one extended family, the Avelar family.

A conflict emerged when some *comuneros* established a new municipality (San Matías) in 1879. The few official title holders now lived in Opico and opposed the separation. In 1880 Mariano Salinas, a community member, asked the governor to divide their lands. But a majority of community members protested that during the nine years of Zaldívar's rule "bayonets drowned [their] calls for justice" and enforced the unfair partition of 1880. They had asked the courts for titles, spending more than 5,000 pesos in the process.[28] They protested in 1891 that nine *comuneros* were titling the land for themselves. The governor claimed he could find no titles in his archive and therefore could not resolve this dispute.[29] A further complication was that Cipriano Castro, owner of hacienda "El Angel," had taken part of the peasants' lands. This group had complained in 1889 that he had tried to claim their lands and charge them rent, whereupon Castro used troops to burn 30 houses and plantings in the valley.[30]

The Masajapa *comuneros* also had conflicts with the new owners of the hacienda "Atapasco," Emilio Alvarez and his brothers. When these *hacendados* surveyed their hacienda, they took part of the Masajapa community's lands and confiscated their cattle. The Alvarez family claimed two valleys in which 297 people lived, including even their houses and school. The residents complained of such harassment and asked for a neutral survey, citing the large number of people in the town (1,439) and the military service of 300 of them.[31] In 1896 officials from this community-turned-municipality complained that the governor, Hans Müller, had intervened unfairly to force them to settle their conflict with the Alvarez family. He demanded their titles, accused them of mismanaging the town's revenues, and jailed them in Opico for several days. The governor said he was only following a court order that allowed him to expel usurpers from lands owned by the Alvarez family. He added that most inhabitants of the town "were evil" and that the town should be abolished.[32] The complaints continued into 1899 when 11 co-owners claimed that the mayor was giving out titles to plots that they themselves owned.[33] The final outcome of these criss-crossing claims is not clear, although the municipality survives to this day.

Local officials attempted to keep oppressive landowners from pushing local peasants too hard. The mayor of the small town of Santo Domingo (So) reported in 1886 that a local landowner, Antonio Vallejo, threatened the peasants (mostly Indians) whose plots bordered on his lands "so that these poor and timid possessors [would] abandon to him their small plots for low prices not for need but out of fear." When he cut off their water supply and his workers threatened them with weapons, the mayor asked the governor to intervene to avoid an uprising.[34] A year later, the town complained again that under Zaldívar they had been dispossessed of "three leagues" of lands, because they supported General Menéndez, who eventually ousted Zaldívar. Zaldívar's appointment for governor, General Belloso, "dispossessed many possessors with threats." After Menéndez took power in 1885, the municipality asked for redress.[35] This exaggerated claim would have meant that all possessors of community land in this town had been dispossessed—an unlikely possibility. Other evidence from Santo Domingo suggests that this municipality either recovered control of its lands or had never lost them in the first place.

In another case, conflicts over the distribution of community lands were tied to the suppression of a major revolt. In Santa Ana City, the Ladino community of the Volcán, which had revolted against local authorities in 1870, apparently lost part of its lands to nearby haciendas in 1886. But many other Volcán *comuneros* seem to have had no problem in securing titles to the plots assigned to them in the early 1880s. In 1895 and 1896, the *comuneros* of La Laguna, part of the original Volcán de Santa Ana community, complained that local *hacendados* (and unspecified others described as foreigners) had appropriated some of the undivided 360 hectares they had owned since "the king's times" in Las Lomas and Planes de La Laguna.[36] Despite various decrees and legal decisions in their favor, the "*hacendados* adjacent to our lands have with some manipulation rendered such provisions illusory." In question were haciendas "San José de las Flores," "La Preza," "El Potrero," "Las Lajas," "Los Naranjos," and hacienda "Vieja." The governor asked the 66 signers of the complaint to prove their membership in the (now defunct) community, but none showed up to prove their case, perhaps out of fear, but more likely because they lacked documents.[37]

The *comuneros* of La Laguna in 1896 again requested a survey for dividing their lands among them, including some who had received none before. It would also resolve the encroachments of nearby haciendas. However, the governor could not find the community's titles in his archive and thus did not authorize a survey.[38] In 1899 the ministry ordered another survey of the lands of the Volcán, but the results are unknown.[39] In 1901, Rafael Reyes, an administrator, author, and liberal intellectual who held various government posts, asked a high government official to intervene in favor of the Santa Ana *"indígenas"* (his term; the community of the Volcán was known since the eighteenth century as a community of *pardos* and later Ladinos) in their attempt to regain control of their lands.[40] He restated the circumstances:

> 1st. Having been favored with those lands the Indians *[sic]* of the Volcán of Santa Ana, and it being impossible to take them away, the judge and other courts could order them returned but no one could force the Indians out without shedding blood. 2nd. The Indians who have been

occupying those lands have rendered important services [to the nation] beginning with overthrowing . . . the Dueñas government. They had to be rewarded. 3rd. The occupation of the lands was with the consent of the authorities. . . . 5th. The government . . . having given these lands to the poor and working people . . . is equivalent to having granted these lands to the Indians of Santa Ana.[41]

Besides revealing the complexity of claim and counterclaim, especially regarding government interests, this letter typifies the position of many liberals on privatization, especially of ethnic communities that had been so important to the polity of the nineteenth century.

Another example from the department of Chalatenango illustrates this kind of dilemma. The Indians of the community of Tejutla came into conflict with the hacienda "Santa Barbara" owned by Mercedes Bosque. In January 1886, the ministry ordered local authorities to protect Bosque from encroachments. In November she complained again that the Indians had "divided portions of her haciendas among the *comuneros* for corn planting."[42] Another complaint in 1887 led to an investigation; the ministry asked the governor not to intervene in her favor and to refer her to the courts. He was to intercede only if violence broke out.[43]

## Internal Conflicts and Privatization in Izalco

The division of lands in Izalco's two Indian communities led to violent confrontations. Most of the conflicts were not with outside forces, but between *comuneros*. The technical difficulties of partitioning and titling extensive lands were complicated by bickering and fragmentation and by the efforts of others to maintain a communal presence or leadership. The division was drawn out over five major administrations, each president making new decisions or reversing those of his predecessor.

At the time of the privatization decrees (1881–1882), the two Indian communities of Izalco held almost 6,750 hectares of land in addition to the 3,240 hectares the town controlled as *ejidos*. This made Izalco one of the largest holders of common lands in the country. Two colonial-era *pueblos* had been united, separated, and then reunited into a single municipality in the nineteenth century, yet they had retained distinct identities and corporate organizations. Of all the western Indian and Ladino communities, theirs was the longest and most tortuous process of privatization. It was complicated by a long tradition of commercial agriculture, by haciendas and other communities on their borders, by simmering resentments between the town's Ladino residents and the Indians, and by the government's solicitude in dealing with Indian communities. But most of all, the extreme conflicts in Izalco reflected the fracturing of the communities themselves.

In the community of Dolores Izalco, a protracted internal struggle over the partition of unused lands, the titling of previously allotted or possessed plots, and the titling of outside tenants led to twenty years of internal conflicts that culminated in a violent confrontation in 1898 in which the previous Indian partition administrator was killed. This conflict hopelessly divided the community; it could no longer maintain any communal coherence or solidarity or defend local lands from outside interests. The complex commercial ties of Izalco's Indian peasants and the political-military alliances of community factions caused the community to dissolve and violence to erupt.[44]

A similar conflict developed in the community of Asunción Izalco, where the first administrator, Simeón Tensún, was unable to carry out his mission, although for different reasons. In 1886 the community had taken a census of its members, but they refused to allow their lots to be measured. The process stalled "as much because the individuals within the community opposed with arms the measure of their individual farms and created obstacles with many complaints to the governor or mayor of Izalco."[45] Tensún complained of the expense of traveling to the capital and charged that the community owed him 4,077 pesos as well as the 1 percent of the land value to which he and his assistants were entitled. Furthermore, some *comuneros* had not only taken away titles by force, but were also collecting rent from Ladino tenants. Even one his assistants had refused to collaborate and would not sign the documents. He accused the *comuneros* of being manipulated by ill-motivated Ladinos. An independent commissioner reviewed the charges and in February 1886 rejected many of the claimed expenses, especially the partitioner's fee, which he thought was exaggerated and erroneously calculated. Finally, the job of distributing and titling had not been carried out. The community's books were then returned to the administrator for correction.[46]

Tensún had sold some large plots to cover the costs of the survey. One lot of 45 hectares was sold to Felipe Velázquez for 100 pesos in 1886. Tensún claimed to have settled on a low price because Velázquez had already bought individual possession rights from two-thirds of the possessors.[47] The *comuneros* titled by Tensún were receiving plots that averaged 3.6 hectares. There was more variation in the distribution of lots than in Dolores, but the average was almost the same. Most plots were valued at 1–2 pesos per *manzana*.[48]

After Tensún's removal, the new partition administrator encountered the usual difficulties. He complained to the president's office that many people would file suit instead of purchasing their lands or paying for their improvements by the partitioner. Other peasants, he warned, were without sufficient land—although the desperate rhetoric was not new to him. He asked the president to allow the community to pay these tenants (probably mostly non-*comuneros*) for their improvements and to free the lands they rented for distribution. To make things worse, Tensún still had not delivered the record books and accounts,[49] so by 1890 the new administrator had not finished the work. In May Cruz Shupán, a respected community leader, petitioned the president's office for a surveyor. The governor explained:

> For some time, the administrators and partitioners of the communities of Dolores and Asunción Izalco have been unable to finish the distribution of lands, because although they have tried to carry it out various times it has only led to new difficulties because the practitioners end their terms at the end of the year and those who substitute them redistribute the lands that their predecessors have already assigned. Because of this, the governorship constantly receives complaints from those who are damaged by loss of a plot that they had already been assigned by the previous practitioner. All of this requires the president's office to name a surveyor who will decide on the lots and thus avoid divisions and conflicts between the members of the communities. To carry out this process with order and formality, I offer myself to assist in whatever way the president's office decides is best.

The government approved the request and designated Carlos Castro as the surveyor.[50]

In this same town a difficult question emerged in 1891 when the members wanted to elect, as in Chalatenango, its regular administrator and assistants—as they had done before the abolition. Cruz Shupán, who had served as partition administrator, complained to the governor that Indians of the former community were meeting and organizing a new leadership, which was expressly prohibited by law. He asked the governor to stop the meetings and the collection of monetary contributions. The mayor reported that some Indian leaders had met several times to discuss whether to elect "community mayor and council members . . . as they call them" who would oversee the community's *cofradías*, but he did not think that this threatened public order.[51]

However, Cruz Shupán was also busy petitioning the president's office to defend the communal lands against those Ladinos and outsiders who were interested in appropriating portions of it, while justifying their actions as answering the need to expand the country's agriculture:

> All of those signed below . . . all indigenous *comuneros* of Asunción Izalco, come to you, Mr. President, with humility to declare that . . . the decree of the National Assembly regarding outside influence upon us Indians . . . is not just . . . that these whom we refer to managed maliciously to trick the president's office by referring to the lack of growth of agriculture due to the lack of land in which to form their plantings. It is true, we don't deny it, that in a country as civilized as our sacred Salvadoran republic, needs to be made great and that this comes from agriculture; but this growth must come through legal means; not as those who are interested in our ancient communal lands intend to do, the Ladinos who are occupying large portions of our lands. . . . It is not our desire, Mr. President, to contravene in the rulings of such a supreme power, but we do hope your office will not act in accordance with this decree because our interests would be damaged and it would not protect our weak masses. . . . [We want] a legal partition as ordered by the decree of February 23, '81, that the partition of community lands will be done by a partitioning judge selected among the most respected members of the community, together with a surveyor, so that without any bias they will give each one the plot of land that is fairly his. . . . To you, Mr. Constitutional President of our republic, we ask and beg humbly, knowing your vast power, that you will put an end to this ancient and persistent suffering.[52]

This eloquent request both accepted and challenged the rules and terms of the partition as established by the government. It is ample evidence that Izalco's peasant Indians not only understood the process and goals of the privatization but also could articulate alternative or critical visions of the process. This petition had 234 signatures, and was (as usual) forwarded to the Ministry of the Interior, apparently without comment. (In 1893 Shupán had to request payment for debts he had incurred as administrator and partition judge, including $600 paid to the surveyor and $290 to the community's legal representative in San Salvador.)[53]

Yet the results of these requests are not clear. In 1894 *comuneros* from Asunción requested the partition of 90 hectares of land that had gone undivided and were now considered national property. There was also a standing request from 1892 to the Ministry of the Interior that previous titles from 1887 be validated and that all undivided lands be distributed. The governor confirmed that the lands in question had not been divided, that many titles remained unofficial, and that other lands had not been distributed.[54] He supported the request for a survey and partition.[55] In 1896 the governor reported that the communities of Izalco had not abided by the 1891 abolition of communities and that they constantly held meetings in which they discussed questions of land distribution and sometimes took land away from *comuneros*. Many members of the community had complained about this. The community had named a mayor, "as if the law of communities was still active."[56] This year 34 *comuneros* of Asunción requested approval of their election of Santiago Cuciste as administrator to finish dividing their lands. The petition was signed by Juan Zaña, the Indian mayor. But the government rejected this petition with the perverse logic that communities had been abolished and could therefore not elect administrators.

The conflicts surrounding a farm owned by Dolores Cuellar, a community member, suggest the internal dynamics of the partition process in Asunción Izalco. In 1893 Cuellar requested the court-ordered eviction of some peasants whom she called tenants on her lands. Some of the so-called usurpers claimed the land as theirs, while others asserted that Gen. Castillo Mora—who owned a claim to debts incurred by Cuellar's deceased husband—had allowed them to use the land. Those who claimed ownership argued that Cuellar could not prove she owned the lands and that under current agrarian law they could not be expelled. They showed titles given to them by the former community administrator. When the mayor refused to hear an appeal, they appealed directly to the governor and the president.[57] In their complaint, the *comuneros* said they had received their titles in 1887 and had planted their plots with cane, beans, and plantains. Their titles, like many others granted by the community administrator, had not been fully validated. They requested that the government validate their titles, together with those of 70 other *comuneros*. They sent former administrator Cruz Shupán to ask the governor to intervene on behalf of the 60 people Cuellar wanted to expel. Finally, an appeals court decided that they had no claim because communities had been abolished.[58]

An 1895 document clarifies this dispute. Dolores Cuellar received control of the lands in question on the death of her husband, Romualdo, who with his family had developed valuable commercial farms on Izalco's community lands. Romualdo had borrowed 2,000 pesos in 1877 from María Salguero, putting up as collateral his sugar cane farm of 180 hectares valued at around 10,000 pesos, including equipment and a mill. When Romualdo either defaulted or died before repaying, Salguero demanded that the farm be sold to cover the debt. The community declared that the lands and equipment were communal property and thus could not be sold, for the mortgage contract was illegal, and accused Romualdo of not paying his rent as a community tenant. Salguero could not be repaid with lands that had never belonged to Romualdo. This led to an auction of the improvements on the land. Jesús Portillo then purchased the claim for 5,000 pesos from Abraham Castillo Mora, who had in turn purchased Salguero's claim in 1884. Unable to take possession or sell the lands, Portillo then asked to become a *comunero*: if the lands in question were to be considered communal and if the decree allowed possessors to title (not purchase) communal lands in Izalco, then he could stake a claim for them.

As it turns out, the *comuneros* whom Cuellar had tried to evict were still in possession in 1895. The community's claim was rejected; although its legal ownership of the lands was acknowledged, *comuneros* could not exercise possession. The final ruling excluded the lands from the 1895 decree that could have allowed the current occupants to title the lands, but at the same time left the door open for judicial action on behalf of the possessors and against Portillo's claim.[59]

While the community of Dolores and Asunción had many internal conflicts, local entrepreneurs who had rented portions of the land were also involved. Besides the neighboring landowners who might be interested in extending or contesting Indian interpretations of boundary markers or plot maps, local officials, lawyers, and military officers attempted to take advantage of the process. Farmers and *hacendados* from Izalco and Sonsonate, such as Benigno Barrientos, Domingo Arce, Wenceslao Herrera, and General Carlos Zepeda, were among the tenants.[60] In 1889 the administrator received permission from the Ministry of the Interior to expel all the tenants from communal plots, but apparently some continued to press claims for the lands they occupied.[61]

One tenant was Ruperto Machado, a local farmer described both as a lawyer and a scribe who while representing the community of Dolores also benefited from the sale of plots. (Machado was also involved in unsuccessful land-related legal conflicts with peasants in Cuisnahuat in 1886.)[62] In 1885 Simeón Morán paid him 200 pesos for representing the community in legal proceedings in San Salvador.[63] Morán was also accused of selling or giving Machado at least 90 hectares of land.[64] However, Machado claimed that the titles allowing him to lease part of Izalco's land constituted a sale, and that the previous partitioner had rented him these lands in 1880. In the confusion and constant contestation of the privatization process, it is very likely that men like Machado and other tenants kept portions of the lands they had been renting.[65]

## Indians in a Ladino Municipality: Privatization in Juayua

The privatization of community lands in Juayua went differently. Juayua's communal lands had come under municipal control before the privatization decree, and its Indian community had become weaker and more marginal to local and national politics than the communities of Izalco and Nahuizalco. Its lands were smaller and did not include large unused tracts. The community of Juayua had been formally abolished after a local revolt against the Ladinos in 1873, and revenues from its lands went to the town. But while the Indians did not lose their farms, some of the (mostly Ladino) tenants who rented plots gained ownership because they were allowed to title them as if they were part of the *ejidos*.[66] Since 1862 Juayua's Indian community had been losing ground to local Ladino peasants, farmers, and merchants. By the late 1860s its unused lands were firmly under Ladino and municipal control. Portions were rented out to Ladinos who developed coffee farms and eventually gained ownership.[67] The Juayua Indian community was clearly more dependent on the town because of earlier municipal control over the communal lands.

In 1881 President Zaldívar suspended the partition process in Juayua and Nahuizalco for fear of revolt.[68] In 1883, however, a survey was conducted to separate the communal lands from the *ejidos* so that possessors could claim their lands according to the different types of usage.[69] As elsewhere, the partitioning of this plot involved internal divisions. The partitioners accused town officials and other *comuneros* of "serving themselves with a large spoon" and allegedly intending to sell part of the land to Ladinos. In 1885 some *comuneros* from Juayua complained to the president's office that a former mayor named Gabino Mata (later identified as a Ladino, although his family belonged to the Indian community), was keeping them from partitioning a large plot known as Los Cañales by threatening them with jail if they continued.[70]

Although most of the former communal lands had been already titled by *comuneros*, an extensive grazing ground had been rented to the Salaverría family since 1877. (The land was rented at 2,000 pesos for 5 years, indicating how profitable cattle raising could be even for a family and a region that were starting to specialize in coffee production.) Despite the family's attempts in 1882 to title these lands as *ejidos*, the municipality and governor, Nazario Salaverría, decided it was illegal to sell them to a tenant. They had "become poor because of the legal disputes over land," they said, and asked the president to order the mayor to help them divide and title their lands. They asked for the release of a *comunero* who had supposedly been jailed by order of the governor.[71]

As a result, the municipality called for the sale of this plot to local peasants.[72] The mayor explained that the plaintiffs had been offered plots, but they had refused them. He also insisted that no lands had been sold to Ladinos, although one plot had been rented to a Ladino.[73] The governor himself protested to the ministry that he knew nothing of threats by local officials against the Indians and had personally offered to resolve their disputes.[74] This dispute and others led to a meeting between the town secretary and councilmen who were Indians. They were satisfied with the neutrality and fairness of the current mayor, Adolfo Cea, but they wanted the return of lands held by Gabino Mata and Apolinario

Magaña.[75] Four years later, Gabino Mata, by then mayor of Juayua, asked the ministry for permission to offer titles to Los Cañales, since Juayua needed money for a new town hall.[76] A new request was filed in 1892, this time by a new municipality led by Cea, and the governor again supported it.[77] A government decree that year finally rejected the petition for titling but allowed Los Cañales to be sold to possessors or auctioned, which implied that the lands had not formally belonged to the Indian community.[78] Ironically, in 1895 the municipality had still not received the funds from the titling, which had gone directly to the local internal customs office, and it appealed to the ministry for payment.[79] In the end the partition of Los Cañales resulted in the formation of 97 titled plots, most of them owned by ex-*comuneros*. The average cost was 8 pesos (with a range of 9 to 30 pesos), much less than the $50 recommended by the decree. Thus most plots were small, probably less than 2 hectares.[80]

## A Successful Ladino Community: The Privatization in Chalchuapa

The Ladinos of Chalchuapa encountered similar difficulties. In 1883 the Ministry of the Interior announced that the community of Chalchuapa had ceased to exist and that the possessors of communal lands had all received their titles. Nevertheless, in 1891 many *comuneros* took advantage of a recent decree that abolished any communities that had survived the 1881 law in order to title their plots.[81] In 1892, 135 *comuneros* who resided in El Ranchador, a large plot that had been part of the town's communal lands, requested titles. Their lands had already been surveyed and divided after 1889, when they were authorized to sell the 403 hectares of the farm to possessors.[82] That same year another petition by 97 *comuneros* from both El Ranchador and Sitio del Niño (another large plot) requested titles to 270 hectares that had come from lands owned by the *cofradía* San José de Chalchuapa. These lands were measured by Francisco Cáceres and were approved by the governor of Santa Ana.[83]

In response to a claim filed by Teodoro Mendoza denouncing the Sitio del Niño lands as *baldíos*, in 1893 the Ministry of the Interior reviewed the status of the lands and issued a decree: they had been communal and were now national property. The lands used to belong to the hacienda "Comecayo" but had been sold in 1780 to the Común de Chalchuapa. After a trial in 1824, the questioned lands were left to the community until the hacienda's missing titles reappeared. Portions of these lands remained undivided and were communal but had not been titled. The governor of Santa Ana was authorized to sell the already distributed plots to the possessors, while the undistributed and unused parts would be sold at public auction as a whole or in lots. The money would be used to construct a new theater in Santa Ana City.[84]

However, in 1893 two large landowners opposed the titling of two plots within the lands possessed and claimed by the former *comuneros*. Doña Petrona de Regalado opposed the titling of lot no. 177, composed of 14 hectares, claiming that it (and a few others) were part of the hacienda "Ayuta." She called for a hearing to solve the dispute. Another wealthy landowner, Alfredo Schlesinger, opposed the titling of plot no. 167, claiming that its 18 hectares had been his since 1882 when he titled them as *ejidos*. He also asked for a hearing. The governor found against both landowners and fined them 15 pesos each for obstructing the division process.

Yet Governor Preza was not entirely sympathetic to the peasants of Chalchuapa, and 21 peasants filed a complaint against him in 1894. Like so many others, they were from other towns but had resided on Chalchuapa's communal lands for decades. They accused the governor of destroying their previous petition for titles and of threatening them with imprisonment. They had seen notices in the official newspaper for the titling of lands they considered their own and wanted to register their opposition within the stipulated period of 15 days. De Regalado continued to complain that lands from her hacienda had been appropriated in the survey and titling of El Ranchador and that those who had titled these lands had not possessed them until after the division was carried out by Cáceres.[85]

Another group of peasants representing 50 families and more than 300 people presented a complaint in 1894. They protested the nationalization of 270 hectares (discussed above) that had come from lands owned by a *cofradía,* and which their families had possessed for 40 years, because they were not divided in 1880–1882. The lands were claimed by petitioners, measured, and mapped into lots, but a local resident and her son attempted to take these lands on the basis of a prior request. Similarly, 124 individuals who possessed lands in Sitio del Niño accused the governor of preventing the titling of lands within the stipulated time frame so that Teodoro Mendoza could "denounce" them as a *baldío* and then sell them to the mayor.

Yet another petition by 76 residents of El Ranchador to the Ministry of the Interior in 1894 charged that they had carried out three surveys at a cost of 12,000 pesos under three different presidents without obtaining titles to their lands. When they finally received the titles, they were taken for revision by the governor and then sent to the president for approval. They requested the return of their titles, pointing out that they planted mostly sugar and coffee—valuable export crops promoted by the government.

An earlier attempt to attach these lands came in 1887 when Anselma Linares de Arcia and her daughters requested the "judiciary" sale of the hacienda "Comecayo," presumably for debts. The real goal was to attach the lands of the Ladino community. (She had made a similar request in 1876.)[86] When the original titles of the community and *cofradías* were examined, the demand was rejected. This attempt followed a proposal in the 1860s to have these lands declared *baldíos*. Another such request was filed by tenants of the hacienda "Comecayo," but was also rejected.

In general, the division and titling of the larger communal lands of Chalchuapa was a fragmented process in which the commune had no centralized representation. This may be explained by Chalchuapa's economic success and reliance upon intensive coffee and sugar production. A plethora of requests for land by small, sometimes overlapping groups of peasants had begun in the 1880s. Questions relating to the titles and status of the communal lands continued into the 1890s.

At the end of this drawn-out process, the ministry provided an ambiguous (and astounding) interpretation of the criss-crossing claims and complaints regarding the lands of El Ranchador. Apparently, 427 hectares were within the 2,925 hectares of the hacienda "Comecayo." These had been sold to a *cofradía* in Chalchuapa, but in the early nineteenth century a conflict emerged over 180 hectares of the land. Since the hacienda's titles had been lost or the claim by the new owners was spurious, the lands were left in possession of the *cofradía* until new evidence emerged. As a result, the ministry concluded that the lands were neither communal nor municipal nor *baldíos* but belonged to the church, since the 1835 transaction that gave the community control was not legal. The church, seldom a participant in processes of this kind, surprisingly found itself favored by the government's ruling. We do not know the practical result for either the peasant possessors, the church, or other claimants. A similar ruling was made on other parts of the lands that the Chalchuapa Ladino community had held for over a century.[87]

The fate of the hundreds of peasants who possessed lands in these parts is not clear. In Chalchuapa in particular, most of those in possession of plots had been tenants of the Ladino community, which had progressively enlarged its holdings and had rented to outsiders since the early nineteenth century. Given the extent of Chalchuapa's communal lands, the decades of possession, and the purchase of new tracts, probably few peasants lost access to their lands. The reams of titles for farms in Chalchuapa's municipal archive tend to confirm this. But if legal documentation was nonexistent or ambiguous, or when community lands bordered on haciendas, or if substantial portions had been rented to "outside" farmers and peasants, conflicts and disputes emerged and sometimes led to the dispossession of peasants.

## Conclusion: Privatization, Peasantization, and the Decline of Ethnic Communal Solidarity

There is no doubt that the privatization of community lands weakened the internal organization and coherence of ethnic peasant communities. Both the economic and the ideological functions of these communities faced serious challenges after individuals titled their plots and did not have to rely on any corporate organization for access to land. Many towns continued to have large indigenous populations and even community organizations, but after the dissolution of community landholding these institutions and practices became more diffuse. Other forces acted to preserve ideologies and community practices for some. In some cases they enabled an Indian elite to hold on to local power, but with a much reduced power base. Elsewhere, maintaining common lands for grazing or wood extraction provided a continuing basis for communal practices and ideologies. In yet other localities Indian identity became more individualized and entirely detached from any form of corporate organization. Overall, however, a hardened oppositional identity became the marker of Indianness—an identity wrapped in the memory and history of loss, or at least by strong resentment toward those perceived as Ladinos. Many Indian leaders continued to provide access to local networks of support and patronage.

Most possessors of community lands were able to title their plots despite obstacles. Many sold their plots, perhaps hoping or expecting to claim new ones. The privatization of farms on municipal *ejidos* was much less problematic because it was not mediated by an ethnic or corporate institution whose legal status, titles, and legitimacy were constantly challenged from the outside and subject to internal problems. Because corporate representation had been institutionalized for ethnic groups, communities became dependent on government supervision, approval, and direction, thus reinforcing the tendency for litigious action that emerged in the colonial period and was carried into the republican era. While the original problems associated with communal and *ejido* land use had little to do with the development of agrarian capitalism per se, the resolution of these problems intersected with the demands of those promoting commercial production, especially for export. Populist expectations from provincial landowners and merchants also played a role in the process. The goal of creating a nation of smallholders and a "rural middle class" was wrought with contradictions and was ultimately impossible, given the conditions inherited from the colony and the nation's own changing landscape at the end of the century. The legacy of this attempt, its failures and successes, together with the country's reactivated haciendas, laid the basis for the next fifty years of agrarian change.

However, communities were autonomous political actors that participated in wider struggles than those concerning land or property. Similarly, the ethnic and communal identification of some groups, while weakened and dissolved in some regions, was strengthened, even if made more marginal to national politics by the turn of the century. Indian identity, while tied to communal landowning, transcended the nineteenth-century institution and in some respects became independent of material forces. Thus in places like Izalco, Nahuizalco, and other municipalities of the west, center, and center-south, Indian identity and organization survived the problems associated with the partition of communal lands. In other places where ethnic identification was less important than village-based ties, a strong sense of peasant communalism persisted, partially because of the continued ties to land created by privatization. This communalism, yet again transformed and redefined, was evident in the 1970s, when the peasant movement surged, and in the 1980s, when a popular insurgency engulfed many parts of the country.

Most observers have emphasized the impositions of outsiders, especially of the coffee-growing elite, in affecting the privatization of community lands. The research presented here demonstrates that conflicts associated with the abolition of communities were far more diverse than those found in classic interpretations of the so-called liberal reforms. While some violence did occur, the process was not a violent land grab by elite landowners. It was a multilayered process that more or less followed legally sanctioned, if often confusing, guidelines. Even when lands were lost to outsiders and violence broke out, the lines between oligarchs and Indian peasants were never clear.

A better explanation for the absence of major peasant revolts in El Salvador after the 1890s is the concatenated decline of peasant community and the consolidation of a freeholding landed peasantry—although the growing centralization and autonomy of the national state also contributed. Conflicts became more individualized or were channeled through personalist or party-based alliances, but the military did not play a significant role, and elections, patronage, and clientelism became the key forms of the transfer of power. (After the privatization, conflicts over land became more violent as ownership became less collective.) It was not until the mid-1920s that increased commercial production based on a liberal-oligarchic model dramatically increased the pressure on many peasants and rural workers, contributing to the labor organizing and political realignments of the 1927–1931 period.

It is not surprising that the only known cases of ethnic communities that served as political factions were in the west, where autonomous agrarian and political community practices had been strongest but where peasants, Indians and Ladino alike, experienced a more concentrated version of the social and political changes wrought in the 1920s. But in both cases, the character of political involvement was drastically different from nineteenth-century mobilization. In the case of the mass organizations known as the Red Leagues (Ligas Rojas) of the 1910s and early 1920s, the Indian communities of western and central El Salvador were subordinated to the clientelist political machines of the country's oligarchic paternalism.[88] And in the 1932 revolt the communities could not draw on their previous political and military clout to pull off a confrontation with a stronger central state controlled by a professional and well-armed military that no longer relied on local bases of power and alliances, much less peasant militias, to determine the balance of power.[89]

# 9 Conclusion

## LAND, CLASS FORMATION, AND
## THE STATE IN SALVADORAN HISTORY

In the colonial period, El Salvador's Indian and Ladino peasant communities were economically secure and active in local and export markets. Peasant communities produced indigo successfully and generally managed to coexist with larger indigo producers. More than half of the indigo crop was cultivated and processed by small and midsize producers, most of whom relied on communal and municipal forms of land tenure and often communal forms of production as well. These peasant communities provided a basis for subsistence farming and solidarity by enabling their members to title lands and develop diverse patterns of land use and agricultural production. Most of these communities acquired lands by grant or purchase in the late eighteenth century, a period of population growth and increased commercial activity. Through corporate organization, they were also able to limit the exactions placed on them by local and Guatemalan landowners, merchants, and state officials. Assured access to land and production for the commercial market gave them great autonomy—although Indian communities had to manage the burdens placed on them directly by the colonial state.

From the time of El Salvador's independence from Spain until 1880, peasant landholding and communal social organization and land tenure continued to expand. At the same time, haciendas declined as viable units of production. The collapse of the colonial state, frequent wars, political instability, and peasant insurgency all contributed to the disruption of elite networks after independence. The systems of credit, labor drafts, taxation, and marketing that had enabled the elite to prosper in the export economy collapsed. The effects of economic decline were felt by creole entrepreneurs, especially the more distant Guatemalan elite. Salvadoran landowners and merchants had only local government to rely on as allies for much of the nineteenth century—a period when increased peasant and community mobilization limited their power.

Until the 1880s boundary disputes between communities and haciendas had been infrequent and there was little competition or conflict over unclaimed lands. Until the end of the century, most hacienda land was not used productively. Because of problems with access to labor, capital, and markets, hacienda production of indigo had decreased sharply since independence. Many landowners were heavily in debt, and some even abandoned their properties. An additional problem for large landowners was the absence of a strong and stable central government to support them in local disputes or to help them make structural improvements. The political and military strength of the peasantry at the local level often gave peasant communities an advantage in land disputes. Some municipalities and communities even purchased haciendas or simply claimed them by right of continued possession.

As a result of the decline of haciendas, expanding population, and political pressure from below, common forms of land tenure became even more important between the 1820s and 1870s. After the 1830s, the state recognized two forms of common land tenure: municipal *ejidos* and lands owned by corporate bodies or communities. Although these were usually separate, in some towns dominated by an ethnic majority, communal lands and *ejidos* were administered as if they were one.

Both liberal and conservative regimes recognized peasants' right to subsistence by sanctioning these two forms of land tenure. The various military factions that controlled the state supported the legal status of common lands and allowed or encouraged their expansion. Liberal republicans of the early nineteenth century, midcentury "conservatives," and the more pragmatic liberals of the 1860s and 1870s all supported municipal and community access to land. Furthermore, the reliance on community-controlled resources made these two forms of common land tenure a fundamental element of Salvadoran peasant life. By the 1860s they had become the dominant feature of the agrarian landscape.

Communities not only were legal landholding bodies, but also controlled access to irrigation systems, set aside land for crop rotation, and protected wooded areas and common grazing lands. They fostered local ethnic and political identities and the defense of local interests, along with forming broader regional or national political alliances. The expansion and institutionalization of common forms of land tenure in these decades not only assured peasant access to subsistence resources, but also nurtured more complex forms of commercial production and political activity. The system even gave many town-dwelling Salvadorans access to land.

Yet community landholding also created significant problems. Emerging internal differentiation and the growth of communities created tensions between Indians and Ladinos. The system relied on local solidarities and administration to organize the use of resources. Communal land use and community organization were never fully democratic or egalitarian, and in the context of expanding market participation, the possibilities for local conflict increased. Peasants' reliance on community or municipal lands exacerbated competition. The increasing use of communal lands by artisans and farmers, and even professionals, also brought tensions.

These bodies had lost some of the corporate privileges and legal protections they had during the colony. A contradiction emerged after independence between community control of land in a context where other corporate privileges, such as the legal and administrative systems of the colonial period, were no longer recognized. A growing commercial economy contributed to economic differentiation among peasant producers, while giving exclusive bodies a monopoly over important resources caused friction with migrating Ladinos and urban entrepreneurs in search of land.

The successes and limitations of the common lands that developed with this system varied greatly across regions. Generalizations are impossible for the entire country because of this diversity. Variations in local practices frustrated the government's attempts to regulate land use, and these differences forced local officials to deal with a complex maze of legal prescriptions, local cultures, and varied patterns of land use at a time when El Salvador was undergoing rapid socioeconomic change. Administrative and political conflicts aroused by the application of national and policies in differing local contexts caused additional problems.

## Peasant Politics and State Formation

Any examination of the history of communities and the peasantry must go beyond questions of land and agriculture. Peasants and artisans played an integral role in nineteenth-century political processes. Peasant communities, especially indigenous groups, were important sources of support for elite factions in their battles for control of the state. Because national state structures were weak before the 1880s, contenders for power needed popular support. The relationship between peasant communities and national factional struggles, together with local agrarian conditions, influenced political and social mobilization. Peasants and artisans had mobilized independently and established important alliances with other social sectors since before independence. They had participated in pro-independence conspiracies during the 1810s, peasant militias had allied themselves with elite political leaders, Indians had revolted against Ladinos, and factional conflicts within communities had broken out during the partition of communal lands.

Conflicts over local issues usually predisposed peasant communities or smaller factions to take certain kinds of action, but the possibility of forging alliances and their success or failure depended on other forces. Landed and communally based peasants were able to mobilize and ally themselves with factional leaders not only to defend their immediate material interests, but also to establish strategic political and ethnic alliances that often transcended the borders of the Salvadoran state.

In El Salvador the so-called liberal revolution of 1871 was not an abrupt rupture of state policies or ideology—not even of political procedure. If we compare, for example, the governments of Francisco Dueñas (1863–1871) and his "liberal" successor, Santiago González (1871–1876), there is little difference in state administration, political participation, local support, economic policy, promotion of exports, and so forth. (Dueñas is often presented as a conservative, but his formal allegiances, ideological posturing, and policies were liberal.) Salvadoran political factions and parties were always weak, inconsistent, and pragmatic, and they usually professed a vague liberalism. The distinction between liberals and conservatives had to do more with concrete factional struggles and posturing in relation to larger isthmian politics. The events of 1871 do not represent the sudden capture of the state by one particular class or class fraction. More than anything, it was a continued string of alliances and interventions involving Guatemala and its local allies—a dense web of struggles and alliances that no historian has yet been able to unravel.

The national state was not the best institution from which to form and strengthen an economic oligarchy. Most presidents and their principal officers lost the property they had accumulated during their rule—that is, new rulers exiled or killed their predecessors and expropriated their farms, while using their position to acquire properties for themselves. Government officials also took care of the president's agricultural enterprises later in the century. If anything, national power served more to protect racketeering for unstable, competitive, and factionalized political elites, most of whom began as military officers and maintained their power on that basis.[1] Most wealthy Salvadorans were busy with their investments, and few were compelled to participate in the politics of the military caudillos. Those landlords or capitalists who have been cited as evidence of the oligarchy's control of the state actually experienced the opposite trajectory by the 1880s—men who started off as military officers became involved in factional politics and used this power to succeed in agricultural production. This applies to many in the economic oligarchy. Members of the Gallardo, Salaverría, Regalado, Menéndez, Guirola families and others were high-ranking military officers in the late nineteenth century.

The 1880s and 1890s represent a period of transition to a more successful centralizing project still led by diffuse and shifting alliances among the fragmented political class, the military, and the economic elite—all complicated and made unstable by continued contestation from below and by larger Central American interventionism. By 1900 the country had a stronger central state, built upon a few new pillars: (1) the virtual dissolution of corporate and municipal power centers, (2) the creation of a centrally controlled professional army (ending the reliance on militias),

(3) top-level political and economic negotiation and alliances unmediated by local power centers, and (4) the cumulative benefits of successful state institutions themselves (taxation, finance, infrastructure, repression, law, and communications). The Araujo regime of 1911–1913 epitomizes the consolidation of this trend because of its significant reform of the state and the country's political institutions. But this did not entail, as many have argued, the violent subordination of peasants, their dispossession or proletarianization, or their entrapment in a sort of Foucaldian social prison.[2]

## Coffee and the Expansion of the Commercial Economy

After the 1860s the agrarian landscape became more complex as an increasing number of people produced goods and crops for local, regional, and foreign markets. Even before independence, El Salvador had the highest level of peasant and community participation in Central America in markets involving cacao, cattle, and indigo, including an extensive system of commercial fairs. Agricultural production expanded as idle lands were slowly incorporated by larger landowners; farms were developed on municipal and community lands by entrepreneurs and small-scale producers; peasants became more involved in export production; Indians became entrepreneurs, both communally and individually; and an investment sector emerged, led by merchants, many of them immigrants. The coffee economy expanded, along with balsam extraction, cattle raising, and the manufacture of cigars, textiles, hats, and liquor. Other products, such as silver, sugar, rice, rubber, and hides, became important exports. Some of the expansion was promoted by state policies, including the distribution of trees, seeds, and knowledge to agrarian producers of all classes; export and import incentives; road building; and other infrastructural investments.

Commercial expansion was the product of many forces between the 1850s and the 1880s, including the U.S. Civil War, expansion of Pacific steamship services, the California gold rush, and the opening of the Panama Railroad. Market production responded to the complex interaction of local conditions with the improved access to new markets. But because of the diffuse and regionally circumscribed character of these undertakings, these "engines" of commercialization were incipient and vulnerable to the vagaries of foreign markets and local conditions. Not until the early twentieth century did these trends become a more unified form of agrarian capitalism that began to consolidate markets for land and labor—a process tied to the emergence of a distinct but still heterogeneous agrarian bourgeoisie.

Within the coffee sector—the strongest, most successful part of this emerging commercial economy—the concentration of production that developed in the twentieth century was not characteristic of this earlier period. In many municipalities many peasants were growing small amounts of coffee by the 1880s, while other areas were altogether dominated by smaller coffee farms. Typically, most localities had some combination of estate, peasant, and farmer-based coffee growing. The proliferation of small-scale processing equipment before the 1890s facilitated this mixed pattern of settlement and enabled at least some small producers to raise the value of their beans before they sold them to merchants or larger growers. For these small producers, the principal challenge was not competition over land but the risks involved in participating in the commercial economy. They were vulnerable to losing their lands if a sudden decline in the price of coffee prevented them from paying their debts to merchants or other grower-processors.

Combined with the development of the agrarian economy, the export sector also benefited an emerging class of capitalist entrepreneurs who typically combined different forms of investment. The most successful ones controlled the processing, marketing, and export of coffee, rather than production. This set them apart from a wider and more diverse sector of agriculturists who depended on them for access to credit and markets. However, while the Salvadoran economy between the 1920s and the 1970s was marked by an extreme concentration of land, capital, and wealth in the hands of a small elite, it is fallacious to project these traits backward in time. The economic elites of the 1860–1917 period had their own character. For the incipient Salvadoran landowning and export bourgeoisie at the turn of the century, coffee was the principal but not the sole source of wealth and accumulation. Many other activities were important to the formation of this class: cattle raising, cane growing, sugar and liquor production, balsam export, the import trade, and even speculation with the national debt. Furthermore, important middle sectors coexisted with and benefited from the emerging agro-export economy.

This complexity of internal markets is reflected in the use of railroads. Whereas rail construction in Central America has been associated with export production and foreign capital, in El Salvador the situation was more complex. While coffee gave rail bulding an initial impetus and guaranteed a minimum level of use, by the 1920s an east-west rail line had integrated much of El Salvador's territory, leaving coffee as one of various products carried to market. In 1913 coffee constituted only 20 percent of the gross tonnage; sugar accounted for 8 percent, and other food and manufactured products 72 percent.[3]

The more advanced mechanized mills that brought coffee production to the industrial stage developed slowly but were in place by the first decade of the twentieth century. They allowed the upper echelons of the landowning elite and their merchant counterparts to tap an increasing share of the revenue from the export economy by controlling credit and marketing. After the 1920s this also facilitated their control of land when indebted farmers lost their mortgaged farms to them. This emerging concentration of processing and credit in the early twentieth century also began to direct part of the profits, but not the risks, to those who could invest in modern *beneficios* and their own export ventures.

Until the 1920s coffee production was a very regionally circumscribed activity, occupying less than 60,000 hectares of land. While at least half of the country's departments had some part in coffee production, coffee trees were concentrated in certain areas of just three departments. Thus large sectors of the population were at first unaffected by the expanding coffee economy. The expansion of agro-export activities did not adversely affect regions of older settlement, allowing a symbiotic relationship to emerge. Furthermore, many who worked on midsize and larger coffee farms were not only seasonal workers but largely females and immigrants, at first mostly women from Guatemala but later from within El Salvador (this was the first significant kind of wage labor for women outside of food preparation and some artisanal activities). The remaining laborers, especially after the turn of the century, were both full-time wage workers and seasonal peasant workers. This contradicts the prevailing view that the mobilization of labor in El Salvador's coffee sector required coercive mechanisms.

## The Privatization of Common Lands

Local tensions—especially in the west—between an expanding commercial economy and the limitations and problems inherent in the common land system encouraged the full-scale privatization of common lands after 1879. This process has traditionally been understood as a result of the coffee elite's need for more lands and a landless peasantry ready to sell its labor cheaply. But the case is more complex. By the 1870s the common land system was hindering the development of commercial agriculture for *all* social sectors, for both peasants and members of the elite who had set up their farms on these lands. The system often led to conflicts and arbitrary measures by local and national officials that resulted in the loss of investments. Also, communally owned land could not be used as collateral for loans.

The laws of 1879–1882 only legitimated de facto ownership. In the suburbs of Nueva San Salvador and Santa Ana, where enterprising elites and peasants had developed the most dynamic coffee economies, landholding was secure and virtually private, even though most farms were located in municipal *ejidos*. Therefore, lands that were initially used in the coffee and sugar industries, with a few important exceptions, were not "torn" away from Indian communities, as some historians insist. Instead, in most regions the expansion of coffee production created multiple internal frontiers, developing *baldíos* and forested highlands by means of government concessions or market mechanisms.

In addition to the expansion of coffee production, other forces created additional pressure for privatization. Both elite and plebeian liberals saw the semifeudal ethnic privilege that was intrinsic to the common land system as incompatible with republican forms of sovereignty, citizenship, and property. In its simplest formulation, equal citizens should not have unequal access to material resources and opportunity. This concept was initially consistent with republican support for the common land system, which guaranteed that peasants would have land. However, continued control by peasants, especially Indian communities, of large tracts kept poor Ladino settlers from gaining access to land. Also, many urban entrepreneurs and farmers had established valuable farms on lands they rented from indigenous communities, and these tenants stood to benefit from the security provided by private ownership, even if they had to pay the communities for their lands. Furthermore, some ambitious community members (as well as outside farmers or speculators) looked enviously at their communities' extensive unused lands.

Liberal legislators and state administrators sought to create a layer of entrepreneurial farmers with secure access to land. State administrators hoped that privatizing and distributing common lands among peasants and entrepreneurs would bring more land into production and boost agricultural investment, thus increasing access to land through market mechanisms. Enterprising peasants and farmers, it was hoped, in pursuit of their own interests, would promote the national interest as well—one defined clearly in agrarian and commercial terms. These pressures and contradictions led to the abolition of all forms of common land tenure in 1881 and 1882.

The privatization involved municipal *ejidos,* ethnic communal lands, and state-owned *baldíos.* Many municipalities received additional grants of land that were distributed at low or no cost to residents, especially poorer peasants. Most *ejido* tenants considered the privatization a positive step, since most could now own their plots or farms at low cost and even claim additional lands for later sale. The privatization of most *ejidos* was carried out without major conflicts, but the privatization of Indian and Ladino community lands was more difficult. Communal ownership and the communities themselves were abolished, their lands to be distributed equally among all members, including any unused portions. Costs and revenues from the distribution were also divided, although many large plots were sold to outsiders to cover expenses. This encouraged corrupt dealings and the loss of valuable lands. Some conflicts even led to violence.

Community disentailment met much resistance. Indians believed that their lands were part of a social order inherited from the colony and legitimated by tradition; abolition of their communities was a challenge to their identity and corporate organization. This attitude was compounded by the (well-founded) fear that Ladinos would try to take advantage of the process. Some communities ignored the privatization decree of 1882;

others were riven by preexisting divisions and larger factional alliances that led to violence. For these and other reasons, the privatization of communal lands extended over two and a half decades.

Some Indian communities were the biggest losers in the process, not because their members lost most of their lands to outsiders, but because the primary basis for communal coherence was weakened, either abruptly or in the protracted conflicts of the 1880–1900 period. Altogether, privatization loosened the ties of ethnic solidarity while making ethnic organization increasingly defensive, elitist, and hierarchical. Landowning Indians were more likely to distance themselves socially from Indian peasants who lost access to land and became wage laborers or tenants. Individual landholding also was a centrifugal force, as former *ejidatarios* and community members were free to use their resources without group sanction.

Differentiation among peasants, competition within the peasantry—especially between Indians and Ladinos—and attempts by local officials (especially military officers) to benefit from their local influence were responsible for most of the strictly agrarian conflicts of this period. Most conflicts over land were not caused directly by the expansion of coffee or the privatization of lands alone, but must be understood in the context of larger changes in the agrarian economy as well as local politics.

Privatization extended to state-owned *baldíos* as well, which, because of the nucleated pattern of settlement encouraged by the use of common lands, were very extensive. Possessors of untitled lands and speculators alike were encouraged to stake and title their claims. Vast tracts were sold to claimants, many of whom where urban speculators or investors. *Baldíos* and the remnants from unsold common lands were sold in plots of different sizes, but all at low prices. Possessors were given first right to claim ownership and at times were granted amnesties to facilitate their titling. Old haciendas—many of them vast—were also brought into this process and purchased wholesale or subdivided for new owners. However, most landowners or investors seeking new lands were not driven by the immediate need to expand production but rather by attempts to preempt each other in acquiring portions of a shrinking mass of unused land.

The long-term results of the privatization were more contradictory than legislators expected. As anticipated, thousands of peasants became proprietors, while many entrepreneurs and farmers gained control over their farms and extended their holdings. But the division of lands also froze peasants into differentiated layers, intensifying important differences among them and relegating poorer peasants to plots that would not guarantee their heirs a continued subsistence. As a result of market participation as well as local political events, peasants became highly differentiated within localities, creating a sector of peasants who were vulnerable to losing their lands because of debts to merchants or other landowners. Furthermore, the economic survival of future generations was threatened, as the small farms or plots were divided among family members in the context of a closing agrarian frontier.[4] This combined legacy of a commercially active peasantry with secure but fixed access to land yet increasingly limited opportunities for expansion had important consequences for the period after 1918 when commercial agriculture expanded dramatically.

Altogether, the privatization of *baldíos, ejidos*, and communal lands facilitated the development of commercial agriculture, but this did not mean that land was quickly concentrated in the hands of the export elite. On the contrary, privatization increased the number of property owners and created a large, differentiated class of landowning peasants and farmers. This contradicts the view that the land concentration of the late twentieth century was a direct inheritance from the colonial period or the late nineteenth-century liberal era. Peasant proprietors and their heirs, however, were still vulnerable. The typical plot titled by small-scale producers allowed for subsistence as well as market production, but farms of this size partially laid the basis for the increased *minifundismo* that prevailed by the mid-twentieth century. In a way, the success of the *ejido* and communal land system in providing reasonable access to land created a pattern of intensive land use that made peasants less able to privatize larger, unused plots. The accelerated acquisition of extensive state lands and haciendas in this same period and throughout the country by an emerging elite and by rich peasants and farmers barred poorer peasants from further expansion by virtually closing the agricultural frontier in the first decade of the twentieth century. The inheritance of a successful and dynamic peasantry became within decades the diminishing toe-hold of a minority of peasants whose growing numbers of descendants could only become migrant workers or tenants on other people's lands.

## Implications for the Study of Salvadoran History

Although the continued successes of El Salvador's export economy after the 1860s did not necessarily lead to the impoverishment, marginalization, or proletarianization of most peasants, its intensification in the 1920s had important consequences. After 1920, when population had grown significantly and a new cycle of agro-export production had begun under the aegis an increasingly self-conscious, wealthy, and integrated agrarian elite, more and more peasant families had to subdivide their plots or send family members out to work as seasonal laborers or tenant farmers to make ends meet.[5] As a result, during the 1920s permanent proletarianization—as opposed to occasional participation in the labor market—increased more rapidly because of the closing of internal agricultural frontiers and the increased demand for labor. But proletarianization was still a gradual process and generally not characterized by coercion or direct state intervention.

Furthermore, the somewhat vulnerable and besieged midsize commercial farmers who had survived privatization, notably the trend toward concentration and dispossession, provided a fertile recruiting ground for support for authoritarian politics in the 1930s. The wealthy merchants and landowners had no alternative political project to propose—they had never participated very much in the country's political affairs, instead passively supporting the defensive transformation of the state and social policies by new military rulers and their civilian allies in the rural and urban middle sectors. A policy of maintaining the primacy of coffee at any social cost, including placing intentional limits on manufacturing investments and other potentially competing agrarian interests in the 1930s, gave the country's farmers and larger landowners a degree of state-supported stability, while it also helped to consolidate the antidemocratic alliance. This policy, maintained through the boom and bust cycles of the 1920s, was institutionalized during the 1930s transition. Felix Choussy, an agronomer and government official closely identified with the coffee economy, formulated this perspective most clearly, including opposition to urbanization.[6] During these years many peasants—not yet a majority, but a growing population sector—became directly dependent on large landowners as tenants. This trend contributed to the privatization of power in rural areas and facilitated the militarization of the Salvadoran state that began during the Hernández Martinez regime of the 1930s. Middle and large-scale landowners sought in the state a strong partner who could enforce labor and land contracts in the countryside.

Other structural features characteristic of mid-twentieth-century Salvadoran society and economy began to appear in the 1920s. The production of coffee doubled during the decade, just as other commercial, elite-controlled agricultural investments also boomed. Production, processing, and landowning in general became more concentrated with the powerful market crises of 1921 and 1929–1932, leaving many peasants landless or in debt. Furthermore, the failure to seek alternatives to the mono-export coffee economy after these crises began a pattern of state-society relations in which the agro-export producers and merchants held a form of veto power over state policies. The enduring reliance on coffee (and cotton after the 1950s), regardless of the social cost, left many peasants and farmers marginalized from both participating in the export economy and benefiting from the state's social and economic policies. The process of technological modernization and economic growth that began after World War II only exacerbated this trend, setting up some of the conditions for the peasant insurgency of the 1980s.

Other processes that culminated in this period contributed to the failure of liberal and radical reformers to consolidate an antiauthoritarian coalition after their successes of the late 1920s. Throughout the nation, Indian and peasant communities were weakened greatly by privatization, and even localities that were able to maintain forms of ethnic communal solidarity and identity into the 1930s were increasingly marginalized from national politics. In places like Izalco and Nahuizalco, smaller Indian communes continued to exist on the basis of Indian landownership and community hierarchies. Here Indian communes played a role as local clients of national political elites. But the 1932 revolt signaled the final breakdown of this sort of clientelistic alliance that consolidated in the 1920s but had deep roots in the nineteenth century. The level of repression unleashed against the peasant population after their attempt to seize control of the region demonstrated the intense contempt of certain white and Ladino elites and middle sectors who had heretofore tolerated what in their view was the arrogant and unjustified claims of remaining Indian groups for corporate representation, land and labor rights, and local political autonomy.

In the 1930s population growth and reduced exports exacerbated the structural tendencies inherited from the 1920s toward declining incomes, landlessness, and dependence. Growing numbers of poor or landless peasants now had to rely on other landowners for access to land and wages, but this was more and more difficult as the export economy stagnated, unemployment rose, and wages fell. In this decade, the number of tenants and residents on farms and haciendas increased dramatically. However, precisely because coffee production leveled off, these economic problems had little to do with the product but with larger agrarian patterns. Typically, the largest agricultural properties were diversified, and the farms and haciendas that produced the most coffee had twice as much land dedicated to other uses. By the 1930s the wealthiest entrepreneurs had purchased many of the best properties—including large haciendas—from an older generation of owners, while also patching together farms from smaller plots. Landless workers earned subsistence-level wages on these estates and had access to small plots for food production. Increasingly, control of land became the key to procuring cheap labor for raising coffee and other agricultural endeavors.

The society that had evolved in El Salvador by the end of the nineteenth century was one in which differences in power and wealth were mediated and determined by various local factors. Peasants and rural workers were not an undifferentiated, homogeneous mass that provided only cannon fodder for the wars waged by the elite, cheap labor for their plantations, and coerced votes for their candidates. The conditions that led to the radical concentration of wealth in a few hands by the mid-twentieth century were not a direct, inevitable result of El Salvador's earlier agrarian history.

It would be a mistake to insist that coffee and the landholding transition at the end of the century were structural causes of the authoritarianism that took hold in the 1930s, when the Salvadoran elite and middle sectors supported military rule and repression in response to the worker-peasant mobilizations of the late 1920s and the Indian-communist revolt of 1932. This research points to the autonomy of the political process in the 1920s and 1930s rather than its roots in the agrarian economic structure or the elite's control of land in the 1870–1920 period. The development of coffee, the privatization of common lands, the creation of a wage labor market, and the increased commercialization of agriculture did not mechanically create El Salvador's peculiar form of authoritarian politics that emerged in the mid-twentieth century.

If anything, the most important element of continuity between the 1830s and the 1930s, one that has a decisive bearing on the history of twentieth-century El Salvador, is the military and the political factionalism associated with it. The military and its institutions have regularly acted as a social and political force that excludes all other social actors, including the so-called oligarchy itself.[7] The short-lived civilian-led reform, combined with controlled patronage and the paternalistic populism of the 1911–1931 period, might be considered the anomaly in need of explanation—a brief interruption in a long-standing pattern of military and authoritarian rule that dates back to the 1830s. From this perspective, the consolidation of the national state under the politics of military factionalism between the 1880s and 1910s established patterns that the reformist politics of the following two decades were not able to change.

Political determinants, especially local ethnic and class relations, were important causes of the social and economic changes described in this study. The changes of the nineteenth century were not rigidly determined by crops, demographic density, or the power of the elite. Instead, the transition to a free-holding peasantry and the emergence of a coffee export economy were determined at the local level through small-scale interactions that involved complex local balances of power, negotiation, conflict, and competition.[8] We cannot understand the transition to an authoritarian-oligarchic society of the post-1932 period without examining the history of local agrarian relations. Here we find the keys to understanding El Salvador's experiment with liberal democratization and its collapse at the end of 1931. After the military coup of 1931 and the suppression of the 1932 revolt by local elites and the state, an antidemocratic coalition of commercial farmers, exporters, rural middle sectors, and the military purged the state of its liberal elements and reaffirmed and rigidified the old populist and clientelistic ties to peasants and artisans. Thus arose a militarized authoritarian state with deep clientelistic connections to the elite, the country's middle sectors, and peasants at the local level. The new state became the crucial arbiter of the country's development, establishing a shifting but basically enduring alliance with the country's landholding and agro-export elites, while keeping a balance between the financial-processing-export oligarchy and the middle sectors that produced coffee. By the 1970s this system, despite significant open-ings and closings along the way, was cemented by the military's control over the state.[9] It is in the political arena—the complex balance of power between different social sectors and the state—rather than in the struc-ture of landownership or coffee production that we find the key to the country's authoritarian political history.

The results of this study strongly suggest that market mechanisms, investment in underutilized haciendas, and the claiming of state lands ex-plain much of the concentration of land at the top of El Salvador's narrow class pyramid.[10] El Salvador's wealthy elite, much maligned for support-ing authoritarian and violent solutions to popular demands for reform, require closer attention on two points: First, scholars should examine the crisis of tenancy and the role of midlevel landowners in expelling ten-ants and sharecroppers between the 1950s and the early 1970s,[11] trigger-ing the political crisis that followed. Newly created landless workers provided significant support for the revolutionary movement. Midlevel landowners were more likely to favor state repression in the polarized political climate of those years—a situation analogous to the 1929–1932 crisis.[12] Second, El Salvador's elite accumulated property not only by com-ing to own the land that peasants and workers could not claim, but also by cannibalizing or blocking the upward mobility of other less-capitalized groups of investors and entrepreneurs who saw their possibilities limited by a small number of families who controlled export, marketing, and credit.

While there has been some debate about the origins of peasant sup-port for the FMLN in the 1980s, it is clear from the experience of many communities in Cabañas, Chalatenango, and the northern reaches of San Vicente, San Miguel, Cuscatlán, and Morazán, that numerous smallhold-ers, impoverished after decades of neglect by the state and compressed into ever smaller farms, provided significant if not crucial support to the insurgency after 1981. Members of peasant villages, often the victims of army massacres and subjected to forced displacement, do not fit the image of the landless and seasonal wage workers that is often considered the main source of rebel support. Recent field work by anthropologists supports this perspective by showing that local peasant communities with well-established—if marginal—access to land, and often with a strong sense of ethnic or local identity, provided considerable support to the

FMLN.[13] For these communities, the struggle for liberation was defined more often as a war against a uncaring, repressive, and authoritarian state than as a struggle against a landowning oligarchy, which very often had no presence or a direct impact on these relatively "backward" peasant communities. Recent studies of the military-dominated state in El Salvador also reinforce this argument by stressing the heavy militarization of Salvadoran society and the state beginning in the 1930s.[14]

It is my hope that this research into El Salvador's past will contribute to a better understanding of El Salvador's future options. One of my goals has been to demonstrate that El Salvador's agrarian history was not determined unilaterally by its elites or the state, and that no single transition was the cause of the changes of the following period. May the results presented here encourage scholars to pay more attention to the 1929–1970 period and its contributions to El Salvador's contemporary agrarian and political problems, especially the great concentration of land and income by a few hundred extended families. As the country faces the challenge of distancing itself from fifty years of repressive authoritarian rule and the widespread impoverishment of much of its population, perhaps an enriched understanding of the country's past will bring new visions for its future.

Appendix Tables

Abbreviations Used in Notes

Note on Sources

Notes

Glossary

Bibliography

Index

# APPENDIX TABLES

Appendix Table 1. Coffee Production in Ahuachapán Municipalities, 1876–1912 (in *quintales*)

|                  | 1876  | 1892   | 1912    |
|------------------|-------|--------|---------|
| Ataco            | 8,000 | 10,000 | 25,000  |
| Ahuachapán       | 5,000 | 18,000 | —       |
| Atiquizaya       | 4,599 | 17,000 | 20,000  |
| Apaneca          | 1,390 | 1,200  | 15,000  |
| Turín            | 1,800 | 350    | —       |
| San Pedro Pustla | 681   | 3,900  | 6,000   |
| Tacuba           | 320   | 4,600  | 1,000   |
| Jujutla          | 258[a]| 800    | 2,800[b]|
| El Refugio       | 300   | 500    | —       |
| Guaimango        | 50    | 300    | —       |
| Total            | 20,298| 57,900 | 70,650  |

*Sources:* "Cuadro estadistico de las producciones agricolas de los pueblos de Ahuachapán," 1876, AGN-CG-AH; "Informe que el señor Gobernador del Departamento de Ahuachapán dirige al Ministro de Gobernación," 1892, AGN-CG-AH; Fonseca, *Monografías . . . Ahuachapán.*

a. Data for 1882.

b. Data for 1910.

Appendix Table 2.  Coffee Production in Sonsonate, 1893–1916
(in *quintales*)

|  | 1893 | 1908 | 1916 |
|---|---|---|---|
| Juayua | 10,000 | 30,000 | 10,000[a] |
| Salcoatitán | 6,000 | 3,721 | 4,000 |
| Izalco | 3,000 | 25,000 | 15,000 |
| Nahuizalco | 1,000 | 2,000 | 1,120[a] |
| Santa Catarina | 1,000 | 1,600 | 6,000[a] |
| Armenia | 300 | 1,280 | 1,435 |
| San Julián | 300 | 2,825 | 3,392 |
| Ishuatan | 1,410 | 2,400 | — |
| Sonsonate | 20 | — | — |
| Cuisnahuat | — | 10 | — |
| Total | 21,600 | 67,866 | 43,347 |

*Sources:* "Cosecha de café en el Departamento de Sonsonate," March 1916, AGN-CG-SO; "Informe de comercio y agricultura correspondiente al Distrito de Izalco," 7 February 1893, AGN-CG-SO; "Informe de Comercio y agricultura del Distrito de Sonsonate," 1893, AGN-CG-SO; Barbarena, *Monografías . . . Sonsonate,* 14; El Salvador, *Memoria.*

a. Crops damaged by winds and/or insects.

Appendix Table 3.  Coffee Production in Usulután, 1884

|  | Trees in Production | Almácigo | Quintales Produced |
|---|---|---|---|
| Santiago de María | 650,000 | — | 5,838 |
| Tecapa | 566,200 | 504,000 | — |
| Jucuapa | 300,000 | 200,000 | — |
| Tecapán | 101,860 | — | 1,025 |
| El Triunfo | 15,200 | — | — |

*Source:* Manuel Castro, "Informe del Secretario de la Junta de Agricultura de Jucuapa," *Boletín de Agricultura* 2 (20 October 1884): 326.

Appendix Table 4.  Peasants Who Settled in Baldío Cara Sucia,
Ahuachapán, 1896

| Settler's Origin | No. of Years in Possession | No. of Dependents | Plot Size (hectares) |
|---|---|---|---|
| Ahuachapán | 7 | 1 | 8.0 |
| Ahuachapán | 7 | 2 | 1.3 |
| Ahuachapán | 7 | 1 | 0 |
| Ahuachapán | 7 | 0 | 0 |
| Ahuachapán | 2 | 4 | 2.0 |
| Ahuachapán | few months | 6 | 5.4 |
| Ahuachapán | few months | 4 | 2.0 |
| Apaneca[a] | 4 | 4 | 0.7 |
| Apaneca | 1 | 4 | 1.4 |
| Apaneca | 1 | 5 | 2.7 |
| Apaneca | 1 | 5 | 2.7 |
| Atiquizaya | 3 | 2 | 4.7 |
| Chalchuapa | 8 | 6 | 4.0 |
| Chalchuapa[b] | 8 | 9 | 4.0 |
| Chalchuapa | 8 | 9 | — |
| Chalchuapa | 8 | 9 | — |
| Chalchuapa | 8 | 1 | — |
| Chalchuapa | 2 | 4 | 2.0 |
| Chalchuapa | 2 | 4 | 8.0 |
| Guatemala | 6 | 3 | — |
| Guatemala | 5 | 5 | 2.0 |
| Guatemala[c] | 4 | 8 | 10.0 |
| Guatemala | 4 | 0 | — |
| Guatemala | 4 | 0 | — |
| Guatemala | 2 | 6 | 0.7 |
| Guatemala | 2 | 1 | 0.7 |
| Guatemala[d] | 2 | 0 | — |
| Guatemala | 1 | 2 | 2.7 |
| Guatemala | 1 | 6 | 0 |
| Guatemala | 1 | 5 | 0.7 |
| Salcoatitán | 8 | 2 | 9.4 |
| Salcoatitán[e] | 8 | 2 | — |
| Salcoatitán | 8 | 10 | 10.0 |
| Salcoatitán | 8 | 5 | 4.0 |

Appendix Table 4. (continued)

| Settler's Origin | No. of Years in Possession | No. of Dependents | Plot Size (hectares) |
|---|---|---|---|
| Santa Ana | 8 | 14 | 6.7 |
| Santa Ana | 8 | 2 | 9.4 |
| Santa Ana | 6 | 6 | 2.0 |
| Santa Ana<sup>e</sup> | 5 | 0 | — |
| Santa Ana | 1 | 2 | 0 |
| Santa Ana | few months | 6 | 0 |

*Source:* "Posedores de terrenos en la Soledad y Hachadura del baldío Cara Sucia formado para averiguar cuanto queda para los invalidos," 1896, AGN-CG-AH.

   a. Rents land.

   b. Works with next three.

   c. Father of next two settlers, who work for him.

   d. Works with previous settler, his brother.

   e. Works with previous person.

## Appendix Table 5. Coffee Production in Western Departments, 1854–1868

| | Department | Trees in Production (in feet) | Trees Planted (in feet) | Quintales Produced |
|---|---|---|---|---|
| 1854 | Santa Ana/Ahuachapán | — | — | 300 |
| 1855 | Santa Ana/Ahuachapán | 500,000 | 1,000,000 | 900–1000 |
| 1857 | Santa Ana[a] | 123,000 | 317,000 | — |
| | Ahuachapán[b] | 312,284 | 116,000 | 250 |
| 1858 | Santa Ana | 143,120 | 446,300 | 2,263 |
| | Ahuachapán | 314,713 | 154,160 | 1,159 |
| 1859 | Santa Ana | 143,120 | 444,800[c] | 2,263 |
| 1860 | Santa Ana | 256,000 | 372,000 | — |
| | Ahuachapán | 346,260 | 326,510 | — |
| 1861 | Santa Ana | 612,047 | 661,021 | 6,600 |
| | Ahuachapán | 468,025 | 124,739 | 4,653 |
| | La Libertad | 206,850[d] | — | — |
| 1862 | Sonsonate | — | 625,871[e] | — |
| | La Libertad | — | — | 600 |
| 1865 | Santa Ana | — | — | 9,276 |
| | Ahuachapán | — | — | 3,812 |
| 1866 | Santa Ana/Ahuachapán | — | — | 16,000/est. |
| | Sonsonate/Ahuachapán | — | 5,000[f] | — |
| 1867 | Santa Ana | 1,466,619 | 1,094,546 | 32,585 |
| | Ahuachapán | 587,224 | 489,194 | 6,647 |
| | La Libertad | — | — | 2,926[g] |
| 1868 | Santa Ana | 436,619 | 2,079,546 | — |
| | La Libertad | 658,800 | 1,174,000 | 18,612 |

*Sources:* Monterrey, *Historia de El Salvador,* vol. 1; López, *Estadística,* 73, 76; *Gaceta de El Salvador,* 13 March 1861, p. 4; *Gaceta Oficial,* 9 April 1862, p. 2; 12 April 1862, p. 7; 9 April 1862, p. 2; 12 April 1862, p. 7; 23 April 1862, p. 5; *Memoria de Gobernación y de Relaciones,* 1861, 17; Bustamante, *Cronología;* 17; *El Constitucional,* 22 November 1866; 6 June 1867, p. 2; "Informe del Gobernador de La Libertad," 1867, AGN-CDM Rollo BN-29; Ipiña, "Estadística," 6, 12.

a. Might include Ahuachapán municipalities.

b. Ahuachapán and Atiquizaya only.

c. 1,598,500 in nursuries.

d. Might include both trees in production and planted; only for Nueva San Salvador.

e. Both planted and in nursuries.

f. Produced by 139 farms.

g. Only in Nueva San Salvador. Crop damaged by high winds.

Appendix Table 6.  Indigo Production, 1740–1910

| | Pounds Produced | Est. Land in Use | |
| --- | --- | --- | --- |
| | | Hectares | Caballerías |
| 1740 | 364,000 | 4,100 | 93 |
| 1772 | 808,990 | 9,200 | 209 |
| 1780 | 517,790 | 5,900 | 134 |
| 1785 | 900,000 | 10,200 | 232 |
| 1790 | 1,001,000 | 11,400 | 259 |
| 1791 | 1,001,000 | 11,400 | 259 |
| 1795 | 848,120 | 9,600 | 218 |
| 1800 | 955,599 | 10,900 | 250 |
| 1801 | 865,410 | 9,900 | 225 |
| 1802 | 805,350 | 9,200 | 210 |
| 1803 | 556,124 | 6,300 | 140 |
| 1804 | 247,312 | 2,800 | 60 |
| 1808 | 827,190 | 9,400 | 210 |
| 1809 | 667,030 | 7,600 | 170 |
| 1812 | 409,500 | 4,700 | 110 |
| 1813 | 233,870 | 2,700 | 60 |
| 1814 | 384,930 | 4,400 | 100 |
| 1815 | 375,830 | 4,300 | 100 |
| 1818 | 302,120 | 3,400 | 80 |
| 1830 | 1,200,000 | 13,600 | 310 |
| 1849 | 1,050,000 | 12,000 | 270 |
| 1851 | 1,050,000 | 12,000 | 270 |
| 1852 | 1,500,000 | 17,000 | 390 |
| 1853 | 1,162,000 | 13,500 | 310 |
| 1854 | 1,009,652 | 11,500 | 260 |
| 1855 | 1,050,000 | 12,000 | 270 |
| 1856 | 1,168,000 | 13,000 | 300 |
| 1857 | 1,117,500 | 13,000 | 300 |
| 1858 | 1,280,400 | 14,500 | 330 |
| 1859 | 1,605,450 | 18,200 | 410 |
| 1860 | 1,375,050 | 15,600 | 350 |
| 1861 | 1,980,600 | 22,500 | 510 |
| 1862 | 2,186,550 | 24,800 | 560 |
| 1863 | 1,121,105 | 12,700 | 290 |
| 1864 | 1,237,400 | 14,000 | 330 |
| 1865 | 1,584,000 | 18,000 | 410 |
| 1866 | 1,979,850 | 22,500 | 510 |
| 1867 | 2,250,000 | 25,600 | 580 |
| 1868 | 2,131,500 | 24,200 | 560 |

Appendix Table 6. (continued)

| | Pounds Produced | Est. Land in Use | |
|---|---|---|---|
| | | Hectares | Caballerías |
| 1869 | 2,477,550 | 28,200 | 640 |
| 1870 | 2,619,749 | 29,800 | 610 |
| 1871 | 2,308,317 | 26,200 | 580 |
| 1872 | 2,786,576 | 31,700 | 720 |
| 1873 | 1,802,037 | 20,500 | 470 |
| 1875 | 1,160,700 | 12,700 | 290 |
| 1876 | 1,561,699 | 18,000 | 410 |
| 1877 | 1,429,000 | 16,200 | 350 |
| 1879 | 1,186,894 | 12,700 | 290 |
| 1880 | 1,174,550 | 12,700 | 290 |
| 1883 | 1,812,594 | 20,600 | 470 |
| 1891 | 1,133,350 | 12,700 | 290 |
| 1892 | 1,438,050 | 16,200 | 350 |
| 1901 | 1,187,835 | 13,400 | 300 |
| 1910 | 412,802 | 4,600 | 100 |

*Sources:* Alfaro, *Memoria;* Barbarena, "Nuestra industria añilera," 511; Castro, "Estadística"; *Diario Oficial,* 27 December 1855; 22 June 1859; 10 November 1880, p. 259; 3 December 1880, p. 267; 12 December 1880, p. 242; Dirección General de Estadistica, *La República,* 115. *Gaceta del Salvador,* 30 March 1859; Gobernador de Cabañas, Jacinto Colocho, "Informe al Ministro de Gobernación," 31 December 1908, AGN-CM-MG; Gobernador de Chalatenango, "Carta al Ministro de lo Interior sobre feria de santos," 8 November 1867, AGN-CDM Rollo BN-30; Gobernador de Chalatenango, Aquilino Duarte, "Informe al Ministro de Gobernación," 26 August 1898, AGN-CM-MG; Gobernador de Chalatenango, Manuel Indireo, "Informe al Ministro de Gobernación," 31 December 1908, AGN-CM-MG; Gobernador de Morazan, Francisco Ortiz, "Informe al Ministro Fomento y Beneficiencia," 21 January 1890, AGN-CM-MG; Gobernador de San Miguel, "Informe al Minstro de lo Interior," 5 August 1870, AGN-CDM CDM Rollo BN-36; Gobernador de Santa Ana, "Informe al Ministro de Gobernación," 1899, AGN-CM-MG; González, *Lecciones;* Guzmán, *Apuntamientos;* Haefkens, *Viaje;* Juarros, *Compendio;* Lindo Fuentes, *Weak Foundations;* Monterrey, *Historia;* Mora, *Memoria . . . (1883);* Pinto Soria, *Estructura;* Rubio Sánchez, *Historia;* Scherzer, *Travels;* Sermeño Lima, "Los movimientos," 387–88; Smith, "Indigo production."

*Notes:* Land use estimated from Scherzer, *Travels,* 1:130–31; some production estimates are calculated from data for all of colonial Guatemala.

# ABBREVIATIONS USED IN NOTES

| | |
|---|---|
| AGA | Archivo de la Gobernación de Ahuachapan |
| AGN | Archivo General de la Nación, San Salvador |
| AGS | Archivo de la Gobernación de Sonsonate |
| AGSA | Archivo de la Gobernación de Santa Ana |
| AGSV | Archivo de la Gobernación de San Vicente |
| AMA | Archivo Municipal de Armenia |
| AMAh | Archivo Municiapal de Ahuachapan |
| AMC | Archivo Municipal de Coatepeque |
| AMCh | Archivo Municipal de Chalchuapa |
| AMI | Archivo Municipal de Izalco |
| AMJ | Archivo Municipal de Juayua |
| AMNSS | Archivo Municipal de Nueva San Salvador |
| AMS | Archivo Municipal de Sonsonate |
| AMSA | Archivo Municipal de Santa Ana |
| AMSJN | Archivo Municipal de San Juan Nonualco |
| AMSV | Archivo Municipal de San Vicente |
| AN | Asamblea Nacional |
| BG | Biblioteca Gallardo, Nueva San Salvador |
| CA | Colección Alcaldias |
| CB | Colección Barrios |
| CC | Colección Colonial |
| CDC | Colección Clasificados |
| CDM | Colección de Documentos Microfilmados |
| CG | Coleción Gobernaciones |
| CI | Colección Indiferentes |

| | |
|---|---|
| CImp | Colección Impresos |
| CJ | Colección Judicial |
| CM | Colección Ministerios |
| CPC | Colección de Documentos Pre-clasificados |
| CQ | Colección de Documentos Quemados |
| CT | Colección Tierras |
| CTR | Colección Transcripciones |
| MG | Ministerio de Gobernación |
| MA | Ministerio de Agricultura |
| SPE | Supremo Poder Ejecutivo |
| UCA-CVJ | Colección Victor Jerez–Universidad Centroamericana, San Salvador |
| USNA | United States National Archives, Washington, D.C. |

# NOTE ON SOURCES

Because the sources used in the tables in chapters 2 and 3 that refer to *ejido* and community land titles are too numerous to be cited individually, I will provide a general description of these sources and their location. First, the Archivo General de la Nación of El Salvador possesses a collection of colonial and nineteenth-century common land titles and other related documents in its Colección Tierras (AGN-CT). These materials are indexed and microfilmed. Still others are at the AGN in typescript form. A few titles are available in municipal archives: Izalco, Ahuachapán, Armenia, San Vicente, Tepecoyo, etc. Others have been reprinted in now-defunct journals like *Revista Tzunpame* and *Revista del Departamento de Historia*. There are indications that all of the nation's existing common land titles and related judicial cases were copied into the Registro de la Propiedad's books during the late 1890s, but I have not been able to confirm this. Copies of titles and related information also appear in judicial documents relating to land issues. These are in the AGN's Ministerio de Gobernación section and also in the municipal or departmental sections. A few published sources, cited in the text, provide some information on common lands. Among the most Important are the *Estadística General de la República del Salvador,* Antonio Ipiña's *Estadística del Departamento de Sonsonate* (1866) and the *Memorias* of the Ministerio de Gobernación.

The following list is not comprehensive but a sample of the more important sources on the expansion and management of common lands during the nineteenth century. Other important sources are the *Memorias de Gobernación* and the *Diario Oficial* (in its various incarnations). For a longer discussion of archival sources in El Salvador, see Aldo Lauria-Santiago, "Historical Research and Sources on El Salvador," *Latin American Research Review* 30, no. 2 (spring 1995): 151–76.

## *Selected List of Primary Sources*

Acuerdo de Francisco Dueñas, presidente constitucional de la República, 4 February 1871, AGN-CDM Rollo BN-37.

Acuerdo del SG sobre terrenos en Atiquizaya, 11 November 1870, AGN-CDM Rollo BN-36.

Acuerdo del SPE sobre pago a la municipalidad de Aguacayo por tierras denunciadas como baldías, 1867, AGN-CPC.

Alcalde de Zacatecoluca, Salvador Ramos, Carta al Gobernador de La Paz, 20 May 1867, AGN-CQ Rollo BN-29.

Apoderado jeneral de la Municipalidad de Verapaz, Antonio José Castro, Solicitud al Supremo Poder Ejecutivo, 21 September 1872, AGN-CDM Rollo MI-23.

Apuntes de los vienes de campo de la hacienda de San Jose títulos y demas generales que pertenecen al común de ladinos de este pueblo, 1826?, AMCh.

Balbino Rivas, Carta al Ministro de Hacienda y Guerra, 1867, AGN-CDM Rollo BN-29.

Bartolo Arana, Síndico de Caluco, Solicitud al SPE sobre ejidos en Caluco, 8 Feburary 1871, AGN-CDM Rollo BN-37.

Carta al Gobernador del Departamento, 27 May 1868, AGN-CDM Rollo BN-33.

Carta de Joaquín Mejía al Supremo Gobierno solicitando título de tierras de Usulutan, 23 November 1867, AGN-CPC.

Carta de la municipalidad de El Guayabal al SPE sobre donación de tierras a El Guayabal, 16 August 1867, AGN-CC [A3.3-9 Exp. #16].

Ceción hecha por el Supremo Gobierno a favor de la municipalidad de Tecapán de 15 caballerías de tierra del baldío nombrado el Palmital, 1860, 1867, AGN-CT Sección/Caja:10 Folder/Doc:10.

Cecion del supremo gobierno a favor del pueblo de Santa Mariá de los Remedios de un terreno baldío nombrado La Laguna y Mejicapa, 1864, AGN-CT Sección/Caja:10 Folder/Doc:10.

Certificación de acta de la Municipalidad de Tonocatepeque, 18 February 1869, AGN-CDM Rollo BN-32.

Certificación de venta de la Hacienda San Cristobal, 24 September 1859, AGSV.

Certificación expedida por el Juez General de Hacienda al Escribano Francisco Gavidia, 3 July 1860, AGN-CDM Rollo BN-22.

Comunicando a la intendencia de esta Dpto haber recibido 500 pesos de Verapa a buena cuenta de la tierras ejecutadas en la hacienda San Francisco, 16 February 1840, AGN-CPC.

Correspondencia del Gobernador de Ahuachapán, 1872, AGN-CG-AH.

Diligencias de remedida de las tierras de la hacienda Santa Rita el potrero pertenecientes a la comunidad de Ladinos, 1869, AGN-CT Sección/ Caja:6 Folder/Doc:6.

Diligencias seguidas por los cófrades del señor San José con respecto a recuperar las tierras del canton Ayutepeque pertenecientes al comun de Ladinos del pueblo de Chalchuapa, 1809-14, AMCh.

Escritura de venta de la cuarta parte del baldío Isla otrogada por el agrimensor Matias Peraza a la municipalidad de Opico, 2 April 1867, AGN-CM-MG.

Estupianián, Baltasar. *Memoria con que el Sr. Ministro de Gobernación Doctor Don Baltasar Estupinián, dió cuenta a la honorable Asamblea Nacional (1885–1886)*. San Salvador: Imprenta Nacional, 1887. 117.

Expediente de remedida de las tierras ejidales y communales de Armenia, 1873, AGN typescript.

Feliciano Alvarez, Solicitud de la Municipalidad de San Pedro Pustla, 8 February 1871, AGN-CDM Rollo BN-37.

Joaquin Angel Mejía, Solicitud al SPE de título a propiedad de seis caballerías para ejidos en Usulutan, 23 November 1867, AGN-CPC.

Medición de las tierras nombrada Bongo y Rillitos para ejidos del pueblo de Tecapán, 1877, 1847, AGN-CT Sección/Caja:10 Folder/Doc:10.1.

*Memoria de Gobernación y de Relaciones, 1861*. San Salvador, 1862. (BGA).

Montes, Segundo. *El agro salvadoreño (1973–1980)*. San Salvador: UCA Editores, 1986.

Municipalidad de Sonzacate, Carta al Presidente Dueñas agradeciendo haber cedido para ejidos el terreno Nahuizalquillo al pueblo de Sonzacate, 28 March 1867, AGN-CPC.

Sobre concesión de tierras a San Esteban, 1874, AGN-CM-MG.

Sobre el baldio Coyolar en Chinameca, 1867, AGN-CDM Rollo BN-30.

Solicitud al SPE, 22 September 1868, AGN-CDM Rollo BN-31.

Solicitud de Don. Miguel Hernández como apoderado de la Municipalidad de San Miguel para que el S. G. ceda en favor de sus ejidos la Hda. Guadalupe, 6 October 1873, AGN-CDM Rollo BN-47.

Solicitud de la Municipalidad del Guayabal al SPE sobre título del terreno Tecomatepe, 1867, AGN-CDM Rollo BN-29.

Solicitud de la Municipalidad de Sonzacate al SPE sobre título del terreno Nahuizalquillo, 1867, AGN-CQ Rollo BN-27.

Solicitud de los vecinos del barrio de Santa Lucía, Santa Ana, 1867, AGN-CQ.

Solicitud sobre terrenos para ejidos en San Buenaventura, 1867, AGN-CPC.

Título de propiedad de 20 caballerías de tierras que le fueron otorgadas a la municipaldiad de Juayua en 1876, 1876, AGN-CT Sección/Caja:2 Folder/Doc:2.2.

Título de tierras llamadas el sitio San José, Santiestevan, y tierras valdias del volcan, pertenecientes a la municipalidad de San Miguel, 1857, AGN-CM-MG.

Título ejidal de San Juan Opico, typescript, 1826, AGN.

Título ejidal de San Miguel Jujutla, 1831, 1861, AGN.

Título ejidal de Tepecoyo, 1868, AMTep.

# NOTES

## Chapter 1. *Introduction*

1. See Roseberry, *Anthropologies and Histories.*

2. Stern ("Feudalism, Capitalism, and the World System," 871) clarifies the need for reconceptualizing history on the Latin American "periphery" and considering "popular strategies of resistance and survival" alongside the European-dominated world system and elite actions.

3. See Roseberry, "Beyond the Agrarian Question."

4. For example, Torres Rivas, *Interpretación del desarollo social centroamericano*; Menjivar, *Acumulación originaria*; Cardoso, "Historia económica del café"; Burns, "The Modernization of Underdevelopment," and Flores Macal, *Origen, desarollo y crisis.* Dunkerley, *The Pacification of Central America* and *Power in the Isthmus,* and Bulmer-Thomas, *The Political Economy of Central America.* The *Historia general de Centroamerica* reproduces aspects of this perspective.

5. See, for example, Guardino, *Peasants, Politics, and the Formation of Mexico's National State*; Mallon, *Peasant and Nation*; Kourí, "The Business of the Land"; Thomson, "Popular Aspects of Liberalism"; Ducey, "Liberal Theory and Peasant Practice"; Neils Jacobsen.

6. See Gould, *To Lead as Equals* and *To Die in This Way*; Forster, "Campesino Struggles"; Dore, "Coffee, Land and Class Relations."

7. Browning, *El Salvador,* 169.

8. Ibid., 172, emphasis added.

9. Ibid., 206; see also A. Torres, "Tierras y colonización."

10. See Topic, "Putting Back the Pieces"; Roseberry, "Beyond the Agrarian Question"; Roseberry, "Introduction."

11. Yarrington, "Public Land Settlement," reaches similar conclusions. See also Roseberry, "Beyond the Agrarian Question"; Roseberry, "Introduction."

See Samper, *Generations of Settlers;* and Gudmundson, "Peasant, Farmer, Proletarian," "Peasant Movements," and *Costa Rica Before Coffee.*

12. See Montgomery, *Revolution in El Salvador;* Dunkerley, *Power in the Isthmus and The Pacification of Central America.*

13. See Molina and Palmer, *The History of Costa Rica;* and Acuña and Molina Jiménez, *Historia económica y social de Costa Rica.* For a contrast between El Salvador and Costa Rica, see Dunkerley, *Power in the Isthums;* Cardoso, "Historia económica del café"; Williams, *States and Social Evolution.* An exceptional use of empirical research is Samper, "El significado social de la caficultura costarricense y salvadoreña."

14. See Gudmundson, *Costa Rica before Coffee.*

15. See Burns, "The Modernization of Underdevelopment"; Ching, "From Clientelism to Militarism"; and Suter, *Prosperität.*

16. See Samper, "El significado social de la caficultura costarricense y salvaodoreña."

17. See Montgomery, *Revolution in El Salvador;* and Dunkerley, *Power in the Isthmus.*

18. See Cabarrús, "El Salvador."

19. See Pearce, *Promised Land;* Cabarrús, *Génesis de una revolución;* Binford, *The El Mozote Massacre.*

20. Dirección General de Estadística y Censos, *Primer censo agropecuario;* on the political importance of middle-sector landholders, see Cabarrus, *Génesis de una revolución.*

21. Wilson, "The Crisis of National Integration," 7, 39.

22. Dana G. Munro, cited in Wilson, "The Crisis," 29.

23. Palmer, *Central America and Its Problems,* 110.

24. Ibid., 29.

25. Thompson, *Rainbow Countries,* 98–99.

26. Karl Sapper, cited in Wilson, "The Crisis," 30.

27. Lambert de Sainte-Croix, *Onze mois,* 249.

28. Morrill, *Rotten Republics,* 116.

29. Thompson, *Rainbow Countries,* 94, 96, 99.

30. Foster, *A Gringo in Mañana-Land,* 222.

31. Koebel, *Central America,* 18.

32. Dirección General de Estadística, *La República de El Salvador,* 114.

33. Carpenter, *Lands of the Caribbean,* 114.

34. Vanni *(Salvador)* used statistics provided by the head of El Salvador's National Statistics Office.

35. Ibid., 96–97.

36. West and Augelli, *Middle America,* 411–12.

37. But see Castro, *La población de El Salvador;* Escalante Arce, *Codice Sonsonate;* Fowler, "The Political Economy of Indian Survival"; Fowler, "Cacao, Indigo, and Coffee"; Flores Macal, "La hacienda colonial"; Fernández

Molina, *Colouring the World in Blue;* Smith, "Indigo Production"; Smith, "Forced Labor"; Macleod, *Spanish Central America*; Fowler, *Caluco.*

38. See Martínez, *La Patria del Criollo,* 701, n. 59; Taracena Arriola, "Contribución al estudio del vocablo 'ladino'"; Adorno, "The Indigenous Ethnographer."

39. For comparisons, see Lockhart and Altman, *Provinces of Early Mexico*; and von Mentz, *Pueblos de indios, mulatos y mestizos, 1770–1870.*

## Chapter 2. *Peasants, Indigo, and Land During the Late Colonial Period*

1. See Wolf, "Types of Latin American Peasantries."

2. See Solórzano Fonseca, "Las comunidades indígenas"; and Solórzano Fonseca, "Centroamerica en el Siglo XVIII."

3. An 1782 report estimated that two-thirds of the crop came from producers of 6 to 100 pounds. See Smith, "Indigo Production," 186, 197.

4. Pinto Soria, *Estructura agraria,* 10–11.

5. Fernández Molina, "Colouring the World."

6. Floyd, "Los comerciantes guatemaltecos," 33; Pinto Soria, *Raices historicas,* 122, n. 234; Juarros, *Compendio,* 21; Fernández Molina, "Colouring the World," 181.

7. Browning, *El Salvador,* 76–79. See "Título Ejidal de San Miguel," for a similar conflict around the city of San Miguel which led to official recognition of hacienda enroachment upon the city's ejidos (typescript, 1803, BGA).

8. Fiehrer, "The Baron de Carondelet," 176–77.

9. Scherzer, *Travels,* 1:130–31.

10. Fiehrer, "The Baron de Carondelet," 163.

11. Cortés y Larraz, *Descripción geográfico-moral, passim.*

12. Fiehrer, "The Baron de Carondelet," 181; Fernández Molina, "Colouring the World," 119, 132.

13. Fernández Molina, "Colouring the World," 173, 175–77.

14. Larrazabal, "Apuntamientos sobre la agricultura," 44.

15. Fernández Molina, "Colouring the World," 125.

16. See Fiehrer, "The Baron de Carondelet," 232.

17. See Monterrey, *Historia de El Salvador,* 1:52–53.

18. Fiehrer, "The Baron de Carondelet," 155.

19. Solano, "Tierra, comercio y sociedad."

20. Monterrey, *Historia de El Salvador,* 1:52.

21. Larrazabal, "Apuntamientos sobre la agricultura," 49.

22. Browning, *El Salvador,* 84; Pinto Soria, *Estructura agraria,* 10, n. 30; Cortés y Larraz, *Descripción geográfico-moral,* insert.

23. Rubio Sánchez, *Historia;* Squier, *Notes on Central America;* Scherzer, *Travels.*

24. Smith, "Forced Labor."

25. Castro, *La población de El Salvador*, 237.

26. Fiehrer, "The Baron de Carondelet," 196.

27. Gutiérrez y Ulloa, *Estado general.*

28. Pinto Soria, *Raices historicas,* 85, n. 156.

29. Browning, *El Salvador,* 84.

30. Ots Capdequí, *España en América,* chap. 1; Ots Capdequí, *Nuevos Aspectos,* 170, 241–42. On community land titles in Guatemala, see Martínez Palaez, *La patria del Criollo,* chap. 4. See also Fonseca, *Costa Rica colonial,* chaps. 2–4.

31. Wortman, *Government and Society in Central America,* 192–93.

32. Browning, *El Salvador,* 96–101.

33. Pinto Soria, *Guatemala en la decada de la independencia,* 11, 46–47, n. 16; Torres-Rivas and Pinto, *Problemas,* 118, nn. 7–8, 10; Flores Macal, "La hacienda."

34. Juarros, *Compendio,* 20.

35. See Fiehrer, "The Baron de Carondelet"; Macleod, *Spanish Central America*; Cardona Lazo, *Monografias departamentales,* 113; Fernández Molina, "Colouring the World," 176–77.

36. Flores Macal, "La hacienda," 360–61.

37. Pinto Soria, *Raices historicas,* 83–85; Castro, *La población de El Salvador,* 368–69, n.5.

38. Browning, *El Salvador,* 72–76, 85.

39. "Informe del Intendente D. José Ortiz de la Peña," San Salvador, 18 December 1787, quoted in Pinto Soria, *Estructura agraria,* 33, n. 21.

40. See Solórzano Fonseca, "Las comunidades indígenas."

41. Gálvez, "Relación geográfica"; Solano, "Tierra, comercio y sociedad," 332.

Chapter 3. *The Formation of Peasant Landholding Communities, 1820s–1870s*

1. See Ducey, "Liberal Theory and Peasant Practice."

2. Ulloa, *Codificación,* 153.

3. Lindo Fuentes (*Weak Foundations*, 90) assumes that this law was enforced.

4. "Solicitud al Supremo Poder Ejecutivo de la Municipalidad de Apastepeque para autorizar compra de tierras ejidales," 15–19 November 1860, AGN-CC [A3.11-1 Exp. #.5].

5. "Solicitud al SPE," 22 September 1868, AGN-CDM Rollo BN-31.

6. "Título de propiedad de 20 caballerías de tierras que le fueron otorgadas a la municipalidad de Juayua en 1876," 1876, AGN-CT Sección 2

Folder/Doc:2.2>; "Carta al Ministro de Hacienda sobre cesión de tierras a Juayua," AGN-CPC, 1872; "Certificación de venta de la Hacienda San Cristóbal," 24 September 1859, AGSV.

7. "Decreto sobre distribución de tierras en Chinameca," *Diario Oficial*, 2 April 1881.

8. "Acuerdo del Supremo Gobierno sobre terrenos en Atiquizaya," 11 November 1870, AGN-CDM Rollo BN-36.

9. "Carta aceptando la cesión de 100 caballerías de tierra del gobierno," 22 January 1886, AGN-CQ.

10. Smith, "Financing the Central American Federation."

11. Menéndez, *Recopilación*, 161.

12. Ibid., 82–84.

13. *Gaceta Oficial*, 21 November 1860, p. 1.

14. El Salvador, *Colección de leyes*, 58.

15. *Gaceta de El Salvador*, 1 June 1862, p. 1; Gobernador de La Paz, "Carta al Ministro de lo Interior," 1867, AGN-CDM Rollo BN-27.

16. "Informe del Gobernador del departamento de Sonsonate," *Diario Oficial*, 23 February 1865, p. 1.

17. Squier, *Notes on Central America*, 326.

18. Menéndez, *Recopilación*, 270. "Orden a los alcaldes mandando a quienes viven en despoblado a avecindarse en los pueblos o cascos de las Haciendas," 14 January 1847, AGN-CC [G1.1-9 Exp. #14]; "Circular a los Gobernadores sobre la reducción de los habitantes del campo y poblados," 1 March 1847, AGN-CC [G1.2-9 Exp. #72]; "Informe del Gobernador del Departamento de San Vicente," *Gaceta Oficial*, 6, 11, 21 June 1862.

19. Ulloa, *Codificación*, 157–58.

20. "Libro de Notaría de Hipotecas de San Miguel," AGN-CI, 1864.

21. *Diario Oficial*, 6 April 1878, p. 335; Menéndez, *Recopilación*, 162–64.

22. See Gobernador de Sonsonate, Francisco Herrera, "Carta al Ministro de lo Interior," 12 November 1870, AGN-CDM Rollo BN-36; "Certificación del Alcalde de Analco, Rafael Ramires," 25 October 1872, AGN-CDM Rollo BN-44.

23. Chacón, *El Presidente*, 45, 48.

24. "Informe del Gobernador de San Vicente," *Gaceta Oficial*, 11–21 June 1862, pp. 2–3.

25. "Informe del Comisionado Visitador de los Pueblos de la República," *Gaceta Oficial*, 19 December 1860, p. 4.

26. "Informe del Gobernador del Departamento de San Vicente," *Gaceta Oficial*, 11–13 June 1862.

27. "Informe del Gobernador de San Vicente," *Gaceta Oficial*, 11–21 June 1862, pp. 2–3.

28. "Informe del Gobernador de San Vicente," *Gaceta Oficial*, 11–21 June 1862.

29. "Informe del Gobernador de San Miguel," *Gaceta Oficial,* 30 April 1862, p. 2.

30. "Acuerdo Supremo del 5 de Mayo," *Gaceta Oficial,* 7 May 1862, p. 1.

31. "Los señores Juan Panameño, Paz Mira y Luisa Ramires, piden se les ponga en poseción de unos terrenos," 24 April 1867, AGN-CDM Rollo BN-28. "Carta del Gobernador de San Vicente al Presidente de la Republica sobre que los Vecinos de Apastepeque se quejan de que fueron despojados de sus terrenos por la municipalidad," 27 March 1867, AGN-CPC. "Carta al Sr. Presidente de la República sobre terrenos en Apastepeque," 1867, AGN-CDM Rollo BN-29.

32. Menéndez, *Recopilación,* 162–64.

33. Montes, *El agro salvadoreño (1973–1980),* 54.

34. "Solicitud al SPE sobre censos en Tecapa," 1871, AGN-CQ.

35. "Sobre tierras en San Esteban," 1861, AGN-CM-MG.

36. "Informe de la Gobernación de Sonsonate," *El Constitucional,* 1 February 1866, p. 1.

37. Lindo Fuentes, *Weak Foundations,* 90; Monterrey, *Historia del Salvador,* 2:331.

38. Monterrey, *Historia de El Salvador* 2:345, 349.

39. Informe del Gobernador de Sonsonate, *El Constitucional,* 23 February 1865, 23 February 1867.

40. See Ducey, "Liberal Theory and Peasant Practice"; Escobar Ohmstede and Schryer, "Las Sociedades Agrarias"; and Kourí, "The Business of the Land."

41. "Fianza del Señor don Miguel Vasquez en seguridad de los representantes del común de Mejicanos de esta ciudad," 3 June 1877, AGN-CA-SO.

42. Gobernador de Sonsonate, Antonio Ipiña, "Carta al Ministro de lo Interior sobre el común de indígenas de Juayua," 22 July 1867, AGN-CDM Rollo BN-29.

43. Browning, *El Salvador,* 89–90.

44. "Carta al Ministro de lo Interior del Supremo Gobierno ordenando la organización de los indios de Juayua," 22 July 1867, AGN-CPC; "Título general de los terrenos ejidales y comunales de Juayua," 1862, AGN-Col. Tierras-Caja 2/Doc. 2.

45. Gobernador de San Salvador, "Informe al Ministro de lo Interior," 31 December 1870, AGN-CDM Rollo BN-36.

46. Mora, *Memoria,* 112.

47. See Cardenal, *El poder eclesiástico,* 147–59. See also Rodríguez Herrera, "Una aproximación."

48. The only evidence of extensive individual privatization of community lands before the 1870s is in Cojutepeque. "La Situación de El Salvador en la paz," *Gaceta del Salvador* 4:12, 6 June 1857.

49. Contreras, *Memoria,* 217.

50. "Carta de los vecinos de Chalchuapa al SPE denunciando que la municipalidad pretende quitarles los terrenos de su comunidad de Ladinos," 11 July 1867, AGN-CPC.

51. "Expediente de partición de las tierras de la hacienda San Juan Masajapa," 20 March 1891, AGN-CM-MG.

52. "Título de las tierras de Izalco sacados a solicitud del Común de Asunción," 1866, AMI.

53. López, *Estadística general*, 54.

54. "Solicitud al Excelentisimo Señor Presidente," 9 December 1868, AGN-CDM Rollo BN-32.

55. See Escalante Arce, *Códice Sonsonate*, 2:138.

56. Calculated from the "Plano topógrafico de los terrenos de la comunidad de Mejicanos de Sonsonate formado por el Agrimensor José C. López," May 1882, AGN-CM-MG.

57. "Padrón General del barrio de Mejicanos," 15 December 1853, AGN-CA-SO.

58. "Libro de actas del común de Mejicanos 1870," AGN-CA-SO.

59. "Libro de cuentas del común de Mejicanos," 1878, AGN-CA-SO.

60. "Los ladinos de ambos Izalcos sobre que se les asignen algunas tierras de las de los comunes de indígenas," AGN-CA-SO, 1820. "Los vecinos de Asunción Izalco han presentado ante el Supremo Gobierno quejas de exesos por parte de los vecinos de Dolores," 2 April 1852, AGN-CPC.

61. "Documentación de la solicitud de las comunas de Dolores y Asunción Izalco para que se les entregaran las listas de las personas que deben pagar canon," 28 July 1870, AGN-CPC.

62. Lauria-Santiago, "'That a Poor Man Be Industrious.'"

63. "Diligencias seguidas por los cofrades del señor San José con respecto a recuperar las tierras del canton Ayutepeque pertenecientes al comun de Ladinos del pueblo de Chalchuapa," 1809–1814, AGN; "Título ejidal de Chalchuapa," Typescript, 1755, BGA, 1866; "Interdicto de posesión de un terreno contra la municipalidad de Atiquizaya por los Señores Aniceto Sifuentes y María Santos," AGN-CG-AH, 1864; "Juicio civil entre el Sr. Pantaleón Rodríguez y la municipalidad de Atiquizaya por despojo de un terreno," AGN-CG-AH, 1864; "Diligencia en que consta estar arreglada la cuestion de limites entre El Progreso y Chalchuapa," AGN-CM-MG, 1896.

64. López, *Estadística general*, 46; "Informe de la comisión del Supremo Gobierno para visitar los pueblos de la República," *Gaceta Oficial*, 7 November 1860, p. 4.

65. "Solicitud de los Ladinos de Chalchuapa al SPE," 25 March 1867, AGN-CQ.

66. "Carta de los vecinos de Chalchuapa al SPE denunciando que la municipalidad pretende quitarles los terrenos de sus comunidad de Ladinos," 11 July 1867, AGN-CPC.

67. *El Constitucional,* 28 February 1867, p. 1.

68. "Solicitud de los Ladinos de Chalchuapa al SPE," 1867, AGN-CDM Rollo BN-27. For evidence of Chalchuapa's economic successes, see *El Constitucional,* 10 January 1867; López, *Estadística general,* 72–73; *Gaceta Oficial,* 12 April 1862; 31 December 1876, p. 787; 12 April 1862; 31 December 1876, p. 787. By 1883 Chalchuapa held 44% of all the coffee trees in the Department of Santa Ana (Mora, *Memoria [1883]*). Chapters 6 and 8 provide further discussion of Chalchuapa.

69. See Martínez Palaez, *La Patria del Criollo,* 289.

70. López, *Estadística general,* 67.

71. "Esteban Castañeda y Desiderio Moreno del común del Volcan de Santa Ana al Supremo Poder Ejecutivo protestando persecución por el Gobernador por estar legalizando los títulos del común," 5 November 1867, AGN-CPC.

72. "Solicitud al Señor Presidente de la República," 5 December 1872, AGN-CDM Rollo BN-46.

73. "Testimonio de las medidas de los terrenos llamados San Juan Buena Vista y Santa Barbara Tahuilapa de la comunidad del Volcan de Santa Ana," 1872, AGN-CT Sección 3, Folder 3.1.

74. "El común del pueblo de Atiquizaya se queja contra la municipalidad," 31 July 1851, AGN-CG-AH.

75. "Carta del alcalde de Nahuizalco al Ministro General del Supremo Gobierno sobre la nulificación de las elecciones municipales," 1854, AGN-CPC.

76. "Solicitud de la municipalidad de Nahuizalco sobre suprimir el pago de Canon por pastoreo y reestablecer el tributo," 1872, AGN-CC [M1.6(872) I-65 Exp. #65]; Secretario Municipal de Nahuizalco, F. Pareja, "Carta al alcalde municipal y gefe del distrito de Sonsonate," 27 November 1872, AGN-CDM Rollo BN-45.

77. "Expediente de remedida de las tierras ejidales y comunales de Armenia," Typescript, 1873, AGN.

78. "Título general de los terrenos ejidales y comunales de Juayua," 1862, AGN-CT Sección 2, Doc. 2.

79. Antonio García, "Carta al Gobernador del Departamento," 3 February 1868, AGN-CDM Rollo BN-31.

80. "Informe de la Comisión del Supremo Gobierno para Visitar los Pueblos de la Republica," *Gaceta Oficial,* 7 November 1860, p. 4.

81. See Pineda, "Avisos de lo tocante," 323–24, 326–28.

82. Cortés y Larraz, *Descripción geográfico-moral;* see also Macleod, *Spanish Central America;* Browning, *El Salvador;* Fowler, "The Political Economy of Indian Survival."

83. See "Documentos relativos a la escasa producción del cacao en la Villa de la Santísima Trinidad de Sonsonate," 1732, UCA-CVJ.

84. See Adams, *Cultural Surveys.* Adams also identifies the strong pockets of Indian peasant landowners in the western region, especially in Sonsonate.

85. AGN-CDM, *passim.*

86. *Gaceta Oficial,* 23 August 1855.

87. Ibid., quoted in Lainez, *Cojutepeque,* 378.

88. Gobernador de Sonsonate, "Informe de la visita oficial a los pueblos del Departamento," 20 September 1913, AGN-CG-SO.

89. Scherzer, *Travels,* 51–52.

90. Domville-Fife, *Guatemala,* 283.

91. El Salvador, Dirección General de Estadística, *Anuario Estadístico,* 1911–1924; Halle, *Transcaribbean,* 78–79.

92. "Padrón General del barrio de Mejicanos," 15 December 1853, AGN-CA-SO,

93. Mora, *Memoria (1883),* 155, 161, 165.

94. Scherzer, *Travels,* 1:236–37.

95. Montgomery, *Narrative of a Journey,* 160.

96. Gobernador de Sonsonate, "Informe de la Visita Oficial a los Pueblos del Departamento," 20 September 1913, AGN-CG-SO.

97. Ibid., 180.

98. Ipiña, *Estadística,* 7.

99. López, *Estadística general,* 121.

100. "Informe del Goberandor de Sonsonate," *El Constitucional,* 23 February 1865, p. 1.

101. "Informe del Gobernador de Sonsonate," *El Constitucional,* 1 February 1865, p. 2.

102. "Cuadro estadístico de las producciones agricolas de los pueblos de Ahuachapán," 1876, AGN-CG-AH.

103. "Razón de las personas que satisfacen censo anual a los fondos de la municipalidad de Sonsonate," May 16 1835, AGN-CA-SO; "Solicitud al SPE sobre censos en Tecapa," 1871, AGN-CQ; "Diligencias en que manda el Gobernador se de informe sobre lo que ha hecho por despojo que ha hecho la municipalidad de sus terrenos," 26 September 1879, AGN-CG-SO; Benjamin Trabanino, "Carta al Gobernador de La Libertad," 29 July 1870, AGN-CDM Rollo BN-35; "Certificación de la municipalidad de Nueva Concepción pidiendo autorización para canon de tierras ejidales," 6 December 1860, AGN-CC [A3.4-14 Exp. #4]; "Don Lorenzo Villedas solicita un terreno en estos *ejidos,*" 1876, AGN-CG-AH.

104. *Gaceta Oficial,* 23 April 1862, p. 5; 29 January 1863, p. 4; Castro, "Estadística"; "Primer semestre de las cuentas de los pueblos del departamento de La Libertad," 1867, AGN-CDM Rollo BN-29; "Sobre ingresos y egresos del Departamento," 23 March 1853, AGN-CPC.

105. "Testimonio del censo estadístico que se paga a las municipalidades del pueblo de San Pedro Pustla," AGN-CG-AH, 1880.

106. "Carta del gobernador de Cuscatlán sobre reducir los censos por ejidos a los habitantes del Valle de Estansuela," 2 March 1850, AGN-CPC.

107. Mora, *Memoria,* 124–25.

108. Sotero Díaz y Valentín Grande, representantes de los labradores del comun de ejidos de Zacatecoluca, "Diligencias de solicitud para que se les exima del impuesto municipal de un real por manzana de terreno a los labradores del comun de ejidos de Zacatecoluca," 1867, AGN-CPC.

109. See McCreery, "An Odious Feudalism."

110. The property of the Ladino peasants is described in "Carta al Gobernador sobre ejidos en Osicala," 1867, AGN-CDM Rollo BN-27.

111. Laferrière, *De Paris à Guatémala*, 226–27. In 1875, for example, the small town of San Antonio rented out three plots of 800, 524 and 557 tareas to farmers from outside of the town. "Exhorto dirigido por el Alcalde Municipal de San Antonio," 1875, AGN-CG-SO.

112. "Razon de las personas que satisfacen censo anual a los fondos de la Municipalidad de Sonsonate," May 16 1835, AGN-CA-SO.

113. "Diligencias en que manda el Gobernador se de informe sobre lo que ha hecho por despojo que ha hecho la municipalidad de sus terrenos," 26 September 1879, AGN-CG-SO.

114. "Carta al Alcalde de Cuisnaguat," 31 October 1870, AGN-CDM Rollo BN-36.

115. Cambranes find similar rentals of municipal lands to farmers and other investors (*Coffee and Peasants*, 84–85).

116. See Browning, *El Salvador*, chap. 5.

117. See chapters 7 and 8 on the abolition of ejidos and communities; see also Browning, *El Salvador*, chap. 5.

118. *El Constiticional*, 5 March 1864, p. 6.

119. Alcalde de Nueva San Salvador, José López, "Carta al Ministro de Gobernación sobre uso de los ejidos," 15 July 1867, AGN-CDM Rollo BN-29.

120. "Carta de el Alcalde de Nueva San Salvador al Ministro General del Supremo Gobierno sobre la asignación a Santa Tecla de los Ejidos de el Simarrón," 28 July 1856, AGN-CC [A3.5-10 Exp. #9]; Gallardo, *Papeles históricos*, 5:45–50.

121. Browning, *El Salvador*, 176–80.

122. Jerez Bustamante, *Cronología;* Browning states that by 1879 "virtually all of the ejidos had been occupied" (*El Salvador*, 178).

123. The original decree of 1855 specified four reales per 100 tareas but this was later increased (Monterrey, *Historia de El Salvador*, 2:164). Browning doubts that the *canon* tax was collected at all—but there is evidence that for the earlier decades at least as late as 1867 the tax was indeed collected (*El Salvador*, 178).

124. Alcalde de Nueva San Salvador, José López, "Carta al Ministro de Gobernación sobre uso de los ejidos," 15 July 1867, AGN-CDM Rollo BN-29.

125. "Carta al SPE sobre terrenos en Nueva San Salvador," 10 November 1870, AGN-CDM Rollo BN-36; *Diario Oficial*, 1878.

126. Jerez Bustamante, *Cronología*, 14, 17, 23, 29.

127. *Gaceta Oficial*, 7 May 1862.

128. Jerez Bustamante, *Cronología*, 49.

129. *Diario Oficial*, 2 July 1880.

130. Chacón, *El Presidente*, 91.

## Chapter 4. *The Peasantry and Commercial Agriculture, 1830s–1880s*

1. For a similar discussion of peasant market participation during the nineteenth century, see Klein, *Haciendas and Ayllus*; Larson and Harris, *Ethnicity, Markets, and Migration.*

2. Lindo Fuentes, *Weak Foundations*, chap. 1.

3. Smith, "Indigo Production," 181–211; Chacón, *El Presidente*, 178.

4. Fernández Molina asserts that small producers "practically monopolized production in 1834" ("Colouring the World," 220).

5. Fernández Molina confirms the arguments presented here; it is also a pattern found in Mexico. See Tutino, *From Insurrection to Revolution*; Ducey, "Liberal Theory and Peasant Practice," 79.

6. Chief of State San Martín lost seven properties in Sonsonate, while Morazán gained an estate worth 20,000 pesos. Lindo-Fuentes, *Weak Foundations*, chap. 2; Fernández Molina, "Colouring the World," 220.

7. Laferrière, *De Paris à Guatémala*, 148.

8. Baily, *Central America*, 84; Dunlop, *Travels in Central America*, 19, 24.

9. "Pidiendo cuatro a seis familias de las dispersas del pueblo de Santiago Nonualco," 185?, AGN-CPC.

10. "Informe de la Gobernación del Departamento de San Vicente," *El Constitucional*, 9 September 1864, p. 3.

11. Castro, "Estadística de la jurisdicción de San Vicente"; Laferrière, *De Paris à Guatémala*, 148; "Informe de la Gobernación del Departamento de San Vicente," *El Constitucional*, 9 September 1864, p. 3.

12. Duke to Porter, 15 November 1885, Department of State, Despatches from U.S. Consuls in San Salvador, USNA.

13. Lorenzo Merino, "Solicitud al Supremo Poder Ejecutivo," 10 February 1870, AGN-CDM Rollo BN-34; Fernández Molina, "Colouring the World," 220). See Pedro de Aycinena to Gerardo Barrios, 29 June 1860, AGN-CB-Vol. 3, no. 5.

14. "Sobre el pago de habilitación de añiles," 10 July 1871, AGN-CQ.

15. "Comunicando a la intendencia de esta Departamento haber recibido 500 pesos de Verapa a buena cuenta de la tierras ejecutadas en la hacienda San Francisco," 16 February 1840, AGN-CPC.

16. "Solicitud de Don Miguel Hernández como apoderado de la Municipalidad de San Miguel para que el Supremo Gobierno ceda en favor de sus ejidos la Hacienda Guadalupe," 6 October 1873, AGN-CDM Rollo BN-47.

17. González, *Geografía de la America Central*, 171.

18. Secretario de Estanzuelas, Pio López, "Carta al Gobernador," 14 November 1872, AGN-CDM Rollo BN-44.

19. Cárdenas, *Sucesos migueleños*, 253, 257. Mora, *Memoria del Ministerio de Gobernación y Fomento (1883)*, 233.

20. See Tutino, *From Insurrection to Revolution*.

21. Barbarena, *Monografías . . . La Paz*, 19.

22. "Certificación de venta de la Hacienda San Cristóbal," 24 September 1859, AGSV.

23. "Libro de Notaría de Hipotecas de San Miguel," 1864, AGN-CI.

24. Salaverría, "La hacienda colonial de San Juan Buenavista."

25. "Expediente de partición de las tierras de la hacienda San Juan Masajapa," 20 March 1891, AGN-CM-MG; "Los vecinos de San Martin piden que el Gobierno los proteja contra Dn Cipriano Castro quien les exije impuestos y les hostiliza por los terrenos de la hacienda El Angel," 16 December 1885, AGN-CQ; Browning reviews the colonial conflicts over lands in Opico and the surrounding haciendas, but interprets the process in terms limited to an Indian-Ladino opposition (*El Salvador*, 99–110). Ironically, he stresses the encroachments made upon Indian possessions and autonomy, while failing to note the success of the emerging Ladino peasantry, a sector that had much more in common with the Indian peasantry than with the elite.

26. "Sobre notificar a varios de los propietarios de la hacienda las Salinas de Ayacachapa, la resolución dada por el Supremo Govierno en la solicitud que hicieron para la division de dichas tierras," 31 July 1886, AGN-CG-SO; Ministerio de Gobernación, F. Vaquero, "Carta al Gobernador de Sonsonate sobre los terrenos de la municipalidad de Nahuizalco en la hacienda Los Trozos," 16 March, 1887, AGN-CG-SO; "Sobre tierras en San Esteban," 1861, AGN-CM-MG.

27. "Autos de remedida de la hacienda Espiritu Santo," typescript, 1845, BGA.

28. "Carta al Juez de Primera Instacia de La Paz sobre la venta de tierras por la Iglesia," 18 May 1877, AGN-CM-MG.

29. Castro, "Estadística de la jurisdicción de San Vicente"; Gobernador de Chalatenango, J. V. Umaña, "Informe al Ministro de Gobernación," 27 September 1905, AGN-CM-MG; Sermeño Lima, "Los movimientos de población." See Lindo Fuentes for a discussion of regional variations in the production of indigo (*Weak Foundations*, 25–26, 54).

30. Browning refers to a form of communal labor (*El Salvador*, 193).

31. El Salvador, *Colección de leyes*, 28; Smith, "Indigo Production and Trade"; Monterrey, *Historia*, 1:52–53. Many of the small producers mentioned by this document did not even own their lands. Instead they rented or simply

possessed suitable ejido or communal lands. "Certificación de actas sobre el cobro del canon anual a los añileros," 21 July 1871, AGN-CQ.

32. Bosque, *Memoria de relaciones,* 9; Browning, *El Salvador,* 150; "Montepiu de Cosecheros de anil," 1835, Harvard Law School Library.

33. For these contracts, see "Libros de Documentos Privados," AMSV.

34. As late as 1870, producers built new *obrajes* in Zaragoza (LL) and this department's governor expected indigo to be the major crop in a short time (Gobernador de La Libertad, José López, "Informe al Ministro del Interior," 15 July 1870, AGN-CDM Rollo BN-35).

35. On the effects of war during this period, see Lindo Fuentes, *Weak Foundations,* chap. 2.

36. Scherzer, *Travels,* 1:202–03.

37. Baily, *Central America,* 70.

38. Squier, *Notes on Central America,* 327.

39. Haefkens, "Viaje a Guatemala y Centroamerica," 1:53.

40. Ibid., 69.

41. Most sugar was produced by tenants of larger landowners or ejidos. J. M. Duke to James Porter, Assistant Secretary of State, 10 June 1886, USNA.

42. López, *Estadística general,* 42, 59, 174.

43. Ipiña, "Estadística," 7.

44. López, *Estadística general,* 179.

45. Browning, *El Salvador,* 193–94.

46. Tempsky, *Mitla,* 416–18.

47. López, *Estadística general,* 184.

48. Ipiña, "Estadística," 4.

49. "Resultado del Padrón de San Pedro Pustla," 1830, AGN-CA-SO.

50. "Cuadro estadístico de las producciones agricolas de los pueblos de Ahuachapán," 1876, AGN-CG-AH.

51. López, *Estadística general,* 86–87; *Gaceta Oficial,* 12 April 1862.

52. "Correspondencia del Gobernador de Ahuachapán," 25 June 1872, AGN-CG-AH; Gobernador de Sonsonate, Francisco Herrera, Carta al Ministro de lo Interior, 12 November 1870, AGN-CDM Rollo BN-36; Feliciano Alvarez, "Solicitud de la Municipalidad de San Pedro Pustla," 8 February, 1871, AGN-CDM Rollo BN-37; "Cartas al Gobernador de Ahuachapán," November 8 1872, AGN-CDM Rollo BN-44.

53. In this year Salcoatitan's ejidos of *38 caballerías* were not in full use (López, *Estadística general,* 166–69).

54. Calculated on the basis of 1,000 trees per manzana (*Gaceta Oficial,* 23 April 1862, p. 5).

55. "Cuadro estadístico de las producciones agrícolas de los pueblos de Ahuachapán," 1876, AGN-CG-AH.

56. "Padrón militar del corriente año, Ataco," 13 May 1888, AGN-CG-AH.

57. López, *Estadística general,* 161, 176; Carlos Castro, "Carta al Gober-

nador de Sonsonate sobre tierras de la Communidad de indígenas de Izalco," 12 December 1887, AGN-CG-SO; Gobernador de Sonsonate, "Carta al alcalde de Izalco sobre usurpación de terrenos cometidas por los Indígenas de Nahuizalco," 23 March 1899, AGN-CG-SO; "Varios individuos comuners de dolores de la ciudad de Izalco se quejan de que Juan Tino, Manuel Lue...y Blas Shul que encabezan una pandilla, los perturban en el ejercicio de sus derechos," 1893, AGS.

58. López, *Estadística general,* 125; "Cuadro de los productos del Departamento de Ahuachapán exportados a Guatemala," 1865, AGN-CG-AH.

59. Clegern notes the significant unregistered sale of indigo and cattle in Honduras and Guatemala (*Origins of Liberal Dictatorship,* 99).

60. "Carta al Gobernador del Departamento de Sonsonate sobre la extración de granos que se realiza por la frontera de Guatemala," 22 March 1854, AGN-CPC.

61. *Diario Oficial,* December 1880 *(De Paris à Guatémala,* 226); Herran, *Notice,* 30; López, *Estadística general,* 159.

62. Guzmán, *Apuntamientos,* 283.

63. "Carta del Gobernador de Sonsonate diciendo que reunio a los comerciantes de esta ciudad para reunir 3,000 pesos del emprestito para mover las fuerzas hacia Nicaragua," 25 March 1857, AGN-CPC; "Carta del Gobernador de Sonsonate, Antonio Ipiña, al Ministro de Hacienda y Guerra pidiendo pago de la escolta necesaria para remitir a la capital a los renuentes a contribuir," 27 February 1857, AGN-CPC.

64. Monterrey, *Historia de El Salvador,* 2:223.

65. "Documentos relativos a la escasa producción del cacao en la Villa de la Santisima Trinidad de Sonsonate," UCA-CVJ, 1732.

66. Haefkens, "Viaje a Guatemala y Centroamerica," 1:69. According to the "Apuntamientos" (45), 200,000–300,000 pesos worth of indigo was purchased in Sonsonate by ships from Peru and Chile. Movimiento de exportación, *Diario Oficial,* 28 March 1878, p. 302.

67. Juarros, *Compendio,* 270; López, *Estadística general,* 154–55.

68. Jarves, *Scenes and Scenery,* 301.

69. Scherzer, *Travels,* 1:158; Jarves, *Scenes and Scenery,* 301.

70. Haefkens, "Viaje a Guatemala y Centroamerica," 1:104.

71. Thompson, *Narrative,* 74.

72. Scherzer, *Travels,* 1:194–96.

73. "Resultados del Censo de Sonsonate," 17 June 1865, AGN-CA-SO.

74. *El Constitucional,* 20 October 1864, pp. 1–2; Lindo Fuentes, *Weak Foundations,* 109–10.

75. A report by the departmental governor noted the planting of 1,200 hectares of cotton trees and 28,000 *quintales* of production. "Carta al Ministro del Interior del Gobierno Politico del Departamento de Sonsonate," 2 January 1865, AGN-CC [G1.2(865) Exp. #7].

76. Foote, *Recollections,* 59.

77. Baily, *Central America,* 80.

78. "Informe de la Gobernación del Departamento de Sonsonate," *Gaceta Oficial,* 24 April 1861, p. 3.

79. Foote, *Recollections,* 65.

80. *Gaceta Oficial,* 10 June 1864, p. 8.

81. Miguel Saízar, "Informe del Gobernador de Sonsonate," *Gaceta Oficial,* April 1862, p. 4.

82. "Informe del Goberndor del Departamento de Santa Ana," *El Constitucional,* 9 September 1864, pp. 1–2.

83. López, *Estadística general,* 41.

84. "Informe de la Comisión del Supremo Gobierno para Visitar los Pueblos de la República," *Gaceta Oficial,* 7 November 1861, p. 4.

85. Mora, *Memoria del Ministerio de Gobernación y Fomento,* 41.

86. "Informe General de la Gobernación del Departamento de Santa Ana," *Gaceta Oficial,* 2 March 1861, pp. 4–5. There was an attempt during the mid 1860s to import Chinese workers, but there is no evidence of its success (El Salvador, *Colección de leyes,* 29).

87. "Informe del Goberanador del Departamento de Santa Ana," *El Constitucional,* 9 September 1864, pp. 1–2.

88. "Informe del Gobernador de Santa Ana," *Gaceta Oficial,* 2 April 1862, p. 2. Another report mentioned that "las plantaciones que se levantan, cada día se resienten de una escasez de brazos." *Gaceta de El Salvador,* 7 March 1861, p. 4.

89. "Censo de Población, Ciudad de Santa Ana," 23 December 1879, AMSA.

90. Castro, "Estadística de la jurisdicción de San Vicente"; "Padrón de Trabajadores de la Ciudad de San Vicente," 1894, AGN-CM-MG.

91. El Salvador, Memoria de Gobernación y de Relaciones (1861) (San Salvador, 1862), 18.

92. *El Constitucional,* 1 June 1865; "Informe del Gobernador de La Libertad," *El Constitucional,* 20 February 1867, p. 1.

93. *El Constitucional,* 5 March 1864, p. 6.

94. See Cortés y Larraz, *Descripción geográfico-moral* and the "respuestas" provided to Cortés y Larraz reproduced in Montes, *Etnohistoria de El Salvador,* vol. 2.

95. Floyd, "Los comerciantes guatemaltecos," 33; Pinto Soria, *Raices históricas,* 122, n. 234; Juarros, *Compendio,* 21.

96. Ots Capdequí, *España en América;* "Título ejidal de Chalchuapa," 1755, BGA, 1866; Solano, "Tierra."

97. Castro, *La población de El Salvador;* Gálvez, "Relación geográfica"; Cortés y Larraz, *Descripción.*

98. Gobernador de Santa Ana, "Datos para el Anuario Americano," 2 December 1916, AGN-CM-MG; Barbarena, *Monografías . . . Santa Ana.*

99. *El Constitucional,* 10 January 1867.

100. López, *Estadística general,* 72–73; *Gaceta Oficial,* 12 April 1862; *Gaceta Oficial,* 31 December 1876, p. 787.

101. Mora, *Memoria . . . (1883),* 58.

102. *El Constitucional,* 6 June 1867.

103. El Salvador, *Memoria presentada por el Ministro de Gobernación,* 85.

104. Escamilla, *Geografía económica;* Castro, *Geografía elemental del Salvador.*

105. These numbers are taken from a local tax list in which small landholders benefited from declaring themselves jornaleros in order to pay a lower tax. "Lista de Impuestos," AGS, 1898–1903.

106. *Gaceta Oficial,* 4 December 1861, p. 1.

107. "Informe de la Gobernación de Chalatenango," *Gaceta Oficial,* 20 October 1864, pp. 1–2.

108. López, *Estadística general,* 102.

109. Ibid., 108.

110. López, *Estadística general,* 120–48.

111. Ibid., 115–18.

112. Scherzer, *Travels,* 1:140.

113. Solano, "Tierra."

114. Gálvez, "Relación geográfica."

115. Haefkens, "Viaje a Guatemala y Centroamérica," 1:75.

116. López, *Estadística general,* 138, 141.

117. Tempsky, *Mitla,* 422–23; Lainez, *Cojutepeque;* Escamilla, *Geografía económica,* 28; Guzman, *Apuntamientos,* 202.

118. José Chávez, "Informe de la Gobernación del Departamento de Cuscatlán," *Gaceta Oficial,* 25 June 1862, pp. 4–6.

119. Gálvez, "Relación geográfica"; Juan López de Velazco. *Geografía y descripción universal de las indias (1571–74),* cited in Barbarena, *Monografía . . . Cuscatlan,* 8–9.

120. Squier, *Notes on Central America,* 46; Haefkens, "Viaje a Guatemala y Centroamérica," 1:75.

121. Brasseur de Bourbourg, "Un viaje."

122. *Gaceta Oficial,* 23 August 1855, rpt. in Lainez, *Cojutepeque,* 378. See Francisco Revelo, Carta al Ministro del Interior, 23 March 1868, AGN-CDM, Rollo BN-31; "La situación de El Salvador en la paz," *Gaceta del Salvador* 4:12, 6 June 1857.

123. Haefkens, "Viaje a Guatemala y Centroamérica," 1:80.

124. Dunlop, *Travels in Central America,* 19.

125. "Informe del Gobernador de San Vicente," *Gaceta Oficial,* 11–21 June 1862, 2–3.

126. Castro, "Estadística de la jurisdicción de San Vicente," 100–01.

127. "Informe de la riqueza publica de este Distrito y ciudad (San Vicente)," 1895, AGN-CM-MG.

128. Flores Macal, "La hacienda colonial," 335–71. Haciendas Concepción Ramirez in San Vicente, San Marcos in Zacatecoluca—Obrajuelo and Buenavista in Zacatecoluca were indigo plantations owned by the marquis of Aycinena.

129. Cortés y Larraz, 188, 190–91.

130. Juarros, *Compendio*, 22–23.

131. Galvez, "Relación geográfica."

132. Haefkens, "Viaje a Guatemala y Centroamérica," 1:54.

133. Informe del Gobernador de San Vicente, *Diario Oficial*,

134. Dawson, *Geografía elemental*, 18–19.

135. González, *Lecciones de geografía*; Guzmán, *Apuntamientos*, 198, 201–02.

136. "Informe de la gobernador del departamento de San Vicente," *Diario Oficial*, 3 November 1864.

137. "Informe del Gobernador de San Vicente," 31 December 1899, AGN-CM-MG.

138. Gobernador de San Vicente, C. J. Aviles, "Informe al Ministro de Gobernación," 15 August 1899, AGN-CM-MG.

139. Fonseca, *Monografías departamentales*, 5, 20, 28,

140. López, *Estadística general*, 10; González, *Lecciones de geografía*, 172.

141. López, *Estadística general*, 10–11.

142. Lindo Fuentes, *Weak Foundations*, 97.

143. Cortés y Larraz, *Descripción*, 194.

144. López, *Estadística general*, 19; Lindo Fuentes, *Weak Foundations*, 90.

145. López, *Estadística general*, 25.

146. "Solicitud al SPE sobre ganados y ejidos en Moncagua," 1860, AGN-CDM Rollo BN-22.

147. Baily, *Central America*, 78; Mrs. Foote, *Recollections*, 60–61.

148. Jackson, "The Technological Development," 223.

## Chapter 5. *Peasant Politics, Revolt, and the Formation of the State*

1. Studies of peasant revolt in nineteenth-century Central America often focus on the relationship between peasant mobilization and Guatemala's Carrera. See Woodward, *Rafael Carrera*; Solórzano Fonseca, "Rafael Carrera"; Ingersoll, "The War of the Mountain"; McCreery, *Rural Guatemala*; and Carmack, *Rebels of Highland Guatemala*.

2. See Alvarenga, *Cultura y Etica*; Williams, *States and Social Evolution*.

3. Mallon, *Peasant and Nation*; Nugent, *Spent Cartridges of Revolution*;

Joseph and Nugent, *Everyday Forms;* Thomson, "Popular Aspects of Liberalism"; Tutino, *From Insurrection to Revolution;* Guardino, *Peasants, Politics.*

4. For example, see Guardino, *Peasants, Politics,* chap. 1.

5. See Lauria-Santiago, "La independencia y el campesinado."

6. Monterrey, *Historia de El Salvador,* 1:224–25.

7. Ibid., 1:225.

8. Ibid., 1:227.

9. According Reyes, "The people threw themselves at the garrison" (*Nociones de historia,* 400).

10. Monterrey, *Historia de El Salvador,* 1:230–32.

11. Reyes, *Nociones de historia,* 400–02.

12. Kincaid, "Peasants into Rebels," 473.

13. Calderón, *Episodios nacionales,* 10–14.

14. Marroquín, *San Pedro Nonualco,* 65.

15. Rodríguez, "Historia y descripción."

16. Cañas y Cañas, *El Caudillo,* 7.

17. See Dominguez Sosa, *Ensayo Histórico;* Kincaid, "Peasants into Rebels."

18. Rodríguez, "Historia y descripción," 249.

19. Reyes, *Nociones de historia;* see also Calderón, *Episodios Nacionales,* 26.

20. Monterrey, *Historia de El Salvador,* 1:233.

21. Rodríguez, "Historia y descripción," 249.

22. Cañas y Cañas, *El Caudillo,* 8–45.

23. De Witt to McLane, Guatemala City, July 31, 1834, in Manning, *Diplomatic Correspondence,* 3:76.

24. Monterrey, *Historia de El Salvador,* 1:244

25. Bancroft, *History of Central America,* 3:169.

26. See Guardino, *Peasants, Politics,* 48; Deaton, "The Decade of Revolt."

27. See Woodward, *Rafael Carrera.*

28. The events of 1835 are known from a government investigation into the events after the neutralization (not defeat) of the faction: *Informe que el secretario.*

29. Ibid.

30. De Witt to Forsyth, U.S. Secretary of State, November 7, 1835, in Manning, *Diplomatic Correspondence,* 3:136.

31. "Decreto del Gobierno de 29 de Mayo de 1835. Dado en San Vicente," AGN-CImp.

32. *Informe que el secretario.*

33. Ibid.

34. Ibid, 6.

35. De Witt to Forsyth, U.S. Secretary of State, November 7, 1835, in Manning, *Diplomatic Correspondence,* 3:136.

36. De Witt to Forsyth, Guatemala City, December 18, 1835, in ibid., 3:137; *Informe que el secretario.*

37. *Informe que el secretario.*

38. De Witt to Forsyth, Guatemala City, 18 December 1835, in Manning, *Diplomatic Correspondence,* 137.

39. *Informe que el secretario.*

40. Ibid.

41. Ibid.

42. Flores Membreño, *Anuario.*

43. "Estado Mayor General del Ejercito de Morazán, Agosto de 1842," ANCR, Serie XII, no. 8286; Leistenschneider and Leistenschneider, *Administración,* 57.

44. Wortman, *Government and Society,* 262–63.

45. Martínez, "Historia," 208–09; Monterrey, *Historia de El Salvador,* 1:266.

46. Reyes, *Nociones de historia,* 417.

47. Woodward, "Liberalism," 115–16.

48. Monterrey, *Historia de El Salvador,* 1:274; "Inventario de los documentos y demás papeles del Archivo Nacional, que se salvaron del incendio de la madrugada del 20 de noviembre de 1889," *Memoria de Gobernación, 1890,* 327.

49. Reyes, *Nociones de historia,* 417; Galdamés Armas, *Hombres y cosas,* 156.

50. Piñeda Alvarado, *Reseña historica,* 8; Reyes, *Nociones de historia,* 444.

51. Reyes, *Nociones de historia,* 449. See also Orellana and Orellana, *Sonsonate histórico,* 36–37; El Salvador, *Atlas censal,* 110.

52. Monterrey, *Historia de El Salvador,* 2:19.

53. Ibid., 2:20; Reyes, *Nociones de historia,* 466–69; Leistenschneider and Leistenschneider, *Administración,* 137.

54. Cardenal, *El poder eclesiástico,* chap. 2.

55. Malaina, *La Compañía de Jesus,* 38.

56. Cojutepeque, *La municipalidad.*

57. L. Dupre to Porter, Dec. 1886, U.S. Department of State, Despatches from U.S. Consuls in San Salvador, USNA.

58. Another case of Indian recruitment of white or Ladino leadership is found in Mendoza, "Páginas historicas."

59. Martínez, "Historia," 229.

60. See Teodoro Moreno to Gerardo Barrios, 22 November 1861, AGN-CB, vol. XVI, doc. 108; Samuel González to Gerardo Barrios, April 1862, AGN-CB, vol. XIV, doc. 131; Teodoro Moreno to Gerardo Barrios, 24 April 1862, AGN-CB, vol. XIV, doc. 132.

61. Gerardo Barrios, "El presidente de la República a los Indígenas de Cojutepeque," leaflet, 15 July 1863, UCA-CVJ.

62. Martínez, "Historia," 230.

63. Larraínzar, *Carta,* 35.

64. Bustamante, *Historia militar,* 88.

65. De Belot, *La Republique*, 33.

66. Mrs. Foote, *Recollections,* 68.

67. Ministerio del Interior, "Carta al Gobernador de San Vicente," 30 December 1868, AGN-CDM, Rollo BN-32.

68. J. S. Molina, Cuartel General de San Vicente, "Carta al Ministro de Hacienda y Guerra," 27 April 1871, AGN-CDM, Rollo BN-38.

69. Martínez, "Historia," 231–32; Reyes, *Nociones de historia,* 576–78.

70. "Solictud de Dionicio Tamallo al Supremo Poder Ejecutivo," 21 September 1872, AGN-CDM, Rollo MI-23.

71. Martínez, "Historia," 233; "Enviando Lista de los indígenas para que los ponga a la disposición del juez de primera instancia para las causa contra los autores y promotores de la asonada del 9," 1872, AGN-CPC; "Borrador de nota al Comandante General de este Departamento General D. Vicente Vaquero," 1872, AGN-CDM, Rollo BN-39.

72. Antonio G. Valdés, "Decreto de El Supremo Gobierno de la República, Cojutepeque," 20 January 1873.

73. Gobernador de La Paz, Agustín Gómez, "Carta al Ministro del Interior sobre los efectos de la revuelta de Cojutepeque en Santiago Nonualco," 1872, AGN-CPC.

74. Alcalde de Santiago Nonualco, Ancelino Colindres, "Carta al Gobernador de La Paz," 12 July 1872, AGN-CDM, Rollo BN-39.

75. Proyecto de formación de pueblos de los valles de Cojutepeque, 10 August 1872, AGN-CDM, Rollo MI-23. "Certificación de acta municipal del pueblo de Monte de San Juan," 17 September 1872, AGN-CDM.

76. Laferrière, *De Paris à Guatémala,* 151–53.

77. Bancroft, *History of Central America,* 3:398–99.

78. Alcalde de Santo Domingo, Antonio Portillo, "Carta al Mariscal Presidente Don Santiago Gonzáles," 22 July 1872, AGN-CDM, Rollo BN-39.

79. *Boletín Oficial # 74,* 28 September 1872, in García, *Diccionario histórico,* A:16.

80. Bustamante, *Historia militar,* 138.

81. But see Alvarenga, *Cultura y ética,* chap. 1.

82. Ibid., chap. 6; Ching, "From Clientelism to Militarism," chaps. 5–6.

83. Galdaméz Armas, *Hombres y cosas,* 154; López, *Estadística.*

84. On Zaldívar, see Bancroft, *History of Central America,* 406–07. Ministro del Interior, Larreynaga, "Borrador de nota al Gobernador de Santa Ana," Agosto 22 1870, AGN-CDM, Rollo BN-35.

85. Gobernador de Santa Ana, "Carta al Ministro del Interior sobre desordenes," August 20, 1870, AGN-CC [G1.2(870) Exp. #13].

86. Galdamés Armas, *Hombres y cosas,* 108.

87. *Boletín Oficial,* 5 December 1870, San Salvador, in García, *Diccionario histórico,* A:38.

88. Monterrey, *Historia de El Salvador,* 2:355.

89. *Boletín Oficial #3,* 12 December 1870, San Salvador, in García, *Diccionario histórico,* A:38–9.

90. *Boletín Oficial #4,* 14 December 1870, San Salvador, in García, *Diccionario histórico,* A:40.

91. *Boletín Oficial #5,* 19 December 1870, San Salvador, in García, *Diccionario histórico,* A:37.

92. Gáldamez Armas, *Hombres y cosas,* 155–58.

93. García, *Dicconario Histórico,* A:44; Gobernador de Sonsonate, Herrera, "Carta al Minstro de Hacda. sobre gastos relacionados con los Volcaneños," 1870, AGN-CDM, Rollo BN-36. Gobernador de Ahuchapán, Francisco Menéndez, "Carta al Ministro de Relaciones Interiores," 4 December 1870, AGN-CDM, Rollo BN-36. *Boletín Oficial #2,* 7 December 1870, San Salvador, reproduced in García, *Diccionario histórico,* A:38. On 9 December the government prohibited the sale of gunpowder in the entire region. Ministro del Interior, "Carta al Adm. del ramo de polvora," 9 December 1870, AGN-CDM, Rollo BN-36. Gobernador de Sonsonate, Herrera, "Carta al Ministro de Hacienda," 10 December 1870, AGN-CDM, Rollo BN-36

94. *Boletín Oficial,* 5 December 1870, San Salvador, in García, *Diccionario histórico,* A:37.

95. "Solicitud al Presidente de la República," 12 June 1867, CDM, Rollo BN-28.

96. "La señora Elena Aldana de Paz solisita aprobar sus pérdidas de 2 de Diciembre de 1870, ocasionados por los sediciosos en valor de 10,374$", 1872, AGN-CDM, Rollo BN-45.

97. *El Constitucional,* 15 December 1870, reproduced in Garcia, *Diccionario histórico,* A:41.

98. Galdamés Armas, *Hombres y cosas,* 165.

99. Belisario Molina, Secretaría de la Corte Suprema de Justicia, "Carta al Ministro del Interior sobre Dueñas," 25 June 1872, AGN-CQ.

100. "Lista de los individuos que voluntariamente han emprestado dinero a esta gobernación para los gastos en la revolución," 12 May 1871, AGN-CQ.

101. Alcalde de Santa Ana, Anastacio Rodriguez, "Carta al Ministro del Interior," 19 November 1872, AGN-CDM Rollo BN-44.

102. Rafael Reyes, "Carta al Dr. Dn. Julio Interiano sobre tierras de indígenas de San Rafael La laguna," 1901, AGN-CM-MG.

103. "Solicitud de Nulificación de Eleccion," 27 December 1872, AGN-CDM.

104. "Descripción de cada uno de los municipios del departamento," 1913, AGN-CG-SO; Gobernador de Sonsonate, "Informe de la Visita Oficial a los pueblos del Departamento," 20 September 1913, AGN-CG-SO. Among the

killed were Braulio Salaverría, Casimiro Dominguez, and a son of Pedro Cea. Orellana and Orellana, *Sonsonate histórico,* 43.

105. "Libro de Actas Municipales," 1873, AMJ.

106. Compare the profiles in Burgess, *Justo Rufino Barrios,* 211.

107. Dominguez Sosa, *Génesis,* 20–21.

108. Martínez, "Historia de Cojutepeque," 326; Figeac, *Recordatorio histórico,* 301; Marcial Esteves, *Relación historica de algunos . . . Ounalaska* (1885).

109. Duke to Porter, 28 May 1885, U.S. Department of State, Despatches from U.S. Consuls in San Salvador, USNA; Estupianián, *Memoria,* 232.

110. Calderón, *Episodios nacionales,* 48.

111. Piñeda Alvarado, *Reseña historica,* 9–11; Marroquín, *San Pedro Nonualco,* 179.

112. "Relación que varios vecinos de Opico hacen de los desordenes ocurridos alli con motivo de la eleccion locales," 24 December 1885, AGN-CQ.

113. "El General Don Francisco Menéndez solicita comprobar las perdidas que sufrio en sus intereses el año de 1876," AGN-CM-MG, 1883.

114. Martínez, "Historia," 240–41; Duke to Porter, 13 June 1885, U.S. Department of State, Despaches from U.S. Consuls in San Salvador, USNA.

115. Dupre to Porter, December 1886, U.S. Department of State, Despaches from U.S. Consuls in San Salvador, USNA.

116. Dupre to Porter, 1 December 1887, U.S. Department of State, Despaches from U.S. Consuls in San Salvador, USNA.

117. Bustamante, *Historia militar,* 88.

118. Orellana and Orellana, *Sonsonate histórico,* 48–50.

119. Larreynaga, *Memoria,* 3–4.

120. Velasco, *Monografía histórica,* 34; Martínez, "Historia," 230–46; *La Union, Suplemento No. 11,* 1890, UES-PEH.

121. "Certificación del Juzagado de Paz de Ilopango," 25 February 1890, AGN-CM-MG; Larreynaga, *Memoria,* 70, 104.

122. Martínez, "Historia," 247.

123. Bustamante, *Historia militar,* 91.

124. Francisco Funes, Gobernador de San Salvador, "Informe del Gobernador al Ministro de Gobernación," 23 December 1890, AGN-CM-MG.

125. "Salvadoreños," leaflet, UES-PEH, 1890.

126. *La Revolución. Alcance al Número 6,* 1890.

127. Plutarco Bowen, "Informe sobre tropas revolucionarias contra Ezeta," 1894, AGN-CC [M1.2-2 Exp. #2].

128. Orellana and Orellana, *Sonsonate histórico,* 50; "Lista de los capitalistas del Departamento de La Libertad con expresión del capital que se les supone," 1893, AGN-CM-MG; "Recibos de Pagos de Emprestitos," 1894, AGN-CG-SO.

129. De Guevarra, *Exploración etnográfica,* 43.

130. Orellana and Orellana, *Sonsonate histórico,* 51.

131. De Guevarra, *Exploración etnográfica,* 42.

132. "Descripción de cada uno de los municipios del departamento," 1913, AGN-CG-SO.

133. See Lauria-Santiago, "Land, Community, and Revolt."

134. Gobernador de Usulután, R. Orellana, "Informe al Ministro de Gobernación," 9 February 1899, AGN-CM-MG; Gobernador de Cabañas, Antolín Olarro, "Informe al Ministro de Gobernación," 5 August 1899, AGN-CM-MG.

135. See Lindo Fuentes, "Los limites del poder en la era de Barrios," in Arturo Taracena, ed. *Construcción de las identidades.*

136. Adams, *Nationalization;* Cardenal, *El poder eclesiástico.*

137. See "Viva El Pueblo Migueleño, Viva el Estado"; "Proclama a los Pueblos de El Salvador"; Leistenschneider and Leistenschneider, *Administración,* 134.

138. See Palmer, "A Liberal Discipline."

139. See Loveman, *The Constitution of Tyranny,* 110–17.

140. De Belot, *La Republique,* 33.

141. Francisco Campos, "Cuerpo de Patriotas de la Ciudad de Izalco," 17 July 1890, AGS.

142. Scherzer, *Travels;* "Memoria del Secretario de Estado en los Deptos de Interior, Hacienda y Guerra," 1867, AGN-CQ.

143. Barbarena, *Descripción geográfica;* Wright, *Salvador,* 46; El Salvador, *Memoria Presentada por el Ministro de Gobernación,* 17–21; Ezeta "Ejercito del Salvador, Cuadro Demonstrativo del Estado General Diario," 1896, AGN.

144. Alcalde de Cuisnahuat, Damian Hernández, "Carta al Gobernador del Departamanto," 10 February 1886, AGS.

145. For another view, see Ching, "From Clientelism to Militarism," esp. chaps. 2–4.

146. See Ducey, "Liberal Theory," 66.

147. Alcalde de Mazahuat, "Carta al Gobernador del Departamento de Sonsonate," 28 November 1886, AGS.

148. "Contra Toribio Melgares y Leandro Hernandez como promotores del desorden ocurrido en esta Villa el 30 del prosimo pasado," 1886, AGN-CI.

149. See Lauria-Santiago, "An Agrarian Republic," chap. 8.

## Chapter 6. *Coffee and Its Impact, 1850–1910*

1. See Arias Peñate, *Los subsistemas;* Bulmer-Thomas, *The Political Economy of Central America;* Fowler, "Cacao"; Slutzky and Slutsky, "El Salvador"; Arce, "El Salvador"; Paige, *Coffee and Power;* Browning, *El Salvador;* and Lindo Fuentes, *Weak Foundations.*

2. See Kerr, "The Role of the Coffee Industry"; Kerr, "La edad de oro";

Cardoso, "Historia económica"; Wilson, "The Crisis of National Intergration"; Guillen Chacón, "Historia y comentarios"; Iraheta Rosales, et al., "La crisis de 1929"; Williams, *States and Social Evolution;* and Lindo Fuentes, *Weak Foundations.*

3. See Lindo Fuentes, "La introducción del café en El Salvador," paper presented at the conference "Las sociedades agrarias centroamericanas, Siglos XIX y XX," Universidad Nacional de Costa Rica, 1990.

4. See Lindo Fuentes, *Weak Foundations,* 116–22; Williams, *States and Social Evolution;* Hall, *El Café;* Pérez Brignoli, *Breve historia;* Pérez Brignoli, *Historia general de Centroamérica;* Cardoso, "Historia económica."

5. Lardé y Larín, *Monografía,* 115; Jiménez, "La República," 287.

6. Bosque, *Memoria de relaciones;* see also Lindo Fuentes, *Weak Foundations,* 116–18.

7. *Gaceta Oficial del Salvador,* 28 July 1858, p. 6; Orellana and Orellana, *Sonsonate histórico,* 44; "Exhorto dirigido por el Alcalde Municipal de San Antonio," 1875, AGN-CG-SO.

8. Lardé y Larín, *Monografía,* 115.

9. Ibid.; "Informe del Gobernador de La Libertad," 1867, AGN-CDM Rollo BN-29.

10. Mrs. Foote, *Recollections,* 59; Lindo Fuentes, *Weak Foundations,* 116–22; Suárez, *Noticias generales,* 12.

11. López, *Estadística,* 166–67, 169–70.

12. Ibid., 174.

13. Ibid., 178.

14. Ibid., 23.

15. Ibid., 128–29, 138, 141; "La situación de El Salvador en la paz," *Gaceta del Salvador* 4:12, 6 June 1857.

16. El Salvador, *Anuario Estadístico;* "Salvador," editor's notes, *Bulletin of the Pan American Union* 12 (March 1902): 636.

17. For an example, see "Informe del gobernador de Usulután," 1921, AGN-CM-MG.

18. *Bulletin of The Pan American Union* (March 1902): 636.

19. See Lindo Fuentes, *Weak Foundations,* 104–05.

20. Figeac, *Recordatorio histórico,* 253; Kerr, "La edad de oro," 13.

21. For examples, see "Certificación de la municipalidad de nueva concepción pidiendo autorización para canon de tierras ejidales," 6 December 1860, AGN-CC [A3.4-14 Exp. #4]; Secretario del Partido de la Nueva San Salvador, Benjamin Trabanino, "Carta al Gobernador del Departamento sobre el cobro del canon anual por tierras ejidales para tierras usadas para café, azucar," 1870, AGN-CC [M1.6(870) I-53 Exp. #53].

22. Mora, *Memoria . . . (1883),* 39, 41.

23. Ibid., 63–67; Trigueros, "Informe."

24. Mora, *Memoria . . . (1883),* 59–60. "Libro de Actas Municipales de

Juayua," 1882, AMJ; Lever refers to resistance to coffee by commercial investors. Lever, *Central America*, 103, 182.

25. See Hall, *El Café*; Palacios, *Coffee*.

26. Lindo Fuentes, *Weak Foundations*; Jacob Bair to Pacific Mail Co., 22 November 1882, *Boletín de Agricultura* 1 (1882): 250.

27. Lindo Fuentes, *Weak Foundations*, 93–97, 159–62.

28. "Credito Agricola," *Boletín de Agricultura* 2 (15 September 1883): 399.

29. *Diario Oficial*, 25 February 1882, p. 194.

30. "Testimonio de hipoteca," 1897, AGN-CM-MG; "Libro de Juicios por cesiones, Sonsonate," 1895, AGS; "Incidente de apelación interpuesta por la indígena María Cuadra del auto proveído . . . previniendole que dentro de ocho dias desocupe la finca situada en el paraje Tescalito en virtud de un pedimento de don Luis Rios," 1893, AGN-CG-SO.

31. See Putnam, *The Southland of North America*, 232–34.

32. "Cosecha de café en el Departamento de Sonsonate," March 1916, AGN-CG-SO; Guzmán, *Apuntamientos*, 231.

33. "El Sr. Dn. Juan Antonio Montiel denuncia los abusos que el Srio. Municipal de la villa de Nahuizalco Sr. don Vicente Escobar comete en el desempeño del destino," 1892, AGN-CG-SO.

34. For examples, see El Salvador, *Memoria . . . (1861)*, 20. "Informe de la Gobernación del Departamento de Sonsonate," *El Constitucional*, 26 August 1864, pp. 1–3. "Libro de Copias y Acuerdos," 1882, AMJ.

35. Mora, *Memoria . . . (1883)*, 141; Vicente Dueñas, "Anexos al Informe sobre las dispocisiones dictadas por las municipalidades en el ramo de agricultura," *Diario Oficial*, 12 December 1880.

36. Ibid., 318.

37. *Gaceta Oficial*, 31 December 1876, 787.

38. Guzmán, *Apuntamientos*, 288.

39. Mora, *Memoria . . . (1883)*, 58.

40. Guzmán, *Apuntamientos*, 288.

41. Narciso Aviles, "Informe del Gobernador del Departamento de Santa Ana," *Diario Oficial*, 5 October 1881, p. 319.

42. Barbarena, *Monografías . . . Santa Ana*, 15.

43. Gobernador de Santa Ana, "Datos para el Anuario Americano," 2 December 1916, AGN-CM-MG.

44. *El Constitucional*, 10 January 1867.

45. El Salvador, *Memoria . . . (1892)*, 85.

46. Escamilla, *Geografía económica*; Castro, *Geografía elemental*.

47. López, *Estadística general*, 72–73; *Gaceta Oficial*, 12 April 1862; *Gaceta Oficial*, 31 December 1876, p. 787. Mora, *Memoria . . . (1883)*, 58; "Lista de Impuestos," AGS, 1898–1903.

48. Barbarena, *Monografías . . . Santa Ana*, 43.

49. Ward, *Libro azul*.

50. See Montes, *El agro.*

51. See *Breves datos históricos de El Congo,* 12; Montes, *El agro,* 55.

52. Barbarena, *Monografía . . . departamento de Santa Ana,* 32–35; López, *Estadística,* 42.

53. "Nomina de los Cafetaleros en los Municipios del Departamento de Santa Ana," 1931, AGN-CM-MG.

54. "Informe del Gobernador de Santa Ana," 1915, AGN-CM-MG. El Salvador, *Memoria . . . (1892),* 82; Gobernador de Santa Ana, "Datos para el Anuario Americano," 2 December 1916, AGN-CM-MG.

55. See Alcalde de Santa Ana, "Carta al Minstro de Gobernación," 5 May 1924, AGN-CM-MG.

56. See "Solicitud al Señor Presidente de la Republica," 5 December 1872, AGN-CDM Rollo BN-36.

57. "Solicitud de Leon Trajo sobre exhonerarse del empleo de primer socio del administrador del comun de Indijenas de aqui," 1871, AGN-CG-AH; López, *Estadística,* 46; Mora, *Memoria . . . (1883),* 125; Scherzer, *Travels,* 236–37.

58. "Don Lorenzo Villedas solicita un terreno en estos ejidos," 1876, AGN-CG-AH.

59. "Cuadro estadístico de las producciones agricolas de los pueblos de Ahuachapán," 1876, AGN-CG-AH.

60. "Informe del gobernador de Ahuachapán," 1900, AGN-CM-MG.

61. Ipiña, *Estadística;* Fonseca, *Monografías . . . de Ahuachapán,* 18–19, 24, 32; "Informe que el señor Gobernador del Departamento de Ahuachapán dirige al Ministro de Gobernación," 1892, AGN-CM-MG.

62. "Informe del gobernador de La Libertad," 1900, AGN-CM-MG.

63. *El Constitucional,* 1 June 1865.

64. Rosignon, "Los cafetales," 120–21.

65. "Libro Compuesto de 96 Fojas . . . en que se notan los títulos de propiedad de terrenos ejidales estendidos por esta alcaldia," 1882, AMNSS.

66. Rosignon, "Los cafetales," 120–21.

67. Ibid.

68. See Alcalde de Nueva San Salvador, "Informe especial de agricultura," 30 January 1885, AMNSS.

69. "Lista de los agricultores, comerciantes y otras clases sociales de la jurisdicción municipal de Nueva San Salvador," 16 July 1898, AGN-CM-MG.

70. Barbarena, *Monografías . . . La Libertad,* 10.

71. Ward, *Libro azul,* 64.

72. Ipiña, "Estadística," 6.

73. "Solicitud de los Señores Nazario Salaverria . . . pididiendo una concesión para construir una via ferrea que una la ciudad de Sonsonate con las poblaciones de Nahuizalco, Salcoatitan y El Progreso," 1897, AGN-CM-AL.

74. Barbarena, *Monografías . . . Sonsonate,* 47–48.

75. Ibid.; Gobernador de Sonsonate, "Informe de la Visita Oficial a los pueblos del Departamento," 20 September 1913, AGN-CG-SO.

76. "Cuadro de los terrenos acotados y distribuidos en Salcoatitan," 29 May 1868, AGN-CA-SO.

77. "Francisco Salaverria acusa a la municipalidad del pueblo de Salcoatitan por haber cedido una parte del terreno de sus finca a Don Pedro Viscarra," 1889, AGN-CG-SO.

78. Gobernador de Sonsonate, "Informe de la Visita Oficial a los pueblos del Departamento," 20 September 1913, AGN-CG-SO.

79. "Copia del Informe que se remite al Director del Museo Nacional para formar un mapa que la República del Salvador debe mandar a la esposición de San Luis," 1903, AGN-CG-SO.

80. Alcalde de Salcoatitan, "Informe al Gobernador de Sonsonate," 30 July 1908, AGN-CG-SO.

81. "Informe de comercio y agricultura del Distrito de Sonsonate," 1893, AGN-CG-SO.

82. "Informe de comercio y agricultura correspondiente al Distrito de Izalco," 7 February 1893, AGN-CG-SO; Alcalde de Armenia, Wenceslao Gomes, "Informe al Gobernador de Sonsonate," December 1892 AGN-CG-SO; "Descripción de la villa de Armenia," 1895, AGN-CG-SO; Gobernador de Sonsonate, "Informe de la Visita Oficial a los pueblos del Departamento," 20 September 1913, AGN-CG-SO.

83. Barbarena, *Monografías . . . Sonsonate*, 60.

84. "Informe de comercio y agricultura correspondiente al Distrito de Izalco," 7 February 1893, AGN-CG-SO.

85. Barbarena, *Monografías . . . Sonsonate*, 64; Gobernador de Sonsonate, "Informe de la Visita Oficial a los pueblos del Departamento," 20 September 1913, AGN-CG-SO.

86. "Informe de comercio y agricultura del Distrito de Sonsonate," 1893, AGN-CG-SO.

87. Ibid.

88. Barbarena, *Monografías . . . Sonsonate*, 37; Alcalde de Nahuizalco, "Carta al Gobernador del Departamento de Sonsonate sobre las perdidas de café," 30 November 1906, AGS.

89. Gobernador de Sonsonate, "Informe de la Visita Oficial a los pueblos del Departamento," 20 September 1913, AGN-CG-SO.

90. Castro, "Estadística."

91. "Informe del Gobernador de San Vicente," 31 December 1899, AGN-CM-MG; "Padrón de trabajadores de la ciudad de San Vicente," 1894, AGN-CM-MG.

92. Rodríguez, "Historia y descripción," 286–87.

93. Gobernador de San Vicente, C. J. Aviles, "Informe al Ministro de Gobernación," 15 August 1899, AGN-CM-MG.

94. *Gaceta Oficial,* 25 January 1862, p. 5; Gobernador de La Paz, A. Castillo G., "Informe al Ministro de Gobernación," 15 January 1900, AGN-CM-MG; Alfaro, *Memoria,* 121; Ward, *Libro azul,* 64; "Informe del gobernador de La Paz," 1917, AGN-CM-MG.

95. "Inspección general de agricultura," *Boletín de Agricultura* 1 (15 May 1882): 111.

96. Barbarena, *Monografías . . . La Paz,* 21–25; G. Hernández, "Informe de la visita oficial del Gobernador del Departamento de La Paz," 1905, AGN-CM-MG.

97. Barbarena, *Mongrafias . . . Cuscatlan,* 32, 34–35, 45, 48–49.

98. Gobernador de Usulután, José de Parker, "Informe al Ministro de Gobernación," 18 January 1894, AGN-CM-MG.

99. "Solicitud del Dr. Dn. Miguel Enrique Araujo sobre que se le venda un terreno que esta poseyendo en los extinguidos ejidos de Santiago de María," 1894, AGN-CM-MG.

100. Ward, *Libro azul,* 64.

101. *Memoria . . . (1892),* 67, 72–73.

102. Simón Sol, "Informe del Comisionado de Santiago de María," *Diario Oficial,* 5 December 1882, p. 730.

103. Ibid.

104. *Memoria . . . (1892),* 341.

105. Guzmán, *Apuntamientos,* 288.

106. Gobernador de Morazán, Francisco Ortiz, "Informe al Ministro Fomento y Beneficiencia," 21 January 1890, AGN-CM-MG.

107. Barbarena, *Monografías . . . Morazán,* 16, 18, 29, 32, 35.

108. El Salvador, *Memoria,* 103.

109. Gobernador de Morazán, Antonio Cardona, "Informe al Ministro de Gobernación," 31 July 1909, AGN-CM-MG.

110. "Informe de la Gobernación de San Miguel," *El Constitucional,* 26 January 1865, pp. 2–3; "El Señor Manuel Godoy solicita información de unos testigos," 1895, AGN-CM-AL.

111. Gobernador de San Miguel, Francisco Mendoza, "Informe Semestral del Gobernador del Departamento de San Miguel," 11 December 1895, AGN-CM-MG.

112. Barbarena, *Monografías . . . San Miguel,* 37.

113. See Cardona, "Población indígena," 2.

114. Mathe to Hamilton Fish, 18 July 1871, Despatches from U.S. Consuls, U.S. State Department, USNA.

115. "Informe del Director de la Escuela y Finca Modelo," *Diario Oficial,* 12 November 1882, p. 654; see also Lindo Fuentes, *Weak Foundations,* 83–84; Mathe to Hamilton Fish, 18 July 1871, U.S. Department of State, Despatches from US Consuls, USNA.

116. Bureau of American Republics, *Coffee in America,* 25.

117. Teodoro Moreno, "Informe del Gobernador Departamental de Santa Ana," *Gaceta del Salvador,* 12 January 1859.

118. Narciso Avilés, "Informe sobre las dispociciones dictadas por los municipios en el ramo de agricultura," *Diario Oficial,* 12 December 1880.

119. *Boletín de Agricultura* 2 (1882): 339.

120. Teodoro Moreno, Diputado y Presidente de la Camara de Senadores, *Diario Oficial,* 13 June 1883, 14:136, p. 569.

121. Laferrière, *De Paris à Guatémala,* 227; see Manuel Guzama to Gerardo Barrios, 22 October 1860, AGN-CB, vol. 1, doc. 50.

122. "Censo de Población, Ciudad de Santa Ana," 23 December 1879, AMSA.

123. Barbarena, *Monografías . . . Santa Ana,* 46.

124. Putnam, *The Southland,* 234.

125. "Marcelina González se queja contra el alcalde de El Progreso por habersele acusado de quebradora del General Castillo," 1890, AGS. Another document from 1884 confirms the wage of 4 reales per day. "Lista de los Trabajadores en la Hacienda San Andres," 1884, AGA.

126. Martin, *Salvador,* 191; "Nomina de la Mina Butters-Divisadero," 1914, AGN-CM-MG; see also Jackson, "The Technological Development of Central America," 214, 289–91.

127. Thompson, *Rainbow Countries,* 98–99.

128. "Informe del gobernador de Usulután," 1921, AGN-CM-MG.

129. "Libros de Inscripción de Jornaleros," 1903–1909, AMSA; "Marcelina González se queja contra el alcalde de El Progreso por habersele acusado de quebradora del General Castillo," 1890, AGS.

130. "Secretaría de la Junta de Agricultura del Distrito de Izalco," *Boletín de Agricultura* 1 (15 January 1882): 49.

131. For a different view, see Alvarenga, *Cultura y ética.*

132. Monterrey, *Historia de El Salvador,* 1:300.

133. See Knight, "Debt Bondage"; Katz, "Labor Conditions."

134. "Se deroga la ley que creo los jueces de agricultura," *Diario Oficial,* 10 March 1882, p. 245.

135. See Alcalde de Izalco, Samuel Velado, "Carta al Gobernador del Departamento," 5 September 1885, AGS.

136. "Libro en que consta el numero de personas que pagan en el presente año los cuatro reales," 1852, AGN-CA-SO.

137. "El Sr. Ignacio se queja de que el alcalde de Ishuatan a mandado sitarlo para que como jornaleros valla a los trabajos de la finca de General Regalado," 1896, AGS; Palmer, *Central America,* 113.

138. Hacienda Chilata, "Lista de mozos quebradores que debe darseles de alta," 18 June 1897, AGS.

139. Ibid.

140. "Informe del gobernador de Usulután," 1900, AGN-CM-MG; Gob-

ernador de Usulután, C. J. Aviles, "Informe al Ministro de Gobernación," 16 December 1908, AGN-CM-MG.

141. "Informe del Gobernador de Ahuachapán," 1900 and 1915, AGA; "Informe del alcalde de Izalco," 1900, AGS.

142. "Informe municipal de Juayua," 28 May 1900, AGS.

143. Abraham Pinel, "Solicitud al Ministro de Gobernación para dos Guardias Nacionales para su finca," 25 November 1919, AGN-CM-MG.

144. See Alvarenga, *Cultura y ética.*

145. "Tres productos agrícolas nacionales," *Boletín de Agricultura* 2 (26 October 1884): 305–06.

146. Ibid.

147. See Sainte-Croix, *Onze mois,* 235.

148. Palmer, *Central America,* 113.

149. "Ojeada sobre la economía rural salvadoreña," *Boletín de Agricultura* 1 (1882): 276, emphasis added.

150. Guzmán, *Apuntamientos,* 269.

151. Martínez Funes, *Album de San Salvador y Santa Ana.*

152. Ward, *Libro Azul,* 164, 246, 305.

153. Barbarena, *Monografías Departamentales . . . San Miguel,* 21. See also "Nomina de los Socios del Banco Internacional del Salvador," 31 January 1898, AGN-CImp.

154. "Clasificación de establecimientos Commerciales," 1902, AGN-CG-SO.

155. Fonseca, *Monografías departamentales,* 40–41.

156. "Solicitud, prima sobre la exportación de azúcar," *Boletín de Agricultura* 1 (1882): 249.

157. *Gaceta Oficial,* 13 July 1861, p. 8.

158. Long, *Railways of Central America.*


Chapter 7. *The Privatization of Land, 1881–1912*

1. For example, Browning, *El Salvador;* Menjivar, *Acumlación,* Torres Rivas, *Interpretación;* Burns, "The Modernization," and Cardoso, *Historia del café;* for a more nuanced view, see Lindo Fuentes, *Weak Foundations.*

2. Browning, *El Salvador,* 176; "Ejidos," *Gaceta del Salvador,* 1 October 1847.

3. Gobernador de La Libertad, "Carta al Ministro del Interior sobre la probabilidad de una revuelta en Opico contra los que propusieron al gobierno abolir las comunidades de Indios y ladinos," 21 October 1872, AGN-CQ.

4. "Ejidos," *Boletín de Agricultura* 1 (15 November 1881): 9–10.

5. "Influencia de la leyes sobre el progreso de la Agricultura," *Boletín de Agricultura* 1 (15 November 1882): 37.

6. "Agricultura Nacional," *Boletín de Agricultura* 1 (1882): 380.

7. See *Diario Oficial*, 28 January 1881.

8. Teodoro Moreno, "Discurso de clausura," *Diario Oficial*, 19 March 1882, 277.

9. "Memoria del Ministerio de Gobernación y Fomento,"*Diario Oficial*, 7 March 1882, 225–27.

10. Mora, *Memoria*, 8–9.

11. Mrs. Foote, *Recollections*, 84.

12. Mora, *Memoria*, 8–9.

13. Browning, *El Salvador*, 175–89.

14. Suarez, *Noticias generales*, 13.

15. Ibid., 52–55.

16. González, *Lecciones;* Guzmán, *Apuntamientos;* see also Reyes, *Apuntamientos.*

17. See, for example, Alcalde de Nueva San Salvador, "Informe especial de agricultura," 30 January 1885, AGST.

18. See Browing, *El Salvador* 205; Lindo Fuentes, *Weak Foundations*.

19. "Sobre notificar a los arrendantes de las tierras Tacuscalex en cumplimiento del Art 1 de la acta de la sesion extraordinaria . . . respecto a la siembra de cacao," 20 December 1879, AGN-CG-SO.

20. Gómez Carillo, *Estudio histórico*, 143.

21. Lever, *Central America*, 182.

22. Ibid.

23. "Borrador del Informe del Gobernador de Sonsonate al Ministro de Gobernación," 1889, AGN-CG-SO.

24. See, for example, Alcalde de Izalco, González, "Carta al Gobernador del Departamento de Sonsonate," 3 August 1890, AGS.

25. *Diario Oficial*, 12 February 1881, 146.

26. *Diario Oficial*, 18 February 1881, 165; *Diario Oficial* 10:47, 24 February 1881, 190.

27. *Diario Oficial*, 24 February 1883; *Diario Oficial* 12:54, 4 March 1882. See Browning, *El Salvador*, chap. 5, for the text of the legislation.

28. "Recibo por pago para título de tierra ejidal," 13 September 1882, AGN-CM-MG.

29. Mora, *Memoria*, 6.

30. *Diario Oficial*, 24 April 1891, 1; see chapter 6 and "Partición de los terrenos comunales de Dolores Izalco," 1890, AGN-CG-SO.

31. *Diario Oficial*, 24 July 1891, 1–2.

32. "Acuerdase denegarles título de propiedad a los poseedores de las tierras llamadas el Volcanillo y Joya del Pilón en San Pedro Nonualco," 1892, AGN-CPC.

33. "Solicitud de devolución de títulos," 1895, AGN-CM-MG.

34. "Solicitud de Juan Ruiz a que se le extienda título de propiedad de un terreno qaue posee en los baldíos de Santa Ana," 1895, AGN-CM-MG.

35. "Solicitudes de Títulos de Propiedad," 1899–1900, AMSA.

36. Mora, *Memoria,* 145.

37. Mora, *Memoria . . . (1883),* 218.

38. Mora, *Memoria,* 139–42.

39. The "Memorias de Gobernación" from 1883 to 1890 provide extensive detail on the procedures and problems surrounding the division, distribution, and titling of the common lands. See Browning, *El Salvador,* 209–11.

40. Larreynaga, *Memoria,* 9.

41. See text in *Diario Oficial,* 24 July 1891, 1–2; *Diario Oficial,* 24 April 1891, 1.

42. "Memorandum para la Memoria de Gobernación," 1901, AGN-CM-MG.

43. "Solicitud de la plebe de Coatepeque para que se les mande a medir y repartir por lotes las tierras de la hacienda San José Las Flores," 1912, AGN-CM-MG.

44. Mora, *Memoria . . . (1883),* 15.

45. Jiménez, *Memoria,* 406, 489.

46. "Certificación de actas sobre ejidos en Lislique," 1882, AGN-CM-MG; "Titulación de tierras en Nueva Esparta," 1882, AGN-CM-MG.

47. Mora, *Memoria,* 18, 120–21.

48. Pedro Galán, "Minuta de los lotes de terrenos no acotados del pueblo de San Miguel de Mercedes," 24 July 1882, AGN-CM-MG; *Diario Oficial,* 9 July 1882, 38.

49. Mora, *Memoria,* 6, 94.

50. Ibid., 9–10.

51. *Diario Oficial,* 15 September 1882, 250.

52. *Boletín de Agricultura* 2 (1 February 1884): 52.

53. Ibid., 33.

54. Ibid., 124.

55. Ibid., 129, 134.

56. Alcalde de Tepepetitan, Santiago Magaña, "Carta al SPE sobre terrenos baldíos," 17 August 1892, AGN-CM-MG.

57. "El sindico municipal de Caluco solicita que un terreno de cinco caballerias . . . se declare comprendido en los extintos ejidos de Caluco," 2 October 1897, AGN-CG-SO.

58. Estupinian, *Memoria,* 46.

59. Gobernador de Cabañas, "Informe de la visita a los municipios del departamento de Cabañas," 15 December 1900, AGN-CM-MG.

60. Mora, *Memoria,* 131.

61. Agustin Palacios Gobernador de San Salvador, "Informe al Minstro de Gobernación," 28 December 1891, AGN-CM-MG.

62. *Diario Oficial,* 1 October 1882, 309.

63. "Minuta de los terrenos baldíos de la jurisdicción de Guaimango," 31 August 1896, AGN-CG-AH.

64. "Borrador de la venta de terrenos en Ahuachapán," 1874, AGN-CG-AH.

65. Mora, *Memoria,* 147.

66. "Baldíos," *Boletín de Agricultura* 2 (15 January 1884): 44.

67. "Memoria con que el Ministro de Hacienda, Guerra y Marina," *Diario Oficial,* 21 April 1882, 369.

68. Ibid., 381.

69. Leopoldo A. Rodríguez, "Historia y descripción de la ciudad de San Vicente, y consideraciones sobre el origen de algunos pueblos de su departamento," *La Universidad* 3 (March–June 1892): 286–87.

70. "Libro de acuerdos del Ministerio de Gobernación," 1893, AGN-CDM Rollo MI-3.

71. "Autorizaciones del SPE sobre titulación de tierras," 1893, AGN-CM-MG.

72. "Solicitud al SPE sobre titulación de terrenos del volcan de San Vicente," 19 October 1892, AGN-CM-MG.

73. Larreynaga, *Memoria,* 134.

74. "Carta aceptando la cesion de 100 caballerias de tierra del gobierno," 22 January 1886, AGN-CQ.

75. P. Bedoya, "Carta al Ministro de Gobernación remitiendo lista de los señores que solicitaron medidas de lotes de terreno," 1894, AGN-CM-MG.

76. "Autorizaciones del SPE sobre titulación de tierras," 1893, AGN-CM-MG and "Libro de acuerdos del Ministerio de Gobernación," 1893, AGN-CM-MG.

77. Larreynaga, *Memoria,* 135–37.

78. "Solicitud de la municipalidad de Santiago sobre la venta del baldío el Tablón," 21 January 1897, AGN-CM-MG.

79. Larreynaga, *Memoria,* 9.

80. *Diario Oficial,* 23 December 1887.

81. Alcalde de Acajutla, J. Agustin Ramirez, "Informe al Gobernador de Sonsonate," 14 December 1892, AGN-CG-SO.

82. Gobernador de Sonsonate, "Carta al Ministro de Gobernación sobre ejidos en Acajutla," March 1893, AGN-CM-AL; "Libro de acuerdos del Ministerio de Gobernación," 1893, AGN-CM-MG.

83. Mora, *Memoria,* 116; "Carta de Antonio Blanco al Supremo Poder Ejecutivo sobre terrenos ejidales," 6 October 1885, AGN-CQ.

84. Jiménez, *Memoria,* 404, 494. "Solicitud al Gobernador del Departamento sobre tierras," 1893, AGN-CM-MG; "Solicitud al Supremo Poder Ejecutivo sobre tierras ejidales," 1893, AGN-CM-SPE; P. Bedoya, "Carta al Goberandor del Departamento sobre la medida de los terrenos nacionales en Tacuba," 1894, AGN-CG-AH.

85. "Don José Angel Velasco y Don José Antonio Aguirre solicita se compulsen las diligencias de venta de diez caballerías de tierras," 1896, AGN-CM-MG.

86. "Solicitud de varios vecinos de Tacuba que se nombre el Ingeniero Espinal para que practique la mensura de cuatro caballerías de terreno," 1896, AGN-CM-MG.

87. "Certificación del acta Municipal en que se solicita el sobrante de los terrenos de Loma Larga para la construcción del mercado de esta ciudad," 1904, AGN-CG-AH.

88. "Medidas de los terrenos de Loma Larga practicada por comisión oficial del Supremo Gobierno por el Ingeniero Don. M. J. Aragon," 1905, AGN-CG-AH.

89. *Diario Oficial* 4:7 1878, 1.

90. *Diario Oficial*, 9 August 1887, 969.

91. "Distribución de los terrenos de Soledad en Cara Sucia a los invalidos," 17 April 1896, AGN-CM-MG.

92. "Solicitud al Gobernador de Ahuachapán sobre tierras," 1897, AGN-CM-MG.

93. Jiménez, *Memoria*, 372.

94. Advertisement, *El Correo Nacional*, 27 October 1891.

95. "Informe del Gobernador de La Libertad," 1900, AGN-CM-MG.

96. "Dueños de terrenos ejidales despachados por el alcalde municipal del Armenia," 1897, AGN-CG-SO. The demographic data is from "Descripción de la Villa de Armenia," 1895, AGN-CG-SO.

97. "Informe de la Municipalidad de Armenia de sus trabajos hechos durante el año de 1887," 1887, AGN-CG-SO.

98. "Testimonios de los títulos que expedio la Alcaldia Municipal de Nueva San Salvador desde 1882 hasta 1884," BGA; Gallardo, *Papeles históricos*, 5:82.

99. "Libro . . . en que se estiende cada título a los poseedores de terrenos ejidales de esta comprension," 1882, AGN-CA-SO.

100. "Minuta de los lotes de terrenos que no fueron titulados en la cual quedarno comprendidos tambien los títulos supletivamente y los valdios," 1896, AGN-CG-AH.

101. "Minuta de los lotes de tierras ejidales del pueblo de Chilanga," 1896, AGN-CM-MG.

102. See Menjivar, *Acumulación;* Browning, *El Salvador*, 190; and Lindo Fuentes, *Weak Foundations*, 125–31.

103. Browning, *El Salvador*, 212–13.

## Chapter 8. *The Abolition of Ethnic Communities and Lands, 1881–1912*

1. Those listed as quickly privatizing their lands were Comunidad de Masajapa (LL), and the Indian communities of Tonocatepeque, Ahuachapán,

Ataco, Atiquizaya, El Paraíso, Dulce Nombre de María, La-Palma, San Ignacio, Ilobasco, Las Charcas o Positos, and Umaña. The communities of Arcatao, San Miguel, San Francisco de Mercedes, Chalatenango, Jocotán, Tejutla, Jucuapa, Cacaopera, Chilanga, and Guatayagua remained undivided. Mora, *Memoria,* 8–9.

2. "Aprobación de partición de terrenos comunales," *Diario Oficial,* 26 October 1882, p. 594, and "Registro de Comuneros," 1880, AMC.

3. "Sobre levantar el plan de los terrenos de la comunidad de La Palma," 8 January 1883, AGN-CQ.

4. Mora, *Memoria,* 59–62.

5. Ibid., 59–60, 62.

6. For examples, see *Diario Oficial,* 26 April 1882, p. 368.

7. Isidoro Figueroa, "Nominas," 27 June 1881, AGS; "Compraventa de terrenos," 1883, AGN-CQ.

8. Ibid., 108–10.

9. "Sobre levantar el plan de los terrenos de la communidad de la Palma," 8 January 1883, AGN-CQ.

10. Mora, *Memoria,* 110.

11. Ibid., 111–13.

12. Ibid., *Memoria,* 111.

13. Ministerio de Hacienda y Credito Publico, "Libro de acuerdos concediendo títulos de terrenos y aprobando nombramientos de agrimensores," 1892, AGN-CM-MH.

14. Contreras, *Memoria,* 121.

15. Ibid., 215.

16. Mora, *Memoria,* 112–13.

17. "Carta del Gobernador de Chalatenango sobre si rije o no la ley deo comunidades y si en consecuencia puede permitir y aprobar el nombramiento de nuevos administradores y socios de dichas comunidades," 11 January 1886, AGN-CQ.

18. Aquilino Duarte Gobernador de Chalatenango, "Informe al Ministro de Gobernación," 26 August 1898, AGN-CM-MG.

19. "El común de ladinos del pueblo de Las Vueltas solicita se reparta con equidad un terreno que poseén," 1893, AGN-CM-MG.

20. Jiménez, *Memoria,* 493.

21. "Carta de Hilaro Hernandez al Supremo Poder Ejecutivo sobre posesión de terrenos," 23 May 1891, AGN-CM-SPE.

22. "Correspondencia del Ministerio de Gobernación," 1892, AGN-CM-MG.

23. "Solicitud de los Comuneros de Chalatenango a que se nombre un ingeniero para que practique la division de sus tierras," 1897, AGN-CM-MG.

24. Ibid.

25. Ibid.

26. "Solicitud al SPE de los Comuneros Indígenas de Chalatanango sobre despojo de sus terrenos," 27 April 1899, AGN-CM-MG.

27. "Suplicatorio al SPE por el Gobernador del Departamento sobre tieras," 1897, AGN-CM-MG.

28. "Carta al SPE sobre tierras," 1893, AGN-CM-SPE.

29. "Expediente de partición de las tierras de la hacienda San Juan Masajapa," 20 March 1891, AGN-CM-MG.

30. "Los Vecinos de San Martin Piden Que el Gbno. Proteja Contra Don Cipriano Castro Quien les Exije Impuestos y les Hostiliza por los Terrenos de la Hacienda el Angel," 16 December 1885, AGN-CQ.

31. "Carta al SPE sobre tierras," 1893, AGN-CM-SPE.

32. "Queja del alcalde municipal de San Matías contra el Gobernador del Departamento de La Libertad Hans Müller," 1896, AGN-CM-MG.

33. "Legajo de cartas sobre tierras del Ministro del Interior," 1899, AGN-CM-MG.

34. Alcalde de Santo Domingo, Dionicio Cortes, "Carta al Sr. Gobernador del Departamento," 11 November 1886, AGS.

35. "Cartas al Gobernador de Sonsonate," 1887, AGN-CG-SO.

36. "Solicitudes de títulos de propiedad de terrenos comunales de Santa Ana," 1886, AMSA.

37. "Solicitud de los comuneros de La Laguna que se titulen los terrenos que poseen," 1895, AGN-CM-MG.

38. "Solicitud de los Sres. Juan Ruiz y Serapio Chavez a que se les mande repartir los terenos comunales existentes entre las haciendas Lajas, Preza y Naranjos," 4 March 1896, AGN-CM-MG.

39. "Memorandum de la Memoria del Ministro de Gobernación," 1899, AGN-CM-MG.

40. Figeac, *Recordatorio histórico*, 280; see also Burns, "The Intellectual Infrastructure," 77.

41. Rafael Reyes, "Carta al Dr. Dn Julio Interiano sobre tierras de Indígenas de San Rafael La laguna," 1901, AGN-CM-MG.

42. Estupianian, *Memoria,* 44, 274.

43. Contreras, *Memoria,* 115.

44. See Lauria-Santiago, "Land, Community, and Revolt."

45. "Escrito por el cual los señores Simeón Tensún juez partidor de los terrenos comunales de Asunción Izalco y Antonio Cuadra socio de la misma, presentan los libros en que estan los travajos que han tenido desde el año de 1881 hasta el de 1885," 1886, AGN-CG-SO.

46. "Escrito por el cual los señores Simeón Tensún juez partidor de los terrenos comunales de Asunción Izalco y Antonio Cuadra socio de la misma, presentan los libros en que estan los travajos que han tenido desde el año de 1881 hasta el de 1885," 1886, AGN-CG-SO.

47. "Certificación sobre acuerdos sobre división de los terrenos comunales de Asunción Izalco," 1886, AGN-CG-SO.

48. "Libro de la división de los ejidos de Izalco (Borradores)" 1882?, AMI; "Libro de Registros de la comunidad de Asunción," 1891, AGN-CG-SO.

49. "El Señor Jesús Pulacho Juez Partidor de la Comunidad de Asunción solicita que el Supremo Gobierno acuerde que la Comunidad pague las mejoras que hubieren en los terrenos cuestionados," 3 September 1888, AGN-CG-SO.

50. Secretario de Estado en el Despacho de Gobernación, Francisco G. de Machón, "Carta al Gobernador de Sonsonate," 15 October 1890, AGN-CM-MG.

51. "Cruz Shupán ex-administrador y Juez partidor de la comunidad de Indígenas de Asunción Izalco da parte que los comuneros se estan reuniendo con el objeto de elejir como ha sido costumbre los empleados del comun, lo cual es indebido," 1891, AGN-CG-SO.

52. "Solicitud de los comuneros de Asunción Izalco," 1891, AGN-CG-SO.

53. "Don Cruz Shupán pide que por el Estado se le mande pagar la suma de 890 que ascendio la medida y partición de un terreno de la comunidad de Izalco en la cual fue partidor el solicitante," 1893, AGN-CG-SO.

54. "Manuel Punche solicita título de propiedad de una manzana de terreno situada en la comunidad de Asunción," 1896, AGN-CG-SO.

55. "Solicitud de varios vecinos de Asunción Izalco," 1895, AGN-CM-MG.

56. "Solicitud de varios Indijenas de la comunidad de Asunción Izalco pidiendo que el señor Gobernador confirme el nombramiento del administrador Santiago Cucisto," 1896, AGN-CM-MG.

57. "Juicio sobre tierras," 1893, AMI.

58. "Tomás Pasasi i otros individuos de la extinguida comunidad de Izalco se quejan de haberles mandado deshauciar de sus legitimas propiedades o mas bien dicho de los terrenos que tienen en los lugares llamados La Chapina i Talcomunca," 1893, AGN-CG-SO.

59. "Solicitud de Jesús Portillo que se derogue el acuerdo que manda vender las tierras de Asunción Izalco o se le incluya en los comuneros del mismo," 1895, AGN-CM-MG.

60. "Partición de los terrenos comunales de Dolores Izalco," 1890, AGN-CG-SO.

61. Larreynaga, *Memoria,* 138.

62. Estupianián, *Memoria,* 229.

63. Libro compuesto de 32 hojas utiles . . . para que el juez partidor de la comunidad de indígenas de Asunción Izalco, Señor Simeon Tensún, lleve la cuente que le corresponde, 1885, AGS.

64. Los infraescritos alcaldes de Dolores Izalco exponen que el administrador señor Simeón Morán no ha concluido aun la partición de nuestros terrenos municipales, 1885, AGS.

65. See Lauria-Santiago, "Land, Community, and Revolt."

66. "Libro de Actas Municipalies de Juayua," AMJ.

67. "Título General de los Terrenos Ejidales y Comunales de Juayua," 1862, AGN-CT-Caja 2/Doc. 2.

68. Mora, *Memoria,* 62.

69. Estupianián, *Memoria,* 235.

70. Gobernador de Sonsonate, "Informe de la Visita Oficial a los pueblos del Departamento," 20 September 1913, AGN-CG-SO.

71. "Solicitud de los vecinos de la Villa del Progreso sobre repartición de terrenos comunales," 1885, AGN-CG-SO.

72. "Libro de actas Municipales de Juayua," AMJ.

73. "Espediente de los Comuneros del Pueblo de Juayua," 31 August 1885, AGN-CG-SO.

74. "Carta al SPE por el pueblo de Juayua sobre tierras comunales," 8 October 1885, AGN-CQ.

75. Secratario de Juayua, Pedro Barrientos, "Carta al Gobernador del Departamento de Sonsonate sobre problemas con los indígenas sobre tierras en Juayua," February 1886, AGN-CG-SO.

76. "Solicitud de la municipalidad de El Progreso/Títulos de los cañales," 1891, AGN-CG-SO.

77. "La municipalidad de la villa del Progreso solicita del Supremo Gobierno le conceda lisencia para titular los terrenos del caserio denominado los cañales," 1892, AGN-CG-SO.

78. "Avaluo de los terrenos en el lugar llamado los Cañales," 1892, AGN-CG-S; Gobernador de Sonsonate, Dionisio Arauz, "Carta al Ministro de Gobernación," 10 June 1892, AGN-CPC.

79. "El Dr. dn Wenceslao Herrador Sindico procurador de la municipalidad de la villa de El Progreso reclama la devolución del dinero que produjo la venta de las tierras," 1895, AGN-CM-MG.

80. "Avaluo de los terrenos en el lugar llamado Los Cañales," 1892, AGN-CG-SO; "Protocolo de título de los terrenos situados en el valle Los Cañales de la jurisdicción de la Villa El Progreso," 1892, AMJ.

81. Mora, *Memoria,* 41.

82. Larreynaga, *Memoria,* 133.

83. "Copia de los expedientes de titulación de los terrenos comunales Ranchador y Sitio del Niño en Chalchuapa," 1894, AGN-CM-MG.

84. "Libro de acuerdos del Ministerio de Gobernación," 1893, AGN-CM-MG.

85. "Copia de los expedientes de titulación de los terrenos comunales Ranchador y Sitio del Niño en Chalchuapa," 1892, AGN-CM-MG.

86. "Incidente de apelación del juicio ejecutivo promovido por doña Anselma Linares de Arcia contra la comunidad de ladinos de Chalchuapa, para que se le entreguen unos terrenos," 1876, AGN-CT Sección/Caja 3.

87. "Copia de los expedientes de titulación de los terrenos comunales Ranchador y Sitio del Niño en Chalchuapa," 1894, AGN-CM-MG.

88. See Alvarenga, *Etica y cultura,* chap. 6.

89. See Ching, "From Clientelism to Militarism."

## Chapter 9. *Conclusion*

1. See Stanley, *The Protection Racket State.*

2. For such an argument, see Alvarenga, *Cultura y ética.*

3. Long, *Railways of Central America.*

4. For a similar discussion of peasant decline in Venezuela, see Yarrington, *A Coffee Frontier.*

5. Tutino, *From Insurrection to Revolution,* calls this process *agrarian compression.*

6. Choussy, *El Café,* 160–61.

7. See Williams and Walter, *Militarization and Demilitarization.*

8. For a similar conclusion, see Yarrington, *A Coffee Frontier.*

9. See Williams and Walter, *Militarization and Demilitarization;* and Montgomery, *Revolution.*

10. On the 1980 agrarian reform, see Ward, "Land Ownership."

11. See Posada and López, "El Salvador 1950–1970."

12. Cabarrús, *Génesis de una revolución.*

13. Personal communication, Henrik Roensbo.

14. Williams and Walter, *Militarization and Demilitarization.*

# GLOSSARY

## Glossary of Terms

| | |
|---|---|
| *agricultor* | farmer |
| *alcabala* | tax |

| | |
|---|---|
| *alcalde* | mayor |
| *añil* | indigo dye; the plant used to produce the dye |
| *baldío* | unclaimed land officially declared as such by a process of "denouncing" (ch 2) |
| *beneficiencia* tax | a tax collected by local governments for medical care and other services to the poor |
| *beneficio* | coffee-processing facility; mill |
| *caballería* | 45 hectares |
| *canon* | rental fee |
| *capellanía* | debt to church with lands as collateral |
| *castas* | mixed-blood persons |
| Central American Federation | Provincias Unidas, the Federated States of El Salvador and Guatemala (1823–1840), held together by a small, fragmented, and mostly unsuccessful political-military faction led first by José M. Arce and then Francisco Morazán. After its breakdown, El Salvador continued ties with Guatemala and Honduras even after declaring itself an independent republic in 1847. |
| *chacra* | suburban farm tilled by city dwellers |
| *cofradía* | confraternity, with religious functions, that provided mutual benefits to its members |
| *componer* | to claim, title, and purchase land, such as outside an existing title or crown land (in colonial times) |
| *composición* | land claimed, titled, or purchased in colonial era |
| *común* | community, as in Indian community |
| to "denounce" | to declare unclaimed land as *baldío*, which then could be titled with government approval |
| *ejidos* | common lands held by towns, a practice dating from the colonial period |
| *finca* | country estate; plantation |
| FMLN | Farabundo Martí National Liberation Front (FMLN), a guerrilla movement of the 1980s |
| "Group of 44" | a group from Santa Ana that included important landowners and entrepreneurs |
| *hacendado* | hacienda owner; landowner |
| hacienda | rural estate; ranch |
| hectare | (ha) 10,000 square meters, or 2.47 acres |

| | |
|---|---|
| Indian | indigenous person, usually identified by formal or loose membership in pueblos or communities dating from the early colonial era |
| *indígena* | native person; Indian |
| Jefe de Estado | Chief of State |
| *jornalero* | day laborer or wage worker |
| *labrador* | small farmer or peasant |
| Ladino | Indians who had left their native communities; originally migrants from other areas who took on the dress and language of Spaniards; can also mean *mestizo* or mulatto |
| *manzana* | .67 of a hectare |
| *mestizo* | person of mixed race |
| *obraje* | indigo-processing site |
| *oro* | processed coffee ready for export |
| *pardo* | in the colonial period a catch-all category to refer to *mestizos,* mulattos, and free blacks |
| peasant | small-scale farmers who produce for subsistence but not necessarily for the market; they can be tenants, share-croppers, owners of land, or "possess" lands without title |
| *peninsulares* | Spaniards, born in the Peninsula |
| to possess land | to occupy land with or without legal sanction |
| *pueblo* | Indian community |
| *quintal* | 100 pounds |
| real | 1/8 peso |
| *regidores* | town council members |
| *sitio* | cattle ranch |
| Supremo Poder Ejecutivo | President's Office |
| to title land | to acquire legal ownership |
| *trapiche* | wooden or metal sugar mill |
| Volcán de Santa Ana (the Volcán) | Ladino peasant community occupying lands within the municipality of Santa Ana on the slopes of the Imatepec volcano |
| *volcaneños* | those who live in the Volcán |

# BIBLIOGRAPHY

Acuña, Victor Hugo, and Iván Molina Jiménez. *Historia económica y social de Costa Rica*. San José: Editorial Porvenir, 1991.

Adams, Richard N. *Nationalization*. Offprint series, Institute of Latin American Studies, no. 60. Austin: Institute of Latin American Studies, University of Texas, 1967.

Adorno, Rolena. "The Indigenous Ethnographer: The 'Indio Ladino' as Historian and Cultural Mediation." In *Implicit Understandings: Observing, Reporting, and Reflecting on the Encounters Between Europeans and Other Peoples in the Early Modern Era,* ed. Stuart B. Schwartz. Cambridge: Cambridge University Press, 1994.

Alfaro, Prudencio. *Memoria con que el Doctor Prudencio Alfaro da cuenta a la Asamblea Nacional de 1895 de los actos del Gobierno Provisional correspondiente a la Cartera de Gobernación en el año de 1894.* San Salvador: Imprenta Nacional, 1895.

Alvarenga, Patricia. *Cultura y ética de la violencia: El Salvador 1880–1932.* San José: EDUCA, 1996.

"Apuntamientos sobre la agricultura y comercio del reino de Guatemala que el Señor Don Antonio Larrazábal diputado en las cortes." In *Economía de Guatemala 1750–1940: Antología de lecturas y materiales,* compiled by Jorge Luján Muñoz, 1:37–82. Guatemala: Universidad de San Carlos de Guatemala, 1980.

Arce, Rafael A. "El Salvador: renta diferencial del café y configuración capitalista." *Teoria y Politica* (1980).

Arias Peñate, Salvador. *Los subsistemas de agroexportación en El Salvador.* San Salvador: UCA Editores, 1988.

Baily, John. *Central America*. London: Trelawney Saunders, 1850.

Bancroft, Hubert Howe. *History of The Pacific States of North America.* San Francisco: The History Company, Publishers, 1887.

301

Barbarena, Santiago I. *Descripción geográfica y estadística de la república del Salvador*. San Salvador: Impresora Nacional, 1892.

———. *Monografías departamentales: Departamento de Cuscatlán*. San Salvador: Imprenta Nacional, 1910.

———. *Monografías departamentales: Departamento de La Paz*. San Salvador: Imprenta Nacional, 1909.

———. *Monografías departamentales: Departamento de Santa Ana*. San Salvador, 1910.

———. *Monografías departamentales: Departamento de Sonsonate*. San Salvador: Imprenta Nacional, 1910.

———. "Nuestra industria añilera," *Revista de Agricultura Salvadoreña* 4 (1 July 1921).

Binford, Leigh. *The El Mozote Massacre: A Compelling Story for Everyone Concerned with the Lives of Third World Peoples*. Tucson: University of Arizona Press, 1996.

Bosque, D. Juan. *Memoria de relaciones*. Cojutepeque, El Salvador: Imprenta El Triunfo, 1857.

Brasseur de Bourbourg, Charles Etienne. "Un viaje a los estados de San Salvador y Guatemala." *Anales de la Sociedad de Geografía e Historia de Guatemala* 1, no. 3 (1925): 203–13.

*Breves datos historicos de El Congo en su 50 aniversario*. Santa Ana (ES): Impresora Nacional, 1983.

Browning, David. *El Salvador: Landscape and Society*. Oxford: Clarendon Press, 1971.

Bulmer-Thomas, Victor. *The Political Economy of Central America Since 1920*. Cambridge: Cambridge University Press, 1987.

Bureau of American Republics. *Coffee in America: Methods of Production and Facilities for Successful Cultivation*. Special Bulletin. Washington, D.C.: Bureau of American Republics, 1893.

———. *Salvador*. Washington, D.C.: Bureau of American Republics, 1892.

Burgess, Paul. *Justo Rufino Barrios*. Guatemala: Editorial Universitaria de Guatemala, 1972.

Burns, Bradford. "The Modernization of Underdevelopment: El Salvador, 1858–1931." *Journal of Developing Areas* 18:3 (April 1984), 293–316.

Bustamante, Gregorio. *Historia militar de El Salvador*. San Salvador: Talleres Gráficos Cisneros, 1935.

Cabarrús, Carlos Rafael. "El Salvador: De movimiento campesino revolución popular." In *Historia política de los campesinos latinoamericanos*, compiled by Pablo González Casanova. 2:77–115. Mexico City: Siglo Veintiuno, 1985.

———. *Génesis de una revolución: Análisis del surgimiento y desarollo de la organización campesina en El Salvador.* Mexico City: Ediciones de la Casa Chata, 1983.

Calderón, Cesar. *Episodios nacionales: Anastasio Aquino y el porque de su rebelión en 1833 en Santiago Nonualco.* San Salvador, 1957.

Cambranes, J. C. *Coffee and Peasants: The Origins of the Modern Plantation Economy in Guatemala, 1853–1897.* South Woodstock: CIRMA, 1985.

Cañas y Cañas, Fernando. *El Caudillo de los Nonualcos, una epopeya nacional.* San Salvador: Imprenta Arevalo, 1939.

Cardenal, Rodolfo. *El poder eclesiástico en El Salvador. 1871–1931.* San Salvador: UCA Editores, 1980.

Cardenas, Joaquín C. *Sucesos migueleños.* San Miguel, El Salvador, 1939.

Cardona, Jorge Alberto. "Población indígena en la Zona Oriental de El Salvador." Unpublished manuscript. San Salvador, 1973.

Cardona Lazo, Antonio. *Monografías departamentales.* San Salvador: Imprenta Nacional, 1939.

Cardoso, Ciro f.s. "Historia económica del café en Centroamérica (siglo XIX)." *Estudios Sociales Centroamericanos* 4, no. 10 (1985).

Carpenter, Frank G. *Lands of the Caribbean.* Garden City, N.Y.: Doubleday, Page, 1925.

Castro, Esteban. "Estadística de la jurisdicción de San Vicente." *Documentos y datos históricos y estadísticos de la República de El Salvador.* El Salvador, Biblioteca Nacional. San Salvador: Imprenta Nacional, 1926.

Castro, Juan Francisco. *Geografía elemental del Salvador.* San Salvador: Tipografía La Unión, 1905.

Castro, Rafael Barón. *La población de El Salvador.* San Salvador: UCA Editores, 1978.

Chacón, Enrique. *El Presidente Dr. Francisco Dueñas y su epoca.* San Salvador: Academia Salvadoreña de la Historia, 1900.

Ching, Erik. "From Clientelism to Militarism: The State, Politics and Authoritarianism in El Salvador, 1840–1940." Ph.D. diss. University of California, Santa Barbara, 1997.

Choussy, Felix. *El Café.* San Salvador, 1934.

Clegern, Wayne M. *Origins of Liberal Dictatorship in Central America: Guatemala, 1865–1873.* Niwot, Colorado: University Press of Colorado, 1994.

Cojutepeque, El Salvador. *La municipalidad y vecindario de la cuidad leal de Cojutepeque a los centro-americanos.* San Salvador: Imprenta del Gobierno, 1863.

*Colección de leyes.* San Salvador, 1868.

Contreras, Santiago. *Memoria con que el Señor Sub Secretario de Estado Encargado del Despacho de Gobernación Dr. D. Santiago Contreras dió cuenta de los actos del Poder Ejecutivo ocurridos en 1887 a la Honorable Asamblea Nacional.* San Salvador: Imprenta Nacional, 1888.

Cortés y Larraz, Pedro. *Descripción geográfico-moral de la diocesis de Goathemala.* Biblioteca "Goathemala," vol. 20. Guatemala: Sociedad de Geografía e Historia de Guatemala, 1958.

Dawson, Guillermo. *Geografía elemental de la República de El Salvador.* 1890.

de Belot, Gustave. *La Republique de Salvador.* Paris: Chez Duntu, Libraire, 1865.

de Guevarra, Concepción Clara. *Exploración etnográfica en el Departamento de Santa Ana.* San Salvador: Ministerio de Educación, 1973.

Deaton, Dawn Fogle. "The Decade of Revolt: Peasant Rebellion in Jalisco, Mexico, 1855–1864." In *Liberals, the Church, and Indian Peasants: Corporte Lands and the Challenge of Reform in Nineteenth-Century Spanis America*, ed. Robert H. Jackson, 65–93. Albuquerque: University of New Mexico Press, 1997.

Dirección de Patrimonio Cultural. Departamento de Historia. *Chalchuapa.* San Salvador: Ministerio de Educación, Dirección de Publicaciones, 1985.

Dirección General de Estadística. *La República de El Salvador.* San Salvador: Imprenta Nacional, 1924.

Dirección General de Estadística y Censos. *Atlas censal de El Salvador.* San Salvador, 1955.

———. *Primer censo agropecuario.* San Salvador: Dirección General de Estadística y Censos, 1954.

Dominguez Sosa, Julio Alberto. *Génesis y significado de la constitución de 1886.* San Salvador, 1958.

———. *Ensayo Histórico Sobre las Tribus Nonualcos y Su Caudillo Anastasio Aquino.* San Salvador: Ministerio de Educación, 1962.

Domville-Fife, Charles William. *Guatemala and the States of Central America.* London: Francis Griffiths, 1913.

Dore, Elizabeth. "Coffee, Land and Class Relations in Nicaragua, 1870–1920." *Journal of Historical Sociology* 8, no. 3 (September 1995): 303–26.

Ducey, Michael T. "Liberal Theory and Peasant Practice: Land and Power in Northern Veracruz, Mexico, 1826–1900." In *Liberals, the Church, and Indian Peasants: Corporte Lands and the Challenge of Reform in*

*Nineteenth-Century Spanis America,* ed. Robert H. Jackson, 65–93. Albuquerque: University of New Mexico Press, 1997.

Dunkerley, James. *The Pacification of Central America.* London: Verso, 1995.

———. *Power in the Isthmus: A Political History of Modern Central America.* London: Verso, 1988.

Dunlop, Robert. *Travels in Central America.* London: Longman, Brown, Green, and Longmans, 1847.

Escalante Arce, Pedro Antonio. *Códice Sonsonate.* 2 vols. San Salvador: Concultura, 1992.

Escamilla, Miguel. *Geografía económica de la República de El Salvador.* San Salvador: Imprenta Melendez, 1908.

Escobar Ohmstede, Antonio, and Frans J. Schryer. "Las Sociedades Agrarias en el Norte de Hidalgo, 1856–1900." *Mexican Studies/Estudios Mexicanos* 8, no. 1 (Winter 1992).

Estupianián, Baltasar. *Memoria con Que el Sr. Ministro de Gobernación Doctor Don Baltasar Estupinian, Dió Cuenta a la Honorable Asamblea Nacional (1885–1886).* San Salvador: Imprenta Nacional, 1887.

Fernández Molina, José Antonio. "Colouring the World in Blue: The Indigo Boom and the Central American Market, 1750–1810." Ph.D. diss., University of Texas, Austin, 1992.

Fiehrer, Thomas Marc. "The Baron de Carondelet as Agent of Bourbon Reform: A Study of Spanish Colonial Administration in the Years of the French Revolution." Ph.D. diss., Tulane University, 1977.

Figeac, José F. *Recordatorio histórico de la República de El Salvador.* San Salvador: Talleres Gráficos Cisneros.

Figueroa Salazar, Amílcar. *El Salvador: elementos de sus historia y sus luchas (1932–1985).* Caracas: Fondo Editorial Tropykos, 1987.

Flores Macal, Mario. "La hacienda colonial en El Salvador, sus orígenes." *Estudios Sociales Centroamericanos* 9, no. 25 (January–April 1980): 335–71.

———. *Origen, desarollo y crisis de las formas de dominación en El Salvador.* San José: SECASA, 1983.

Flores Membreño, Rafael, comp. *Anuario de El Salvador.* San Miguel, El Salvador: Centro Editorial La Nación, 1927.

Floyd, Troy S. "Los comerciantes guatemaltecos, el gobierno y los provincianos, 1750–1800." *Cuadernos de Antropologia* 8 (1968): 37–58.

Fonseca, Pedro Salvador. *Geografía ilustrada de El Salvador.* Barcelona: Impenta Ramón Sopena, 1926.

———. *Monografías departamentales: departamento de San Salvador.* San Salvador: Imprenta Nacional, 1914.

———. *Monografías departamentales: departamento de San Vicente*. San Salvador: Imprenta Nacional, 1914.

Foote, Mrs. *Recollections of Central America and the West Coast of Africa*. London: T. Cautley Newby, 1869.

Forster, Cindy. "Campesino Struggles and Plantation Justice during Guatemala's National Revolution, 1944 to 1954." In *Identity and Struggle at the Margins of the Nation-State: The Laboring Peoples of Central America and the Hispanic Caribbean, 1850–1950*, ed. Aldo Lauria-Santiago and Aviva Chomsky. Chapel Hill: Duke University Press, 1998.

Foster, Harry Latourette. *A Gringo in Mañana-Land*. New York: Dodd, Mead, 1925.

Fowler, William R., Jr. "Cacao, Indigo, and Coffee: Cash Crops in the History of El Salvador." *Research in Economic Anthropology* 8 (1987): 139–87.

———. *Caluco: Historia y Arqueología de un Pueblo Pipil en el Siglo XVI*. San Salvador: Patronato Pro-Patrimonio Cultural, 1995.

———. "The Political Economy of Indian Survival in Sixteenth-Century Izalco, El Salvador." In *The Spanish Borderlands in Pan-American Perspective*, ed. David Hurst Thomas, 3:187–204. Washington, D.C.: Columbian Consequences, Smithsonian Institution, 1991.

Galdamés Armas, Juan. *Hombres y cosas de Santa Ana*. Santa Ana (ES), 1943.

Gallardo, Miguel Angel. *Papeles historicos*. Vols. 1–8. Santa Tecla, 1954–83.

Gálvez, Manuel de. "Relación geográfica de la provincia de El Salvador (1740)." Archivo General del la Nación, Folleto, no. 27, 1966. Mimeo.

García, Miguel Angel. *Diccionario historico enciclopedico de la República de El Salvador*. San Salvador: Impresora Nacional, 1952.

Gómez Carillo, Agustín. *Estudio histórico sobre la América Central*. San Salvador, 1884. <microfilm>.

———. *Historia de la America Central*. Guatemala: Tipogragía Nacional, 1895–07.

González, Dario. *Geografía de la America Central*. San Salvador: Imprenta Nacional, 1876.

———. *Lecciones de geografía*. San Salvador: Imprenta Nacional, 1876.

Gould, Jeffrey L. *To Die in This Way: Nicaraguan Indians and the Myth of Nicaragua Mestiza, 1880–1960*. Durham: Duke University Press, 1997.

———. *To Lead as Equals: Rural Protest and Political Consciousness in Chinandega, Nicaragua, 1912–1979*. Chapel Hill: University of North Carolina Press, 1990.

Guardino, Peter. *Peasants, Politics, and the Formation of Mexico's National State: Guerrero, 1800–1857*. Stanford: Stanford University Press, 1996.

Gudmundson, Lowell. *Costa Rica Before Coffee: Society and Economy on the Eve of the Export Boom*. Baton Rouge: Louisiana State University Press, 1986.

———. "Lord and Peasant in the Making of Modern Central America." In *Agrarian Structure and Political Power: Landlord and Peasant in the Making of Latin America*, ed. Evelyn Huber and Frank Stafford. Pittsburgh: University of Pittsburgh Press, 1995.

———. "Peasant, Farmer, Proletarian: Class Formation in a Smallholder Coffee Economy, 1850–1950." *Hispanic American Historical Review* 69, no. 2 (May 1989): 221–58.

———. "Peasant Movements and the Transition to Agrarian Capitalism: Freeholding Versus Hacienda Peasantries and Agrarian Reform in Guanacaste, Costa Rica, 1880–1935." *Peasant Studies* 10, no. 3 (1983).

Gudmundson, Lowell, and Héctor Lindo-Fuentes. *Central America, 1821–1871: Liberalism Before Liberal Reform*. Tuscaloosa: University of Alabama Press, 1995.

Guillén Chacón, José Antonio. "Historia y comentarios de la tributación cafetalera en El Salvador." Thesis. Universidad de El Salvador, 1963.

Gutierrez y Ulloa, Antonio. *Estado general de la Provincia de San Salvador, Reyno de Guatemala*. San Salvador: Ministerio de Educación Pública. Dirección General de Publicaciones, 1962.

Guzmán, David Joaquin. *Apuntamientos sobre la topografía de la República del Salvador*. San Salvador: Tipografía El Cometa, 1883.

Haefkens, Jacobo. "Viaje a Guatemala y Centroamerica." Vols. 1–3. Socieded de Geografía e Historia de Guatemala, 1969.

Hall, Carolyn. *El Café y el Desarollo Histórico-Geográfico de Costa Rica*. San José: Editorial Costa Rica y Universidad Nacional, 1976.

Halle, Louis J., Jr. *Transcaribbean: A Travel Book of Guatemala, El Salvador. British Honduras*. New York: Logmans, Green and Co., 1936.

Herran, Victor. *Notice sur les cinq états du Centre-Amérique*. Bordeaux: Imprimerie de A. Pechade, 1853.

Huber, Evelyn, and John D. Stephens. "Conclusion: Agrarian Structure and Political Power in Comparative Perspective." In *Agrarian Structure and Political Power*, ed. Huber and Stafford.

*Informe Que el Secretario de Relaciones Hace a la Nación de Orden del Presidente de la República, Sobre la Conducta del Licenciado Nicolas Espinosa, Gefe del Estado del Salvador*. Guatemala: Imprenta Mayor, 1836.

Ingersoll, Hazel Marylyn Bennet. "The War of the Mountain, a Study of Reactionary Peasant Insurgency in Guatemala, 1837–1873." Ph.D. diss., George Washington Unversity: University Microfilms, 1972.

Ipiña, Antonio. "Estadística del Departamento de Sonsonate, 1866." *Boletín de la Dirección General de Estadística de la República de El Salvador* 4, no. 2 (March 1906): 2–14. 1866.

Iraheta Rosales, Gerardo, Vilma Dolores López Alas, and María del Carmen Escobar Cornejo. "La crisis de 1929 y sus consecuencias en los años posteriores." *La Universidad*, no. 6 (1971): 22–74. #755.

Jackson, Harry Franklin. "The Technological Development of Central America, 1823–1913." Ph.D. diss., University of Chicago, 1948.

Jacobson, Nils. "Liberalism and Indian Communities in peru, 1821–1920." In *Liberals, the Church and Indian Peasants: Corporate Lands and the Challenge of Reform in Nineteenth-Century Spanish America*, 123–70. Albuquerque: University of New Mexico Press, 1998.

Jarves, James Jackson. *Scenes and Scenery in the Sandwich Islands, and a Trip Through Central America*. Boston: James Munroe and Company, 1843.

Jerez Bustamante, Victor. *Cronología de Nueva San Salvador, 1768–1955.* Santa Tecla, El Salvador: N.p., 1955.

Jiménez, Domingo. *Memoria con que el Dr. Don Domingo Jiménez da cuenta de los actos del ejecutivo en los ramos de Gobernación y Fomento del año de 1891.* San Salvador: Imprenta Nacional, 1892.

Jiménez, Liliam. "La república: inestabilidad, influencia gutemalteca y consolidación del liberalismo." In *El Salvador,* ed. Silvia Dutrenit, 285–92. Guadalajara, México: Nueva Imagen, 1989.

Joseph, Gilbert M., and Daniel Nugent, eds. *Everyday Forms of State Formation: Revolution and the Negotiation of Rule in Modern Mexico.* Durham: Duke University Press, 1994.

Juarros, Domingo. *Compendio de la historia del Reino de Guatemala, 1500–1800.* Guatemala: Editorial Piedra Santa, 1981.

Junta Central de Agricultura. *Boletín de Agricultura.* San Salvador, 1882–1910.

Katz, Friedrich. "Labor Conditions on Haciendas in Porfirian Mexico: Some Trends and Tendencies." *Hispanic American Historical Review* 54, no. 1 (February 1974): 1–47.

Kerr, Derek. "La edad de oro del café en El Salvador, 1863–1885." *Mesoamerica* 3, no. 3 (June 1982): 1–25.

———. "The Role of the Coffee Industry in the History of El Salvador: 1840–1906." M.A. thesis. University of Calgary, 1977.

Kincaid, A. Douglas. "Agrarian Development, Peasant Mobilization and Social Change in Central America: A Comparative Perspective." Ph.D. diss. Johns Hopkins University, 1987.

————. "Peasants Into Rebels: Community and Class in Rural El Salvador." *Comparative Studies in Society and History* (1987).

Klein, Herbert S. *Haciendas and Ayllus: Rural Society in the Bolivian Andes in the Eighteenth and Nineteenth Centuries.* Stanford: Stanford University Press, 1993.

Knight, Alan. "Debt Bondage in Latin America." In *Slavery and Other Forms of Unfree Labour,* ed. Leonie J. Archer, 102–17. London and New York: Routledge, 1989.

————. "Mexican Peonage: What Was It and Why Was It?" *Journal of Latin American Studies* 18 (May 1986): 41–74.

Koebel, William Henry. *Central America.* New York: T. Fisher Unwin, 1925.

Kourí, Emilio H. "The Business of the Land: Agrarian Tenure and Enterprise in Papantla, Mexico, 1800–1910." Ph.D. diss., Harvard University, 1996.

Laferrière, Joseph. *De Paris à Guatémala; notes de voyages au Centre-Amérique, 1866–1875.* Paris: Garnier Frères, Libraires-Edituers, 1877.

Laínez, Jorge B. *Cojutepeque: Biografía de un pueblo.* San Salvador: Impresora Nacional, 1984.

Lambert de Sainte-Croix, Alexandre. *Onze mois au Mexique et au Centre-Amérique.* Paris: E. Plon, Nourrit and Cie., 1897.

Lardé y Larín, Jorge. *Monografía histórica del Departamento de Santa Ana.* San Salvador, 1955.

Larrainzar, Federico. *Carta sobre los ultimos sucesos de Centro-América.* Mexico City: Imp. Literaria, 1864.

Larreynaga, José. *Memoria de los actos del poder ejecutivo en el ramo de Gobernación durante el año de 1889.* San Salvador: Imprenta Nacional, 1890.

Larson, Brooke, and Olivia Harris, eds. *Ethnicity, Markets, and Migration in the Andes: At the Crossroads of History and Anthropology.* Durham, N.C.: Duke University Press, 1995.

Lauria-Santiago, Aldo. "An Agrarian Republic: Production, Politics, and the Peasantry in El Salvador, 1740–1920." Ph.D. diss., University of Chicago, 1992.

————. "Historical Research and Sources on El Salvador." *Latin American Research Review* 30, no. 2 (Spring 1995): 151–76.

————. "La historia regional del café en El Salvador." *Revista de Historia (San José)* No. 38 (1999).

———. "Land, Community, and Revolt in Indian Izalco, El Salvador, 1855–1905." *Hispanic American Historical Review* 79, no. 1 (February 1999).

———. "'That a Poor May Be Industrious:' Coffee, Community, and Agrarian Capitalism in the Transformation of El Salvador's ladino Peasantry, 1760–1900." In *Identity and Struggle at the Margins of the Nation-State: The Laboring Peoples of Central America and the Hispanic Caribbean, 1850–1950,* ed. Aviva Chomsky and Aldo Lauria-Santiago. Durham, N.C.: Duke University Press, 1998.

Leistenschneider, María, and Freddy Leistenschneider. *Administración del General Francisco Malespin.* San Salvador: Ministerio del Interior, 1980.

Lever, E. A. *Central America or the Land of the Quiches and Chontales.* New Orleans: E. A. Brandao, 1885.

Lindo Fuentes, Héctor. "Los limites del poder en la era de Barrios." In *Identidades nacionales y Estado moderno en Centroamérica,* ed. Arturo Taracena A. and Jean Piel, 87–96. San José: Editorial de la Universidad de Costa Rica, 1995.

———. "Nineteenth Century Economic History of El Salvador." Ph.D. diss., University of Chicago, 1984.

———. *Weak Foundations: The Economy of El Salvador in the Nineteenth Century.* Berkely and Los Angeles: University of California Press, 1990.

Lockhart, James, and Ida Altman. *Provinces of Early Mexico.* Los Angeles: UCLA Latin American Center, 1976.

Long, W. Rodney. *Railways of Central America and the West Indies.* Trade Promotion Series, no. 5. Washington, D.C.: U.S. Government Printing Office, 1925.

López, Lorenzo. *Estadística general de la República del Salvador.* San Salvador: Imprenta Nacional, 1974.

Loveman, Brian. *The Constitution of Tyranny: Regimes of Exception in Spanish America.* Pittsburgh: University of Pittsburgh Press, 1993.

Luna, David. "Análisis de una dictadura fascista latinoamericana: Maximilano Hernández Martínez, 1931–1944." *La Universidad* 94, no. 5 (1969).

———. "Manual de historia económica de El Salvador." San Salvador, 1971.

———. "Un heroico y trágico suceso de nuestra historia." Conference presentation in *El Proceso Político Centroamericano.* San Salvador: Editorial Universitaria, 1964.

Macleod, Murdo J. *Spanish Central America: A Socioeconomic History, 1520–1720.* Berkeley: University of California Press, 1973.

Malaina, Santiago. *La Compañia de Jesús en El Salvador, Centro America, desde 1864 a 1872.* San Salvador: Imprenta Nacional, 1939.

Mallon, Florencia E. *The Defense of Community in Peru's Central Highlands: Peasant Struggle and Capitalist Transition, 1860–1940.* Princeton: Princeton University Press, 1983.

————. *Peasant and Nation: The Making of Postcolonial Mexican and
Peru.* Berkeley: University of California Press, 1995.

Manning, William Ray, ed. *Diplomatic Correspondence of the United States,
Inter-American Affairs: Central America, 1831–1860.* Vol. 3. Carnegie
Endowment for International Peace. Washington, D.C., 1933.

Marroquín, Alejandro Dagoberto. *San Pedro Nonualco.* San Salvador: Editorial Universitaria, December.

Martin, Percy Falcke. *Salvador of the Twentieth Century.* London: E. Arnold,
1911.

Martínez, José María. "Historia de Cojutepeque." In *Papeles Históricos,* ed.
and comp. Miguel Angel Gallardo. Santa Tecla, El Salvador: Editorial
Léa, 1975.

Martínez, Severo. *La Pátria del Criollo.* San José: EDUCA, 1973.

Martínez Funes, Gerardo. *Album de San Salvador y Santa Ana.* Santa Ana,
El Salvador, 1938.

McCreery, David. *Rural Guatemala: 1760–1940.* Stanford: Stanford University Press, 1994.

*Memoria de Gobernación y de Relaciones, 1861.* San Salvador, 1862.

*Memoria de los actos del poder ejecutivo en el ramo de Gobernación.* San
Salvador: Imprenta Nacional, 1891.

*Memoria Presentada por el Ministro de Gobernación, Guerra y Marina
Doctor Domingo Jimenez a la Asamblea Nacional (1892).* San Salvador: Imprenta Nacional, 1893.

Mendoza, Jeremías. "Páginas historicas del a raza lenca de la República de
El Salvador." In *Cuzcatlan Típico,* ed. María de Baratta, 2:398–402.
San Salvador: Ministerio de Cultura, 1952.

Menendez, Isidro. *Recopilación de la Leyes del Salvador en Centro-
America.* 1855. Guatemala: Imprenta de L. Luna, 1956.

Menjivar, Rafael. *Acumulación originaria y desarollo del Capitalismo en El
Salvador.* San José: Editorial Universitaria Centroamericana, 1976.

Molina, Ivan, and Steven Palmer. *The History of Costa Rica.* San José:
EDUCA, 1988.

Monterrey, Francisco J. *Historia de El Salvador: anotaciones cronológicas.*
2 vols. San Salvador: Talleres Gráficos Cisneros, 1978.

Montes, Santiago. *Etnohistoria de El Salvador.* 2 vols. San Salvador: Ministerio de Educación, 1977.

Montes, Segundo. *El agro salvadoreño (1973–1980)*. San Salvador: UCA Editores, 1986.

Montgomery, George Washington. *Narrative of a Journey to Gauatemala in Central America, in 1838*. New York: Wiley and Putnam, 1839.

Montgomery, Tommie Sue. *Revolution in El Salvador*. Boulder, Colo.: Westview Press, 1982.

Montis, Rafael. *Informe documentado de los trabajos de la Dirección é Inspección General de Hacienda durante el año de 1896*. San Salvador: Imprenta Nacional, 1897.

Mora, Adán. *Memoria del Ministerio de Gobernación y Fomento*. San Salvador: Imprenta Nacional, 1883.

———. *Memoria del Ministerio de Gobernación y Fomento (1883)*. San Salvador: Imprenta Nacional, 1884.

Morrill, Gulian Lansing. *Rotten Republics, A Tropical Tramp in Central America*. Chicago: M. A. Donahue, 1916.

Orellana, Alejandro, and Carlos Orellana. *Sonsonate historico e informativo*. San Salvador: Imprenta Nacional, 1960.

Ots Capdequí, José María. *España en América: El régimen de tierras en la época colonial*. Mexico City; Fondo de Cultura Económica, 1959.

———. *Nuevos Aspectos del Siglo XVII Español en América*. Bogota: Editorial Centro, 1946.

Palacios, Marco. *Coffee in Colombia, 1850–1970*. Cambridge: Cambridge University Press, 1980.

Palmer, Frederick. *Central America and Its Problems; an Account of a Journey from the Rio Grande to Panama*. New York: Moffat, Yard and Company, 1910.

Palmer, Steven. "A Liberal Discipline: Inventing Nations in Guatemala and Costa Rica, 1870–1900." Ph.D. diss., Columbia University, 1990.

Pearce, Jenny. *Promised Land: Peasant Rebellion in Chalatenango, El Salvador*. London: Latin America Bureau, 1986.

Perez Brignoli, Hector. *Breve historia de Centroamerica*. Madrid: Alianza Editorial, 1985.

Périgny, Maurice de. *Les cinq républiques de l'Amérique Centrale*. Paris: Pierre Roger, 1912.

Piñeda Alvarado, Abraham. *Reseña Historica de Santiago Nonualco*. Santiago Nonualco, El Salvador: N.p., 1959.

Pinto Soria, Julio César. *Guatemala en la decada de la independencia*. Guatemala: Editorial Universitaria, 1978.

———. *Estructura agraria y asentamiento en la Capitania General de Guatemala*. Guatemala: Editorial Universitaria, 1981.

———. *Raices historicas del estado en Centroamerica*. Guatemala: Editorial Universitaria de Guatemala, 1983.

Pinto Soria, Julio César, Héctor Pérez Brignoli, and Víctor H. Acuña Ortega. *Historial General de Centroamérica*. Ed. Edelberto Torres-Rivas. Madrid: Comunidades Europeas Sociedad Estatal Quinto Centenario/FLACSO, 1993.

Posada, Marcelo Germán, and Mario López. "El Salvador 1950–1970: latifundios, integración y crisis." *Revista de Historia de América,* no. 115 (January–June 1993): 37–62.

Putnam, George Palmer. *The Southland of North America*. New York and London: The Knickerbocker Press, 1914.

Reyes, Rafael. *Apuntamientos estadísticos sobre la República de El Salvador.* San Salvador: Imprenta Nacional, 1888.

———. *Nociones de historia del Salvador.* San Salvador: Imprenta del Dr. Francisco Sagrini, 1885.

Robinson Wright, Marie. *Salvador*. New York: L'Artiste, 1893.

Rodríguez, Leopoldo A. "Historia y descripción de la ciudad de San Vicente, y consideraciones sobre el origen de algunos pueblos de su departamento." *La Universidad* serie 3, no. 5–8 (March–June 1892).

Rodríguez Herrera, América. "Una aproximación al estudio de las Cofradías en El Salvador." *Estudios Sociales Centroamericanos* 51 (September–December 1989): 97–117.

Roseberry, William. *Anthropologies and Histories: Essays in Culture, History, and Political Economy*. New Brunswick, N.J.: Rutgers University Press, 1989.

———. "Beyond the Agrarian Question in Latin America." In *Confronting Historical Paradigms: Peasants, Labor, and the World System in Africa and Latin America,* ed. Frederick Cooper et al. Madison: University of Wisconsin Press, 1993.

———. "Introduction." In *Coffee, Society, and Power in Latin America,* ed. William Roseberry, Lowell Gudmundson, and Mario Samper Kutschbach. Baltimore: The Johns Hopkins University Press, 1995.

———. *"La Falta de Brazos:* Land and Labor in the Coffee Economies of Nineteenth-Century Latin America." *Theory and Society* 20 (1991): 351–82.

Rubio Sánchez, Manuel. *Historia del añil o xiquilite en Centro América.* San Salvador: Ministerio de Educación, 1976.

Salaverría, Joaquin. "La hacienda colonial de San Juan Buenavista." Unpublished paper. San Salvador.

Samper K., Mario. "El significado social de la caficultura costarricense y salvaodoreña: Análisis histórico comparado a partir de los censos cafetaleros." In *Tierra, café y sociedad,* ed. Héctor Pérez Brignoli and Mario Samper. San José: FLACSO, 1994.

―――. *Generations of Settlers: Rural Households and Markets on the Costa Rican Frontier, 1850–1935.* Boulder, Colo.: Westview Press, 1990.

Scherzer, Carl. *Travels in the Free States of Central America: Nicaragua, Honduras, and San Salvador.* London: Longman, Brown, Green, Longmans, and Roberts, 1857.

Sermeño Lima, José. "Los Movimientos de Población y Sus Relaciones Socioeconómicas en El Salvador." *ECA,* nos. 387–388 (January–February 1981): 33–41.

Slutzky, Daniel, and Esther Slutsky. "El Salvador: estructura de la explotación cafetalera." *Estudios Sociales Centroamericanos,* no. 30 (September–December 1972).

Smith, Robert S. "Financing the Central American Federation, 1821–1838." *Hispanic American Historical Review* 48, no. 4 (November 1962): 483–510.

―――. "Forced Labor in the Guatemalan Indigo Works." *Hispanic American Historical Review* 36, no. 3 (August 1956): 319–28.

―――. "Indigo Production and Trade in Colonial Guatemala." *Hispanic American Historical Review* 39, no. 2 (1959): 181–211.

Solano, Francisco de. "Areas lingüísticas y población de habla indígena de Guatemala en 1772." Revista Española de Antropologia Americana 4 (1969): 145–200.

―――. "Autoridades indigenas y población india en la Audiencia de Guatemala en 1572." Revista Española de Antropologia Americana 7, no. 2 (1972): 133–50.

―――. "Castellanización del indio y areas del castellano en Guatemala en 1772." Revista de la Universidad de Madrid 19, no.72 (1970): 289–340.

―――. "La economía agraria de Guatemala, 1768–1772." Revista de Indias 31, nos. 123–24 (Enero–Junio 1971): 285–327.

―――. "La población indigena de Guatemala, 1492–1800." Anuario de Estudios Americanos 26 (1969): 279–355.

―――. "Población y areas linguisticas en El Salvador 1772." Revista Española de Antropologia Americana 5 (1970): 275–315.

―――. "Tierra, comercio y sociedad: Un análisis de la estructura social agraria centroamericana durante el Siglo XVIII." *Revista de Indias* 31 (July–December 1971): 311–65.

Solórzano Fonseca, Juan Carlos. "Centroamerica en el Siglo XVIII: Un intento de explicación economica y social." *Estudios Sociales Centroamericanos* 11, no. 32 (1982): 11–22.

———. "Las comunidades indigenas de Guatemala, El Salvador y Chiapas durante el siglo XVIII: los mecanismos de explotación economica." *Anuario de Estudios Centroamericanos* 11, no. 2 (1985): 93–130.

Squier, Ephraim George. *Notes on Central America; Particularly the States of Honduras and San Salvador: Their Geography, Topography, Climate, Population, Resources, Productions, Etc., Etc. and the Proposed Honduras Inter-Oceanic Railway.* New York: Praeger, 1969.

———. *The States of Central America.* New York, 1858.

Stanley, William. *The Protection Racket State: Elite Politics, Military Extortion, and Civil War in El Salvador.* Philadelphia: Temple University Press, 1997.

Stern, Steve J. "Feudalism, Capitalism, and the World System in the Perspective of Latin American and the Caribbean." *American Historical Review* 93, no. 4 (October 1988): 829–72.

Suarez, Francisco de Paula. *Noticias generales sobre la república del Salvador, reunidas y publicadas por F. de P.S.* Lima: Tipografía de "la Patria," 1874.

Suter, Jan. *Prosperität und Krise in einer Kaffeerepublik.* Frankfurt: Vervuert, 1996.

Taracena Arriola, Arturo. "Contribución al estudio del vocablo 'ladino' en Guatemala (S. XVI-XIX)" in Jorge Lujan Muñoz, *Historia y antropología, Ensayos en honor de J. Daniel Contreras.* Guatemala: Facultad de Humanidades, USAC, 1982, 89–104.

———. *Invención criolla, sueño Ladino, pesadilla indígena: Los Altos de Guatemala: de región a Estado, 1740–1850.* San José: Editorial Porvenir, 1997.

Tempsky, Gustav Ferdinand von. *Mitla: A Narrative of Incidents and Personal Adventurs on a Journey in Mexico, Guatemala, and Salvador in the Years 1853 to 1855.* London: Longman, Brown, Green, Longmans and Roberts, 1858.

Thompson, George Alex. *Narrative of an Official Visit to Guatemala from Mexico.* London, 1929.

Thompson, Wallace. *Rainbow Countries of Central America.* New York: E. P. Dutton and Co., 1924.

Thomson, Guy P. "Popular Aspects of Liberalism in Mexico, 1848–1888." *Bulletin of Latin American Research* 10, no. 3 (1991): 265–92.

Topic, Steve. Paper presented at the Third Congress on Central American History, Ciudad Universitaria "Rodrigo Facio" de la Universidad de Costa Rica, 15–19 July 1996.

Torres, Abelardo. "Tierras y colonización." Regimen de Tenencia de la Tierra y Condiciones de Trabajo Agricola en El Salvador. San Salvador: Instituto de Estudios Economicos, Universidad de El Salvador, 1961.

Torres Rivas, Edelberto. *Interpretación del desarollo social centroamericano*: Procesos y estructuras de una sociedad dependiente. San José: EDUCA, 1981.

Torres-Rivas, Edelberto, and Julio Cesar Pinto. *Problemas en la formación del estado nacional en Centroamérica*. San José: ICAP, 1983.

Tutino, John. *From Insurrection to Revolution in Mexico: Social Bases of Agrarian Violence, 1750–1940*. Princeton: Princeton University Press, 1986.

Ulloa, Cruz. *Codificación de Leyes Patrias, Desde la Independencia Hasta el Año de 1875*. San Salvador: Imprenta Nacional, 1879.

United States, Department of State. *Despatches from U.S. Consuls in San Salvador*. Washington, D.C., 1868–1906. <microform> T-237, 10 rolls.

———. "Despatches from U.S. Consuls in Sonsonate, El Salvador." Washington, D.C.: National Archives, 1868–87. <microfilm Roll #T440>.

Vanni, Manfredo. *Salvador: condizioni naturale ed economiche*. Rome: Fretelli Treves, 1926.

Velasco, Miguel Angel. *Monografía historia de la cuidad de Sensuntepeque, Departamento de Cabañas*. Sensuntepeque, El Salvador: Imprenta Mercurio, 1949.

Vilanova, Santiago Ricardo. *Apuntamientos de historia patria eclesiastica*. San Salvador: Imprenta Diario del Salvador, 1911.

Von Mentz, Brigida. *Pueblos de indios, mulatos y mestizos. 1770–1870*. Ediciones de la Casa Chata, 1988.

Ward, Cubie Edward. "Land Ownership in the Coffeee Growing Region of El Salvador: The Impact of the Liberal Land Reform, 1880–1980." Ph.D. diss., University of Texas, Arlington, 1994.

Ward, L. A., ed. and comp. *Libro azul de El Salvador*. San Salvador: Bureau de Publicidad de la America Latina, 1916.

Wellman, Frederick Lovejoy. *Coffee: Botany, Cultivation, and Utilization*. London, 1961.

West, Robert C., and John P. Augelli. *Middle America, Its Lands and Peoples*. N.J.: Prentice Hall, 1989.

Williams, Philip J., and Knut Walter. *Militarization and Demilitarization in El Salvador's Transition to Democracy*. Pittsburgh: University of Pittsburgh Press, 1997.

Williams, Robert G. *Export Agriculture and the Crisis in Central America*. Chapel Hill: University of North Carolina Press, 1986.

———. *States and Social Evolution: Coffee and the Rise of National Governments in Central America*. Chapel Hill: University of North Carolina Press, 1995.

Wilson, Alan Everett. "The Crisis of National Integration in El Salvador. 1919–1935." Ph.D. diss., Stanford University, 1969.

Wolf, Eric R. "Types of Latin American Peasantries." *American Anthropologist* 57 (1953): 452–71.

Woodward, Ralph Lee. "Liberalism, Conservatism, and the Response of the Peasants of La Montaña to the Government of Guatemala, 1821–1850." *Plantation Society in the Americas* 1 (1979).

———. *Rafael Carrera and the Emergence of the Republic of Guatemala, 1821–1871*. Athens: University of Georgia Press, 1993.

Wortman, Miles L. *Government and Society in Central America*. New York: Columbia University Press, 1982.

Yarrington, Doug. *A Coffee Frontier: Land Society, and Politics in Duaca, Venezuela, 1830–1936*. Pittsburgh: University of Pittsburgh Press, 1997.

Zamora Castellanos, Pedro. *Vida militar de Centro America*. Guatemala: Editorial del Ejercito, 1966–67.

# INDEX

Cuellar, Dolores, 211–12
Cuellar, Romualdo, 212
Cuscatlán, 75, 96–97, 112, 149; Indian revolts in, 116–17

Dardano, Félix, 146
De Belot, Gustave, 117
De Regalado, Doña Petrona, 216
De Witt, Charles G., 109
Demographics: of Chalchuapa, 94–96; in Cojutepeque, 98; of Cuscatlán, 96–97; and definition of ethnicity, 58–61; and indigo production, 21; of Santa Tecla, 68–69; women farm workers, 92
Dependency theories, 4
Dolores, 51–52
Domville-Fife, Charles William, 59
Dueñas, Francisco, 43, 79, 225–26; land policies of, 46–47, 55, 63, 69; opposition to, 121–22; and revolts, 116–17, 120
Duke, Rafael Guirola, 146
Dunlop, Robert, 72–73

Economy: change from colonial to state financial structures, 34; changes in, 102–03; of cities in western El Salvador, 88–94; coffee processing and exports in, 138; of coffee production, 136–37; of Cojutepeque, 97; crises, 235; diversified, of agricultural bourgeoisie, 161–62; effects of coffee production on, 132–33, 150–51; effects of independence on, 71–74; effects on coffee production, 133, 135; of El Salvador, 158; extent of influence of coffee production, 8–9; importance of indigo production in, 76–77; of indigo production, 76; instability of, 223; national, attempts to stabilize, 93; role of coffee production in, 227–30; role of indigo production in, 18–19; of Santa Ana: effects of coffee production on, 140; occupations, 92; ties to Guatemala's, 87; of western El Salvador, 79–88
Egalitarianism, and land policies, 43–45, 165, 230
*Ejidos*, 35–43, 55–56; abolition of, 151–52, 166–68, 183–84; acquisition by commercial investors, 144; administration of, 42, 45–50, 82, 86–87; agriculture on, 98–994; coffee production on, 134–35; coffee production on, 137, 140, 146–47; conflicts with ethnic communities over, 56; confused with common lands, 52, 56, 216; confused with *composición*, 64; criticism of, 165–69; distribution of, 164; and ethnic divi-

sions, in San Vincente, 99; history of, 25–30, 35–36; incentives for expanding commercial agriculture on, 170; in La Libertad, 143–44; privatization of, 171–83, 176–83, 187–88, 192–94, 231; around San Vincente City, 100; compared to privatization of common lands, 96–99, 200; effects of, 191; and privatization of common lands, 204; quality of, 81; separating common lands from, 46, 214; uses of, 43, 45, 63–69; private, 41–42; in western El Salvador, 82–86
El Salvador: agrarian history of, 1–11; coffee production in western departments, 133, 138–48, 154; eastern departments, 149–50, 155; economy of, 34, 79–80, 136–37, 158; geography of, 11–13, 77; relative ethnicity of regions, 60–61; wage labor in, 152–53; western departments, 32, 56, 77–96, 126–27. *See also* Government; State
Elections, in state formation, 130
Elites, 4, 105, 221; agricultural, 161, 234, 235; and coffee production, 4–5, 132–33, 146, 160; effects of coffee production on development of, 4–5; effects of land privatization on, 189–91, 193, 233; and land privatization, 163, 220, 230; politics of, 124, 126–27, 226; and power of military, 237–38; relations with peasants, 55, 121; use of common lands, 63–69; wealth of, 146, 223, 228
Escalón, Quirino, 85, 126
Espinosa, Nicolás, 108
Espinoza, Nicolás, 42–43, 108–10
Ethnic communities. *See* Indian communities; Ladino communities; Peasant communities
Ethnic tensions, 7; competition for land, 27; conflicts over land use, 42–43, 44, 55–56, 65, 130–31, 142; elites mediating, 105; Ladinos *vs.* Indians, 61–63, 111, 142; during land privatization, 208, 213–15, 231–32; over common lands, 47, 51–52; over land, 55, 87; and push for land privatization, 165; relations among groups, 57–63; and revolts against Zaldívar, 124; in San Vincente, 99; solidarity and sovereignty within, 119; thought of as homogenized, 31–32; used by political leaders, 108
Ethnicity: definitions of, 57–59, 61, 63; effects of land privatization on, 219–20
Export agriculture. *See* Commercial agriculture
Exports, 88, 98; cattle, 91; coffee, 132–34, 137–38, 157; development of regional trade, 99–101; manufactured/craft